Praise for *The David Story*

"The most compelling version of [the David] story since the King James Bible. While reclaiming that translation's ceremonious aura, and even the cadenced gravity of the Hebrew itself, Alter offers a modern rendering, strong in its lexical precision and literary finesse, that conveys the range of David from a crafty, contradictory politique to the representative of humankind, embattled yet enduring. . . . Masterful."
—Robert Fagles, Arthur W. Marks '19 Professor of
Comparative Literature, Princeton University,
and award-winning translator of *The Iliad* and *The Odyssey*

"A masterpiece of contemporary Bible translation and commentary by one of the world's leading Bible scholars. . . . [Alter's] work is assured and authoritative, lyrical and lucid. For any reader whose experience of the Bible is limited to the stately but archaic English of the King James version—or one of its progeny—the experience of *The David Story* may seem like reading the Bible for the first time. . . . David comes alive in all of his color and complexity. . . . Alter approaches the Bible with the full arsenal of contemporary Bible scholarship. . . . At the same time, [he] is a gifted translator, a poet with an ear for both ancient Hebrew and modern English."
—Jonathan Kirsch, *Los Angeles Times Book Review*, Best Books of 1999

"Alter's translation is bravely Hebraic, offering the heft and rhythm of the original verses. . . . [His] commentary excels in the attention it devotes to narrative technique and to features of the text that are only available to the reader who knows Hebrew. . . . [His commentary is] far more illuminating for the general reader than more traditionally philological and historical commentaries."
—Raymond Scheindlin, *Forward*, Arts and Letters front-page review

"A compelling literary translation. . . . In many instances, [Alter's] translation surpasses King James's by more accurately reproducing the rhythm, syntactical arrangement, and word plays of the Hebrew text."

—*Library Journal*

"Superb commentary." —Hillel Halkin, *The New Republic*

"The King David who emerges from these pages is a masterful (and sometimes cunning) politician, a bold (and often opportunistic) warrior and a devoted (but also vindictive) ruler—the surprisingly human centerpiece of an ancient story few modern novelists can match for sheer drama." —Herbert Kupferberg, *Parade*

"In this eminently readable translation and commentary of the David story . . . [Alter] skillfully breathes a fresh spirit and sense of urgency into this ancient narrative. . . . A genuinely original contribution."

—*Choice*

"A powerful accomplishment." —*San Francisco Chronicle*

"It is one of the masterpieces of world literature, brought masterfully to life by a great scholar and critic of our own generation."

—Jonathan Magonet, *The Jewish Chronicle*

ALSO BY ROBERT ALTER

THE
DAVID STORY

A TRANSLATION WITH COMMENTARY

OF 1 AND 2 SAMUEL

ROBERT
ALTER

W · W · NORTON & COMPANY

NEW YORK   LONDON

The author gratefully acknowledges permission from Yehuda Amichai for use of
the four-line poem that begins "When Samuel was born. . . ." (PATUAH
SAGUR PATUAH, Tel Aviv, 1998, p. 34) on p. xv of the Introduction,
translation by the author.

For information about permission to reproduce selections from this book,
write to Permissions, W. W. Norton & Company, Inc.,
500 Fifth Avenue, New York, NY 10110

The text of this book is composed in 11/14.5 and 10/12 Fairfield LH Light
with the display set in Bodega Serif Light
Composition and manufacturing by the Haddon Craftsmen, Inc.
Book design by Margaret M. Wagner

Library of Congress Cataloging-in-Publication Data
Bible. O.T. Samuel. English. Alter. 1999.
The David story : a translation with commentary of 1 and 2 Samuel / Robert Alter.
p. cm.
Includes bibliographical references and index.
ISBN 0-393-04803-9
1. Bible. O.T. Samuel—Commentaries. I. Alter, Robert.
II. Title.
BS1323.A48 1999
222'.4077—dc21 99-21116
CIP

ISBN 0-393-32077-4 pbk.

W. W. Norton & Company, Inc.
500 Fifth Avenue, New York, N.Y. 10110
www.wwnorton.com

W. W. Norton & Company Ltd.
Castle House, 75/76 Wells Street, London W1T 3QT

In memory of Judah M. Eisenberg

(1938–1998)

Man of science and humane culture

Cherished friend of my youth

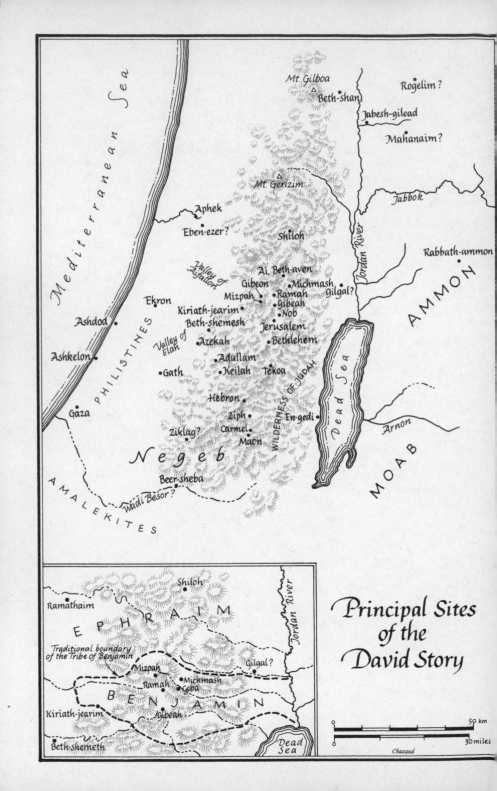

Principal Sites
of the
David Story

TO THE READER

I. THE STORY OF SAMUEL, SAUL, AND DAVID

The major sequence that runs, according to the conventional book and chapter divisions of later editorial traditions, from 1 Samuel 1 to 1 Kings 2 is one of the most astounding pieces of narrative that has come down to us from the ancient world. The story of David is probably the greatest single narrative representation in antiquity of a human life evolving by slow stages through time, shaped and altered by the pressures of political life, public institutions, family, the impulses of body and spirit, the eventual sad decay of the flesh. It also provides the most unflinching insight into the cruel processes of history and into human behavior warped by the pursuit of power. And nowhere is the Bible's astringent narrative economy, its ability to define characters and etch revelatory dialogue in a few telling strokes, more brilliantly deployed.

It must also be said, after nearly two centuries of excavative scholarship, that the precise literary history and authorship of this great narrative remain beyond recovery. To specialists who have exercised painstaking analysis in order to expose an intricate patchwork of sources and historical layers in the book as a whole and in most of its episodes, it may seem a provocation or an expression of ignorance to speak at all of the story of Samuel, Saul, and David. Even a reader looking for unity must concede that certain passages are not of a piece with the rest. The most salient of these is the coda placed just before the end of the David story (2 Samuel: 21–24), which comprises material from four different sources, none of them reflecting the style or perspective of the David story proper. It may be unwise to think of these disparate passages as intrusions because creating a purposeful collage of sources was demonstrably a standard literary procedure in ancient Israel. In any case, the architectonic cohesion of the narrative from the birth of Samuel to the death of David has been made increasingly clear by the innovative literary commentary of the past two decades, and much of the richness and complexity of the story is lost by those who imagine this book as a stringing together of virtually independent sources: a prophetic Samuel narrative, a cycle of Saul stories, a history of the rise of David, and so forth.

Readers should not be confused by the conventional division into books. The entities 1 and 2 Samuel are purely an artifact of ancient manuscript production. Scrolls used by scribes were roughly the same length, and when the Hebrew Bible was translated into Greek in the third century B.C.E., a single scroll was not long enough to encompass the whole book, so it was divided into two parts in no way intrinsic to the original composition. (The Talmud speaks of a single Book of Samuel.) It is also demonstrable that the first two chapters of 1 Kings, as I shall try to show in my commentary, are the real conclusion of the book, subtly echoing earlier moments in the story and evincing the same distinctive literary mastery. Later redactors placed these two episodes at the beginning of Kings so that they could serve as a preface to the story of Solomon.

But if the ancient editors passed this material down to posterity as a book, what are we to make of its composite nature? Two fundamental issues are involved: the presence of the so-called Deuteronomist in the book, and the introduction of purportedly independent narratives. In regard to the second of these two considerations, the baseline for modern scholarly discussion was set in a 1926 monograph by the German scholar Leonhard Rost. He concentrated on what he saw as two independent narratives—an Ark Narrative (1 Samuel 4–7:1, plus 2 Samuel 6) and a Succession Narrative (2 Samuel 9–20 and 1 Kings 1–2). The argument for an originally independent Ark Narrative has a good deal of plausibility: there are some stylistic differences in this segment; human agents, at the center of the surrounding narrative, are marginal; miraculous intervention by God, not in evidence elsewhere, is decisive; and the figure of Samuel with which the story began temporarily disappears. The Ark Narrative is often thought to be the oldest component of the Book of Samuel, perhaps actually pre-Davidic, because it does not envisage a royal cult in Jerusalem and has no interest in the more political concerns of the larger story. Even in this case, however, the narrative in question has to be read in the context of the comprehensive literary structure into which it has been integrated, whether by editorial ingenuity or by the allusive artistry of the author of the David story. Thus, the old priest Eli, sitting at the gate awaiting the news of disaster from the battlefield (news which will include the death of his sons), generates a haunting avatar in the aging David at Mahanaim, sitting between the two gates of the walled city, anxiously awaiting the messenger from the battlefield who will tell him of the death of his son. A second scene of receiving catastrophic tidings is tied in with Eli: the old priest hears an uproar in the town, asks what it means, and then a messenger arrives to give him a breathless report of the terrible defeat, just as the usurper Adonijah, at the end of the David story, will hear an uproar in the town and then a breathless report from an eyewitness of the developments that have destroyed his hopes for the throne.

The argument for an independent Succession Narrative, long embraced by scholarly consensus, is shakier. Rost's contention that it is stylistically distinct from the preceding text is unconvincing, and his notions of style are extremely vague. One may question whether the succession to the throne is actually the central concern of this sequence of episodes, which are more powerfully focused on David's sin and the consequent theme of the unfolding of the prophet's curse on the house of David. (This theme has a certain affinity with Greek tragedy, as Faulkner, ultimately a better reader of the David story than Rost, keenly understood in *Absalom, Absalom!*) The powerful imaginative continuities in the representation of David from agile youth to decrepit old age speak for themselves. To read, for example, David's grim response to the death of his infant son by Bathsheba (2 Samuel 12) as part of an independent Succession Narrative, unrelated to his previous public utterances and acts in a purported History of the Rise of David, is to do palpable violence to the beautiful integrity of the story as the probing representation of a human life. Over the past two decades, admirable work has been done by scholars from different points of the geographical and methodological map to illuminate the fine and complex interconnections among the various phases of the story of David, Saul, and Samuel. The most notable contributions are those of the Dutch scholar J. P. Fokkelman, the North American Robert Polzin, and the Israeli Shimon Bar-Efrat, and I shall frequently follow their precedent or build on their insights in my comments on the text.

The other pervasive question about the stratification of this book involves its Deuteronomistic editing. No one knows with certainty when the main part of the original narrative was written, though there is good reason to place it, as a recurrent scholarly view does, quite close to David's own time, in the first half of the tenth century B.C.E. (Gerhard von Rad proposed the court of Solomon as the setting for the composition of the story.) Samuel is set into the larger history that runs from Joshua to the end of 2 Kings and that scholarly usage designates as the Deuteronomistic History. The book was probably edited at the time of King Josiah's cultic and theological reforms in the late seventh century B.C.E., though it may well have undergone a secondary Deuteronomistic redaction in the Babylonian Exile, during the sixth century B.C.E. But to what extent is Samuel a product of the work of the Deuteronomist? The bulk of the story shows no traces of the peculiar brand of nationalist pietism that marks the Deuteronomistic movement—its emphasis on the purity and the centralization of the cult, its insistence on a direct causal link between Israelite defection from its covenant with God and national catastrophe, and its distinctive and strikingly formulaic vocabulary for expressing this outlook. The compelling conclusion is that the Deuteronomistic editors did no more with the inherited narrative than to provide some minimal editorial framing and transition (far less than in the Book of Judges) and to interpolate a few brief passages. Thus I strenuously disagree with Robert Polzin, one of the most finely perceptive readers of this book (in his two volumes *Samuel and the Deuteronomist* and *David and the Deuteronomist*). Exercising great ingenuity, Polzin sees the historical perspective of the Deuteronomist manifested in all the minute details of the story.

Let me cite a rare moment when the Deuteronomist has patently inserted a bit of dialogue of his own contrivance into the story that probably antedates his editing by more than three centuries, for the contrast with what immediately follows will vividly illustrate the kind of world that defines David, Joab, Saul, Abner, and all these memorable figures steeped in the bitter juices of politics and history. On his deathbed, David summons Solomon in order to convey to him an oral last will and testament (1 Kings 2):

I am going on the way of all the earth. And you must be strong, and be a man. *And keep what the LORD your God enjoins, to walk in His ways, to keep His statutes, His commandments, and His dictates and His admonitions, as it is written in the Teaching of Moses, so that you may prosper in everything you do and in everything to which you turn. So that the LORD may fulfill His word that He spoke unto me, saying, 'If your sons keep their way to walk before Me in truth with their whole heart and with their whole being, saying, no man of yours will be cut off from the throne of Israel.'* And, what's more, you yourself know what Joab son of Zeruiah did to me, what he did to the two commanders of the armies of Israel, Abner son of Ner and Amasa son of Jether—he killed them and spilled the blood of war in peace, and put the blood of war on his belt that was round his waist and on his sandals that were on his feet. And you must act in your wisdom, and do not let his gray head go down in peace to Sheol.

Every word in the italicized section of the passage shows the fingerprints of the Deuteronomist. The phraseology is almost identical with recurrent phraseology in the Book of Deuteronomy: the heavy stress on "keeping" and "commandments," whole strings of terms such as "walk in His ways," "His statutes, His commandments, and His laws and His dictates," "so that you may prosper in everything you do," "to walk before me in truth with their whole heart and with their whole being." The very mention of the "Teaching [*torah*] of Moses" is a Deuteronomistic rallying point that would scarcely have been invoked in the tenth century. Stylistically, moreover, these long-winded sentences loaded with didactically insistent synonyms are nothing like the sentences spoken by characters in the David story.

Why did the Deuteronomist interpolate these lines of dialogue? The most plausible inference is that, given his brand of pious monotheism, he was uncomfortable with the way the founding king of the divinely elected dynasty speaks on his deathbed. It is, after all, a will and testament worthy of a Mafia chieftain. David and Joab go back together half a century. David has been repeatedly dependent on Joab's resourcefulness and ruthlessness as his principal strong man, but he also feels himself to have been terribly wronged by his henchman—above all, in Joab's self-interested and treacherous murders of two army commanders whom David had embraced (and also in his killing of Absalom, against the king's explicit orders, which David refrains from mentioning). The image of Joab splashed in blood from waist to feet strongly recalls the narrative report of his butchering Amasa with a stealthy sword thrust to the belly, and invokes the recurrence of spilled blood as material substance and moral symbol throughout the story. When David enjoins the proverbially wise Solomon to act in his wisdom, the quality in question is not the wisdom of the Torah of Moses but rather the wisdom of a Talleyrand. Soon after David's death, Solomon will show how adept he is in exercising that faculty of wary calculation. The Deuteronomistic editor could not delete this material but he sought to provide a counterweight to its unblinking realism by first having David on his deathbed speak in a high moral tone. In fact, nobody in the David story talks like this. The dialogues show nothing of this hortatory style, nothing of this unalloyed didacticism. It is not that the writer is devoid of any ideological viewpoint: he believes in a morally imperative covenantal relationship between God and Israel; he believes in the authority of prophecy; and he believes in the divine election of the Davidic line. But one must hasten to say that he believes in all these things only with enormous dialectic complication, an order of complication so probing that at times it borders on subversion.

The dialectic complication of national ideology is a phenomenon worth explaining, for it brings us to the heart of the greatness of the David story. Biblical scholarship by and large has badly underread this book by imagining that ideological strands can be identified like so many varieties of potatoes and understood as simple expressions of advocacy. In this fashion, it is repeatedly claimed in the critical litera-

ture that one component of the book is prophetic, promoting the interests of prophetic circles; that another is "Saulide"; that a third is basically a narrative apologetic for the Davidic dynasty; and so forth. All of
this strikes me as badly misconceived, and it is blind to the complexity
of vision of this extraordinary writer.

The representation of the prophet Samuel is instructive in this connection. It has been conjectured that a "prophetic" writer, active perhaps a century or two after the reported events, is responsible for this
portion of the book as well as for the ones in which Nathan the
prophet figures. But there is scant evidence in the text for the construction of this hypothetical entity. It is rather like assuming that
Shakespeare must have been a "royalist," or perhaps even royal, writer
in order to have written *Henry IV.* What, in fact, is the writer's attitude
toward Samuel? There is no question that he is shown to be a prophet
confirmed in his vocation by God Himself, as the dedication scene, in
which God calls to him in the night at the Shiloh sanctuary (1 Samuel
3) makes clear. It is concomitantly stressed that Samuel has been chosen to exercise a spiritual authority that will displace the priestly
authority of the house of Eli, on which an irrevocable curse is pronounced soon after the report of Samuel's birth. The entire people
becomes subservient to Samuel, and they feel that only through the
initiative of the prophet (however grudging) can they get the king they
want. In all this, one could claim that the story is confirming a
prophetic ideology by reinforcing the notion of the indispensability of
prophetic authority to Israelite national life.

Yet as in the case of Saul, David, and all the principal figures around
them, Samuel is a densely imagined character, and, it must be said, in
many respects a rather unattractive one. The Israeli poet Yehuda
Amichai neatly catches the dubiety of the mature Samuel in a wry little
poem: "When Samuel was born, she said words of Torah, / 'For this lad
I prayed.' / When he grew up and did the deeds of his life, / she asked,
'For this lad I prayed?' " The prophet Samuel may have God on his side,
but he is also an implacable, irascible man, and often a palpably self-
interested one as well. His resistance to the establishment of the
monarchy may express a commitment to the noble ideal of the direct
kingship of God over Israel, but it is also motivated by resentment that

he must surrender authority, and the second of his two antimonarchic speeches is informed by belligerent self-defensiveness about his own career as national leader. When he chooses Saul, he wants to play him as his puppet, dictating elaborate scenarios to the neophyte king, even setting him up for failure by arriving at an arranged rendezvous at the last possible moment. He is proud, imperious, histrionic—until the very end, when he is conjured up by Saul as a ghost on the eve of the fatal battle at Mount Gilboa.

It would be misleading, I think, to imagine that any of this is intended to discredit the idea of prophetic authority. Samuel is invested with prophetic power by an act of God. But the writer understands that he is also a man, all too human, and that any kind of power, including spiritual power, can lead to abuse. Samuel toys with the idea of creating a kind of prophetic dynasty through his two sons, even though they are just as corrupt as the two sons of Eli, whose immoral behavior seals the doom of their father's priestly line. Is Samuel's choice of Saul really dictated by God, or rather by his own human preconceptions? (He is on the point of making the same mistake twice when he is ready to anoint David's eldest brother Eliab, another strapping young man who seems to stand out from the crowd.) When he insists it is God's will that the entire population and all the livestock of Amalek should be slaughtered, and then offers King Agag as a kind of human sacrifice to the LORD, does he act with divinely authorized prophetic rightness, or, as Martin Buber thought, is he confusing his own human impulses with God's will? The story of Samuel, then, far from being a simple promotion of prophetic ideology, enormously complicates the notion of prophecy by concretely imagining what may become of the imperfect stuff of humanity when the mantle of prophecy is cast over it.

The representation of David is another instance, far more complex and compelling, of the complication of ideology through the imaginative reconstruction of historical figures and events. Before I try to explain how that process is played out in the David story, a few words are in order about the relation of this entire narrative to history.

As with almost every major issue of biblical studies, there have been sharp differences among scholars on this particular question. On the one hand, Gerhard von Rad in the 1940s and others after him have seen the David story as the beginning of history writing in the Western tradition. On the other hand, one group of contemporary scholars, sometimes known as minimalists, is skeptical about whether there ever was a King David and likes to say that this narrative has about the same relation to historical events as do the British legends about King Arthur. The gritty historical realism of the story—what Hans Frei shrewdly identified as its "history-like" character—surely argues against the notion that it is simply legendary. Were David an invention of much later national tradition, he would be the most peculiar of legendary founding kings: a figure who early on is shown as a collaborator with the archenemies of Israel, the Philistines; who compounds adultery with murder; who more than once exposes himself to humiliation, is repeatedly seen in his weakness, and oscillates from nobility of sentiment and act to harsh vindictiveness on his very deathbed. (On this last point, the editorial intervention of the Deuteronomist that we observed suggests that he had inherited not a legendary account but a historical report that made him squirm.) If, moreover, the bulk of the story was actually composed within a generation or two, or perhaps three, after the reported actions, it is hard to imagine how such encompassing national events as a civil war between the house of Saul and the house of David, the Davidic campaigns of conquest east of the Jordan, and the usurpation of the throne by Absalom with the consequent military struggle, could have been invented out of whole cloth.

This narrative nevertheless has many signs of what we would call fictional shaping—interior monologues, dialogues between the historical personages in circumstances where there could have been no witness to what was said, pointed allusions in the turns of the dialogue as well as in the narrative details to Genesis, Joshuah, and Judges. What we have in this great story, as I have proposed elsewhere, is not merely a report of history but an imagining of history that is analogous to what Shakespeare did with historical figures and events in his history plays. That is, the known general contours of the historical events and of the principal players are not tampered with, but the writer brings to bear the resources of his literary art in order to imagine deeply, and critically, the concrete moral and emotional predicaments of living in history, in the political realm. To this end, the writer feels free to invent an inner language for the characters, to give their dialogues revelatory shape, to weave together episodes and characters with a fine mesh of recurrent motifs and phrases and analogies of incident, and to define the meaning of the events through allusion, metaphor, and symbol. The writer does all this not to fabricate history but in order to understand it.

In this elaborately wrought literary vehicle, David turns out to be one of the most unfathomable figures of ancient literature. He begins as the fair-haired boy of Israel—if the term "red" or "ruddy" in his initial description refers to hair color, it might be something like auburn. Everyone seems to love him. He is beautiful, he is musical, and he is brave and brilliantly resourceful on the battlefield. He is also, from the start, quite calculating, and it can scarcely be an accident that until the midpoint of his story every one of his utterances, without exception, is made on a public occasion and arguably is contrived to serve his political interests. The narrative repeatedly reveals to us the churning fears and confusions within Saul while blocking access to David's inner world. Beset by mortal dangers, David is constantly prepared to do almost anything in order to survive: with the help of his devoted wife Michal, wordlessly fleeing Saul's assassins; playing the drooling madman before the Philistine king Achish; serving as vassal to the Philistines, massacring whole towns in order to keep his real actions unknown to his overlords; profiting politically from the chain of violent deaths in the house of Saul while vehemently dissociating himself from each of the killings. He is, in sum, the first full-length portrait of a Machiavellian prince in Western literature. The Book of Samuel is one of those rare masterworks that, like Stendhal's *Charterhouse of Parma,* evinces an unblinking and abidingly instructive knowingness about man as a political animal in all his contradictions and venality and in all his susceptibility to the brutalization and the seductions of exercising power.

And yet, David is more than a probing representation of the ambiguities of political power. He is also an affecting and troubling image of human destiny as husband and father and as a man moving from youth to prime to the decrepitude of old age. The great pivotal moment of the whole story in this regard is when he turns to his perplexed courtiers, after putting aside the trappings of mourning he had assumed for his ailing infant son, now dead, and says, "I am going to him. He will not come back to me." These are the very first words David pronounces that have no conceivable political motive, that give us a glimpse into his inwardness, revealing his sense of naked vulnerability to the inexorable mortality that is the fate of all humankind. For the rest of the story, we shall see David's weakness and his bonds of intimate attachment in fluctuating conflict with the imperatives of power that drive him as a king surrounded by potential enemies and betrayers.

The story of David, in turn, cannot be separated from the story of the man he displaces, Saul. (The moral and psychological complication with which both men are imagined argues powerfully against the simplification of sorting out the book into "Davidide" and "Saulide" narratives.) As a number of observers have proposed—perhaps most vividly, in a series of ballads, the early twentieth-century Hebrew poet Saul Tchernichovsky—Saul is the closest approximation of a tragic hero in the Hebrew Bible. A farm boy from Benjamin seeking his father's lost donkeys, he is overtaken by a destiny of kingship of which he had not dreamed and that at first he tries to escape. Ambivalence and oscillation are the hallmarks of the story of Saul, and the writer may have been led to mirror this condition in his abundant use of paired or even tripled episodes: three different coronation scenes are required for the reluctant Saul; two tales of Saul among the prophets, the first elevating him at the beginning of his career and the second devastating him at the end; two incidents of Saul's hurling his spear at David; two encounters with the fugitive David, who spares his life and receives a pledge of love and a kind of endorsement from Saul, still not to be trusted by David as the older man veers wildly between opposed feelings.

The stories of Saul and David interlock antithetically on the theme of knowledge. Saul, from first to last, is a man deprived of the knowledge he desperately seeks. At the outset, he has to turn to the seer Samuel in order to find his father's asses. In subsequent episodes, he has no luck with oracles and divination in guiding him on his military way, and he tries to coerce fate by imposing a rash vow of fasting

on his troops in the midst of battle. He seizes on the report of informers in his pursuit of David, but David continues to elude him. At the
very end, on the eve of his last battle, he tries oracle and prophecy and
dreams in order to find out what the impending future will be, but all
fail, and he is compelled to resort to the very art of necromancy that he
himself had made a capital crime. The knowledge he then receives
from the implacable ghost of Samuel is nothing but the news of his
own imminent doom.

David, on the other hand, at first seems peculiarly favored with
knowledge. The position that he is brought to the court to fill is for a
man "skilled in playing" (the literal meaning of the Hebrew is *"knowing
to play"*) and "prudent in speech." In what follows, David demonstrates
impressive prudence and agile resourcefulness. It also emerges that
once he has become a fugitive, he is rapidly equipped with an oracular
ephod and a priest to use it and so, in contrast to Saul, has a direct line
of communication with God in making his key decisions. Much later
in the story, when things have begun to fall apart, the wise woman from
Tekoa will tell David, "My lord is wise as with the wisdom of a messenger of God, to know everything in the land" (2 Samuel 14:20). By this
point, however, it has become painfully evident that her words are a
gesture of deference to the king that is ironically contradicted by fact.
The knowing David of the earlier part of the narrative has become the
king isolated in his palace. He must even send intermediaries to discover the identity of the naked beauty bathing on the rooftop in view of
his palace, though she seems to be the daughter of one of the members
of his own elite guard. He is singularly unaware of his son Amnon's lust
for his half sister Tamar, then of Absalom's plot to murder Amnon in
revenge, then of Absalom's scheme to usurp the throne. The pitiful
image of the shivering, bedridden David, ignorant of the grand feast of
self-coronation arranged by his son Adonijah, then reminded or perhaps rather persuaded by Bathsheba and Nathan that he has promised
the throne to Solomon, is the ultimate representation of the painful
decline of knowledge in this once perspicacious figure, the brilliant
successor to the purblind Saul.

Who could have written a story like this, and what could his motives
have been? The way this question is typically posed in biblical studies

is to ask what interests the writer could have been serving, but it seems to me that framing the issue in those terms involves a certain reductionism which harks back to the historical positivism of the nineteenth century. Although it is safe to assume that no biblical author wrote merely to entertain his audiences, and although there is no evidence of a class of professional storytellers in ancient Israel analogous to the bards of Greece, the social location and political aims of the biblical writer remain unclear. (The prophets, who sometimes incorporated autobiographical passages in their writing, and who stand out sharply as critics of society and often of the royal establishment, are the one clear exception to this rule.) Scholars of the Bible often speak of "schools" or "circles" of biblical writing (prophetic, priestly, Wisdom, Davidic, and so forth), but in fact we have no direct knowledge of such groups as cultural institutions. The one school or movement for which a very strong case can be made is the Deuteronomistic movement. In this instance, a comprehensive, uncompromising reform of cultic practice, theology, and law was instituted during the reign of Josiah, around 622 B.C.E. The Book of Deuteronomy was composed, with abundant satellite literature to come after it, as a forceful literary instrument of the reform. In the great speeches of Deuteronomy, literature has patently been marshalled to inculcate an ideological program. Yet the very contrast we observed in 1 Kings 2 between the didacticism of the Deuteronomist and the worldly realism of the author of the David story argues for the idea that the latter had very different aims in mind from the simple promotion of a political program.

My guess is that the author of the David story thought of himself as a historian. But even if he frequented the court in Jerusalem, a plausible but not at all necessary supposition, he was by no means a writer of court annals or chronicles of the kings of Judea, and, as I have argued, he was far from being an apologist for the Davidic dynasty. I would imagine that he was impelled to write out of a desire to convey to his contemporaries and to posterity a true account of the significant events involved in the founding of the monarchy that governed the nation. It is conceivable that he had some written reports of these events at his disposal or at any rate drew on oral accounts of the events. Perhaps he had spoken with old-timers who were actual participants, or, if one places him very early, he himself might have been an observer of some of what he reports. He also did not hesitate to exploit etiological tales (Saul among the prophets) and folk tales (David slaying the giant Goliath) in order to flesh out his historical account and dramatize its meanings. Though committed to telling the truth about history, his notion of historical factuality was decidedly different from modern ones. His conception of history writing involved not merely registering what had happened and who had been the principal actors but also reflecting on the shifting interplay between character and historical act, on the way social and political institutions shape and distort individual lives, on the human costs of particular political choices.

The author of the David story was in all likelihood firmly committed to the legitimacy of the Davidic line. In the book he wrote, after all, God explicitly elects David once Saul has been rejected and later promises that the throne of David will remain unshaken for all time. But the author approaches the David story as an imaginative writer, giving play to that dialectic fullness of conception that leads the greatest writers (Shakespeare, Stendhal, Balzac, Tolstoy, Proust, to name a few apposite instances) to transcend the limitations of their own ideological points of departure. Even though the vocational identity of "imaginative writer" was not socially defined in ancient Israel as it would be in later cultures, the accomplished facts of literary art in many cultures, ancient and modern, suggest that the impulse of literary creation, with the breadth of vision that at its best it encourages, is universal.

The person who wrote this story is not only a formidably shrewd observer of politics and human nature but also someone who manifestly delights in the writerly pleasures of his craft and is sometimes led to surprising insights by his exploration of those pleasures. He has an ear for dialogue, and for the contrastive treatment of the two interlocutors in particular dialogues, that Joyce might have envied. Though both narrator and characters are sparing in figurative language, the metaphors he gives them are telling, and sometimes set up electrically charged links between one moment of the story and another. This writer has a keen sense of the thematic uses of analogy between one episode and another, as when he gives us Amnon lying in a pretended sickbed so that he can summon his sister Tamar to serve his violent lust, right after the story of David's rising from his siesta bed to see the bathing Bathsheba and then summon her to the palace for his illicit pleasure. (Both prohibited sexual acts lead to murder and political disarray.) Like most of the great masters of narrative art, the author of the David story is constantly asking himself what it must be like concretely—emotionally, psychologically, morally, even physically—to be one or another of these characters in a particular predicament, and it is this salutary imaginative habit that generates many of the dialectic complications of the historical account. Saul on the last night of his life is not merely represented as fearful of the Philistine foe but driven by desperation into the necromancer's den. This last gesture of grasping for knowledge denied makes the fate of the defeated king seem wrenching, indeed, tragic. David's flight from Absalom is not merely a story of political intrigue and opposing interests but also a tale of anguished conflict between father and king in the same man, culminating in David's horrendous stutter of grief over Absalom's death and followed by Joab's harsh rebuke to him for his behavior.

One of the hallmarks of this whole writerly relation to the historical material is the freighted imagining of the detail not strictly necessary to the historical account. Let me offer one brief instance that may stand for all the others. David's first wife Michal, it will be recalled, is married off by her father Saul to a man named Paltiel son of Laish after David's flight from his father-in-law's assassins. We know nothing about Paltiel except his name, and nothing about Michal's feelings concerning the union with him imposed by her father. When Abner, the commander of the forces of the house of Saul, comes to transfer his fealty to David and end the civil war, David stipulates that Michal daughter of Saul must first be sent back to him. (Presumably, his motive is strictly political.) Michal is duly removed by royal decree from Paltiel, with no word or emotion of hers reported by the writer. What he does give us are these few, indelible words: "And her husband went with her, weeping as he went after her, as far as Bahurim. And Abner said to him, 'Go back!' And he went back." (2 Samuel 3:16). To a sober historian, this moment might well seem superfluous. To a great imaginative writer like the author of this story, such moments are the heart of the matter. Paltiel never even speaks in the story, but his weeping speaks volumes. He is a loving husband caught between the hard and unyielding men who wield power in the world—Abner, Saul's tough field commander, and his adversary turned ally, David, who insists on the return of the woman he has acquired with a bloody bride price because he calculates that as Saul's daughter she will bolster his claim to be Saul's legitimate successor. The tearful Paltiel walking after the wife who is being taken from him, then driven back by the peremptory word of the strongman with whom he cannot hope to contend, is a poignant image of the human price of political power. If history, in the hackneyed aphorism, is the story told by the victors, this narrative achieves something closer to the aim that Walter Benjamin defined as the task of the historical materialist, "to brush history against the grain." Lacking all but the scantiest extrahistorical evidence, we shall probably never know precisely what happened in Jerusalem and Judea and the high country of Benjamin around the turn of the first millennium B.C.E., when the Davidic dynasty was established. What matters is that the anonymous Hebrew writer, drawing on what he knew or thought he knew of the portentous historical events, has created this most searching story of men and women in the rapid and dangerous current of history that still speaks to us, floundering in history and the dilemmas of political life, three thousand years later.

2. THE TEXT

From what do you translate the Bible? This abrupt question, which has been put to me several times since I ventured into doing a new English version of Genesis, is either very naive (from what language?) or quite challenging (from what text?). Any text, sacred or profane, that has been handed down for nearly three thousand years is likely to be the worse for wear, and unfortunately the textual perplexities in Samuel abound to a degree that makes all but the archaic poetic insets in Genesis seem relatively transparent. There are many instances of what appears to be haplography—in which the scribe's eye has inadvertently skipped over a repeated phrase or clause or letter and thus deleted it, and also some evident cases of its inverse, dittography, in which a phrase, a clause, or individual words or letters have been inadvertently repeated in the copying process. There is a sprinkling of otherwise unknown Hebrew terms that might conceivably be rare words or might simply reflect words garbled in transcription. And from time to time one encounters a whole clause in the Hebrew that looks like gibberish because the syntactic or even grammatical link between one word and the next has somehow been scrambled.

Elaborate analytic and reconstructive studies have been devoted to the text of Samuel. The troubling question that underlies all such efforts is what alternative there is to the Masoretic Text, the received Hebrew text of the book (*masoret* is Hebrew for "tradition"). The Masoretic Text of the Bible was established by a school of grammarians and textual scholars in Tiberias sometime between the seventh and the tenth centuries C.E., which is to say, more than a millennium and a half after the likely original composition of the book we are considering. The Tiberian scholars sorted out textual variants and decided which readings were to be deemed authoritative; they added a system of vowel points ("vocalization") to the consonantal Hebrew text and a set of symbols for cantillation that also served as demarcations of syntactic and semantic units. The oldest integral manuscript of the Hebrew Bible that has been preserved is the Aleppo Codex, dating from around the year 1000 C.E. Among the scrolls discovered in the caves at Qumran overlooking the Dead Sea is a copy of Samuel, partly decomposed, found in Cave IV. The fragmentary Qumran Samuel scroll, more than a thousand years older than the Aleppo Codex, has provided plausible alternatives to quite a few opaque formulations in the Masoretic Text. However, one cannot assume that it is invariably more authoritative, because the scribe or subtradition responsible for it, after all, may have resolved some difficulties in the inherited text by a clarifying reformulation of it.

Beyond these precious parchment scraps of Hebrew manuscript from a moment just after the biblical period proper, alternatives to the Masoretic Text are provided by the so-called ancient witnesses, that is, the earliest translations of the Hebrew Bible in late antiquity into Greek, Latin, Syriac, and Jewish Aramaic, together with citations from the Bible in Josephus. The assumption scholars make in using these different versions is that in particular instances the ancient translators may have been working from a more reliable Hebrew text than transmitted to us by the Tiberian Masoretes. The oldest of these translations, the Greek, or Septuagint, done in Alexandria in the third century B.C.E., is the one that scholars have drawn on most heavily for solutions to puzzles in the Masoretic Text. (It should be said that the Septuagint has its own difficulties of transmission and exists in several different textual versions.) In my own translation, I have resorted to alternative readings from the Septuagint a little more often than I would have liked simply because careful consideration in many instances compelled me to conclude that the wording in the Masoretic Text was unintelligible or self-contradictory. Nevertheless, as a matter of methodological principle I strenuously disagree with the practice of those biblical scholars who put the Masoretic Text and the Septuagint on an equal footing and choose variants between the two strictly on the basis of what seems to them the more attractive reading. The Greek translators obviously had before them an older version of the book than appears in the Masoretic Bible, but there is no reason to assume that it was invariably a better version. And the fact remains that the Greeks were translators, obliged as translators to clarify obscure points, resolve contradictions, and otherwise make the Hebrew text with which they labored intelligible to their Greek readers.

My own practice, then, as translator has been to follow the Masoretic Text as long as it made some sense, even if a seductive variant beckoned from the Septuagint or elsewhere. When the received text struck me as really unviable, even by an interpretive stretch, I considered alternatives from the ancient witnesses, feeling a little more confident in those instances in which a variant reading in the Septuagint was explicitly confirmed by the Hebrew text from Qumran. Ultimately, all such decisions depend on the interpreter's discretion, and I have tried to keep in mind the tried-and-true textual principle that the more difficult reading is more likely to be the authentic one, because transmitters of texts tend to regularize and simplify features that seem out of the ordinary. In all instances in which my translation diverges from the Masoretic Text, I have offered an indication, usually with an explanation, in my notes that I was adopting a different reading.

Let me give one illustration of a moment in which it seemed to me that the case was fairly compelling for turning to a variant in the Septuagint. In 1 Samuel 14:18, Saul, at the head of his army, is wondering what course of action he should take against the Philistines. We are told, in the Masoretic Text (this rendering is quite literal), "And Saul said to Ahijah, 'Bring forth the Ark of God.' For the Ark of God on that day was, and the Israelites." It is immediately evident that the second sentence here is fragmentary, each of its two clauses breaking off abruptly, with the syntactic link between them unclear. An even greater perplexity is the presence of the Ark of God on the battlefield and its use (as the context makes clear) for inquiry of an oracle. After the earlier disaster in carrying the Ark to the front and after the lethal consequences of its return from Philistia to Israel, the people had firmly concluded that the dangerous Ark should be left at Kiriath-jearim (1 Samuel 5), and the later narrative strongly implies that it remained ensconced there until the victorious David came to take it up to Jerusalem. There is, moreover, no indication elsewhere in the Bible that the Ark was ever used as an instrument of divination. The oracular device that was repeatedly employed was a cultic object called the ephod, and that is what appears in the Septuagint reading of this verse, which I decided to adopt: "And Saul said to Ahijah, 'Bring forth the ephod.' For on that day he was bearing the ephod before the Israelites." Admittedly, there can be no certainty in such matters, but when the received text combines in a single verse a blatantly contradictory narrative datum and syntactic incoherence, it is not unreasonable to conclude that an ancient version free of both defects may reflect the original wording of the story.

The one other alternative to the Masoretic Text is emendation, without warrant from the ancient witnesses. In this regard I have exerted the greatest caution, again assuming that if the received text made any sense, it should stand. I have limited my very infrequent emendations (including the adoption of the emendations of others) to revocalizing certain words—one should remember that the vocalization is an artifact of scholars working well over a thousand years after the composition of the text—or to changing one or two consonants. These rare emendations are duly noted in the commentary. But as a rule, I have kept in mind Samuel Johnson's eminently sensible remark on the emendation of a much more recent text in his *Preface to Shakesepeare*: "To alter is more easy than to explain, and temerity is a more common quality than diligence." This is prudent advice but a little too pat. Sometimes diligence devolves into mere ingenuity in the effort to rescue the text as it stands, and when I felt that was happening, I at least considered the possibility of trying to restore the text instead of interpreting its received version.

3. THE TRANSLATION

This English version of Samuel follows the same principles of Bible translation that I tried to implement in my translation of Genesis. Since I explained those principles at some length in the introduction I wrote to Genesis, let me simply repeat here the brief summary I wrote of what seems to me an appropriate modern equivalent for the ancient Hebrew style.

If one keeps in mind the strong element of stylization of the ancient language even in its own time, there is no good reason to render biblical Hebrew as contemporary English, either lexically or syntactically. This is not to suggest that the Bible should be represented as fussily old-fashioned English. However, a limited degree of archaizing coloration is entirely appropriate, employed with other strategies for creating a language that is stylized yet simple and direct, free of the overtones of contemporary colloquial usage but with a certain timeless homespun quality. An adequate English version should be able to indicate the small but significant modulations in diction in the biblical language. A suitable English version should avoid at all costs the modern abomination of elegant synonymous variation, for the literary prose of the Bible turns everywhere on significant repetition, not variation. Similarly, the translation of terms on the basis of immediate context—except when it becomes grotesque to do otherwise—is to be resisted as another instance of the heresy of explanation. Finally, the mesmerizing effect of these ancient stories will scarcely be conveyed if they are not rendered in cadenced English prose that at least in some ways corresponds to the powerful cadences of the Hebrew.

I would like to comment briefly on just two issues with which I did not deal directly in my remarks about translating Genesis—literalism and semantic precision. My notion of an effective translation of the Bible involves a high degree of literalism—within the limits of reasonably acceptable literary English—both in regard to representing the word choices and the word order of the Hebrew. Such adherence to the verbal contours of the original is in large part justified by the fact that the Hebrew choice of terms, operating within the limits of a rigorously restricted vocabulary, is so finely apt and the Hebrew syntax is often so beautifully expressive, as I explained with illustrative detail in my introduction to Genesis. What is clearer to me now is that the precedent of the King James Version has played a decisive and constructive role in directing readers of English to a rather literal experience of the Bible, and that this precedent can be ignored only at considerable cost, as nearly all the English versions of the Bible done in recent decades show. The men responsible for the 1611 version authorized by King James, following the great model of William Tyndale a century earlier, produced an English Bible that often, though by no means invariably, evinced a striking fidelity to many of the literary articulations of the Hebrew text. This success of course reflected their remarkable sense of English style (nothing traduces the power of the original more egregiously than the nonstyle cultivated by the sundry modern versions), but it was also a consequence of their literalism. The literalism was dictated by their firm conviction as Christians that every word of the biblical text was literally inspired by God. That belief led them to replicate significant verbal repetition in the original, avoiding elegant synonymity, and to reproduce in English many of the telling word choices of the biblical writers. It also encouraged them to convey Hebrew idioms in English as though they had always been indigenous English idioms—a trick that may now be beyond us but that is worth trying to emulate. Finally, as a matter of cultural history, it is through the language of the King James Version that nearly four centuries of

English speakers have experienced the Bible, and it has had a pro-found effect on literary English from Herbert to Blake to Melville to Joyce, Faulkner, and Hemingway. This history makes it difficult, I sus-pect, for any English version that wrenches itself entirely from the underlying conception of translation embodied in the King James Ver-sion to be read as an authentically literary rendering of the Bible.

I am not proposing that contemporary translators of the Bible should deliberately mine the King James Version for phrasing or some-how imitate it word for word (like José Luís Borges's Pierre Menard, who through successive drafts laboriously reproduces the entire *Don Quixote* word for word, imparting layers of irony and new meaning because he is doing this in the twentieth century). The fundamental notion, however, of a subtly stylized, eloquent, Hebraizing English that formally echoes the ancient language in some of its features seems to me vital. In my own procedure as translator, I was careful not to look at the King James Version or at any other translation until I had com-pleted a draft of the section on which I was working. From time to time, I would then discover that in a particular choice of phrase I had, like Pierre Menard, reinvented verbatim my seventeeth-century prede-cessor. Only rarely did I change my own wording by deliberately adopt-ing a formulation from the King James Version. And just a few times, I used a phrase from the 1611 translation because it was both famous and beautiful and, whatever the scholarly challenges, still philologically defensible—as, for example, David's anxious words to his generals before the battle with Absalom's army, "Deal gently for my sake with the young man, even with Absalom" (my version, somewhat pared down in consonance with the compactness of the Hebrew, reads, "Deal gently for me with the lad Absalom"). The commitment to liter-alism, in sum, that I have sought to honor, in keeping with the prece-dent of the great seventeenth-century English version, is not, as many modern treatments of the Bible assume, an impediment to the literary experience of the ancient narratives but, on the contrary, its necessary vehicle.

The effort to convey something of the eloquence of the Hebrew, its shifting levels of diction, its rhythmic power, and its expressive syntax by no means precludes a concern for philological precision. The bibli-

cal writers, like great writers elsewhere, chose their terms very scrupu-
lously. Their choices are all the more telling because they occur, as I
have noted, in a narrative tradition that imposes limits on the range of
vocabulary that can be used. It is unfortunate that the nuanced meanings of the stories are often thrown slightly out of focus by translators
who, even in a philologically informed age, too often settle for loose
approximations of the original. I have indicated in my notes particular
instances where a juster English equivalent than the customary one is
required, but let me offer a few quick examples here. The leaders of
the Philistine towns are referred to in the Hebrew as *seranim*, evidently
a Philistine loanword (which, because of the origins of the Philistines
in the Greek sphere, some have thought may be related to the Greek
tyrannos, itself a term evidently drawn from one of the languages of
Asia Minor). This term is usually represented in English as "lords," but
the story makes clear that the *seranim* are not a general class of nobility
but the regents of the five principal Philistine towns, for there are only
five of them. In order at least to intimate this distinction, I call them
"overlords." On the Israelite side, there are several references to the
be'alim of one town or another. In the existing English versions, this
term usually comes up, again, as the all-purpose "lords," or simply as
"men." The Hebrew word means "master" or "owner" and is not necessarily associated with the idea of nobility. In a social context, it probably suggests something like a prominent and powerful citizen, so in my
rendering the *be'alim* of the town are its "notables." Amnon, pretending
to be desperately ill, asks Tamar to prepare him *biryah*, repeatedly represented in the various English versions as "food." But the general term
for food would be *'okhel* or, in a common synecdoche, *lehem* ("bread").
By contrast, *biryah* is the food you give a person who has been fasting
or who is physically failing in order to make him *bar'i* (hale, fat). The
choice of term adds a nuance of urgency to Amnon's demand, one
which I try to mirror by calling what he wants from Tamar "nourishment." In my final example, after David has volunteered to confront
Goliath, Saul attempts to dress him in his own *madim*. This has been
loosely rendered as "tunic" (Revised English Bible) or "garment" (New
Jewish Publication Society). The King James Version is closer in calling it "armor," though *madim* (the form is plural) are not armor but

rather a particular kind of clothing that is worn during the performance of a public duty, whether priestly or military or diplomatic (like the torn garments of David's ambassadors in 2 Samuel 10, whose diplomatic privilege is violated when the uncouth Ammonites cut their *madim* in half). Kyle McCarter, Jr. in the Anchor Bible Samuel tries to get this nuance through "uniform" (which happens to be the meaning of *madim* in Israeli Hebrew), but it is highly unlikely that uniforms, which were devised for modern regimented armies, were worn in ancient Israel. My own choice was "battle garb," which seemed semantically right and sounded appropriate as diction, and in keeping with this decision, I have the ambassadors of the later story wearing "diplomatic garb."

Objections can of course be raised to any of these solutions. The underlying principle, however, is that the literary force of the original resides verbally not merely in a complex of aesthetic effects (the "eloquence" of the prose) but also in a rigorously precise vocabulary that nicely defines actions, instruments, persons, and motives. Narrative interpretation and philological analysis are not competing activities but mutually instructing moments in a single dynamic process of understanding. It is this reciprocity between the literary and the lexical that I have striven to embody in my English version of Samuel.

4. THE COMMENTARY

One minimal but necessary constituent of the commentary was dictated by the special problems of presenting an ancient and often translated text to readers of modern English. As a translator, I felt obliged to annotate particular choices that might seem surprising or even peculiar to readers of the Bible—divergences from the Masoretic Text and English renderings that swerve from the precedent of earlier translations. Given my commitment, moreover, to a rather literal representation of the Hebrew (more literal, in fact, than the King James Version), I also thought it appropriate to indicate the places where the requirements of intelligible English usage compelled me, reluctantly, to recast a Hebrew idiom in more indigenously English terms. And where the

Hebrew has a wordplay or soundplay that I was unable to intimate in the English, I have provided a brief notation. Beyond such issues of translation, because this is a story written in the early Iron Age in a culture quite different from ours, it made sense to provide some general orientation about cultural contexts for the modern reader, who is likely to have no more than a hazy idea about what was involved in a sacrificial feast or a sheep-shearing festival, what were the mechanisms of Israelite divination, what were the prevalent beliefs about ghosts and the underworld, what were the geostrategic conditions of warfare under which the reported battles took place. Some information of this sort is needed simply in order to follow what is going on the story, but I have consciously sought to limit the explanations of cultural practices and historical context to a necessary minimum. Scholarly commentaries and ancillary guides, dictionaries and encylopedias of the Bible can offer the curious reader a wealth of informative details about ancient Israel and its Near Eastern neighbors, but that is not my purpose.

What I have chiefly tried to do, beyond the sort of explanatory notes to which I have just referred, is to throw light on this book as someone trained in literature and deeply excited by the extraordinary narrative art of the David story, which becomes the vehicle for a penetrating representation of human nature, politics, and history. My comments for the most part are directed to issues that at best are only marginally touched on in the standard scholarly commentaries: the handling of dialogue, the opening or blocking of access to the thoughts and feelings of the characters, the intricate system of motif and analogy that links different episodes, the subtle means through which motive and moral quandary are intimated, the multifarious ways in which the terrible dilemmas of political life are pondered through narrative representation. With these concerns in mind, I did not think it appropriate to try to engage the abundant text-critical scholarship (much of it German) on Samuel that has attempted to sort out the purported historical layers and variegated literary components of the book. I have borrowed an occasional insight from one or another of the medieval Hebrew exegetes, though by and large they have less to say on this text than they do on the Pentateuch. Several recent scholars who bring literary perspectives to bear have been helpful to my own reading and are acknowledged in the commentary on specific points where I was indebted to them: the Israelis Shimon Bar-Efrat and Moshe Garsiel, both writing in Hebrew; and the two scholars who have produced the most perceptive close readings of the Book of Samuel, J. P. Fokkelman and Robert Polzin (though I share neither Fokkelman's commitment to structuralist analysis nor Polzin's notion of a pervasive Deuterono-mistic viewpoint).

The temptations to comment at great length on the minute details of this inexhaustible story are great, but I have deliberately kept the commentary to fairly modest proportions. I would rather emulate the cogent concision of my favorite commentators, both medieval—Rashi and Abraham ibn Ezra—than in any way aspire to the encyclopedic pro-portions of modern biblical scholars, whose commentaries typically stand in a ratio of ten to one, a hundred to one, or even (this is not an exaggeration) a thousand to one, to the text expounded. In the transla-tion itself, I have mustered whatever literary and linguistic resources I could call on in order to attempt to convey in English at least some-thing of the power, the subtlety, the incisiveness of language, and the rhythmic momentum of the Hebrew narrative that has cast its spell for nearly three thousand years over audiences who could follow it in its original language. The commentary is conceived as handmaiden to the translation. It is, I freely confess, the work of an unrepentant literary critic, but its principal aim is to serve the story, to highlight its literary force by offering a kind of analytic supplement to the translator's effort at fashioning an English style that might in some degree answer to the finely wrought Hebrew.

A NOTE ON TRANSLITERATION

We have only an approximate idea of the pronunciation of Hebrew in the biblical period. The transliteration in this commentary by and large reflects the way the language is pronounced by speakers of Hebrew now, with the exception of *w* for biblical *waw* (modern Hebrew *vav*), adopted in order to avoid confusion with the *v* that is used here for the consonant *bet* when it lacks the *dagesh* that makes it a hard *b*. Most of the diacritical marks used in scholarly transliteration are avoided because they would be obstacles rather than guides to the general reader. There are three exceptions: ʾ indicates the Hebrew letter *ʾaleph,* probably a lightly aspirated consonant in the biblical period and no longer pronounced. ʿ indicates the Hebrew letter ʿ*ayin,* pronounced as a glottal stop in the biblical period. Ḥ is used for Hebrew *ḥet,* a light fricative something like the Spanish *j* in *mujer. Kh* represents Hebrew *khaf,* a heavier fricative closer to the German pronunciation of *ch* in words such as *machen.* In accordance with the general effort to keep the transliteration simple, consonants that are supposedly doubled by being marked with a *dagesh* are not doubled in the English transcription because there is no audible difference in the way anyone pronounces them today. Thus the word for battle garb is represented as *madim,* not *maddim.*

ACKNOWLEDGMENTS

The manuscript was read with scrupulous care by Michael André Bernstein, Stanley Burnshaw, Carol Cosman, Steve Forman, and Thomas G. Rosenmeyer. I am fortunate to have had such intelligently attentive readers. They saved me from a good many lapses of judgment in the translation as well as sins of omission and commission in the commentary. In some instances, I stubbornly persisted in my own peculiar decisions despite suggestions to the contrary, so these wise counselors and friends should not be held responsible for anything that may seem amiss to certain readers. I am especially grateful to Steve Forman, my editor, for encouraging me in this project from the start and for offering several helpful general proposals about the presentation of the material. Although on questions of Hebrew philology I kept my own counsel, I did run a few of my original notions by Shalom Paul of the Hebrew University of Jerusalem, and I appreciated getting confirmation of my hunches from a scholar with such a splendid mastery of ancient Near Eastern languages and cultural contexts.

Secretarial and research costs were covered by income from the Class of 1937 Chair of Hebrew and Comparative Literature at the University of California at Berkeley, and a Humanities Research Fellowship from the Berkeley campus provided a sabbatical salary supplement that enabled me to take off a semester in order to complete preparation of the manuscript. Janet Livingstone did an admirable job in translating my scribbled drafts into elegantly readable computer printouts, with the commentary neatly answering the translated text above it.

I SAMUEL

CHAPTER 1

And there was a man from Ramathaim-zophim, from the high country of   1
Ephraim, and his name was Elkanah son of Jeroham son of Elihu son
of Tohu son of Zuph, an Ephraimite. And he had two wives; the name   2
of the one was Hannah and the name of the other, Peninnah. And

---

The story of Hannah provides an instructive illustration of the conventions of
narrative exposition that govern a large number of biblical stories. First the main
character, or characters, are identified by name, pedigree, and geographical location. The only verb used is "to be" (verses 1–2). In this instance the standard biblical story beginning, "there was a man," is in part a false lead because the real
protagonist of the story is Elkanah's wife Hannah. Then there is a series of
reported actions in the iterative tense—that is, an indication of habitually
repeated actions (verses 3–7). (In all this, compare Job 1.) The narrative then
zooms in to a particular moment, one of those annually repeated events of Hannah's frustration at Shiloh, by way of Elkanah's dialogue (verse 8), which could
not plausibly be an iterative event. At this point, we have moved from prelude to
story proper. The writer himself seems quite conscious of this play between
recurring units of time and specific moments in time: the word *yamim*, "days,"
but often as in verse 3 with the sense of "annual cycle," is used five times, together
with the singular *yom*, in an iterative sense, at the beginning of verse 4. (These
recurrences are complemented by "year after year," *shanah beshanah*, in verse 7.)

2. *And he had two wives.* The reference to two wives, one childbearing, the
other childless, immediately alerts the audience to the unfolding of the familiar annunciation type-scene. The expected sequence of narrative motifs of the
annunciation scene is: the report of the wife's barrenness (amplified by the
optional motif of the fertile co-wife less loved by the husband than is the
childless wife); the promise, through oracle or divine messenger or man of
God, of the birth of a son; cohabitation resulting in conception and birth. As
we shall see, the middle motif is articulated in a way that is distinctive to the
concerns of the Samuel story.

3 Peninnah had children but Hannah had no children. And this man
would go up from his town year after year to worship and to sacrifice to
the LORD of Hosts at Shiloh, and there the two sons of Eli, Hophni and
4 Phineas, were priests to the LORD. And when the day came round,
Elkanah would sacrifice and give portions to Peninnah his wife and to
5 all her sons and her daughters. And to Hannah he would give one double portion, for Hannah he loved, and the LORD had closed her womb.
6 And her rival would torment her sorely so as to provoke her because
7 the LORD had closed up her womb. And thus was it done year after
year—when she would go up to the house of the LORD, the other
would torment her and she would weep and would not eat.

8 And Elkanah her husband said to her, "Hannah, why do you weep and
why do you not eat and why is your heart afflicted? Am I not better to
9 you than ten sons?" And Hannah arose after the eating in Shiloh and

---

3. *the two sons of Eli.* The reference is initially puzzling but points forward to
the focus on proper and improper heirs to the priesthood in Samuel's story.

5. *and to Hannah he would give one double portion.* The Hebrew phrase, which
occurs only here, means literally "one portion [for the?] face," and has perplexed commentators. The conclusion of several modern translators that the
phrase means "only a single portion" makes nonsense out of the following
words that the allotment was an expression of Elkanah's special love. It seems
wisest to follow a long tradition of commentators who take a cue from the
doublative ending of ʾapayim, the word for "face" (perhaps even a textual corruption for another word meaning "double") and to construe this as a double
portion to Hannah who, alas, unlike Peninnah, has no children.

7. *and thus was it done.* The Hebrew is literally "thus did he do," but the impersonal masculine active singular is often used in this kind of passive sense.
   the other. The Hebrew simply says "she," but the antecedent is clearly
Peninnah.

8. *am I not better to you than ten sons?* The double-edged poignancy of these
words is that they at once express Elkanah's deep and solicitous love for Hannah and his inability to understand how inconsolable she feels about her affliction of barrenness. All the annunciation stories must be understood in light of
the prevalent ancient Near Eastern view that a woman's one great avenue to
fulfillment in life was through the bearing of sons. It is noteworthy that Hannah does not respond to Elkanah. When she does at last speak, it is to God.

after the drinking, while Eli the priest was sitting in a chair by the doorpost of the LORD's temple. And she was deeply embittered, and 10 she prayed to the LORD, weeping all the while. And she vowed a vow 11 and said, "LORD of Hosts, if you really will look on your servant's woe and remember me, and forget not your servant and give your servant male seed, I will give him to the LORD all the days of his life, no razor shall touch his head." And it happened as she went on with her prayer 12 before the LORD, with Eli watching her mouth, as Hannah was speak- 13 ing in her heart, her lips alone moving and her voice not heard, Eli thought she was drunk. And Eli said to her, 14

"How long will you go on drunk?
Rid yourself of your wine!"

---

11. *I will give him to the LORD.* Hannah's prayer exhibits a directness of style, without ornament or conventional liturgical phrasing, and an almost naive simplicity: if you give him to me, I will give him to you. This canceling out of the two givings is reconciled by the introduction of another verb at the end of the story: Hannah "lends" to God the child He has given her.

no razor shall touch his head. As an expression of her dedication of the prayed-for child, Hannah vows that he will be a Nazirite (like Samson), a person specially dedicated to God who took a vow of abstinence from certain activities. (The literal meaning of the Hebrew is "no razor will go up on his head.") The Nazirites also refrained from wine, which throws an ironic backlight on Eli's subsequent accusation that Hannah is drunk. A few biblical texts link Nazirite and prophet.

14. *How long will you go on drunk?* The central annunciation motif of the type-scene is purposefully distorted. Since Hannah receives no direct response from God—she prays rather than inquires of an oracle—Eli the priest should be playing the role of man of God or divine intermediary. But at first he gets it all wrong, mistaking her silent prayer for drunken mumbling, and denouncing her in a poetic line (marked by semantic and rhythmic parallelism) of quasi-prophetic verse. When in verse 17 he accepts her protestation of innocent suffering, he piously prays or predicts—the Hebrew verb could be construed either way—that her petition will be granted, but he doesn't have a clue about the content of the petition. The uncomprehending Eli is thus virtually a parody of the annunciating figure of the conventional type-scene—an apt introduction to a story in which the claim to authority of the house of Eli will be rejected, and, ultimately, sacerdotal guidance will be displaced by prophetic guidance in the person of Samuel, who begins as a temple acolyte but then exercises a very different kind of leadership.

15 And Hannah answered and said, "No, my lord! A bleak-spirited woman
am I. Neither wine nor hard drink have I drunk, but I poured out my
16 heart to the LORD. Think not your servant a worthless girl, for out of
17 my great trouble and torment I have spoken till now." And Eli
answered and said, "Go in peace, and may the God of Israel grant your
18 petition which you asked of Him." And she said, "May your servant but
find favor in your eyes." And the woman went on her way, and she ate,
19 and her face was no longer downcast. And they rose early in the morning and bowed before the LORD and returned and came to their home
in Ramah. And Elkanah knew Hannah his wife and the LORD remem-
20 bered her. And it happened at the turn of the year that Hannah conceived and bore a son, and she called his name Samuel, "For from the
LORD I asked for him."

21 And the man Elkanah with all his household went up to offer to the
22 LORD the yearly sacrifice and his votive pledge. But Hannah did not go

---

15. *bleak-spirited.* The Hebrew, which occurs only here as a collocation, is literally "hard-spirited."

20. *She called his name Samuel.* There is a small puzzlement in the Hebrew
because it is the name Saul, *Sha'ul,* not Samuel, *Shmu'el,* that means "asked"
(or "lent"). This has led some modern scholars to speculate that a story originally composed to explain the birth of Saul was transferred to Samuel—perhaps because Saul's eventual unworthiness to reign made it questionable that
he should merit a proper annunciation scene. But it must be said that the only
evidence for this speculation is the seeming slippage of names here. That
could easily be explained, as by the thirteenth-century Hebrew commentator
David Kimchi, if we assume Hannah is playing on two Hebrew words, *sha'ul
me'el,* "asked of God."

21. *the yearly sacrifice.* The annual cycle of iterative actions invoked at the
beginning is seemingly resumed, but everything is different now that Hannah
has born a son, and she herself introduces a change in the repeated pattern.
   votive pledge. Although this is the same Hebrew term, *neder,* that is used
for Hannah's vow at the beginning of verse 11, its most likely referent here is a
vowed thanksgiving offering on the part of the husband for his wife's safe
delivery of a son.

up, for she had said to her husband, "Till the lad is weaned! Then I will bring him and we will see the LORD's presence, and he shall stay there always." And Elkanah her husband said to her, "Do what is right in your 23 eyes. Stay till you wean him, only may the LORD fulfill what your mouth has uttered." And the woman stayed and nursed her son till she weaned him. And she took him up with her when she weaned him, 24 with a three-year-old bull and one *ephah* of flour and a jar of wine, and she brought him to the house of the LORD, and the lad was but a lad.

---

22. *Till the lad is weaned.* The word for "lad," *na͑ar*, is quite often a tender designation of a young son. Though it typically refers to an adolescent, or even to a young man at the height of his powers (David uses it for the usurper Absalom), it evidently can also be used for an infant. Nursing and weaning (compare the end of this verse and the beginning of the next verse) are insisted on here with a peculiar weight of repetition and literalness. This usage surely intimates the powerful biological bond between Hannah and the longed-for baby and thus points to the pain of separation she must accept, whatever the postponement, according to the terms of her own vow. In the Ark Narrative that follows, there will be a surprising recurrence of this image of nursing mothers yearning for their young. At this point, the only other indication of her feelings about the child is the term "lad" that she uses for him.

we will see the LORD's presence. Or, even more concretely, "the LORD's face." The anthropomorphism of this ancient idiom troubled the later transmitters of tradition sufficiently so that when vowel points were added to the consonantal text, roughly a millennium after the biblical period, the verb "we will see" (*nir͡eh*) was revocalized as *nir͡uh* ("he will be seen"), yielding a more chastely monotheistic "he will appear in the LORD's presence."

23. *what your mouth has uttered.* The Masoretic Text has "His word." But a fragment of Samuel found in Cave 4 at Qumran reads "what your mouth has uttered," which, referring directly to Hannah's vow at Shiloh, makes much better sense since God, after all, has made no promises.

24. *a three-year-old bull.* This is again the reading of the Qumran Samuel text. The Masoretic Text has "three bulls," but only one bull is sacrificed in the next verse, and three-year-old beasts were often designated for sacrifice.

25, 26 And they slaughtered the bull and they brought the lad to Eli. And she
said, "Please, my lord, by your life, my lord, I am the woman who was
27 poised by you here praying to the LORD. For this lad I prayed, and the
28 LORD granted me my petition that I asked of Him. And I on my part
granted him for the asking to the LORD; all his days he is lent to the
LORD." And she bowed there to the LORD.

---

25. *they slaughtered the bull . . . they brought the lad.* The plural subject of
these verbs is evidently Elkanah and Hannah. The simple parallelism of the
brief clauses is eloquent: both the bull and the child are offerings to the LORD,
and Samuel's dedication to the sanctuary is, surely for the parents, a kind of
sacrifice. It may be relevant that the term "lad," *naᶜar,* is precisely the one used
for Isaac when he is on the point of being sacrificed and for Ishmael when he
is on the brink of perishing in the wilderness. Perhaps that background of
usage also explains the odd insistence on "the lad was but a lad" at the end of
the preceding verse. Given the late weaning time in the ancient world, and
given Hannah's likely impulse to postpone that difficult moment, one might
imagine the child Samuel to be around the age of five.

26. *Please, my lord.* As in their previous encounter, Hannah's speech is full of
deference and diffidence in addressing the priest—a reverence, we may
already suspect, that he does not entirely deserve.

27. *For this lad I prayed . . .* She spells out the act of petition and its precise fulfillment, insisting twice on the root *sh-ʾ-l,* "to ask." The Hebrew is literally:
"my asking that I asked of Him."

28. *granted him for the asking to the LORD; all his days he is lent to the LORD.*
The English here is forced to walk around an elegant pun in the Hebrew: in
the *qal* conjugation, *sh-ʾ-l* means to ask or petition; in the *hiphᶜil* conjugation
the same root means to lend; and the passive form of the verb, *shaʾul,* can
mean either "lent" or "asked."
  and she bowed. The translation again follows the reading of the Samuel
fragment discovered at Qumran. The Masoretic Text reads "and he bowed" (a
difference of one initial consonant in the Hebrew), but it is Hannah, not Elkanah, who has been speaking for the last two verses.

CHAPTER 2

A nd Hannah prayed and she said:
   "My heart rejoiced through the LORD,
       my horn is raised high through the LORD.

According to the standard collagelike convention of biblical narrative composition, Hannah's psalm has been set into the story at a later stage in the editorial process than the original tale, and it gives evidence of having been taken
from a familiar repertory of thanksgiving or victory psalms. The reference to
the anointed king at the end of the poem assumes the institution of the
monarchy, not established until two generations after the moment when Hannah is said to pronounce this prayer. It is clearly the invocation in verse 5 of
the barren woman who bears seven that encouraged the introduction here of
this particular text. But the larger thematic assertion in the poem of God's
power to reverse fortunes, plunging the high to the depths and exalting the
lowly, is a fitting introduction to the whole Saul-David history. This psalm
(verses 1–10) and David's victory psalm (2 Samuel 22) echo each other and act
as formal "bookends" to the extended narrative sequence that includes the
stories of Samuel, Saul, and David.

1. *my horn is raised high.* This archaic Hebrew animal imagery is worth preserving literally in English, as did Tyndale and the King James Version. The
idea seems to be that the animal's horn is its glory and power, held high, perhaps in triumph after goring an enemy into submission. There is a sequence
of body parts at the beginning of the first three versets of the poem, two literal
and the middle one metaphorical: "my heart," "my horn," "my mouth." The
raising high of the horn is crucial to the thematic unfolding of the poem,
which reiterates a pattern of vertical movement, elevation and descent, that
manifests God's power to reverse the fortunes of humankind. The upraised
horn at the beginning returns in the envelope structure of the last line, a
prayer that the LORD "raise high His anointed's horn." That final image, in
turn, involves a hidden pun, because the Hebrew "horn" (*qeren*, actually one

My mouth is wide to bolt down my foes;
　　for I was gladdened by Your deliverance.

2　There is no one holy like the LORD,
　　for there's no one beside You,
　　　　and there is no bastion like our God.

3　Do not go on talking high and mighty—
　　arrogance slips from your mouth—
　for a God all-knowing is the LORD,
　　and His is the measure of actions.

4　The warriors' bow is shattered
　　and stumblers gird up strength.

5　The sated are hired for bread
　　and the hungry cease evermore.
　The barren woman bears seven
　　and the many-sonned woman is bleak.

6　The LORD deals death and grants life,
　　brings down to Sheol and lifts up.

7　The LORD impoverishes and bestows wealth,
　　plunges down and also exalts.

---

of the rare Semitic terms cognate with Indo-European—*cornu/horn*) is also
the receptacle containing the oil with which the king is anointed.

　My mouth is wide to bolt down my foes. The Hebrew does not express but
implies "bolt down." The conventional rendering of this idiom as "gloated" is
an evasion of its intimation of predatory violence.

4. *shattered.* The verb used is restricted to poetry; a noun derived from it
means "rubble" or "tiny broken fragments," hence the sense seems to be more
extreme than the standard term "to break."

5. *the hungry cease evermore.* The Masoretic Text is rather cryptic. This translation revocalizes the last Hebrew word of the line ʿad ("until," or by a long
conjectural stretch, "prey") as ʿod, an adverb indicating persistence through
time. The Masoretes attached the word to the beginning of the next clause,
where, however, its semantic function is equally unclear.

He raises the poor from the dust,   8
   from the dungheaps the wretched He lifts
to seat among princes,
   a throne of honor He bequeaths them.
For the LORD's are the pillars of earth,
   upon them He founded the world.
The steps of His faithful he watches,   9
   and the wicked in darkness turn dumb,
      for not by might will a man prevail.
The LORD shatters his adversaries,   10
   against them in the heavens He thunders.
The LORD judges the ends of the earth:
   may He grant strength to His king
      and raise high His anointed's horn."

And Elkanah went to Ramah to his home while the lad was ministering   11
to the LORD in the presence of Eli the priest. And the sons of Eli were   12

---

8. *to seat among princes.* The language here might anticipate the monarchic flourish at the end of the poem. "Throne" (*kis²e*) in the next line can mean either throne or chair. Robert Polzin has made an elaborate argument for seeing not only Hannah's prayer but all of the early chapters of 1 Samuel as a grand foreshadowing of the fate of the monarchy with the old and failing Eli, who will die falling off his chair or throne, as a stand in for the Davidic kings.

9. *the wicked in darkness turn dumb.* The verb obviously refers to death—the underworld in other psalms is sometimes called *dumah*, the realm of silence or speechlessness, a noun cognate with the verb *yidamu* used here. Those who talked high and mighty, their mouths spewing arrogance (verse 3), are now forever silenced.

10. *The LORD shatters his adversaries.* The Masoretic Text reads, "LORD, Your adversaries are shattered." But the Samuel fragment from Qumran has God as the subject of a verb in the singular (a difference of only one letter) with the adversaries as the object. This makes better syntactic sense, especially since it is God who is thundering against the enemies in the second half of the line. The verb *shatter* is the same one used for the warriors' bow in verse 4

13 worthless fellows; they did not know the LORD. And this was the priests' practice with the people: each man would offer his sacrifice, and the priest's lad would come when the meat was boiling, a three-pronged
14 fork in his hand. And he would thrust into the cauldron or the pot or the vat or the kettle, whatever the fork would pick up, the priest would take away with it. Thus they would do to all the Israelites who came there to
15 Shiloh. Even before they had burned off the fat, the priest's lad would come and say to the man who was sacrificing, "Hand over meat to roast
16 for the priest, for he won't take boiled meat from you, only raw." And the man would say, "Let them burn off the fat now and then take you whatever you want," and he would say, "No! For you shall hand it over now,
17 and if not, I will take it by force." And the lads' offense was very great
18 before the LORD, for they scorned the LORD's offering. And Samuel was
19 ministering in the presence of the LORD, a lad girt in linen ephod. And a little cloak would his mother make him and would bring up to him year

---

14. *the cauldron or the pot or the vat or the kettle.* This catalogue of implements is quite untypical of biblical narrative (and in fact the precise identification of the sundry cooking receptacles is unsure). The unusual specification serves a satiric purpose: Eli's sons are represented in a kind of frenzy of gluttony poking their three-pronged forks into every imaginable sort of pot and pan. This sense is then heightened in the aggressiveness of the dialogue that follows, in which Eli's sons insist on snatching the meat uncooked from the worshipers, not allowing them, as was customary, first to burn away the fat.

18. *ephod.* A short garment, chiefly of linen, worn by priests. The Hebrew term has a second meaning, a device for divination manipulated by the officiating priests, and that is the evident sense of ephod when it recurs in verse 28.

19. *and a little cloak would his mother make him.* This is a poignant instance of the expressive reticence of biblical narrative. We have been told nothing about Hannah's feelings as a mother after her separation from the child for whom she so fervently prayed. This minimal notation of Hannah's annual gesture of making a little cloak for the son she has "lent" to the LORD beautifully intimates the love she preserves for him. The garment, fashioned as a gift of maternal love, stands in contrast to the ephod, the acolyte's official garb for his cultic office. Moreover, the robe (*meᶜil*) will continue to figure importantly in Samuel's life, and even in his afterlife, as we shall have occasion to see.

year after year. The phrase takes us back to the iterative tense of the beginning of the story.

after year when she came up with her husband to offer the yearly sacrifice. And Eli would bless Elkanah and his wife and would say, "May the 20
LORD bestow on you seed from this woman in place of the loan she has
lent to the LORD," and they would go back to their place. For the LORD 21
singled out Hannah and she conceived and bore three sons and two
daughters. And the lad Samuel grew up with the LORD.

And Eli was very old. And he heard of all that his sons did to all the 22
Israelites, and that they lay with the women who flocked to the
entrance of the Tent of Assembly. And he said to them, "Why do you do 23
such things of which I hear—evil things about you from all these people? No, my sons! For it is not good, what I hear that the LORD's people 24
are spreading about. If a man offends against man, God may intercede 25
for him, but if against the LORD a man should offend, who can intercede for him?" And they did not heed their father's voice, for the LORD
wanted to put them to death. And the lad Samuel was growing in good- 26
ness with both the LORD and with men.

And a man of God came to Eli and said to him, "Thus says the LORD! 27
Did I not reveal myself to your father's house when they were in Egypt,
slaves to Pharaoh's house? And did I not choose him from all the tribes 28

---

22. *and that they lay with the women*   This whole clause is missing in the
Qumran scroll and in one version of the Septuagint; in fact, sexual exploitation was not mentioned in the initial narrative report of the sons' misdeeds.
There is, however, a consonance between their appetitive impulse in snatching the meat and grabbing the women, perhaps reinforced by the satiric, and
phallic, image of thrusting forks into bubbling pots.
    flocked. The Hebrew verb might also mean "ministered."

27. *A man of God came to Eli.* This enunciation of a curse on the house of Eli,
at the very beginning of the Samuel story, is introduced at precisely the corresponding place in the narrative as the denunciation and admonition of the
divine messenger at the beginning of Judges (Chapter 2). An analogous curse
will be pronounced by Nathan the prophet on the house of David (2 Samuel
12) and will be enacted in the subsequent narrative.
    slaves to Pharaoh's house. The Masoretic Text lacks "slaves to" but it is
attested in the Qumran Samuel scroll, in the Septuagint, and in the Targum
of Yonatan ben Uziel.

of Israel as a priest for me, to go up to My altar, to burn incense, to
carry an ephod before Me? And I gave to your father's house all the
29 Israelites' burnt offerings. Why do you trample on My sacrifice and My
offering which I have commanded, and you honor your sons more than
Me, to batten upon the first portions of each offering of Israel My peo-
30 ple? Therefore, says the LORD God of Israel, I indeed said, 'Your house
and your father's house will walk before Me forever,' but now, says the
LORD, forbid I should do it! For those who honor Me will I honor, and
31 my spurners shall be dishonored. Look, a time is coming when I will
cut down your seed and the seed of your father's house, and there shall
32 be no elder in your house. And you shall look with a jaundiced eye at all
the bounty bestowed upon Israel, and there will be no elder in your
33 house for all time. And no man of you will I cut off from My altar, to
make your eyes waste away and your spirit ache, and the increase of

---

29. *My sacrifice and My offering which I commanded.* The Masoretic Text reads
"which I commanded [as a?] habitation [*maᶜon*]." Since that makes no sense,
and all attempts to rescue a meaning seem forced, I have assumed that *maᶜon*
is an excrescence, perhaps inadvertently transposed by a scribe from verse 32,
where it also occurs rather enigmatically. Several points in the curse pronounced by the man of God look textually defective.

30. *will walk before Me.* The biblical idiom suggests dedicated service of a deity.
    honor . . . dishonor. The Hebrew terms mean, etymologically, "heavy" and
"light" (that is, "weighty" and "worthless"). These antonyms will recur at
strategic moments in the Ark Narrative and in the story of David.

32. *look with a jaundiced eye.* The received text at this point is very doubtful,
yielding, literally, a nonsense chain: "you will look narrow habitation." This
translation adopts an emendation that has considerable scholarly currency:
ᶜ*ayin* instead of *maᶜon* (a difference of one consonant in the Hebrew). That
yields the idiom *tsar-ᶜayin*, "jealously" or "with a jaundiced eye." But the Qumran text and one version of the Septuagint lack the entire clause.

33. *no man of you will I cut off.* The usual understanding of these words is that
God will leave them alive to witness in pain the destruction of the family. This
interpretation seems a bit strained because in the next verse God promises to
destroy both of Eli's sons on a single day. Perhaps the clause originally read,
"every man of you will I cut off," though this phrasing is not reflected in any of
the ancient versions.

your house shall fall by the sword of men. And this is the sign for you— 34
that which comes upon your two sons, Hophni and Phineas, on a single day the two of them shall die! And I will set up for Myself a stalwart 35
priest, according to my heart and my spirit he shall act, and I will build
him a stalwart house and he will walk before My anointed for all time.
And it will happen that whoever remains from your house shall come 36
to bow before him for a bit of silver and a loaf of bread, and he shall say,
"Add me on, pray, to one of the priestly details for a crust of bread to
eat."

---

fall by the sword of men. Again, both the Qumran fragment and Version B of
the Septuagint confirm this reading, which seems much likelier than the
Masoretic Text's cryptic "shall die [as?] men."

35. *a stalwart priest . . . a stalwart house.* The Hebrew *ne'eman* in the first
instance means "faithful" or "trustworthy," in the second instance, "well-
founded," "enduring." The present translation draws on an older sense of
"stalwart," which can be applied to structures and inanimate objects as well as
to people. The probable referent of the prophecy is the house of Zadok, which
was to become the priestly line in the Davidic monarchy.

before my anointed. Like Hannah's psalm, this whole passage of prophecy
appears to presuppose a historical context in which the monarchy was an
established fact.

CHAPTER 3

And the lad Samuel was ministering to the LORD in Eli's presence, and the word of the LORD was rare in those days, vision was not spread about. And it happened on that day that Eli was lying in his place, his eyes had begun to grow bleary, he could not see. The lamp of God had not yet gone out, and Samuel was lying in the temple of the LORD in which was the Ark of God. And God called to Samuel, and he said,

---

1. *the word of the LORD was rare . . . vision was not spread about.* The "word of the LORD" is often a technical term referring to oracular message. Inquiring of the oracle would have been a priestly function, and so there is an intimation here of some sort of breakdown in the professional performance of the house of Eli. But the same phrase also is used to announce prophecy, and "vision" is a prophetic term: the whole episode concerns the transition from priestly to prophetic authority.

2. *he could not see.* Eli's blindness not only reflects his decrepitude but his incapacity for vision in the sense of the previous verse. He is immersed in permanent darkness while the lad Samuel has God's lamp burning by his bedside.

3. *The lamp of God had not yet gone out.* Since the sanctuary lamp would have burned through most of the night, this may be an indication, as Kyle McCarter, Jr. has proposed, that the scene occurs close to dawn. But the symbolic overtones of the image should not be neglected: though vision has become rare, God's lamp has not yet gone out, and the young ministrant will be the one to make it burn bright again (see verses 19–21, plus 4:1a). The actual lamp would have been a concave earthenware vessel filled with oil.

"Here I am." And he ran to Eli and he said, "Here I am, for you called   5
me," and he said, "I did not call. Go back, lie down." And he went and
lay down. And the LORD called once again, "Samuel!" And Samuel rose   6
and went to Eli and said, "Here I am, for you called me." And he said,
"I did not call, my son. Go back, lie down." And Samuel did not yet   7
know the LORD and the word of the LORD had not yet been revealed
to him. And the LORD called still again to Samuel, a third time, and   8
he rose and went to Eli and said, "Here I am, for you called me." And
Eli understood that the LORD was calling the lad. And Eli said to   9
Samuel, "Go lie down, and should someone call to you, say, 'Speak,
LORD, for Your servant is listening.'" And Samuel went and lay down
in his place. And the LORD came and stood poised and called as on   10
each time before, "Samuel, Samuel!" And Samuel said, "Speak, for
Your servant is listening." And the LORD said to Samuel, "I am about to   11
do such a thing in Israel that whoever hears of it, both his ears will ring.

---

5. *he ran to Eli, and he said "Here I am."* These words make clear that the previous "Here I am" is not a direct response to God but rather the boy's calling
out from the inner chamber of the sanctuary to Eli in the outer room, thinking
that it is Eli who called him. Samuel's thrice-repeated error in this regard
reflects not only his youthful in experience but, as the sixteenth-century
Hebrew exegete Yosef Karo has proposed, the general fact that "the word of
the LORD was rare," revelation an unfamiliar phenomenon.

6. *"Samuel!"* In an intensifying pattern, as the folk-tale structure of three repetitions with a final reversal unfolds, God's address is now represented more
immediately in dialogue instead indirectly as in verse 4. The third time, God
will say, "Samuel, Samuel!"
"I did not call, my son." Until this point, we have been told nothing
about Eli's relationship with Samuel. The introduction of this single term of
affection, "my son," reveals the fondness of the blind and doomed Eli for his
young assistant. His own biological sons have of course utterly betrayed his
trust.

9. *"Speak, LORD, for Your servant is listening."* This is virtually a formula of deferential response to superior authority. When Samuel repeats these words in
verse 10, he omits *"Lord,"* perhaps, as Shimon Bar-Efrat has suggested, in diffidence about addressing God.

12   On that day I will fulfill against Eli all that I have spoken concerning
13   his house, from beginning to end. And I have told him that I was passing judgment on his house for all time because of the sin of which he
knew, for his sons have been scorning God and he did not restrain
14   them. Therefore I have sworn against the house of Eli, that the sin of
the house of Eli will not be atoned by sacrifice and offering for all
15   time." And Samuel lay until morning, and he opened the doors of
the house of the LORD, and Samuel was afraid to tell the vision to Eli.

---

12. *all that I have spoken concerning his house.* This clause, and the one beginning "I have told him" in the next verse, refer back to the prophecy of doom
pronounced by the man of God in Chapter 2.

13. *his sons have been scorning God.* The Masoretic Text reads, "his sons have
been scorning for themselves [*lahem*]," but the last Hebrew word has long
been recognized as a *tiqun sofrim,* a scribal euphemism for *ʾelohim,* God—
that is, the scribes were loath to write out so sacrilegious a phrase as scorning,
or cursing, God. The verb here is commonly used in the sense of "to damn" or
"to express contempt." In this case, the sons' contempt would have been
expressed by their snatching of choice portions from the sacrificial meat.
    he did not restrain them. The Hebrew *kihah* occurs only here as a transitive
verb in the *piʿel* conjugation, though it is fairly common as an intransitive verb
in the *qal* conjugation, meaning "to grow weak," "to become dark," or, as with
the eyes of Eli in verse 2, bleary. The transitive sense of the verb would then
be something like "to incapacitate," to prevent someone from doing something. Its unusual usage in this sentence is obviously meant to align Eli's failing in parental authority with the failing of his sight.

11.–13. It is noteworthy that God's first message to Samuel is a prophecy
of doom. Its content not only indicates the overthrow of the priestly authority
of the house of Eli and the implicit move to a different sort of authority to be
embodied by the prophet Samuel, but it also adumbrates the rather dour and
dire role Samuel will play as leader, in relation to both Israel and to Saul.

15. *and Samuel lay until morning.* The verb does not necessarily imply that he
fell asleep again after this riveting revelation, and if in fact the whole scene takes
place close to dawn, there would be little time before the first light roused him.
    he opened the door of the house of the LORD. He resumes his usual business
as faithful temple ministrant, almost as though he wanted to shrug off the
divine revelation that implied a more portentous role for him than that of
priestly acolyte.

And Eli called to Samuel and said, "Samuel, my son," and he said, 16
"Here I am." And he said, "What is the thing He spoke to you? Pray, do 17
not conceal it from me. Thus and more may God do to you if you conceal from me anything of all the things He spoke to you." And Samuel 18
told him all the things and he did not conceal from him, and he said,
"He is the LORD. What is good in His eyes let Him do."

And Samuel grew up and the LORD was with him, and He let not fall to 19
the ground any of his words. And all Israel, from Dan to Beersheba, 20
knew that Samuel was stalwart as a prophet to the LORD. And the 21
LORD continued to appear in Shiloh, for the LORD was revealed to

---

Samuel was afraid to tell the vision. The divine message is called a vision
though it was conveyed through words rather than images. The term used
here, *mar²eh*, is different from *hazon*, the word that occurs in verse 1, though
both refer to sight, the faculty Eli lacks.

17. *Thus and more may God do to you.* This is a set idiom for abjuration: may
terrible things befall you if you fail to perform what I require of you.

18. *What is good in His eyes let Him do.* Old Eli's response is pious resignation
to the prophecy of doom. He of course is aware of his sons' misdeeds and of
his own failure to intervene successfully.

19. *He let not fall to the ground any of his words.* The antecedent of "his" is
ambiguous, but since the point of the narrative report is to confirm Samuel's
prophetic authority, the more likely reading is that God did not allow any of
Samuel's words to go awry but fulfilled all of His prophet's predictions.

20. *from Dan to Beersheba.* That is, from the far north, near Phoenician territory, to the Negeb in the south.
    stalwart. Or, "faithful." That is, Samuel's authority as prophet was recog-
nized by all Israel.

21. *and the LORD continued to appear . . . the LORD was revealed.* This emphatic
indication is an obvious counterpoint to the first verse of the chapter: instead
of being withheld, divine communication is now regular and repeated through
the person of Samuel.

4:1a   Samuel in Shiloh through the word of the LORD, and Samuel's word was upon all Israel.

4:1a. Although the conventional chapter division attaches this brief clause to the next episode, it is clear that it is actually a final summary of Samuel's new authority at the end of his dedication story. The next words of the text (Chapter 4:1b) in fact refer to a military initiative undertaken by the Israelites without Samuel's authorization.

CHAPTER 4

And Israel went out in battle against the Philistines, and they encamped by Eben-ezer, while the Philistines were encamped at Aphek. And the Philistines drew up their lines against Israel, and the battle forces were deployed, and Israel was routed by the Philistines, and they struck down in the lines in the field about four thousand men.

1b
2

1b. *the Philistines.* The Philistines were part of the general incursion of the so-called Sea Peoples from the Aegean—the prophet Amos names Crete as their land of origin—into the Eastern Mediterranean region perhaps less than a century before the early eleventh-century setting of our story. (There is some evidence that they first migrated to Anatolia, then moved southward.) They established a powerful presence in Canaan on the coastal plain, concentrated in the region a little south of present-day Tel Aviv. They were intrepid warriors (note the martial exhortation of verse 9) and also exercised a mastery of military science and military technology. In the coastal plain, they were able to deploy iron chariots (which seem to have been lacking among the Israelites) as well as infantry. Perhaps their failure to extend their minikingdom of five allied cities more than a dozen or so miles eastward from the coast was related to a loss of the strategic advantage of chariots as they went up into the high country.

2. *the Philistines drew up their lines, and the battle forces were deployed.* Interestingly, the language of strategic deployment is attached only to the Philistines. "Battle forces" is, literally, "battle." Although the precise indications of these terms are unclear, their use elsewhere in the Bible makes it evident that they had a technical military application.

the lines. The Hebrew, *ma'arakhah*, is a singular, with the sense of "battle formation" or "front line."

3   And the troops came into the camp, and the elders of Israel said, "Why has the LORD routed us today before the Philistines? Let us take to us from Shiloh the Ark of the Covenant of the LORD, that it may come
4   into our midst and deliver us from the hands of our enemies." And the troops sent to Shiloh and they bore from there the Ark of the Covenant of the LORD of Hosts Enthroned on the Cherubim, and there the two sons of Eli were with the Ark of the Covenant of God—Hophni
5   and Phineas. And when the Ark of the Covenant of the LORD came into the camp, all Israel let out a great shout, and the earth resounded.
6   And the Philistines heard the sound of the shouting and said, "What is the sound of this great shouting in the camp of the Hebrews?" And they knew that the Ark of the LORD had come into the camp.

---

3. *Let us take to us.* The addition of this seemingly superfluous personal pronoun suggests how the elders arrogate to themselves a sacred object for their own purposes, conceiving the Ark magically or fetishistically as a vehicle of power that they can manipulate for military ends.

the Ark of the Covenant of the LORD. This would have been a large case made of acacia wood, with carved cherubim on its top, containing the stone tablets of the Law given at Sinai. As the material residue of the defining encounter between God and Israel, these tablets were viewed as the most sacrosanct possession of the nation. Hence the horror at the end of this episode over the news that the Ark has been captured by the Philistines.

4. *troops.* The Hebrew has a collective noun, ⁵am, "people," which in military contexts refers to the ordinary soldiers.

the Ark of the Covenant of the LORD of Hosts Enthroned on the Cherubim. This extravagantly full title is a kind of epic flourish reflecting the power that the elders of Israel attribute to the Ark. "Hosts," bearing its older English sense of "armies," underscores the LORD's martial nature. The cherubim are fierce winged beasts imagined as God's celestial steeds, and so the carved cherubim on the Ark are conceived as the earthly "throne" of the invisible deity.

Hophni and Phineas. In an odd stylistic tie, each time the two sons are mentioned in this chapter, their proper names are stuck on at the very end of the sentence, as though their precise identity were being isolated for opprobrium.

6. *the camp of the Hebrews.* "Hebrews" is generally the designation of the Israelites when they are named by other peoples.

And the Philistines were afraid, for they thought, "God has come into 7
the camp." And they said, "Woe to us! For it was never so in times gone
by. Woe to us! Who will save us from the hands of these mighty gods? 8
They are the very gods who struck Egypt with every blow in the wilderness. Muster strength and be men, O Philistines, lest you become 9
slaves to the Hebrews as they were slaves to you. Be men and do battle!"
And the Philistines did battle and Israel was routed, and every man fled 10
to his tent and the blow was very great, thirty thousand foot soldiers of
Israel fell. And the Ark of the LORD was taken, and the two sons of Eli 11
died—Hophni and Phineas. And a man of Benjamin ran from the lines 12
and came to Shiloh that day, his garments torn and earth on his head.

---

7. *God has come into the camp.* Here ²*elohim* is the subject of a verb in the singular, but in verse 8, in proper polytheistic fashion, the Philistines use the
same term but construe it grammatically as a plural, "gods."

8. *every blow.* The Hebrew *makah* also means "plague," an obviously appropriate sense here, but it is important that the writer uses the same word in verse
10, though with a military meaning, for a theological irony is intended in the
pun: they feared the might of the LORD Who struck such terrible blows
against Egypt, and then they themselves strike a blow against Israel, which
actually does not have God in its midst, only His sacred paraphernalia. Here
as elsewhere in the Bible, the national fiction is maintained that all the peoples of Canaan were intimately familiar with the Exodus story and deeply
impressed by it.

9. *Muster strength and be men.* There may be a pointed antithesis in their
speech between "gods" and "men." In any case, they summon stirring rhetoric
to rouse themselves from their fear of a supernatural adversary and to go out
to do battle.

12. *his garments torn and earth on his head.* This disheveled appearance is not
because of the fighting but reflects the customary signs of mourning.

13 He came, and, look, Eli was seated in a chair by the road on the
lookout, for his heart was trembling over the Ark of God, and the
14 man had come to tell in the town and the whole town cried out, and
Eli heard the sound of the outcry and said, "What is this sound of
15 uproar?" The man had hurried, and he came and told Eli. And Eli
was ninety-eight years old, his eyes were rigid and he could not see.
16 And the man said to Eli, "I am the one who has come from the lines,
I from the lines fled today." And he said, "What happened, my son?"

---

13. *Eli was seated in a chair by the road.* Similarly, in Chapter 1, he was
seated in a chair in the temple—in both instances a token of his infirmity,
his passivity or incapacity as leader. The Hebrew phrase behind "by the
road" is textually problematic, as is the related phrase attached to the word
"gate" in verse 18. Scholarly opinion differs as to whether Eli is sitting
by the road, by the gate, or, like David in 2 Samuel 18, above the gate. The
last of these possibilities would best explain his breaking his neck when he
falls, but it is by no means the inevitable meaning of the Hebrew, and the
Hebrew preposition in verse 18 actually indicates *through* the gate.

his heart was trembling over the Ark of the LORD. Apprehension over the fate
of his scurrilous sons is not mentioned.

14. *What is this sound of uproar?* Eli's question pointedly, and ironically, parallels the question asked by the Philistines in verse 6 about the jubilant uproar
from the Israelite camp. At the very end of the David story (1 Kings 1), the
usurper Adonijah will ask virtually the same question about an uproar that
spells disaster for him and his followers.

15. *his eyes were rigid.* The idiom for Eli's blindness has a stark finality here
that it does not have in 3:2. Presumably a good deal of time has elapsed since
that moment of the young Samuel's dedication as prophet, and the process of
blindness is now complete. It is because Eli can see nothing that he must ask
with particular urgency about the reason for all the shouting.

16. *I am the one who has come from the lines, I from the lines fled today.* This odd
repetition may reflect a stammer of nervousness or confusion, as Shimon Bar-
Efrat has proposed.

And the bearer of tidings answered and said, "Israel fled before the 17
Philistines, and what's more, there was a great rout among the troops,
and what's more, your two sons died—Hophni and Phineas—and the
Ark of God was taken." And the moment he mentioned the Ark of God, 18
Eli fell backward from his chair through the gate and his neckbone was
broken and he died, for the man was old and heavy. And he had judged
Israel forty years. And his daughter-in-law, Phineas's wife, was big with 19
child, and when she heard the report about the taking of the Ark, and
that her father-in-law and her husband were dead, she crouched down
and gave birth, for her birth pangs overwhelmed her. And as she was on 20
the point of death, her attendant women spoke up, "Fear not, for you
have born a son." And she did not answer or pay heed. And she called 21
the boy Ichabod, which is to say, "Glory is exiled from Israel"—for the

---

17. The report of the battle moves from a general indication of the defeat, to
the admission of a rout, to the death of Eli's two sons, and, finally, to what is
assumed to be the worst catastrophe, the capture of the Ark. It should be
noted that 1 and 2 Samuel are in part organized around a series of interechoing
scenes in which a messenger brings ill tidings. The bearer of ill tidings to
Adonijah at the very end of this long narrative also nervously repeats *wegam*,
"what's more" as he recounts the catastrophe.

18. *and he had judged Israel forty years.* This notice, with its use of the formulaic forty years, is odd because Eli certainly has not been a judge, either in the
military-charismatic or the juridical sense. This sentence could be an attempt
to establish a carry-over from the Book of Judges, or it could be an inadvertent
editorial repetition of the Judges formula.

19. *big with child.* The Hebrew says literally "was pregnant to give birth."
    she crouched down. In the ancient Near East, women generally gave birth
in a kneeling position, leaning on a special birthing stone—examples have
been uncovered by archeologists—called in Hebrew a *mashber*.

21. *Ichabod . . . Glory is exiled.* The Hebrew name is conventionally construed
to mean "Inglorious," though Kyle McCarter, Jr. has argued that the more
probable meaning is "Where is glory?" or "Alas for glory!" In any case, it is a
most peculiar name—the dying mother, overcome by the loss of the Ark
(which affects her much more than her husband's demise), inscribing the
national catastrophe in her son's name. Where one must agree unhesitatingly

22 taking of the Ark and for her father-in-law and her husband. And she said, "Glory is exiled from Israel, for the Ark of God is taken."

---

with McCarter is that the verb in this verse and the next should be rendered as "exiled" and not, as it is customarily translated, as "departed." Exile is what it clearly denotes, and it is surely significant that this whole large sequence of stories that will provide an account of the founding of Israel's dynasty and the crystallization of its national power begins with a refrain of glory exiled from Israel. It is also noteworthy that the term for "glory," *kavod*, is transparently cognate with *kaved*, "heavy," the adjective used to explain Eli's lethal tumble from his chair—the leader who might be supposed to represent Israel's glory exhibits only deadly heaviness.

CHAPTER 5

A nd the Philistines had taken the Ark of God and brought it from   1
Eben-ezer to Ashdod. And the Philistines took the Ark of God and   2
brought it to the house of Dagon and set it up alongside Dagon. And   3
the Ashdodites arose on the next day and, look, Dagon was fallen forward to the ground before the Ark of the LORD. And they took Dagon

---

The Ark Narrative at this point leaves behind the house of Eli, Samuel, and
the paramount question of Israel's leadership in order to tell a bizarre satiric
story of a battle between cult objects—the potent Ark of the Covenant, which
is conceived as the conduit for the cosmic power of the God of Israel, and the
idol of Dagon, vainly believed to be a real deity by the Philistines. The dominant tone of the story is a kind of monotheistic triumphalism; accordingly,
themes from the story of the plagues of Egypt are replayed, though in a virtually scatological key.

1. *from Eben-ezer to Ashdod.* The Ark is carried down from Eben ezer, in the
western part of the territory of Ephraim (roughly ten miles from the coast and
just a little to the north of present-day Tel Aviv) to Ashdod, on the Mediterranean, in the heart of Philistine territory.

2. *Dagon.* This god is now generally thought to be a vegetation or fertility god,
its name cognate with the Hebrew *dagan,* "grain" (and not, as was once widely
imagined, with the Hebrew *dag,* "fish").
    set it up alongside Dagon. Either to amplify the power of their own deity or
to express the subservience of the God of Israel to Dagon.

3. *and, look, Dagon was fallen forward to the ground.* This clause and the parallel one in the next verse reflect the visual perspective of the Ashdodites when
they come into the temple early in the morning and make their shocking discovery. Tyndale's translation gets into the spirit of the scene, though with a
certain creative licence, by rendering this, "lay grovelling upon the ground."

4 and set him back in his place. And they arose the next morning
and, look, Dagon was fallen forward to the ground before the Ark of
the LORD, and Dagon's head and both his hands were chopped off
5 upon the threshold—his trunk alone remained on him. Therefore
the priests of Dagon, and all who enter the house of Dagon, do not
6 tread on the threshold of the house of Dagon to this day. And the
hand of the LORD was heavy upon the Ashdodites and He devastated
them, and He struck them with tumors, Ashdod and all its territories.

---

4. *his trunk alone remained on him.* The Masoretic Text has cryptically, "Dagon
alone remained on him," but several of the ancient translations appear to have
used a version which read *gevo,* "his trunk," instead of *Dagon.* Dagon's first
downfall might be attributed to a natural, accidental cause—the idol's somehow slipping from its pedestal. This second incident, in which the hands and
head of the idol have been chopped off, offers to the Philistines clear proof of
divine intervention. Hacking the hands and feet off war prisoners was a well-
known barbaric practice in the ancient Near East, and similar acts of mutilation are attested in the Book of Judges.

5. *Therefore.* This is the introductory formula for etiological explanations. An
observed Philistine practice of skipping over the sanctuary threshold, as a special measure for entering sacred space, is reinterpreted as a reminiscence of
the victory of Israel's God over Dagon.

6. *the hand of the LORD was heavy upon the Ashdodites.* The word *kaved,* previously associated with Eli's corpulence and linked by root with *kavod,* "glory,"
recurs here in a clause that introduces the first of several echoes of the
plagues against Egypt.
   tumors. Many translations render this as "hemorrhoids," and there is a little
confusion in the Masoretic Text: the consonantal written version *(ketiv)* has
"tumors," but the tradition for reciting the text *(qeri)* indicates "hemorrhoids."
This confusion is compounded because the Septuagint, seconded by Josephus,
includes a plague of mice not in evidence in the Masoretic version, and the
golden mice of the next chapter look very much like a response to just such a
plague. The fact, moreover, that hemorrhoids are a humiliating but not lethal
disorder and are not spread by epidemic, whereas the Philistines protest that
they are dying, gives support to an interpretation at least as old as Rashi: the
plague in question is bubonic plague, carried by rats (metamorphosed in this
story into mice, and associated with the epidemic but perhaps not clearly
understood as the bearers of the disease); the tumors are the *buboes* of bubonic
plague, which might especially afflict the lower body, including the rectal area.

And the people of Ashdod saw that it was so, and they said, "Let not the 7
Ark of the God of Israel stay among us, for His hand is hard upon us and
upon Dagon our god." And they sent and gathered to them all the Philis- 8
tine overlords and they said, "What shall we do with the Ark of the God of
Israel?" And they said, "To Gath let the Ark of the God of Israel be
brought round." And they brought round the Ark of the God of Israel. And 9
it happened after they had brought it round that the hand of the LORD
was against the city—a great panic. And He struck the people of the city,
young and old, and they had tumors in their secret parts. And they sent 10
the Ark of God on to Ekron, and it happened when the Ark of God came
to Ekron that the Ekronites cried out, saying, "They have brought round
to me the Ark of the God of Israel to bring death to me and my people."
And they sent and gathered all the Philistine overlords and they said, 11
"Send the Ark of the God of Israel back to its place, and let it not bring
death to me and my people." For there was death panic throughout the
city, the hand of God was very heavy there. And the people who did not 12
die were struck with tumors, and the town's outcry rose to the heavens.

---

8. *overlords.* The Hebrew term *seranim* is a Philistine loanword and is applied
only to Philistines as a touch of local color (like calling Spanish aristocrats
"grandees"). Some scholars have linked the word with the Greek *tyrannos.*
Since there is only one *seren* for each Philistine city, they are clearly more than
just "lords."

   Gath. The Ark is carried around to three of the five Philistine cities. The
other two are Gaza and Ashkelon.

9. *the hand of the* LORD *was against the city—a great panic.* This apposition
reflects the Hebrew syntax, which sounds a little peculiar, but there is not
convincing evidence of a defective text here.

   they had tumors in their secret parts. The verb *yisatru* is peculiar. This translation follows Rashi, Kimchi, and the King James Version in linking it with
seter, secret place.

12. *the town's outcry rose to the heavens.* This clause balances on the edge of an
ambiguity. "The heavens" *(hashamayim)* can be simply the sky or the abode of
God. Is God, Who has been present in the story through His acts, His heavy
hand—but not, as it were, in person—listening to the anguished cries of the
Philistines, or is this merely an image of the shrieks of the afflicted Philistines
echoing under the silent vault of the heavens?

CHAPTER 6

1, 2 **A**nd the Ark of the Lord was in Philistine country seven months. And the Philistines called to the priests and the soothsayers, saying, "What shall we do with the Ark of the Lord? Tell us how shall we send it back 3 to its place." And they said, "If you are about to send back the Ark of the God of Israel, do not send it back empty handed, for you must give back to Him a guilt offering. Then you will be healed and there will be 4 atonement for you. Why should His hand not relent from you?" And they said, "What guilt offering should we give back to Him?" And

---

This chapter—the episode actually ends in the first verse of Chapter 7—which concludes the Ark Narrative also brings to a climax the traits that set it off from the larger narrative of Samuel, Saul, and David in which it is placed. Instead of the sharply etched individual characters of the surrounding narrative, we have only collective speakers and agents. Instead of the political perspective with its human system of causation, the perspective is theological and the culminating events of the story are frankly miraculous. God, Who does not speak in this narrative, manifests His power over Philistines and Israelites alike through supernatural acts in the material realm, as the strange tale of the cart and the golden images vividly demonstrates.

3. *send back.* The Hebrew *meshalhim* is the same verb repeatedly used for Pharaoh's sending Israel out of Egypt and thus sustains the network of allusions to the Exodus story. In Exodus, the Israelites, too, were told that they would not leave Egypt "empty handed" but would take with them golden ornaments despoiled from the Egyptians.

there will be atonement for you. The Masoretic Text has "it will become known to you" (*wenodʿa lakhem*), but the reading of both the Qumran Samuel scroll and the Septuagint, *wenikaper lakhem*, "and it will be atoned for you," makes far better sense.

they said, "The number of the Philistine overlords is five. Five golden tumors and five golden mice. For a single plague is upon all of you and upon your overlords. And you shall make images of your tumors and images of your mice that are ravaging the land, and you shall give glory to the God of Israel—perhaps He will lighten His hand from upon you and from upon your god and your land. And why should you harden your hearts as Egypt and Pharaoh hardened their hearts? After He made sport of them, did they not let the Hebrews go, and off they went? And so, fetch and make one new cart, and two milch cows that no yoke has touched, and harness the cows to the cart, but bring their calves back inside.

5

6

7

---

5. *you shall give glory to the God of Israel—perhaps He will lighten His hand.* Once again, the writer harks back to the play of antonyms, *kavod/kaved* (glory/heavy) and *qal* (light, and in other contexts, worthless). Glory has been exiled from Israel with the capture of the Ark: now, with the restitution of the Ark together with an indemnity payment of golden images, glory will be restored. This process helps explain the insistence on the term "give back" associated with the guilt offering.

6. *harden your hearts.* This phrase is not only an explicit link with the Exodus story, but it also continues the play on glory/heaviness because the literal Hebrew idiom is "make your heart heavy" (the verb *kabed*).

let the Hebrews go. The Hebrew says "let them go," but the lack of antecedent for the pronoun would be confusing in English.

7. *a new cart.* It is to be an undefiled instrument made specifically for this ritual purpose.

that no yoke has touched. The cows, too, are uncompromised by use in ordinary labor, though the more important point is that they are entirely devoid of experience as draft animals, so that their ability to pull the cart straight to Beth-shemesh would have to be a manifestation of God's intervention, or of the intrinsic power of the Ark.

their calves back inside. This, of course, is the crux of the test: the milking cows will have to go against nature in plodding forward into Israelite territory with their calves behind them, shut up in the manger and waiting to be fed.

8 And you shall fetch the Ark of the LORD and set it on the cart, and the golden objects that you give back to Him as a guilt offering you shall place in a chest at its side, and you shall send it away and off it will go.
9 And you will see—if on the road to its own territory, to Beth-shemesh, it will go up, He it was Who did us this great evil, and if not, we shall know that it was not His hand that afflicted us but chance that came upon us."

10 And so the men did: they took two milch cows and harnessed them
11 to the cart, but their calves they shut up inside. And they placed the Ark of the LORD on the cart and the chest and the golden mice
12 and the images of their tumors. And the cows went straight on the way, on the way to Beth-shemesh, on a single road they went, lowing as they went, and they veered neither right nor left, with the Philistine overlords walking after them to the border of Beth-shemesh.

---

8. *chest.* The Hebrew *ʾargaz* appears only here. Postbiblical Hebrew consistently understood it as "chest," though some scholars, on the basis of Semitic cognates, have argued for the meaning of "pouch." It may be more plausible that precious objects would be placed in orderly fashion in a chest rather than piled up in a pouch.

11. *the Ark of the LORD . . . and the chest and the golden mice and the images of the tumors.* This whole scene has a certain grotesquely comic and incongruous effect: Israel's most sacred cult object drawn in a cart by two cows with swollen udders, and alongside the Ark golden images of vermin and tumors.

12. *straight on the way, on the way to Beth-shemesh, on a single road they went . . . and they veered neither right nor left.* Against the spareness and swift efficiency of normal Hebrew narrative style, the writer here lavishes synonyms and repetitions in order to highlight the perfect geometry of the miracle: against all conceivable distractions of biology or sheer animal unknowingness, the cows pursue an arrow-straight northwest trajectory from Ekron to Beth-shemesh.
lowing as they went. This small but vivid descriptive detail is an even more striking exception to the stringent economy that governs biblical narrative. The last thing one would expect in a biblical story, where there is scant report of the gestures of the human actors, is a specification of sounds made by draft animals. The point, however, is that the milch cows—more driven by the Ark than hauling it—are going strenuously against nature: their udders full of milk for the calves they have been forced to leave behind, they mark with

And the men of Beth-shemesh were harvesting the wheat harvest in   13
the valley, and they raised their eyes and saw the Ark, and they rejoiced
at the sight. And the cart had come to the field of Joshua the Beth-   14
shemeshite and it came to rest there, and a great stone was there, and
they split up the wood of the cart, and the cows they offered up as a
burnt offering to the LORD. And the Levites had brought down the Ark   15
of the LORD and the chest that was with it, in which were the golden
objects, and they placed them on the great stone, and the men of Beth-
shemesh offered up burnt offerings and sacrificed sacrifices on that
day to the LORD. The five Philistine overlords saw, and they returned to   16
Ekron on that day. And these are the golden tumors that the Philistines   17
gave back as guilt offering to the LORD: for Ashdod, one; for Gaza, one;

---

maternal lowing their distress over the journey they cannot resist. There is a
peculiar resonance between this episode and Hannah's story in Chapter 1.
There, too, a nursing mother does not want to be separated from her young,
and, as we noted, special emphasis is placed on the physical acts of nursing
and weaning. (The connection between the two episodes is underscored in
the Hebrew, which literally calls the cows' young their "sons," not their
calves.) In both stories, sacrifice is offered after mother and young are separated. Here, of course, the mothers become the objects of the sacrifice; in
Hannah's story, it is a bull, and, in symbolic rather than literal fashion, the son
as well. Though all these correspondences seem too pointed to be coinciden-
tal, it is unclear whether they represent the literary artifact of the redactor, or
an allusion by the author of the Samuel story to the Ark Narrative.

13. *the men of Beth-shemesh were harvesting.* The Hebrew uses an ellipsis:
"Beth-shemesh were harvesting."

14. *the cows they offered up.* One connection between the Ark narrative, with
its concern for sanctity, and the Samuel-Saul-David cycle, with its preoccupation with politics, is a kind of brooding sense of the cruel price exacted for
dedication to the higher cause. The milch cows are burned on the improvised
altar; Hannah and her son Samuel must be separated in *his* dedication to the
sanctuary; and later both Saul and David will pay terrible costs in their personal lives for their adhesion to power.

17. *and these are the golden tumors.* The introductory formula suggests a kind
of ritual or epic catalogue, so that we know there is in fact one golden image
corresponding to each of the five Philistine cities, just as the soothsayers had
stipulated.

18   for Ashkelon, one; for Gath, one; for Ekron, one. And the golden mice
were the number of all the Philistine towns, from the fortified cities to
the unwalled villages. And the great stone on which they set the Ark of
19   the LORD is to this day in the field of Joshua the Beth-shemeshite. And
He struck down men of Beth-shemesh, for they had looked into the
Ark of the LORD, and he struck down from the people seventy men
[fifty thousand men], and the people mourned, for the LORD had
20   struck down the people with a great blow. And the people of Beth-
shemesh said, "Who can stand before this holy LORD God, and to

---

18. *the golden mice were the number of all the Philistine cities.* This appears to
contradict the explicit directions in verse 4, that there should be exactly five
golden mice. Kimchi resolves the discrepancy by proposing that, in the event,
as added insurance for all the villages (since the mice had overrun the fields),
the Philistines went beyond their instructions and fashioned multiple images
of the mice.

   and the great stone. The Masoretic Text reads ²*avel* (brook or meadow)
instead of ²*even* (stone), but both the Septuagint and the Qumran scroll have
the latter reading. The Masoretic Text also has "and to" (*weᶜad*) preceding this
word, but that is probably an inadvertent scribal duplication of the preposition
that occurs twice before in the verse.

19. *fifty thousand men.* This figure makes no sense because Beth-shemesh was
a small agricultural village. It appears in all the ancient versions, but Josephus
seems to have possessed a text in which only the much more plausible number seventy appeared. The fact that the Hebrew has no indication of "and"
between "seventy" and "fifty thousand" is further evidence that the latter
number is an intrusion in the text.

   a great blow. As in 4:8, the Hebrew for "blow" can also mean "plague." If
there is a historical kernel to this whole story, an epidemic ravaging the
Philistines could have easily spread to the bordering Israelites, perhaps even
through the agency of the cart and the Ark.

20. *Who can stand before this holy LORD God?* Throughout the Ark narrative,
including what may be its epilogue in 2 Samuel 6, runs an archaic sense of
God's sacred objects as material precipitates of an awesome and dangerous
power. This notion led Leonhard Rost, one of the earliest scholars to argue for
an entirely distinct Ark Narrative, to assume that the author must have been a
priest, though that is hardly an inevitable inference, as these attitudes were
widely held in ancient Near Eastern cultures. The phrase "stand before"
means idiomatically "to serve."

whom will He go up away from us?" And they sent messengers to the   21
inhabitants of Kiriath-jearim, saying, "The Philistines have brought
back the Ark of the LORD. Come down and carry it up to you." And the   7:1
men of Kiriath-jearim came and carried up the Ark of the LORD and
brought it to the house of Abinadab on the hill, and Eleazar his son
they consecrated to watch over the Ark of the LORD.

---

will He go up. The Hebrew could equally be construed as "will it go up,"
referring to the Ark. From the point of view of the terrified speakers, it may
amount to the same thing.

21. *and they sent messengers to Kiriath-jearim.* There seems to be no question
of sending the Ark back to Shiloh, which has led to the scholarly inference
that the Shiloh sanctuary was destroyed in the wake of the defeat at Aphek.
The destruction of Shiloh is in fact attested in other sources.

CHAPTER 7

2 And it happened from the day the Ark dwelled in Kiriath-jearim that the days grew many and became twenty years, and the whole house of Israel was drawn after the LORD. And Samuel said to the whole house of Israel, saying, "If with your whole heart you now return to the LORD,

---

This chapter, which offers a summary account of Israel's religious reformation and military ascendancy under Samuel's rule, serves as a bridge between the Ark Narrative and the great narrative of the founding of the monarchy that will occupy the rest of 1 and 2 Samuel and the first two chapters of 1 Kings.

2. *twenty years.* This is half the formulaic figure of forty years that recurs so frequently in the Book of Judges. The period of twenty years could refer to the time until David brings the Ark up to Jerusalem, though given the immediate narrative context, the more likely reference is the time until Samuel assembles the tribes at Mizpah. During this period, the presence of the Ark at Kiriath-jearim inspires the people to cultic loyalty to God.

was drawn after. The Hebrew *yinahu* is anomalous. The usual meaning of this verbal root, to weep, makes little sense here (though it was followed by the King James translators). The present translation adopts the proposal of Rashi, who may simply have been interpreting from context. The Hebrew could also be a scribal error for *yinharu,* which clearly means "to be drawn after."

3. *with your whole heart.* This phrase, and Samuel's language here in general, is notably Deuteronomistic, and the narrative line in this chapter follows the Deuteronomistic theological assumption that cultic faithfulness leads to military success. Neither this language nor this assumption is much in evidence in the main body of the Samuel-Saul-David narrative.

put away the alien gods from your midst and the Ashtaroth, and set
your heart firm for the LORD and serve Him alone, that He may rescue
you from the hand of the Philistines." And the Israelites put away the 4
Baalim and the Ashtaroth and they served the LORD alone.

And Samuel said, "Assemble all Israel at Mizpah that I may intercede 5
for you before the LORD. And they assembled at Mizpah and they drew 6
water and spilled it before the LORD and they fasted on that day and
there they said, "We have offended the LORD." And Samuel judged
Israel at Mizpah. And the Philistines heard that the Israelites had 7
assembled at Mizpah, and the Philistine overlords came up against
Israel, and the Israelites heard and were afraid of the Philistines.

Ashtaroth. The form is a feminine plural of Ashtoreth (Astarte), the
Canaanite fertility goddess. The plural either indicates a plurality of god-
desses or—more likely—the multiple *icons* of Astarte.

4. *Baalim.* This is the masculine plural of Baal, the principal Canaanite male
deity

5. *Mizpah.* Mizpah appears as a point of tribal assembly at two significant
junctures in the Book of Judges. The name means "lookout" and in the
Hebrew has a definite article.

6. *they drew water and spilled it before the LORD.* This act is a small puzzle
because a water-drawing ritual is otherwise known only from the late Second
Temple period (through Mishnaic sources), and there it is associated with fertility and the fall festival of Sukkot. The context makes clear that in this
instance it must be a rite of penitence or purification. Rashi puts it succinctly:
"It can only be a symbol of abnegation, that is, 'Behold we are in your presence like this water spilled forth.' "

7. *the Philistines heard that the Israelites had assembled.* Either the Philistines
assumed that the assembly was a mustering of the tribes for war, which might
not have been far off the mark (compare the assembly at Mizpah at the end of
Judges 10), or they decided to seize this opportunity of the gathering of Israel
for cultic purposes in order to attack the assembled tribes.

8 And the Israelites said to Samuel, "Do not hold still from crying out for us to the LORD our God, that He deliver us from the hand
9 of the Philistines." And Samuel took one suckling lamb and offered it up whole as a burnt offering to the LORD, and Samuel cried out to the LORD on behalf of Israel, and the LORD answered him.
10 And just as Samuel was offering up the offering, the Philistines drew near to do battle with Israel, and the LORD thundered with a great sound on that day upon the Philistines and panicked them,
11 and they were routed before Israel. And the men of Israel sallied forth from Mizpah and pursued the Philistines and struck
12 them down as far as below Beth-car. And Samuel took a single stone and set it up between Mizpah and Shen, and he called its name Eben-ezer and he said, "As far as here has the LORD helped us."

---

9. *one suckling lamb*. The Hebrew is literally "milk lamb" (*teleh ḥalav*). The choice of the sacrificial animal strikes an odd little echo with the two milch cows sacrificed at the end of the Ark Narrative and with the emphasis on nursing and weaning in Samuel's own infancy.

10. *the LORD thundered . . . and panicked them*. The key terms restate a recurrent pattern in 1 Samuel: God's hand, or God's voice (the thunder), comes down on the enemy, and the enemy is smitten with "panic" (*mehumah*). Compare, also, the end of Hannah's poem: "the LORD shatters His adversaries, / against them in the heavens He thunders." Essentially, it is God Who does battle, with the Israelite foot soldiers merely mopping up after His celestial bombardment. This Deuteronomistic view will fade from the Saul and David narratives.

12. *Shen*. If the Masoretic Text is correct (the Septuagint reflects a different place-name), this name means "cliff," and like Mizpah, it is preceded by a definite article.
   Eben-ezer. The name means "stone of help," with "help" bearing a particularly martial implication. This place may not be the same as the one where the Ark was captured. In any case, the recurring name is meant to signify the righting of old wrongs.
   As far as here. The Hebrew phrase could be either temporal ("up till now") or spatial, but the placing of a stone as a marker makes the latter more likely: as far as this point the LORD granted us victory.

And the Philistines were brought low and they no longer came into   13
Israelite country, and the hand of the LORD was against the Philistines all
the days of Samuel. And the towns that the Philistines had taken from   14
Israel were returned to Israel, from Ekron as far as Gath, and their territories Israel retrieved from the hand of the Philistines. And there was
peace between Israel and the Emorite. And Samuel judged Israel all the   15
days of his life. And he would go about from year to year and come round   16
Bethel and Gilgal and Mizpah and would judge Israel in all these places.

---

13. *the hand of the LORD was against the Philistines all the days of Samuel.* Since
under Saul's kingship the Philistines remained a dominant military power, "all
the days of Samuel" could refer only to the period of Samuel's actual leadership. In any case, there are later indications that even under Samuel the
Philistines remained powerful.

14. *peace between Israel and the Emorite.* This seemingly incongruous notice
actually throws light, as Shmuel Avramsky has proposed, on Israel's military-
political situation. The Emorites—a designation often used loosely by the biblical writers for the indigenous Canaanite peoples—had also been dominated
by the Philistine invaders, and Israel's success against the Philistines may
have been facilitated by an alliance, or at least a nonaggression pact, with the
Emorites.

15. *And Samuel judged Israel.* The precise nature of his leadership is left
ambiguous, as befits this transitional figure in Israel's political evolution.
Some of the "judging" may actually be performance of a judicial function, as
the next verse indicates that Samuel operated as a kind of circuit judge,
though he may well have carried out cultic or priestly duties as well (the
towns at which he stopped are all cultic sites). He is also judge in the sense
of "chieftain" or political leader, though he plays this role not as a warrior,
according to the model of the Book of Judges, but as exhorter and intercessor. He is also, as we shall see in the Saul story, a seer and a reprover-
prophet.

16. *from year to year.* This locution for iterative annual peregrination takes us
back to Hannah and Elkanah at the very beginning of the Samuel story.

17　And his point of return was Ramah, for there his home was, and there
he judged Israel. And he built there an altar to the LORD.

---

17. *his point of return was Ramah.* The Hebrew says literally "his return was
Ramah." This is evidently the same place as Ramataim Zofim, where his parents lived. Samuel's circuit is an uneven ellipsis roughly twenty miles across in
the northern part of the territory of Benjamin (Saul's tribe) and the southern
part of the territory of Ephraim, in north-central Israel. It is far from encompassing all the tribal territories.

CHAPTER 8

And it happened when Samuel grew old that he set his sons up as judges ₁
for Israel. And the name of his firstborn son was Joel and the name of his ₂
secondborn was Abijah—judges in Beersheba. But his sons did not go in ₃
his ways and they were bent on gain and took bribes and twisted justice.

And all the elders of Israel assembled and came to Samuel at Ramah. ₄
And they said to him, "Look, you yourself have grown old and your sons ₅
have not gone in your ways. So now, set over us a king to rule us, like
all the nations." And the thing was evil in Samuel's eyes when they ₆
said, "Give us a king to rule us." And Samuel prayed to the LORD.

---

1. *he set his sons as judges for Israel.* It is a signal expression of the ambiguity of
Samuel's role as leader that he oversteps his mandate as judge (*shofet*—both
judicial authority and ad hoc political leader) by attempting to inaugurate a kind
of dynastic arrangement. The two sons who betray their trust of office are a nice
parallel to Eli's two corrupt sons, who essentially were displaced by Samuel.

2. *judges in Beersheba.* It is a little puzzling that Samuel should send both his
sons from north-central Israel to this city in the south. Josephus evidently was
familiar with a tradition in which one son was sent to Bethel in the north and
the other to Beersheba, a more plausible deployment.

   bent on gain . . . twisted justice. The two verbs are different conjugations of
the same root, *n-t-h*, which means to bend off from the straight and narrow.

6. *the thing was evil in Samuel's eyes.* Samuel is ideologically opposed to the
monarchy because he is committed to the old idea of the ad hoc inspired leader,
shofet, who is a kind of direct implementation of God's rule through the divine
spirit over the unique nation of Israel. God appears to agree with him but yields
to political necessity. It is noteworthy that when the elders' words are replayed
in this verse from Samuel's point of view, the very phrase rejecting covenantal
status that must especially gall him, "like all the nations," is suppressed.

7 And the LORD said to Samuel, "Heed the voice of the people in all
that they say to you, for it is not you they have cast aside but Me they
8 have cast aside from reigning over them. Like all the deeds they have
done from the day I brought them up from Egypt to this day, forsaking
9 Me and serving other gods, even so they do as well to you. So now,
heed their voice, though you must solemnly warn them and tell them
10 the practice of the king that will reign over them." And Samuel said all
the words of the LORD to the people who were asking of him a king.
11 And he said, "This will be the practice of the king who will reign over

---

8. *forsaking Me and serving other gods.* Both the locutions used and the preoccupation with cultic loyalty are notably Deuteronomistic, and the coupling
of the shift in style with this theme leads one to suspect a seventh-century
interpolation here, since there has been no question of idolatry in the immediate context. The elders' expressed concern has been rather with the breakdown of the institution of the judge in Samuel's corrupt sons. The grounds for
the argument for and against monarchy will shift once again in Samuel's
speech (verses 11–18).

10. *asking of him a king.* The Hebrew participle *sho'alim* takes us back to
the verb of asking used in Samuel's naming and points forward to *Sha'ul*,
Saul.

11. *the practice of the king.* This whole episode turns repeatedly on an untranslatable pun. *Mishpat* means "justice," the very thing that Samuel's sons have
twisted by taking payoffs. *Mishpat* also means "habitual behavior," "mode of
operation," or "practice." As a verb the same root means either "to judge" or "to
rule": it is used (in a verbal noun) in the former sense in verses 1 and 2, in the
latter sense in verses 5 and 6. The recurrent scholarly assumption that this
whole attack on the encroachments of the monarchy reflects a knowledge of
Solomon's reign or of later Davidic kings is by no means inevitable: all the
practices enumerated—military conscription, the corvée, expropriation of
lands, taxation of the agricultural output—could easily have been familiar to
an early writer from observing the Canaanite city-states or the larger imperial
regimes to the east and the south.
    who will reign over you. The people had spoken of the king ruling/judging
them (the verb *shafat*); Samuel unambiguously speaks of reigning (*malakh,*
the cognate verb of *melekh,* king).

you: Your sons he will take and set for himself in his chariots and in his cavalry, and some will run before his chariots. He will set for him- 12
self captains of thousands and captains of fifties, to plow his ground and reap his harvest and to make his implements of war and the implements of his chariots. And your daughters he will take as confec- 13

---

your sons he will take. Samuel's speech is solidly constructed as a hammering piece of antimonarchic rhetoric. All the cherished possessions to be expropriated by the king are placed emphatically at the beginning of each clause, followed by the verb of which they are objects. "He will take" (one word in the Hebrew, *yiqah*) is insisted on with anaphoric force. The speech moves systematically from the expropriation of sons and daughters to land and produce to slaves and beasts of burden, ending with the climactic "you will become his slaves." A modern American reader might easily be reminded of the rhetoric of a radical libertarian inveighing against the evils of big government and the encroachments of its bureaucracies and taxation. In no part of his pragmatic argument does Samuel mention the Deuteronomistic themes of abandoning the LORD or betraying His direct kingship.

11.–12. *chariots . . . cavalry . . . captains.* The first item in the indictment of monarchy is military conscription. As is clear in the response of the people (verse 20), the consolidation of national military power under the king is precisely what attracts them to monarchy. All this leads one to suspect that the domination over the Philistines was by no means so comprehensive as claimed by the narrator in Chapter 7.

12. *to plow his ground and reap his harvest.* The Hebrew is literally "to plow his plowing and harvest his harvest."
  to make his implements. After conscripting men to fight and men to perform agricultural service, the king will also draft the artisan class for his purposes—ironsmiths, carpenters, wheelwrights, and so forth.
  his chariots. Samuel's emphasis from the start on chariots signals the political shift he envisions, for chariots were the instruments of the monarchies with which Israel contended, whereas the Israelites in this early stage did not have this sort of military technology at their disposal, at least according to the Book of Judges.

14 tioners and cooks and bakers. And your best fields and your vineyards
15 and your olive trees he will take and give to his servants. And your
seed crops and your vineyards he will tithe and give to his courtiers
16 and to his servants. And your best male and female slaves and your
17 cattle and your donkeys he will take and use for his tasks. Your flocks
18 he will tithe, and as for you, you will become his slaves. And you will
cry out on that day before your king whom you chose for yourselves
19 and he will not answer you on that day." And the people refused to
heed Samuel's voice and they said, "No! A king there will be over
20 us! And we, too, shall be like all the nations and our king will rule
21 us and go out before us and fight our battles." And Samuel listened to
all the words of the people and he spoke them in the LORD's hearing.

---

14. *give to his servants.* "Servants" in a royal context would be the functionaries
of the royal bureaucracy, whose service to the king was in fact often rewarded
by land grants.

16. *your cattle.* The Masoretic Text has "your young men" (*baḥureikhem*), but
the reading of the Septuagint, *beqarkhem*, "your cattle," is much more likely,
given the fact that the sons and daughters have already been mentioned and
that the next term is "your donkeys."

18. *you will cry out . . . and he will not answer you.* The language used here in
relation to the king is precisely the language used elsewhere in relation to God
(compare 7:9, where the people implore Samuel to "cry out" on their behalf to
God). Cries to *this* power will not be answered.

19. *A king there will be over us.* They do not say, "We will have a king" but "A
king will be over us."

20. *rule us.* Again, the people use the ambiguous key verb, *shafat,* "to
rule/judge."
     go out before us. This phrase reflects a specific military idiom—the full ver-
sion of it is, literally, "to go out and come in before us," that is, to lead in battle,
to execute maneuvers. The military power that can accrue to the nation
through the king is what is uppermost in the minds of the people.

And the LORD said to Samuel, "Heed their voice and make them a 22
king." And Samuel said to the men of Israel, "Go every man to his
town."

---

22. *Go every man to his town.* Though God has just instructed Samuel to com-
ply with the people's demand for a monarchy, Samuel's immediate response
instead is to send them back to their homes. His acquiescence remains grudging: he appears to be buying time, perhaps with the claim that he needs to
find a suitable candidate. The reluctance will persist, and grow, after he has
encountered Saul and anointed him.

CHAPTER 9

1 And there was a man of Benjamin whose name was Kish son of Abiel son of Zeror son of Bechorath son of Aphiah, a Benjaminite, a man of great means. And he had a son whose name was Saul, a fine and goodly young fellow, and no man of the Israelites was goodlier than he, head 3 and shoulders taller than all the people. And some asses belonging to Kish, Saul's father, were lost, and Kish said to Saul his son, "Take, pray, 4 with you one of the lads, and rise, go seek the asses." And he passed through the high country of Ephraim and he passed through the region of Shalishah, but they did not find them. And they passed through the region of Shaalim, and there was nothing there, and they passed 5 through the region of Benjamin, but they did not find them. They were just coming into the region of Zuf when Saul said to his lad

---

1. *And there was a man of Benjamin whose name was Kish.* The formulaic phrasing—"there was a man," followed by name, home region, and genealogy—signals to the audience that we are beginning a discrete new story within the larger narrative. (Compare the beginning of Hannah's story in 1:1–2.)

2. *head and shoulders taller than all the people.* The Hebrew says literally "from his shoulders taller than all the people." Saul's looming size, together with his good looks, seems to be an outward token of his capacity for leadership, but as the story unfolds with David displacing Saul, his physical stature becomes associated with a basic human misperception of what constitutes fitness to command.

5. *they were just coming . . . when.* This relatively infrequent indication of simultaneous actions occurs four times in this single episode. The writer seems to want to highlight a crucial series of temporal intersections and concatenations as Saul moves unwitting toward his destiny as king.
   Zuf. This is, of course, Samuel's home region.

who was with him, "Come, let us turn back, lest my father cease
worrying about the asses and worry about us." And he said to him,   6
"Look, pray, there is a man of God in this town, and the man is
esteemed—whatever he says will surely come to pass. Now then, let
us go there. Perhaps he will tell us of our way on which we have gone."

Come, let us turn back. According to the general principle of biblical narrative that the first reported speech of a character is a defining moment of characterization, Saul's first utterance reveals him as a young man uncertain about
pursuing his way, and quite concerned about his father. This concern, especially in light of the attention devoted to tense relations between fathers and
sons in the ensuing narrative, is touching, and suggests that the young Saul is
a sensitive person—an attribute that will be woefully submerged by his experience of political power. But as this first dialogue unfolds, it is Saul's uncertainty that comes to the fore because at every step he has to be prodded and
directed by his own servant.

6. *there is a man of God in this town . . . whatever he says will surely come to
pass.* The fact that neither Saul nor his servant seems to have heard of Samuel
by name (and the town, too, is left unnamed) has led many scholars to conclude that this story comes from a different source. But, as Robert Polzin has
vigorously argued, the palpable shift between Chapter 8 and Chapter 9 may
rather reflect "the varying play of perspectives (between narrator and reader,
between reader and character and between character and character) that
forms the stuff of sophisticated narrative." Saul's entire story, until the night
before his death on the battlefield, is a story about the futile quest for knowledge of an inveterately ignorant man. Samuel may have been presented before
as the spiritual leader of all the tribes, but this particular Benjaminite farm
boy knows nothing of him, and Saul's servant, who presumably has also spent
all his time on the farm, has picked up merely a local rumor of his activity but
not his name. From the rural-popular perspective of both, and in keeping with
the themes of knowledge and prediction of this story, Samuel is not a judge
and political leader but a "man of God" and a "seer" (compare verse 9) who
can predict the future.
  he will tell us of our way on which we have gone. The Hebrew verb clearly
indicates some sort of past action and not, as one might expect, "on which we
should go." Perhaps they feel so lost that they need the seer to tell them where
they have been heading. In the event, it is toward a kingdom, not toward lost
asses.

7   And Saul said to his lad, "But look, if we are to go, what shall we bring
to the man? For the bread is gone from our kits and there is no gift to
8   bring to the man of God. What do we have?" And the lad answered
Saul once again and he said, "Look, I happen to have at hand a quarter
of a shekel of silver that I can give to the man of God, that he may
9   tell us our way." In former times in Israel, thus would a man say when
he went to inquire of God, "Come, let us go to the seer." For the
10   prophet today was called in former times the seer. And Saul said to his
lad, "What you say is good. Come, let us go." And they went on to
11   the town in which the man of God was. They were just coming up
the ascent to the town when they met some young women going out
to draw water, and they said to them, "Is there a seer hereabouts?"

---

7. *But look, if we are to go, what shall we bring . . . ?* The diffident Saul is on the
point of quitting before the encounter. He needs the counsel, and the provi-
dent quarter-shekel, of his servant in order to move forward and make the portentous connection with Samuel.

   bread. As in general biblical usage, a synecdoche for "food."

9. *In former times in Israel.* This terminological notice simultaneously alerts
the audience to the gap between the time of the story (the eleventh century
B.C.E.) and the audience's own time (at the very least, two or three generations
later) and underscores the ambiguity of Samuel's transitional role as leader: he
is variously called judge, man of God, seer, and prophet, and he also performs
priestly functions.

   to inquire of God. The idiom means to inquire of an oracle.

10. *What you say is good.* Saul the future leader follows someone else's lead—
here, a slave's.

11. *they met some young women going out to draw water.* The wells would have
typically been outside the walls of the city. The encounter between a young
man in foreign territory with young women (*nećarot*) drawing water seems to
signal the beginning of a betrothal type-scene (compare Rebekah, Rachel, and
Zipporah at their respective wells). But the betrothal scene is aborted. Instead
of a betrothal feast, there will be a sacrificial feast that adumbrates a rite of
coronation. The destiny of kingship to which Saul proceeds will lead to grim-
mer consequences than those that follow in the repeated story of a hero who
finds his future bride at a well.

And they answered them and said, "There is. Look, he is straight ahead 12
of you. Hurry now, for today he has come to town, for the people have a
sacrifice today on the high place. As soon as you come into town, you 13
will find him before he goes up on the high place to eat. For the people
will not eat till he comes, as he will bless the sacrifice and then the
guests will eat. So go up, for today you will find him." And they went up 14
to the town. They were just coming into the town when Samuel came
out toward them to go up to the high place. And the LORD had dis- 15
closed to Samuel the day before Saul's arrival, saying, "At this time 16
tomorrow I will send to you a man from the region of Benjamin
and you shall anoint him prince over My people Israel and he

12.–13. The reply of the young women is notable for its garrulousness. One
talmudic sage sought to explain this trait with a simple misogynistic formula:
"women are talkative" (*Berakhot* 48 b), whereas, more amusingly, the
Midrash proposes that the young women kept repeating themselves because
they were so smitten by Saul's beauty. The clues in the immediately preceding narrative context suggest a less fanciful explanation: seeing the evident
signs of confusion and incomprehension in Saul's face, the women take elaborate measures to spell out where Samuel is to be found and what Saul
should do in order to be sure not to miss him. In all this, it is noteworthy, as
Polzin has observed, that Samuel, having agreed to find a king for Israel, has
made no move whatever toward that purpose. Instead, the future king "finds"
him.

the high place. The *bamah* was an elevated place, a kind of open-air natural
altar, perhaps sometimes with a structure erected alongside it (see the "hall"
in verse 22), where sacrifices were generally offered in the period before the
centralization of the cult in Jerusalem. The kind of sacrifice involved here is
one in which parts of the animal would be burned on the altar and the rest
eaten in a ceremonial feast.

16. prince. The Hebrew *nagid* is not used to refer to leaders before this
moment in Israelite history and is used only rarely after the very early years of
the monarchy. It is a term that suggests the exercise of political power in a
designated role of leadership rather than in the manner of the ad hoc charismatic leadership of the *shofet*, or judge. But God, in keeping with this transitional moment and perhaps even in deference to Samuel's keen resentment of
the monarchy, pointedly does not use the word "king."

shall deliver My people from the hand of the Philistines. For I have
17 seen the plight of My people, yes, their outcry has reached Me." And
Samuel saw Saul, and the LORD answered him, "Here is that man of
18 whom I said to you, 'This one will govern My people.'" And Saul
approached Samuel in the gateway and said, "Tell me, pray, where is
19 the house of the seer?" And Samuel answered Saul and said, "I am the
seer. Go up before me to the high place, and you will eat with me
today, and I shall send you off in the morning, and whatever is in your
20 heart I shall tell you. And as to the asses that have been lost to you now
three days, pay them no heed, for they have been found. And whose is
all the treasure of Israel? Is it not for you and all your father's house?"

---

he shall deliver My people. Again, the previously reported ascendancy over
the Philistines seems to have vanished, and God endorses military effectiveness as the rationale for the monarchy.

the plight of My people. The Masoretic Text lacks "the plight of," though the
phrase appears to have been in the version used by the Septuagint translators.
It is conceivable that what we have here is not an inadvertent scribal omission
but an ellipsis.

17. *And Samuel saw Saul.* The seer sees the divinely designated object of his
sight, and God immediately confirms that this is the man. Or, in the light of subsequent developments, Samuel is persuaded that he has received direct instruction from God. All the knowledge is on Samuel's side rather than on Saul's.

18. *Where is the house of the seer?* Addressing the very seer himself, Saul picks
up no clues that Samuel is anything but an ordinary passerby. He also
assumes that the seer has a house in the town, though the young women have
said that the seer has come to town for the sacrifice. (The scholarly assumption that the unnamed town must be Samuel's hometown, Ramah, is not
entirely compelling.)

20. *as to the asses.* It is at this point that Samuel reveals his access to supernatural knowledge: no one has told him that Saul was looking for asses, but
Samuel knows both of the lost animals and where to find them.

whose is all the treasure of Israel? This is a deliberately oblique reference to
kingship: if all the choice possessions of Israel are to be yours, why worry
about a few asses? Although the Hebrew term *hemdah* can mean "desire," it
more often has the sense of "desired, or valued, thing," as in the common
idiom, *kley hemdah,* "precious objects."

And Saul answered and said, "Am I not a Benjaminite, from the small-   21
est of the tribes of Israel, and my clan is the least of all the tribe of Benjamin? So why have you spoken to me in this fashion?" And Samuel   22
took Saul and his lad and brought them into the hall, and he gave them
a place at the head of the guests, about thirty men. And Samuel said to   23
the cook, "Bring the portion that I gave to you, about which I said, 'Set
it aside.' " And the cook lifted up the thigh and put it before Saul. And   24
Samuel said, "Here is what is left. Put it before you and eat, for it has
been kept for you for the appointed time as I said to the people I
invited." And Saul ate with Samuel on that day. And they came down   25
from the high place into the town, and they made a bed for Saul on the

---

21. *a Benjaminite, from the smallest of the tribes of Israel*. The young Saul is no
doubt overcome by Samuel's hint of a throne, but the language is also part of an
etiquette of deference. In fact, Benjamin was one of the most powerful tribes,
and given Kish's affluence, his clan would scarcely have been so humble.

all the tribe of Benjamin. The Masoretic Text has "tribes" but the Septuagint
reflects the more logical singular. The plural form is in all likelihood a scribal
replication of the plural in "tribes of Israel" at the beginning of the verse.

22. *a place at the head of the guests*. Samuel offers no explanation to the assembled company as to why this signal honor is accorded to the strangers.

23. *Set it aside*. The Hebrew reads literally "Put it by you."

24. The text here seems clearly defective at two different points. The phrase
"lifted up the thigh" is followed by an anomalously ungrammatical form of
"and that which is on it" (*wehe'aleyha*). It seems best to delete this word, as
does Version B of the Septuagint. The phrase "as I said to the people" is no
more than an interpretive guess about an asyntactic chain of three words in
the Hebrew, which literally are "saying the-people I-invited."

25. *they made a bed for Saul on the roof and he slept*. The Masoretic Text has
"he spoke with Saul on the roof and they rose early." The present translation
follows the far more plausible reading of the Septuagint: the report of speech
on the roof is odd because no content or explanation for it is given, and the rising early is contradicted by the fact that in the next phrase Samuel calls up to
Saul on the roof in order to rouse him. Evidently, a scribe substituted the
common word *wayidaber*, "he spoke," for the more unusual word *wayirbedu*,
"they made a bed" (the same consonants with the order reversed). *Wayishkav*,
"and he slept," differs from *wayashkimu*, "and they rose early," by one consonant in the unvocalized text.

26 roof, and he slept. And as dawn was breaking, Samuel called out to Saul on the roof, saying, "Arise and I shall send you off." And Saul
27 arose, and the two of them, he and Samuel, went outside. They were just going down past the edge of the town when Samuel said to Saul, "Tell the lad to pass on before us." And he passed on. "As for you, stand now that I may let you hear the word of God."

---

the roof. Presumably, the encounter takes place during the warm season, and the roof would be a cool sleeping place.

27. *Tell the lad to pass on before us.* Every step that Samuel takes here in conferring the kingship on Saul is clandestine. He speaks to him only after they have reached the outskirts of the town, and he is sure first to get Saul's servant out of earshot. This course of action is rather puzzling because the people, after all, have already publicly declared to the prophet that they want him to choose a king for them. Samuel's need to proceed in secrecy may reflect his persistent sense that the monarchy is the wrong path for the people, or it might be an expression of doubt as to whether this strapping young Benjaminite is really the right man for the job, despite the unambiguous indication that the prophet has just received from God.

CHAPTER 10

And Samuel took the cruse of oil and poured it over his head and kissed   1
him, and he said, "Has not the LORD anointed you over His inheritance
as prince? When you go away from me today, you shall find two men by   2
Rachel's Tomb in the region of Benjamin at Zelzah, and they will say to
you, 'The asses that you went off to seek have been found, and, look,
your father has put aside the matter of the asses and is worrying about
you, saying, What shall I do about my son?' And you shall slip onward   3

---

1. Anointment is the biblical ritual of conferring kingship, like coronation in
the later European tradition. Samuel carries out this act secretly, on the outskirts of the town, conferring on Saul, in keeping with the term God has used,
the title *nagid*, "prince," rather than "king."

2. *When you go away from me today* . . . This elaborate set of instructions and
predictions is, as Robert Polzin has argued, a strategy for asserting continued
control over the man Samuel has just anointed. Every predictive step manifests Samuel's superior knowledge as prophet, and all the instructions reduce
the new king to Samuel's puppet.
   Rachel's Tomb. The burial site of the mother of Benjamin, the eponymous
founder of the tribe, underscores Saul's own tribal affiliation.
   at Zelzah. This otherwise unattested name may not be a place-name but an
error in transcription in the Masoretic Text.
   your father has put aside the matter of the asses and is worrying about you.
According to the fixed procedure of verbal recycling in biblical narrative, the predicted words of the two men are nearly identical with Saul's first words to his servant. One should note that in the scenario Samuel lays out for him, Saul has no
opportunity to respond to his father's concern for his absence: on the contrary,
his new regal obligations rush him onward toward a daunting rite of initiation.

3. *Slip onward.* The Hebrew verb *halaf* suggests passing through a medium
and may well indicate the clandestine nature of Saul's movements.

from there and you shall come to the Terebinth of Tabor, and there three men will find you who are going up to God at Bethel, one bearing three kids and one bearing three loaves of bread and one bearing a jug

4 of wine. And they will greet you and give you two loaves of bread, and

5 you shall take from their hand. Afterward you shall come to Gibeath-Elohim, where the Philistine prefect is. And as you come into town there, you shall encounter a band of prophets coming down from the high place, preceded by harp and drum and flute and lyre, and they

---

the Terebinth of Tabor. Evidently, a cultic site.

three men . . . three kids . . . three loaves of bread. The triple three is a folk-tale pattern. It also manifests a mysterious design clearly grasped by Samuel, who annunciates this whole prediction, and into which Saul is thrust unwitting. The three men bear meat (or animals that can be turned into meat), bread, and wine—the three symbolic staffs of life. They will offer Saul the primary of the three, bread (in counterpoint to the "worthless fellows" at the end of the episode who give the new king no tribute).

5. *Gibeath-Elohim.* The name means Hill of God, but it would seem to be the same as the Gibeah of Judges 19, in which the Benjaminites perpetrated a lethal gang rape, and is also known as Gibeath-Benjamin and Gibeath-Saul.

the Philistine prefect. This glancing reference to a Philistine garrison deep within Benjaminite territory is still another indication of the Philistines' military ascendancy. That might be another reason for keeping the anointment secret, at least until the new king can consolidate military force around him. The Masoretic Text has a plural "prefects," but three different ancient translations reflect a singular.

a band of prophets. These are professional ecstatics who would whip themselves into a frenzy with the insistent rhythms of the musical instruments mentioned—a phenomenon familiar in enthusiastic religious sects worldwide—and then would "prophesy," become caught up in ecstatic behavior, which could involve glossolalia ("speaking in tongues"), dancing, writhing, and the like. The chief connection between these figures and the later literary prophets is the idea that both are involuntarily inhabited by an overpowering divine spirit.

harp. The Hebrew word for this instrument, *nevel,* is identical with the word for "jug" used at the end of verse 3 (the homonymity may be explained by a perceived lyre shape in the jug). It is a fairly common procedure in biblical narrative to link segments in immediate sequence by using this sort of pun as a linchpin. Here it has the effect of intimating an uncanny link between the first and second stages of the script Samuel is designing for Saul.

will be speaking in ecstasy. And the spirit of the LORD shall seize you, 6
and you shall go into ecstasy with them and you shall turn into another
man. And when these signs come upon you, do what your hand finds to 7
do, for God is with you. And you shall go down before me to Gilgal, 8
and, look, I shall be coming down to you to offer burnt offerings and to
sacrifice communion sacrifices. Seven days shall you wait until I come
to you, and I shall inform you what you must do." And it happened as 9
he turned his back to go off from Samuel, that God gave him another
heart and all these signs came to pass on that day.

---

6. *you shall turn into another man.* The drastic nature of this process is surely
meant by Samuel to be startling: nothing less will do in order to transform this
diffident farmer's son into a king than to be devastated by the divine spirit, vio-
lently compelled to radical metamorphosis. This whole story of Saul among
the prophets is repeated, with very significant changes, in Chapter 19, near
the end of his tortuous career. As we shall have occasion to see, the seeming
repetition, far from being a regrettable "doublet" produced in redaction, is
entirely purposeful: the same etiological tale is rotated 180 degrees to show us
first Saul being invested with the spirit, and with the monarchy, and then
divested of the monarchy by the spirit.

7. *do what your hand finds.* The biblical idiom means do whatever is within
your power.

8. *you shall go down before me to Gilgal . . . Seven days shall you wait.* The third
stage in the set of predictions/instructions that Samuel announces to Saul is in
fact not carried out till much later. Saul's divergence from the prophet's script
adumbrates his future failures of obedience in relation to Samuel. Robert Polzin
has made the shrewd argument that the unfulfilled prediction also reflects
Samuel's failure as a prophet, and that he has actually placed Saul in a double
bind by telling him that he may do whatever he wants because God is with him
and yet "has paradoxically commanded strict royal dependence upon prophetic
direction." Samuel, in other words, seems to want both a king and a puppet.

9. *as he turned his back.* The Hebrew *shekhem* is also the word for "shoulder,"
and so reminds us of Saul's regal stature, head and shoulders above all the
people.
    God gave him another heart and all these signs came to pass. These words are
a kind of proleptic headnote for the narrative report that follows, and it is not
implied that the transformation and the signs occurred the very moment Saul
turned to go.

10 And they came there to Gibeah, and look, a band of prophets was coming toward him, and the spirit of the LORD seized him and he went into
11 ecstasy in their midst. And so, whoever knew him from times gone by,
saw, and, look, with the prophets he spoke in ecstasy, and each would
say to his fellow,

> "What has befallen the son of Kish?
> Is Saul, too, among the prophets?"

---

10. *and they came there to Gibeah.* There is no report of the first of Samuel's
predicted encounters, with the three men bearing kids, bread, and wine. It is
unclear whether this reflects merely a narrative ellipsis or whether this, too, is
an unfulfilled prophecy. The report of the meeting with the two men who
announce that the asses have been found is also omitted. In any case, the
transformative meeting with the band of ecstatics is obviously the chief focus
of the writer's attention.

the spirit of the LORD seized him. This same phrase, or a slight variant of it,
is repeatedly used in the Book of Judges to indicate the inception of the
judge's enterprise as charismatic military leader. There is some overlap with
Saul's taking on the kingship, which will also involve military leadership, but
the report of ecstasy or "prophesying" is a new element, with its more radical
implication that the new leader must become "another man."

11. *Is Saul, too, among the prophets?* This evidently proverbial question, its
full origins scarcely remembered, is the perplexity that generates the etiological tale. The question seems to be proverbial of a case of extreme incon-
gruity (like the English "bull in a china shop")—what on earth is a man like
Saul doing among the prophets? The tale then comes to explain how the
saying arose. But the etiological tale, together with its antithetical counterpart in Chapter 19, figures significantly in the literary design of the Saul
story. Even the characterizing theme of Saul's repeated exclusion from predictive knowledge is inscribed in the question, "Is Saul, too, among the
prophets?" The people ask their question about Saul in a line of poetry (con-
sisting of two parallel versets, or hemistichs). The verse form explains why
Saul is first referred to as "son of Kish" because in poetry based on parallelism, it is the fixed procedure for treating proper names to use the given
name in one verset and, in lieu of a synonym, the patronymic in the other.
Thus, the claim made by some scholars that "son of Kish" is derogatory has
no basis.

And one man from there would answer and say, "And who is their father?"   12
Therefore it became a proverb, "Is Saul, too, among the prophets?" And he   13
ceased from his ecstasy and came to the high place. And Saul's uncle said   14
to him and to his lad, "Where did you go?" And he said, "To seek the asses.
And we saw that they were nowhere and we came to Samuel." And Saul's   15
uncle said, "Tell me, pray, what did Samuel say to you?" And Saul said to   16
his uncle, "He indeed told us that the asses had been found." But the
matter of the kingship of which Samuel had spoken he told him not.

And Samuel mustered the people to the Lord at Mizpah. And he said   17, 18
to the Israelites, "Thus said the Lord God of Israel: 'I brought Israel up

---

12. *who is their father?* The reference is obscure. The least convoluted explanation makes the prophets the antecedent of "their." The meaning then would be that unlike Saul, whose father is Kish, a landholder and a man of substance, the ecstatics are a breed apart, with no father anyone can name (the leader of a band of prophets was called idiomatically their father). The prevalent attitude toward such prophets was ambivalent: they were at once viewed as vehicles of a powerful and dangerous divine spirit, and as crazies (compare Hosea 9:7).

14. *Saul's uncle.* The appearance, without introduction, of an uncle (and not Saul's father, who after his brief initial appearance is never brought into the narrative proper) is puzzling. It has been proposed that this uncle is Ner the father of Abner, who will become Saul's commander in chief, but if that is the case, why is he left unnamed here?

16. *But the matter of the kingship . . . he told him not.* Saul's studied reticence confirms the clandestine character of his anointment.

17. *And Samuel mustered the people.* This national assembly is the second of three episodes that inaugurate Saul's kingship. One should not leap too quickly to the conclusion that these are merely a stitching together of variant sources. From the writer's viewpoint, the institution of the monarchy, with Saul as first king, is both a difficult and a dubious process, and it cannot happen all at once. First there is the clandestine anointment, followed by an initiatory experience, under the nose of the Philistine prefect. Then there is a public proclamation of the king, at which time sufficient forces can be marshalled to bolster him against the Philistines.

18. *Thus said the Lord God of Israel.* Samuel begins his speech with the so-called messenger formula, which is used to initiate prophetic messages. His speech is in fact a kind of prophetic denunciation of the people for having "cast aside" God in demanding a king and so is a reprise of his antimonarchic harangue in Chapter 8, even as he implements the choice of a king.

19 out of Egypt and I rescued you from the hand of Egypt and from the hand of all the kingdoms that have oppressed you.' And you on your part have cast aside your God Who delivers you from all your ills and troubles, and you have said, 'No! A king you shall put over us!' And so,

20 stand forth before the LORD by your tribes and your clans." And Samuel brought forward all the tribes of Israel and the lot fell to the

21 tribe of Benjamin. And he brought forward the tribe of Benjamin by its clans and the lot fell to the Matrite clan, and the lot fell to Saul son of

22 Kish, and they sought him but he was not to be found. And they inquired again of the LORD: "Has a man come here?" And the LORD

23 said, "Look, he is hidden among the gear." And they ran and fetched him from there, and he stood forth amidst the people, and he was head

24 and shoulders taller than all the people. And Samuel said to all the people, "Have you seen whom the LORD has chosen? For there is none like him in all the people." And all the people shouted and said,

---

20. *the lot fell.* The Hebrew verb *lakad* that is used for the drawing of lots means to be caught or trapped. As both Polzin and McCarter note, the only other biblical instances of such drawing of lots among the tribes are in order to discover a culprit, and so Samuel has chosen a mechanism associated with incrimination and punishment.

22. *has a man come here?* This translation reads ʿ*ad halom* instead of the Masoretic ʿ*od halom*, which would mean "again here."
Look, he is hidden among the gear. This detail is virtually a parody of the recurring motif of the prophet-leader's unwillingness to accept his mission. Saul the diffident farm boy had expressed a sense of unworthiness for the high office Samuel conferred on him. Now, confronted by the assembled tribes and "trapped" by the process of lot drawing, he tries to flee the onus of kingship, farcically hiding in the baggage.

24. *there is none like him in all the people.* Perhaps especially because Saul has been hauled out from the midst of saddle packs and sundry impedimenta, Samuel now executes a gesture of public relations: look at this strapping, handsome fellow—there is none in Israel who can match him. In the event, he proves wrong about Saul's fitness for the throne, and one may even wonder whether Samuel's proclamation that this is the one God has chosen (confirmed by the narrator's previous report) is not a misperception to justify his own (erring) choice.

"Long live the king!" And Samuel spoke out to the people the practice   25
of kingship and wrote it as a record and placed it before the LORD. And
Samuel sent all the people away to their homes. And Saul, too, had   26
gone to his home in Gibeah, and the stalwart fellows whose hearts God
had touched went with him. And worthless fellows had said, "How will   27
this one deliver us?" And they spurned him and brought him no tribute, but he pretended to keep his peace.

Long live the king. The people's proclamation does not use *nagid* (prince)
but the unambiguous *melekh* (king).

25. *the practice of kingship.* The phrase here, *mishpat hamelukhah* is close
enough to *mishpat hamelekh,* the term used in Chapter 8, and so the reasonable inference is that the content of the speech is a reiteration of the dangers
of encroachment of individual rights by the king that Samuel warned of in the
assembly at Ramah.

26. *stalwart fellows.* The translation follows the Qumran Samuel text and the
Septuagint in reading *giborey haḥayil* instead of the Masoretic *haḥayil,* "the
troop." The phrase, as many commentators have noted, is an obvious antithesis to "worthless fellows" in the next sentence.

27. *How will this one deliver us?* "This one" (*zeh*) is contemptuous.
    but he pretended to keep his peace. The Masoretic Text has two Hebrew
words here, *wayehi kemaḥarish,* which bear this meaning and have the attraction of indicating the inception of court intrigues and calculations at the very
beginning of Saul's reign—he is aware of political dissidence but chooses for
the moment not to react. It must be said, however, that the Qumran Samuel
fragment, supported by allied readings in the Septuagint and Josephus, has
wayehi kemeḥodesh (the graphemes for r and d are quite similar), "And it happened after about a month," affixing these two words at the beginning of the
next episode rather than at the end of this one.

CHAPTER 11

And Nahash the Ammonite came up and encamped against Jabesh-gilead. And all the men of Jabesh said to Nahash, "Make a pact with us, and we shall be subject to you." And Nahash the Ammonite said to them, "This is how I shall make a pact with you—with the gouging out

---

1. *Nahash the Ammonite.* During this period, the Ammonite kingdom, in the region to the east of the Jordan, was the second great military threat to the Israelites, after the Philistines to the west. David would later beseige the Ammonite capital, Rabbath-Ammon (near the site of present-day Amman). This episode, marking the inception of Saul's military activity, has several details that will be echoed later in the David story.

Jabesh-gilead. This Israelite settlement, in the tribal territory of Manasseh, was located several miles east of the Jordan and hence was exposed to Ammonite attack. In the story of the concubine at Gibeah—Saul's home-town—the men of Jabesh-gilead refuse to fight in the civil war against Benjamin, and so some special kinship between them and Saul's tribe is inferrable. The Samuel scroll found in Cave IV at Qumran reports a general campaign by Nahash against the trans-Jordanian Israelites. Here are the verses from the Qumran version (brackets indicate reconstructed letters or words, where there are gaps in the scroll): "[and Na]hash king of the Ammonites oppressed the Gadites and the Reubenites mightily and gouged out the right eye of e[very] one of them and imposed fe[ar and terror] on [I]srael, and there remained not a man of the Israelites be[yond] the Jordan [who]se right eye Nah[ash king of] the Ammonites did n[ot] [gou]ge out. Only seven thousand men [fled from] the Ammonites and came to [J]abesh-gilead. And after about a month"—the words that follow are identical with verse 1 in the Masoretic Text.

2. *the gouging out of the right eye.* Mutilation of captives was a fairly common practice. Josephus explains that the blinding of the right eye would have impaired the ability to fight because the left eye was largely covered by the shield in battle. In any case, submitting to this ghastly mutilation was a mark of great humiliation, or "disgrace" (*ḥerpah*).

of the right eye of every one of you, and I shall make it a disgrace for all
Israel." And the elders of Jabesh said to him, "Let us alone for seven   3
days, that we may send messengers through all the territory of Israel,
and if there is none to deliver us, we shall come out to you." And the   4
messengers came to Gibeath-Saul and spoke the words in the hearing
of the people, and all the people raised their voices and wept. And,   5
look, Saul was coming in behind the oxen from the field, and Saul said,
"What is the matter with the people that they are weeping?" And they
recounted to him the words of the men of Jabesh. And the spirit of God   6
seized Saul when he heard these words, and he was greatly incensed.

---

3. *Let us alone for seven days.* Nahash's seemingly surprising agreement to this
condition is by no means a sign of generosity but must be understood from his
viewpoint as an additional opportunity to humiliate the Israelites: he scarcely
imagines that the disunited tribes will produce a "deliverer," and thus the
impotent tribes will all be forced to witness helplessly the mutilation of their
trans-Jordanian kinsmen.

4. *the messengers came to Gibeath-Saul.* The men of Jabesh-gilead have told
Nahash they would search through "all the territory of Israel." But perhaps
they know something he does not—that Israel already has a tribally acclaimed
ruler and military leader who resides in Gibeah, but who has not yet begun to
act. The scholarly assumption that this entire story blatantly contradicts the
previous account of Saul's election as king and hence must derive from an
independent source is by no means necessary.

6. *the spirit of God seized Saul.* As many commentators have noted, the story
here explicitly follows the model of the inception of the charismatic leader's
career in Judges, when a kind of berserker spirit enters him and ignites him
with eagerness to do battle. Saul's coming in from the field behind the oxen is
also reminiscent of the pattern in Judges in which an agriculturalist (compare
Gideon) is transformed by an access of the spirit into a warrior. Given the
uncertainty about the new monarchic dispensation, it is quite possible that
Saul, after having been proclaimed king at Mizpah, might have returned to his
work in the field, awaiting the occasion when he would begin to act on his
new royal authority. The archetypal tale of the farmer who steps forward to
save the nation in time of crisis will recur in Roman tradition in the story of
Cincinnatus at the plow.

7 And he took a yoke of oxen and hacked them to pieces and sent them
through all the territory of Israel by the hand of messengers, saying,
"Whoever does not come out after Saul and after Samuel, thus will be
done to his oxen!" And the fear of the LORD fell on the people, and they
8 came out as one man. And Saul marshalled them in Bazek, and there
were three hundred thousand Israelites and thirty thousand men of
9 Judah. And he said to the messengers who had come, "Thus shall you
say to the men of Jabesh-gilead: 'Tomorrow deliverance will be yours as
the sun grows hot.'" And the messengers came and told the men of

---

7. *he took a yoke of oxen and hacked them to pieces.* This violent symbolism
doubly distinguishes Saul from the model of the ad hoc warrior-leader in
Judges. The dismemberment of the oxen is an explicit repetition of the dismemberment of the concubine at the end of Judges 19 after she has been
gang raped to death by the men of Gibeah (later the home of Saul). In
Judges, too, the bloody members were used to assemble all the tribes of
Israel to war, though the person who hacked the body to pieces was not a
judge but rather the morally dubious Levite, husband of the dead woman.
The allusion here is exquisitely ambiguous. Is this an act of restitution, a setting right of the ghastly civil war caused by the atrocity at Gibeah, or does it
inaugurate the narrative of Saul's public actions under the shadow of an earlier act of turpitude? Saul also differs from the judges in behaving like a king,
for he prepares for war by instituting a kind of military conscription binding
on all the tribes (the judges depended on volunteers and worked locally).
Kings, like Mafia capos, operate through coercion: Saul, in sending the
hacked-up oxen parts to his fellow Israelites with the threat, "Whoever does
not come out . . . thus will be done to his oxen," is presenting them with an
offer they cannot refuse.

after Saul and after Samuel. The medieval Hebrew commentator Kimchi
offers a shrewd explanation for Saul's adding Samuel to his exhortation:
"Since not all of them had accepted him as king, he said 'after Samuel.'"

the fear of the LORD. This seemingly pious phrase might also mean "a terrible fear," and it is, after all, Saul's frightening threat conveyed by the bloody
oxen parts that moves the people.

8. *Three hundred thousand.* As usual, the inflated figure does not reflect historical reality. The ten-to-one ratio between Israel and Judah reflects the ratio of
ten tribes to one.

Jabesh and they rejoiced. And the men of Jabesh said [to the   10
Ammonites], "Tomorrow we shall come out to you and you may do to
us whatever is good in your eyes." And it happened on the next day that   11
Saul set the troops in three columns. And they came into the camp in
the morning watch and struck down Ammon till the heat of the day,
and so those who remained were scattered and not two of them
remained together. And the people said to Saul, "Whoever said, 'Saul   12
shall not be king over us,' give us these men and we shall put them to
death." And Saul said, "No man shall be put to death this day, for today   13
the Lord has wrought deliverance in Israel."

And Samuel said to the people, "Come, let us go to Gilgal and we shall   14
renew there the kingship." And all the people went to Gilgal and they   15

---

10. *Tomorrow we shall come out to you.* These words are intended to lull the
Ammonites into a false sense of security before Saul's surprise attack in the
last hours before dawn ("the morning watch").

12. *Saul shall not be king over us.* The "not" appears in some variant manuscripts. The Masoretic Text as it stands is usually construed as a question:
"Saul will be king over us?" Robert Polzin tries to save the simple declarative
sense of the Masoretic Text by proposing that after Saul has just powerfully
acted like one of the old-time judges, the people, with the implicit endorsement of Saul, are inclined to retract their own insistence on monarchy and
return to the institution of judgeship. This reading is ingenious, but may create more problems than it solves. The report of continuing dissidence about
Saul's claim to the throne, as at the end of the previous chapter, in fact sets
the stage for much that will follow.

13. *No man shall be put to death this day.* Saul's magnaminity, after his demonstration of coercion and military effectiveness, strikes a positive note at the
beginning of his reign, though he will later prove to be utterly ruthless against
subjects he suspects of disloyalty.

14. *we shall renew there the kingship.* This clause helps make sense of the
triple story of Saul's dedication as king. First there was the clandestine anointment, with no publicly visible consequences. Then there was the tribal
assembly at Mizpah in which a reluctant Saul was chosen by lot and pro-

made Saul King there before the LORD at Gilgal, and they sacrificed
their communion sacrifices before the LORD, and Saul rejoiced there,
and all the men of Israel with him, very greatly.

---

claimed king. After that event, however, he appears to have returned for the
time being to private life. Now, following his signal success in mustering the
tribes and defeating Ammon, Samuel calls for a new assembly to reconfirm
Saul's standing as king, which will then be seen in subsequent episodes manifested in the institutions and power of a regular court.

CHAPTER 12

And Samuel said to all Israel, "Look, I have heeded your voice in all that   1
you said to me and have set a king over you. And so now the king walks   2
before you and I have grown old and gray, and my sons, they are here
with you, and I have walked before you from my youth till this day.
Here I am! Witness against me before the LORD and before His   3
anointed. Whose ox have I taken and whose donkey have I taken,

---

1. *And Samuel said to Israel.* It is not clear whether Samuel's farewell speech
takes place at Gilgal on the ceremony of "renewing the kingship" mentioned
at the end of the preceding chapter, or whether this is a separate occasion. It
does seem in character for Samuel that he would end up converting the coronation assembly into still another diatribe against the monarchy and an apolo-
gia for his own authority as prophet-judge.

I have heeded your voice. The phrase takes us back to the tribal convocation
in Chapter 8, when the grudging Samuel was enjoined by God to heed the
people's voice and make them a king.

2. *the king walks before you.* As we have had occasion to note earlier, this idiom
means to serve or act as a functionary.

my sons, they are here with you. This slightly odd reference to Samuel's sons
is in all likelihood a final verbal gesture toward the dynasty he has failed to
create: Samuel's crooked sons have already disqualified themselves from
assuming his mantle, but here he appears to take a last wistful look at that
prospect—my sons are here among you, but you insist instead on a king.

3. *Whose ox have I taken and whose donkey have I taken.* Samuel's profession of
innocence, as Kyle McCarter, Jr. has aptly noted, picks up antithetically his
admonition against the "practice of the king" in Chapter 8. There he warned
repeatedly that the king would "take" all the people's cherished possessions.
Here he proclaims that he, the prophet-judge, has taken nothing. In both
instances, he shows himself a master of rhetoric.

whom have I wronged and whom have I abused, and from whose hand
have I taken a bribe to avert my eyes from him? I shall return it to you!"
4   And they said, "You have not wronged us and you have not abused us,
5   and you have not taken a thing from any man." And he said to them,
"The LORD is witness against you, and His anointed is witness this day,
that you have found not a thing in my hand." And they said, "He is wit-
6   ness." And Samuel said to the people, "Witness is the LORD, Who
appointed Moses and Aaron and Who brought up your fathers from
7   the land of Egypt! And now, stand forth, that I may seek judgment with
you before the LORD, and I shall tell you all the LORD's bounties that
8   He did for you and for your fathers. When Jacob came into Egypt, and
your fathers cried out to the LORD, the LORD sent Moses and Aaron,
and they brought your fathers out of Egypt and settled them in this
9   place. And they forgot the LORD your God, and He delivered them into
the hand of Sisera commander of Hazor, and into the hand of the Philistines, and into the hand of the king of Moab, and they fought against
10 them. And they cried out to the LORD and said, 'We have offended, for

---

abused. The Hebrew verb means etymologically to crush or smash.

6. *Witness is the Lord.* The Masoretic Text lacks "Witness" (*ʿed*), which is supplied by the Septuagint. (The next clause also looks textually problematic
because the verb rendered here as "appointed," *ʿasah,* actually means "made"
and is not idiomatic.) It is noteworthy that Samuel sets up his entire speech as
a legal disputation between him and the people in which all the evidence, as
they are compelled to admit, stands in his favor.

7. *And I shall tell you.* The Masoretic Text lacks these words, but the next
phrase, "all the LORD's bounties," preceded by the accusative particle *ʾet,*
clearly requires a verb, and the appropriate verb is reflected in the Septuagint.

8. *When Jacob came into Egypt, and your fathers cried out.* The Septuagint
inserts between these two clauses the words "the Egyptians oppressed them."
But the Greek translators may have simply filled out a narrative ellipsis in the
original Hebrew text.

we have abandoned the LORD and served the Baalim and the Ashtaroth. And now, rescue us from the hand of our enemies, and we shall serve You.' And the LORD sent Jerubaal and Bedan and Jephthah and Samuel, 11 and He rescued you from the hand of your enemies all around, and you dwelled in safety. And you saw that Nahash king of the Ammonites had 12

---

10. *we have abandoned the* LORD *and served the Baalim and the Ashtaroth.* Samuel's speech seems to be an intertwining of an early story with a Deuteronomistic (seventh-century or sixth-century) editorial recasting. The vehement opposition to the monarchy would be original, perhaps even going back to the historical figure of Samuel. The Deuteronomistic school on its part was by no means antimonarchic, though it wanted to limit the monarch with the rules of the Book of God's Teaching (the Torah). On the other hand, the sin of idolatry is not an issue in the Samuel story, but it is a Deuteronomistic preoccupation. It is at this point in the speech that we encounter clusters of Deuteronomistic verbal formulas: "abandoned the LORD and served the Baalim," "delivered [literally, sold] into the hand of," "fear the LORD and serve Him and heed His voice," "serve Him truly with all your heart."

11. *Bedan.* The name of this judge is otherwise unknown, but since there is no reason to assume that the list in the Book of Judges is exhaustive, it seems prudent not to emend this into a familiar name.

and Samuel. It makes sense that Samuel would refer to himself by name rather than with the first-person pronoun because he wants to set himself as a matter of official record in the great roll call of judges.

12. *Nahash king of the Ammonites.* Since there had been no question of Nahash in the original demand for a king in Chapter 8, many scholars have inferred that the present episode reflects a different tradition, in which the call for monarchy is specifically linked with the Ammonite incursion reported in Chapter 11. But Moshe Garsiel proposes an interesting political reading that preserves the unity of the text. The original request for a king stresses the need for a military leader but mentions no particular enemy, perhaps because the people fear to name the dominant Philistines. Saul would have initially been instated in the ceremony at Mizpah as a sort of vassal king (or alternatively, leader of an underground movement), for the Philistines had garrisons in the territory of Benjamin. Now, after Saul's military success against the Ammonites, Samuel explicitly associates the call for a monarchy with Nahash's assault on Israel. This meeting at Gilgal would also have been an occasion to enlist the allegiance to Saul of the trans-Jordanian tribes.

come against you and you said to me, 'No! A king shall reign over us,'
13 though the LORD your God was your king. And now, here is the king
you have chosen, for whom you have asked, and here the LORD has put
14 over you a king. If you fear the LORD and serve Him and heed His voice
and rebel not against the LORD's words, and if both you and the king
who reigns over you will follow the LORD your God, He will rescue you.
15 But if you heed not the voice of the LORD and you rebel against the
LORD's words, the hand of the LORD will be against you and against
16 your king to destroy you. Even now, take your stance and see this great
17 thing that the LORD is about to do before your eyes. Is it not wheat harvest today? I shall call unto the LORD and He will send thunder and

---

13. *the king you have chosen, for whom you have asked.* Several times Samuel
plays sardonically on "asked" (*sha'al*) and "Saul" (*sha'ul*). Moshe Garsiel also
suggests a pun as well in "chosen" (*baḥar*) and the introductory designation of
Saul as a "fine fellow" (*baḥur,* literally "chosen one"). Although the story of
the institution of the monarchy indicates that God does the choosing, there is
no real contradiction—Samuel, in his acute discomfort with the monarchy
that has displaced his own authority, readily imputes the choosing to the people, despite his awareness that God has supposedly chosen. God on His part
no more than acquiesces in the people's stubborn insistence on a king. The
ambiguity of Saul's divine election will continue to be manifested in the narrative.

14. *rebel not against the LORD's words.* The Hebrew says literally "against the
LORD's mouth," but the same verb (root *m-r-h*) appears elsewhere with
"words" as object, and the two formulations are variants of the same idiom.
He will rescue you. The Masoretic Text lacks a clause stating what will happen if Israel remains faithful to God. These words (which would reflect a single verb with its suffix in the Hebrew) are supplied from the Septuagint.

15. *against your king to destroy you.* The Masoretic Text reads "against your
fathers" (without "to destroy you"). This makes no sense because it is a prediction of future catastrophe. Some ancient and medieval interpreters construe
the word "as against your fathers," but the Septuagint's reading, reflected in
this translation, is more likely because Samuel repeatedly brackets "you and
your king" sarcastically in this speech.

17. *wheat harvest.* That is, early summer, when no rain falls in Israel.

rain, and mark it and see, that the evil you have done is great in the
eyes of the LORD, to ask for yourselves a king." And Samuel called unto   18
the LORD, and the LORD sent thunder and rain on that day, and all the
people feared the LORD greatly, and they feared Samuel as well. And all   19
the people said to Samuel, "Intercede on behalf of your servants with
the LORD your God, that we may not die, for we have added to our
offenses an evil thing to ask for ourselves a king." And Samuel said to   20
the people, "Fear not. You have done all this evil, but swerve not from
following the LORD and serve the LORD with all your heart. And swerve   21
not after mere emptiness that will not avail or rescue, for they are mere
emptiness. For the LORD will not desert His people for the sake of His   22
great name, as the LORD has undertaken to make you His people. I on   23
my part, too, far be it from me to offend the LORD by ceasing to intercede on your behalf. I shall instruct you in the good and straight way.
Only fear the LORD and serve Him truly with all your heart, for see the   24
great things He has done for you. And if indeed you do evil, both you   25
and your king will be swept away."

---

19. *an evil thing, to ask for ourselves a king.* Through the pressure of Samuel's
oration, this "renewal of the kingship" most peculiarly turns into a collective
confession of the sin of having wanted a king.

21. *swerve not after mere emptiness.* "Swerve" is once again Deuteronomistic
terminology—to veer off from the straight and narrow path of the LORD. The
Masoretic Text inserts "that" *(ki)* after this verb, creating a small problem of
syntax, but the Septuagint deletes the word. The present translation adds the
adjective "mere" to "emptiness" *(tohu)* in order to convey the full pejorative
sense of the noun, which in many contexts suggests futility and is associated
with the emptiness of the desert (compare the *tohu wabohu*, "welter and
waste," of the beginning of Genesis).

23. *far be it from me to offend the LORD by ceasing to intercede on your behalf.* One
should note how deftly Samuel upstages the king whom he has just helped the
people to confirm in office. It is true, his argument runs, that you have made the
sinful error of choosing yourself a king. (Samuel of course makes no allowance
for God's role in the choice, which might express grudging divine recognition of a
new political necessity.) That cannot be reversed, but never fear—I will still be
here to act as the intercessor you will desperately continue to need.

CHAPTER 13

1 Saul was [ ] years old when he became king, and [-] two years he reigned over Israel.

2 And Saul chose for himself three thousand from Israel, and two thousand were with Saul at Michmash and in the Bethel high country, and a thousand were with Jonathan at Gibeath-Benjamin, and the rest of the people he sent away each man to his tent.

3 And Jonathan struck down the Philistine prefect who was in Gibeah and the Philistines heard of it. And Saul blew the ram's horn through-

---

1. *Saul was [ ] years old . . . and [-] two years he reigned.* The Masoretic Text, notoriously defective at this point, says "Saul was a year old . . . and two years he reigned." This whole sentence is absent from the Septuagint, leading one to suspect that the redactor here stitched into the narrative a textual fragment in which there were lacunae in the numbers that he did not presume to fill in.

3. *Jonathan struck down the Philistine prefect.* Though the Hebrew uses the standard idiom for killing someone in battle, the context of Israel's subservience to the Philistines suggests that this was an act of assassination, intended to trigger general rebellion. Jonathan enters the narrative without introduction. The neophyte king had himself seemed a very young man, but with the casualness about chronology characteristic of the biblical storyteller, Saul now has a grown son.

 in Gibeah. The text reads "Geba," but the two names, which continue to alternate, appear to be variants of the same name.

 Saul blew the ram's horn . . . saying, "Let the Hebrews hear!" The ram's horn, which produces shrill, piercing sounds, was often used for a call to arms. The "hearing" of the Israelites is counterpointed to the just-reported "hearing" of

out the land, saying, "Let the Hebrews hear!" And all Israel heard, say- 4
ing, "Saul has struck down the Philistine prefect, and, indeed, Israel
has become repugnant to the Philistines." And the people rallied round
Saul at Gilgal. And the Philistines had assembled to do battle against 5
Israel—thirty thousand chariots and six thousand horsemen and
troops multitudinous as the sand on the shore of the sea. And they
came up and encamped at Michmash, east of Beth-aven. And the men 6
of Israel saw that they were in straits, for the troops were hard pressed
and the troops hid in caves and among thorns and among rocks and in
dugouts and in pits. And Hebrews had crossed the Jordan into the ter- 7
ritory of Gad and Gilead, while Saul was still at Gilgal, and all the

---

the Philistines. "Hebrews" is usually the term used by foreigners for the
Israelites. As J. P. Fokkelman has observed, Saul invokes "a name used in contempt by enemies such as Pharaoh and the Philistines . . . in order to arouse
his people's pride and fortify their will to resist."

4. *Saul has struck down.* Though Jonathan was the assassin, Saul, as political
leader of the rebel forces, is credited with responsibility for the act.

Israel has become repugnant. The literal meaning of the Hebrew idiom is
very much like "to be in bad odor with," but that antiquated English idiom has
a certain Victorian fussiness not suitable to this narrator.

5. *thirty thousand chariots.* This inflated figure is reduced to three thousand in
the Septuagint.

6. *in dugouts.* The Hebrew term *tsariah* appears only here and in Judges 9.
Though the context in Judges has led some interpreters to construe it as a
tower, extrabiblical evidence from Late Antiquity argues for a chamber, or
sepulchre, hewn out of rock.

7 *and Hebrews crossed.* Here the narrator's use of "Hebrews" may have been
encouraged by the attraction of a folk-etymological pun: *ʿivrim* (Hebrews)
ʿavru (had crossed).

Saul was still at Gilgal. This cultic site is, according to a common identification, near Jericho in the Jordan valley. The "Hebrews"—perhaps the general
population and not the army—who cross the Jordan appear to be fleeing the
Philistines to the relative safety of the territory of Gad and Gilead to the
northeast.

8 troops were trembling behind him. And he waited seven days for the
fixed time Samuel had set, and Samuel did not come, and the troops
9 began to slip away from him. And Saul said, "Bring forth to me the
burnt offering and the communion sacrifice," and he offered up the
10 burnt offering. And it happened as he finished offering the burnt offering that, look, Samuel was coming and Saul went out toward him to
11 greet him. And Samuel said, "What have you done?" And Saul
said, "For I saw that the troops were slipping away from me and you on
your part had not come at the fixed time and the Philistines were
12 assembling at Michmash. And I thought, 'Now the Philistines will
come down on me at Gilgal, without my having entreated the LORD's
favor.' And I took hold of myself and offered up the burnt offering."

---

8. *the fixed time Samuel had set.* The words "had set" (one word in the
Hebrew) are lacking in the Masoretic Text but are supplied by two of the
ancient versions. The fact that the Hebrew word in question, *sam*, has the
same consonants as the first two consonants of Samuel's name may have led
to the scribal error. The entire story of Samuel's fixing a period of seven days
for Saul to await him at Gilgal before the offering of sacrifices goes back to
10:8. The fulfillment of that initial instruction to the new king has been interrupted by the election of Saul by lottery, his campaign against the Ammonites,
and the renewal of the kingship at Gilgal. One must assume either that the
order to await Samuel at Gilgal was for an eventual meeting at an unspecified
future time or that one literary strand of the Saul story has been interrupted
by the splicing in of other strands (Chapters 11–12).

the troops began to slip away from him. Battle could not be engaged without
first entreating the favorable disposition of the deity through sacrifice (compare
Saul's words of explanation in verse 12). Saul's men are beginning to give up hope
and desert; so he feels, with good reason, that he can afford to wait no longer.

10. *as he finished offering the burnt offering that, look, Samuel was coming.* The
timing gives the distinct appearance of a cat-and-mouse game played by
Samuel. He is not absolutely late, but he has waited till the last possible
moment—sometime well into the seventh day (or it might even be the eighth
day), by which time Saul has been obliged to take matters into his own hands.

12. *I took hold of myself.* The Hebrew verb *hitʾapeq* means to force yourself to
do, or to refrain from doing, something. The same verb is used when the tearful Joseph "could not hold himself in check" in the presence of his brothers
(Gen. 45:1).

And Samuel said to Saul, "You have played the fool! Had you but kept 13
the commandment of the LORD your God that He commanded you,
now the LORD would have made your kingdom over Israel unshaken
forever. But now, your kingdom shall not stand. The LORD has already 14
sought out for Himself a man after His own heart and the LORD has
appointed him prince to his people, for you have not kept what the
LORD commanded you." And Samuel arose and went up from Gilgal on 15

---

13. *Had you but kept the commandment of the LORD.* The Masoretic Text has a
declarative, "you have not kept," but the structure of the whole sentence
argues strongly for emending *lo* ("not") to *lu* ("if" introducing a clause contrary to fact). Samuel flatly assumes that his own commands and the commandments of the LORD are entirely equivalent. In fact, it is he, not God, who
has given Saul the elaborate instructions about waiting seven days at Gilgal.
In a kind of prophet's tantrum, Samuel insists again and again in this speech
on the words "commanded" and "commandment." (In verse 14, "appointed
him prince" is literally "commanded him prince.")
    made your kingdom . . . unshaken forever. The Hebrew verb *hekhin* means
both to establish and to keep on a firm foundation *(makhon)*, and so it is misleading to translate it only as the initiating "to establish."

14. *your kingdom shall not stand.* Samuel's rage over the fact that Saul has
offered the sacrifice derives from his construing that act as a usurpation of his
own prerogatives as master of the cult (though there are other biblical
instances of kings who offer sacrifices). One suspects that Samuel has set up
Saul for this "failure," and that he would have been content only with a puppet king.
    The LORD has already sought out for Himself a man after His own heart.
Though this would have to be a veiled prediction of the advent of David,
in naturalistic terms, the incensed Samuel is in a way bluffing: fed up with
Saul, he announces to the king that God has already chosen a successor—
about whom Samuel himself as yet knows nothing whatever, nor has he
even had time for a communication from God that there will be a successor.
    appointed him prince to his people. As Polzin shrewdly notes, David
will later use these very words (2 Samuel 6:21) when he angrily tells Saul's
daughter Michal that it is he who has been divinely elected to replace her
father.

his way, and the rest of the troops went up after Saul toward the fighting force and came from Gilgal to Gibeath-Benjamin. And Saul mus-
16 tered the troops remaining with him, about six hundred men. And Saul
and Jonathan his son and the troops remaining with them were staying
at Gibeath-Benjamin, and the Philistines had encamped at Michmash.
17 And a raiding party sallied forth from the Philistine camp in three
columns—one column turned toward the road to Ophrah, to the Shual
18 region, and one column turned toward the road to Beth-horon, and one
column turned toward the border road that looks out over the Zeboim
19 Valley, toward the desert. And no smith could be found in all the land
of Israel, for the Philistines had said, "Lest the Hebrews make sword or
20 spear!" And all Israel would go down to the Philistines for every man to
put an edge on his plowshare and his mattock and his ax and his sickle.

---

15. *on his way, and the rest of the troops went up* . . . This entire clause, up to
the words "from Gilgal," is lacking in the Masoretic Text but reflected in the
Septuagint. Without them, Samuel is illogically reported to go up to Saul's
town, Gibeah (Gibeath-Benjamin, also called Gibeath-Saul), whereas what
he is clearly doing is abandoning Saul while the king and his remaining
handful of troops take up their position at Gibeah before the Philistine
assault.

about six hundred men. By this point, 1,400 have "slipped away."

17. *the Shual region.* The name literally means "Foxland."

18. *Zeboim Valley.* Or, Jackal Valley.

19. *No smith could be found in all the land of Israel.* This bit of background
notation vividly reflects the abject status of the Israelites under Philistine
domination. Ironsmiths are banned among them to prevent their developing
the weaponry needed for rebellion.

20. *his sickle.* The reading used here is, as in the Septuagint, *hermesho,* instead
of the Masoretic *mahareshato,* "his plowshare," which repeats the first term in
the list.

And the price of the sharpening was a *pim* for the plowshares and the   21
mattocks and the three-pronged forks and the axes, and for setting the
goads. And so it was, on the day of battle, that no sword nor spear was   22
found in the hands of all the troops who were with Saul and Jonathan,
but in the hands of Saul and Jonathan his son. And the Philistine garri-   23
son sallied forth to the pass of Michmash.

---

21. *the price of the sharpening was a* **pim.** The italicized term occurs only here
in the Bible, but the archeologists have found stone weights marked *pim*,
which are two-thirds of a shekel (here, evidently, a silver shekel). The
Philistines, then, not only deprive the Israelites of the technology for making
weapons but also reap a profit from their smithless vassals for the mainte-
nance of the agricultural tools they need for their livelihood.

the three-pronged forks. A commonly proposed emendation yields "a third
of a shekel for the forks and the axes and for the setting of the goads." This
change would make sense if in fact the sharpening of these implements were
half the work of sharpening plowshares and mattocks, but that is not entirely
clear.

CHAPTER 14

1   And when the day came round, Jonathan son of Saul said to the lad bearing his armor, "Come, let us cross over to the Philistine garrison which is on the other side there," but his father he did not tell. And 2 Saul was sitting at the outskirts of Gibeah under the pomegranate tree which is at Migron, and the troops that were with him were about six 3 hundred men. And Ahijah son of Ahitub brother of Ichabod son of Phineas son of Eli priest of the LORD at Shiloh was bearer of the 4 ephod, and the troops did not know that Jonathan had gone. And in the pass through which Jonathan sought to cross over to the Philistine gar-

---

1. *but his father he did not tell.* One assumes that his father would have forbidden him to go out on so dangerous a mission, but there is also an implicit contrast between Saul, sitting under the pomegranate tree, hesitant to act in the face of the superior forces of the enemy, and Jonathan, prepared to execute a daring commando raid.

3. *Ahijah son of Ahitub brother of Ichabod.* The genealogy here casts a certain suspect light on Saul: the priest who accompanies him to the battlefield, and on whose prognostication he relies, belongs to the blighted—and rejected—house of Eli.

   bearer of the ephod. The title, *nosᵉe ephod,* is formally parallel to "armor bearer," *nosᵉe kelim,* and so suggests a contrast between Saul, who relies on divination, and Jonathan, who relies on his weapons.

4. *the pass through which Jonathan sought to cross over.* The Philistines and the Israelites are encamped on the tops of two steep hills facing each other, with a deep gully, or *wadi,* running between them. Jonathan and his armor bearer are able to make their way down the slope unseen by taking cover among the crags and under overhangs. But Jonathan realizes that there will be a moment of truth in this tactic, for when they reach the floor of the gully, they will be "exposed" (verse 8) to the Philistine outpost.

rison there was a rocky crag on one side and on the other side, and the
name of the one was Bozez and the name of the other Seneh. The one 5
crag loomed to the north facing Michmash and the other to the south
facing Gibeah. And Jonathan said to the lad bearing his armor, "Come, 6
let us cross over to the garrison of these uncircumcised! Perhaps the
LORD will act for us, for nothing holds the LORD back from deliverance, whether by many or by few." And his armor bearer said to him, 7
"Do whatever your heart inclines—here I am with you, my heart as
yours." And Jonathan said, "Look, we are about to cross over to the 8
men and we shall be exposed to them. If thus they say, 'Stand still until 9
we get to you,' we shall stand where we are and not go up to them. And 10
if thus they say, 'Come up to us,' we shall go up, for the LORD will have
given them in our hand, and that will be the sign for us." And the two 11
of them were exposed to the Philistine garrison, and the Philistines

---

5. *loomed.* The Hebrew *mutsaq* means literally "column." It might conceivably
be a scrambled scribal repetition of the next Hebrew word in the text, *mitsa-
fon,* "from the north."

6. *these uncircumcised.* This designation for the Philistines is of course contemptuous. Its spirit is precisely reflected, from the other side of the ethnic
barrier, in Othello's reference to a Turk he killed in battle as a "circumcisèd
dog."

7. *Do whatever your heart inclines—here I am with you, my heart as yours.* The
translation follows the reading of the Septuagint. The Masoretic Text conveys
the same general idea, though a bit less coherently: "Do whatever is in your
heart, incline you—here I am with you as your heart."

10. *that will be the sign for us.* Readers from the Talmud to our own times have
construed this as a kind of divination. It is far more likely that a further contrast is implied between Saul, who depends on divination, and Jonathan, who
is thinking in pragmatic military terms: if they invite us to come up to them,
that will be our great opportunity; if they order us to await their descent, we
may have no recourse (except, perhaps, flight at the last moment).

said, "Look, Hebrews are coming out of the holes where they've been
12 hiding." And the men of the garrison spoke out to Jonathan and his
armor bearer and said, "Come up to us, and we'll teach you something!"
And Jonathan said to his armor bearer, "Come up behind me, for the
13 LORD has given them into the hand of Israel." And Jonathan climbed up
on his hands and knees with his armor bearer behind him, and they fell
before Jonathan with his armor bearer finishing them off behind him.
14 And the first toll of dead that Jonathan with his armor bearer struck
15 down was about twenty men, with arrows and rocks of the field. And terror shook the camp in the field and all the troops. The garrison and the
raiding party were also shaken, and the earth trembled, and it became
16 dire terror. And the lookouts attached to Saul at Gibeath-Benjamin
saw and, look, the multitude was melting away and going off yonder.

---

11. *Look, Hebrews are coming out of the holes where they've been hiding.* These
words accord perfectly with the report in 13:6 of the Israelites hiding in every
nook and cranny, and also vividly express the contempt of the Philistines for
the Hebrews, whom they depict as so many vermin. The contempt is
extended in the taunting challenge to Jonathan and his lad in the next verse.

13. *Jonathan climbed on hands and knees.* Although it is not easy to reconstruct
the exact tactic of surprise, this notation makes clear that instead of walking
up the slope directly to the Philistine outpost, Jonathan and his armor bearer
manage to slip off to one side and make their way up the slope by a circuitous
route, crouching and crawling in order to take shelter among the rocks, and
thus come upon the outpost undetected.

14. *the first toll of dead.* The literal meaning of the Hebrew is "the first blow."
with arrows and rocks of the field. The translation adopts the reading of the
Septuagint. The Masoretic Text has here, "within about half a furrow long, an
acre [?] of field," but that sequence of Hebrew words looks scrambled.

15. *terror shook.* The Hebrew *haradah* means both terror and shaking.
dire terror. The Hebrew is literally "terror of God," but the latter word, *ʾelohim,* serves as an intensifier. In any case, the idiom functions as a kind of
pun—dire terror is terror caused by God.

16. *going off yonder.* The translation presupposes *halom* ("yonder"), a repeated
word in this episode, instead of the Masoretic *wahalom,* which could mean
either, asyntactically, "and yonder," or "and hitting" (i.e., the Philistines were
going on, hitting each other).

And Saul said to the troops who were with him, "Call the roll, pray, and see who has gone from us," and they called the roll and, look, Jonathan and his armor bearer were absent. And Saul said to Ahijah, "Bring forth the ephod." For on that day he was bearing the ephod before the Israelites. And it happened that as Saul was speaking to the priest, the tumult in the Philistine camp was growing greater and greater. And Saul said to the priest, "Pull back your hand." And Saul and all the troops who were with him rallied and entered into the fighting, and, look, every man's sword was against his fellow—a very great panic. And there were Hebrews who were previously with the Philistines, who had come up with them into the camp, and they, too, turned round to be

---

18. *Bring forth the ephod.* The Masoretic Text, both in this clause and the next, has "Ark of God" instead of "ephod," but the reading of the Septuagint, *ephod*, is compelling on several grounds. We have been informed earlier that the Ark of God was left, not to be moved for the foreseeable future, at Kiriath-jearim. The Ark was not an instrument of divination, like the ephod, and what Saul wants Ahijah to do here is to divine. It is possible that Ahijah's lineal connection with the keepers of the Ark at Shiloh led some early transmitter of the text to align this episode with the earlier story in which the Ark—quite misguidedly—was brought out from Shiloh to the battlefield. The Masoretic Text also reads, asyntactically, "for the Ark of God on that day was, and the Israelites," whereas the Septuagint, far more coherently, has "for on that day he was bearing the ephod before the Israelites."

19. *Pull back your hand.* That is, desist from the act of divination you have begun—it is no longer necessary, for the auditory evidence of the Philistine rout has reached our ears.

20. *and, look, every man's sword was against his fellow.* This spectacle of total, self-mutilating panic (*mehumah*) in the camp of the enemy is a recurrent motif that goes back to Judges (compare the effect of Gideon's surprise attack on the Midianite camp), and is a kind of narrative realization of God's direct intervention in battle to grant victory to Israel. The foundational instance of this motif is the victory at the Sea of Reeds in Exodus.

21. *Hebrews who were previously with the Philistines.* Given the subject status of the Israelites, it is not surprising that some of them would have been conscripted by the Philistines, either as soldiers or to perform menial tasks for the troops. They are referred to here as "Hebrews" because that is how their Philistine masters would have referred to them.

22   with Israel under Saul and Jonathan. And all the men of Israel who
     were hiding out in the high country of Ephraim had heard that the
     Philistines were fleeing, and they, too, gave chase after them in the
23a fighting. And the LORD delivered Israel on that day.

23b, 24 And the fighting moved on past Beth-aven. And the men of Israel were
         hard pressed on that day. And Saul made the troops take an oath, saying,
         "Cursed be the man who eats food until evening, until I take vengeance
25   upon my enemies!" And all the troops tasted no food. And the whole
         country came into the forest, and there was honey on the ground.

---

24. *and the men of Israel were hard pressed.* The explanation for being hard
pressed is not certain. The Hebrew term, *nigas,* most naturally refers to being
at a military disadvantage, but here the Israelites appear to have the upper
hand. The other possibility is that the men are weak from hunger, not having
had the opportunity to eat in their hot pursuit of the Philistines. The oath Saul
exacts would then compound this predicament. It should be said that the
Septuagint reflects a different text for this entire clause: "And Saul committed
a great blunder on that day."
    Cursed be the man who eats food. As we shall have occasion to see later in
the David narrative, it was a fairly common practice (though by no means an
automatic one) for fighting men to take on themselves a vow of abstinence
from food, in order to enter the battle in what amounted to a state of dedicated ritual purity. But Saul in this instance makes a miscalculation, imposing
a fast on hungry men, in an effort to force the hand of divinity. (Thus the Septuagint's version of the first clause of this verse might be regarded as an interpretive gloss on the lapidary formulation of the received text.)

25. *And the whole country came into the forest.* This sounds as odd in the
Hebrew as in translation because "country" (ʾarets) is not an idiomatic term
for "people." Extensive textual surgery yields this conjectural reconstruction
of an original clause: "and there was honeycomb on the ground." An additional
difficulty in this passage is that the common Hebrew term *yaʿar,* forest, has a
rare homonym that means honeycomb. (In verse 27, the term that occurs is
yaʿarah, which is unambiguous both because with the feminine suffix it can
refer only to honeycomb and because it is joined with *devash,* honey.) But the
received text in our verse has the preposition "into" (*bᵉ*), which presumes that
yaʿar means "forest" and not "honeycomb."

And the troops entered the forest and, look, there was a flow of honey, 26
but none touched his hand to his mouth, for the troops feared the vow.
But Jonathan had not heard when his father made the troops swear, 27
and he reached with the tip of the staff that was in his hand and
dipped it into the honeycomb and brought his hand back to his
mouth, and his eyes lit up. And a man from the troops spoke up and 28
said, "Your father made the troops solemnly swear, saying, 'Cursed be
the man who eats food today.' And so the troops were famished." And 29
Jonathan said, "My father has stirred up trouble for the land. See,
pray, that my eyes have lit up because I tasted a bit of this honey. How 30
much better still if the troops had really eaten today from the booty of
their enemies that they found, for then the toll of Philistines would
have been all the greater." And they struck down the Philistines on 31
that day from Michmash to Ajalon, and the troops were very famished.

---

27. *his eyes lit up.* The idiom used for the refreshing effect of a taste of food is
a pointed one because, as Shimon Bar-Efrat has noted, the verb "to light up"
(the Hebrew verb *ʾor*) plays antithetically on Saul's "cursed (*ʾarur*) be the
man."

29. *My father has stirred up trouble.* The verb ʿakhar that is used here is doubly important. Etymologically, it means "to muddy," as in stirring up muck
in a pond. Thus, it is an antithesis to the lighting up of the eyes Jonathan
has just experienced through partaking of food. It is also the verb Jepthah
invokes when he sees it is his daughter who has come out to greet him: "and
you have been among those who stir up trouble for me" (Judges 11:35).
The echo sets up a network of intertextual links with the Jephthah story:
here, too, a father who is a military leader seeks to influence the outcome of
the battle by a rash vow that is an unwitting death sentence on his own
child.

31. *and they struck down the Philistines.* . . . . Although the form of the two verbs
does not indicate it, the narrative logic of the scene compels us to construe
this sentence as a pluperfect summary of the day's action, responding to
Jonathan's reference to the "toll" (literally, "blow") exacted from the
Philistines.

32 And the troops pounced on the booty and took sheep and cattle and calves and slaughtered them on the ground, and the troops ate them

33 together with the blood. And they told Saul, saying, "Look, the troops are offending the LORD by eating together with the blood!" And he said, "You have acted treacherously. Roll a big stone over to me now."

34 And Saul said, "Spread out among the troops, and say to them, "Every man bring forth to me his ox and his sheep and slaughter them here and eat, and you shall not offend the LORD by eating together with the blood." And all the troops brought forth each man what he had in hand

35 that night and they slaughtered it there. And Saul built an altar to the LORD, it was the first altar he built to the LORD.

36 And Saul said, "Let us go down after the Philistines by night and despoil them till daybreak, and we shall not leave a man among them." And they said, "Whatever is good in your eyes, do." And the priest said, "Let us

---

32. *the troops pounced on the booty . . . ate them together with the blood.* The first verb here has pejorative force, being generally used for birds of prey descending on their victims. Biblical law repeatedly prohibits the consumption of meat together with the blood because the blood is regarded as the sacred stuff of life. The slaughtering on the ground here would make it more difficult to allow the blood to drain off, as would have been done in slaughtering on a stone platform or altar. (Note Saul's correction of the practice in verses 33–34.) Jonathan's tasting a bit of honey thus leads to an orgy of gluttonous consumption of meat with blood. This consequence attaches an association of violation of sacred law to Jonathan's act, but the ultimate fault lies with Saul, who by imposing a fast on already famished men has set them up to abandon all restraint the moment the taboo against eating is broken.

34. *what he had in his hand.* This accords with the Septuagint, *ʾasher beyado,* against the Masoretic, "his bull in his hand," *shoro beyado.*

approach God yonder." And Saul inquired of God, "Shall I go down   37
after the Philistines? Will you give them in the hand of Israel?" And He
did not answer him on that day. And Saul said, "Draw near, all you   38
chiefs of the troops, mark and see, wherein is this offense today? For as   39
the LORD lives Who delivers Israel, were it in Jonathan my son, he
would be doomed to die!" And none answered him from all the troops.
And he said to all Israel, "You will be on one side and I and Jonathan   40
my son on the other side." And the troops said to Saul, "What is good in
your eyes, do." And Saul said, "LORD, God of Israel! Why did You not   41
answer Your servant today? If there is guilt in me or in Jonathan my
son, O LORD God of Israel, show Urim, and if it is in Your people
Israel, show Thummim." And the lot fell on Jonathan and Saul, and the

---

37. *and Saul inquired of God . . . and He did not answer him.* Although it was
extremely common for military leaders everywhere in the ancient Near East to
consult an oracle before going into battle, Saul's failed inquiry here participates in a larger pattern in his story: he is constantly seeking knowledge of
what is about to happen (as in his quest for a seer to help him locate the asses
at the very beginning), but this knowledge is repeatedly withheld from him.

38. *wherein is the offense.* Saul assumes that the oracle did not respond
because someone among his troops committed some "offense." The narrator
does not necessarily endorse this assumption.

39. *were it in Jonathan my son.* "It" refers to the just mentioned "offense." Is
this a flourish of rhetorical emphasis, or, as J. P. Fokkelman has suggested,
does it open the possibility that Saul has Jonathan in mind? In the immediately preceding episode, after all, Jonathan has gone out on a military operation without permission. Jonathan now is brought forth as the possible
perpetrator of some further, not yet specified offense, which will prove to be
the tasting of the honey. In any case, there seems to be some deep ambivalence between father and son well before the appearance of David at court.

41. *LORD, God of Israel! Why did You not answer Your servant today? If there is
guilt in me or in Jonathan my son, show Urim, and if it is in Your people Israel,
show Thummim.* This version comes from the Septuagint. The Masoretic Text
here has the short and cryptic "Show Thammim [sic]." Saul's frustrated reference to his failure to receive an answer from the oracle makes a great deal of
narrative sense (see the comment on verse 37). The Septuagint version also
makes intelligible the process of oracular lottery. The Urim and Thummim

42 troops came out clear. And Saul said, "Cast between me and Jonathan
43 my son." And the lot fell on Jonathan. And Saul said, "Tell me, what
have you done?" And Jonathan told him and said, "I indeed tasted from
the tip of the staff that was in my hand a bit of honey. Here I am, ready
44 to die!" And Saul said, "So may God do to me, and even more, for
45 Jonathan is doomed to die!" And the troops said to Saul, "Will Jonathan
die, who has performed this great deliverance in Israel? Heaven forbid,
as the LORD lives, that a single hair of his head should fall to the
ground! For with God has he wrought this day." And the troops saved
46 Jonathan, and he did not die. And Saul went away from pursuing the
Philistines and the Philistines went back to their place.

---

were two divinatory objects attached to the ephod, probably in a special com-
partment. They may have been in the form of stones or tokens with lettering
on them. They provided indication of binary oppositions: thus the question
addressed to the oracle had to take the form of yes or no, x or y. The opposition
may have been underscored by the fact that Urim and Thummim begin,
respectively, with the first and last letter of the Hebrew alphabet. More spec-
ulatively, Urim might be linked with ᵓ*aror*, "to curse," and Thummim with the
root *t-m-m*, whole or innocent.

    the lot fell on Jonathan and Saul. The same idiom of being "caught" by the
lot that was used for Saul's election recurs here in the devolution of the curse
on Jonathan.

    42. *cast between me and Jonathan.* Since the Urim and Thummim can provide
only binary responses, it is necessary to divide again into two alternatives in
order to get an answer.

    43. *Indeed I have tasted . . . a bit of honey.* Jonathan begins by clearly and
emphatically admitting responsibility, using the infinitive absolute followed by
the verb (literally, "taste I have tasted"). But he chooses, with precision, the
minimal verb "taste" rather than "eat" and holds back its minimal object, "a bit
of honey," for the very end of the sentence.

    45. *And the troops said to Saul, "Will Jonathan die . . . ?"* As several commenta-
tors have observed, this is a precise reversal of the incident after Saul's victory
over Nahash, in which the troops sought to kill dissidents and Saul saved their
lives. Now he has become the severe autocrat, and his son's well-earned popularity with the troops saves the prince.

And Saul had taken hold of the kingship over Israel, and he did battle   47
round about with all his enemies, with Moab and with the Ammonites
and with Edom and with the kings of Zobah and with the Philistines,
and wherever he turned he would inflict punishment. And he tri-   48
umphed and struck down Amalek and rescued Israel from the hand of
its plunderers.

And Saul's sons were Jonathan and Ishvi and Malkishua, and the   49
names of his two daughters were Merab the firstborn and Michal the
younger. And the name of Saul's wife was Ahinoam daughter of Ahi-   50
maaz. And the name of his commander was Abiner son of Ner, Saul's
uncle. And Kish, Saul's father, and Ner, Abner's father, were sons of   51

---

47. *Saul had taken hold of the kingship.* The verb used, *lakad,* is the same one
just invoked for the process of being caught, trapped, taken hold of, in the
divine lottery. Saul himself was "caught" for kingship. Now, through conquest,
he catches, or secures, the kingship. There is thus surely an undertone of
ambiguity in this report of his success as monarch.

he would inflict punishment. The Hebrew *yarshiᶜa* usually means to condemn someone as guilty in a court of justice. But notice that a related idiom,
"to do justice," *ᶜasot shephatim,* also means to carry out punitive acts against an
enemy. The Masoretic version is to be preferred to the Septuagint's *yoshiᶜa,*
"he would deliver," because in this narrative, God, not Saul, is represented as
the deliverer. Apparently, the implication is that he carried out punishing
expeditions against Israel's enemies to the east of the Jordan without actually
conquering them, as David was to do.

49. *And Saul's sons . . .* This entire notice of Saul's family and of his conquests
is placed as a formal marker of conclusion to the body of the Saul story. What
follows is the episode that will definitively disqualify him for the throne in
Samuel's eyes, and then David will enter the scene. The episode in which
Saul pronounces a death sentence on his son and heir heralds the climactic
encounter with Samuel over Amalek in which the prophet will pronounce the
end of Saul's incipient dynasty. Eventually, Saul and Jonathan, the parties
jointly indicated by the first cast of the Urim, will perish in battle on the same
day.

50. *Abiner.* A variant vocalization of Abner.

52   Abiel. And the fighting against the Philistines was fierce all the days of
Saul, and when Saul saw any warrior or valiant fellow, he would gather
him to himself.

---

52. *And the fighting against the Philistines.* Saul has greater success on the
eastern front, but he is unable to subdue the Philistines. In the end, they will
destroy him in their victory at Gilboa.
    when Saul saw any warrior . . . he would gather him to himself. This report of
constant military conscription indicates the institutionalization of the monarchy and also accords with Samuel's warning about the burden of conscription
that the king would impose.

CHAPTER 15

And Samuel said to Saul, "Me has the LORD sent to anoint you as king over His people Israel. And now, listen to the voice of the words of the LORD. Thus says the LORD of Hosts, 'I have made reckoning of what Amalek did to Israel, that he set against him on the way as he was coming up from Egypt. Now, go and strike down Amalek, and put under the ban everything that he has, you

1

2

3

---

1. *Me has the LORD sent.* Samuel, by placing the accusative first-person pronoun at the beginning of his speech (normal Hebrew usage would simply attach an accusative suffix to the verb), once again highlights his own centrality to this whole process: it is only because he, as God's unique delegate, has anointed Saul that Saul can claim to be king. In this way, Samuel sets the stage rhetorically for the prerogative of canceling Saul's kingship that he will exercise later in this episode.

listen to the voice of the words of the LORD. This redundant phrasing is a little odd, but it is dictated by the pressure of the thematically fraught key phrase, "listen to the voice," that defines the entire episode. Saul fails to listen as he fails to see.

2. *reckoning of what Amalek did to Israel.* After Amalek massacred the Israelite stragglers (see Deut. 25:18), Israel was commanded to destroy all remnants of the Amalekites.

set against him. This phrase may be an ellipsis for "set ambushes against him."

3. *put under the ban everything he has.* The verb here is in the plural, evidently including the troops together with Saul, though the subsequent verbs in this verse are in the singular. The "ban" (*herem*), one of the cruelest practices of ancient Near Eastern warfare, is an injunction of total destruction—of all living things—of the enemy. Amalek is, of course, the archetypal implacable enemy of Israel, but it should be said that here, as throughout the Samuel story, there is at least some margin of ambiguity as to whether the real source of this ferocious imperative is God or the prophet who claims to speak on His behalf.

---

shall not spare him, and you shall put to death man and woman, infant
and suckling, ox and sheep, camel and donkey.' "

4 And Saul summoned the troops and assembled them at Telaim, two
5 hundred thousand foot soldiers and ten thousand men of Judah. And
6 Saul came up to the city of Amalek and lay in wait in the ravine. And
Saul said to the Kenite, "Go, turn away, come down from amidst the
Amalekite, lest I sweep you away together with him, for you did kindness to all the Israelites when they came up from Egypt." And the Ken-
7 ite turned away from the midst of Amalek. And Saul struck down
8 Amelek from Havilah till you come to Shur, which is before Egypt. And
he caught Agag king of Amalek alive, and all the people he put under
9 the ban with the edge of the sword. And Saul, and the troops with him,
spared Agag and the best of the sheep and the cattle, the fat ones and

---

you shall not spare him. The Hebrew verb *hamal* straddles two senses, to
feel mercy for and to allow to survive, and the ambiguity between the emotional and the pragmatic sense is exploited throughout the story.

4. *summoned the troops.* The word for "summoned" (there are several more
common terms for mustering troops in the Bible) is quite rare, and literally
means "made them listen." The same verb as "to listen" in a different conjugation, it continues to call attention to this thematically weighted activity.

two hundred thousand foot soldiers and ten thousand men of Judah. The
troops from Judah are presumably also foot soldiers, and so an ellipsis is probable: 'and another ten thousand foot soldiers from the men of Judah.'

6. *Go, turn away, come down from amidst.* These overlapping imperative verbs
are obviously meant to underscore the urgency of the command. The Kenites
appear to have been a tribe of migratory metalsmiths (the meaning of their
name) somehow allied with Israel (compare Judges 4–5), though the nature of
the "kindness" they did for Israel is not known.

9. *And Saul, and the troops with him, spared Agag.* The Hebrew says simply
"Saul and the troops spared Agag," but because a singular verb is used with
the plural subject, it signals to the audience that Saul is the principal actor
and the troops only accessories. (This highlighting of the first-mentioned
agent through a singular verb for a plural subject is a general feature of biblical
usage.) When confronted by Samuel, Saul will turn the responsibility for the
action on its head. "Spared" momentarily sounds as though it could mean

the young ones, everything good, and they did not want to put them under the ban. But all the vile and worthless possessions, these they put under the ban.

And the word of the LORD came to Samuel, saying, "I repent that I made Saul king, for he has turned back from Me, and My words he has not fulfilled." And Samuel was incensed and he cried out to the LORD all night long. And Samuel rose early in the morning to meet Saul, and it was told to Samuel, saying, "Saul has gone to Carmel and, look, he has put up a monument for himself, and has turned about and passed onward, and gone down to Gilgal." And Samuel came to Saul, and Saul said to him, "Blessed be you to the LORD! I have fulfilled the word of the LORD." And Samuel said, "And what is this sound of sheep in my ears, and the sound of cattle that I hear?"

10, 11

12

13

14

"had mercy on," but then it is also attached to cattle and sheep. There is a morally scandalous pairing in the selective massacre Saul and his troops perpetrate: they kill all the defective animals and every man, woman, child and infant, while sparing the good, edible animals and the king (perhaps with the idea that some further profit can be extracted from him).

the fat ones. The Masoretic Text has *mishnim* (two-year-olds?), but, in a reversal of consonants, the Syriac and the Targum reflect *shmenim*, fat ones.

11. *Samuel was incensed.* The reasons for his rage are wonderfully unspecified, or perhaps overdetermined. He may well be incensed with Saul, or with the people who coerced him into this whole distasteful monarchic business in the first place, or even with God for making him heed the people.

12. *Carmel.* This is not the Carmel near Haifa but a town in the tribal territory of Judah, in the general vicinity of Hebron.

he has put up a monument for himself. This would be a victory marker, probably in the form of a stele.

14. *this sound of sheep, and the sound of cattle.* "Sound" and "voice" are the same word in Hebrew (*qol*), and so the thematic key word of the episode comes to the fore: Saul had been enjoined to listen to the voice of the LORD; now Samuel tells him that all that can be heard (the same verb as "listen" in Hebrew) is the bleating and mooing "voice" of the very flocks which, according to God's word, should have been destroyed.

15 And Saul said, "From the Amalekite they have brought them, for the troops spared the best of the sheep and the cattle in order to sacrifice to
16 the LORD your God, and the rest we put under the ban." And Samuel said, "Hold off, that I may tell you what the LORD spoke to me this
17 night." And he said, "Speak." And Samuel said, "Though you may be small in your own eyes, you are the head of the tribes of Israel, and the
18 LORD has anointed you king over Israel. And the LORD sent you on a mission and said to you, 'You shall put under the ban the offenders,
19 Amalek, and do battle against them till you destroy them all.' And why did you not listen to the voice of the LORD, for you pounced on the booty

---

15. *they have brought them.* Saul first uses a vague third-person plural, entirely shifting the responsibility to unnamed others who have done the bringing.

the troops spared the best of the sheep and the cattle. In verse 9, of course, it was expressly reported that Saul, with the troops as accessories, spared the flocks.

in order to sacrifice to the LORD your God. This pious justification for the act was nowhere in evidence in the narrator's initial account of it (verses 8–9). Although it is common enough in biblical usage when addressing a holy man to say "the LORD your God," that locution, invoked twice in this story by Saul, stresses the distance between him and God and his sense that it is Samuel who has proprietary claims on the divinity.

17. *though you may be small in your own eyes.* Samuel is obviously harking back to Saul's initial expression of unworthiness for the throne ("from the smallest of the tribes of Israel," 9:21), as if to say, Well, you may not really amount to much, as you yourself said at the outset, but you nevertheless have taken upon yourself the solemn responsibility of king.

18. *mission.* Literally, "a way."

till you destroy them all. The Masoretic Text, illogically, has "till they destroy them all," but the second-person suffix is supplied in some of the ancient versions.

19. *why did you not listen to the voice of the LORD?* Samuel hammers home the thematic point of the whole confrontation: Saul, actually the initiator, proclaims he has listened to the voice of the people (verse 24)—as, ironically, Samuel himself was enjoined by God to do in Chapter 8—instead of to the voice of God. This antithesis is more pointed in the Hebrew because the general meaning of the word for "troops," *ʿam*, is "people."

you pounced on the booty. Samuel uses the same verb for greedy predation that was used to describe the orgy of meat-eating after the breaking of the vow of fasting in Chapter 14.

and did evil in the eyes of the LORD?" And Saul said to Samuel, "But I   20
listened to the voice of the LORD and went on the way the LORD sent
me, and I brought back Agag king of Amalek, but Amalek I put under
the ban. And the troops took from the booty sheep and cattle, the pick   21
of the banned things, to sacrifice to the LORD your God at Gilgal." And   22
Samuel said,

> "Does the LORD take delight in burnt offerings and sacrifices
>   as in listening to the voice of the LORD?
> For listening is better than sacrifice,
>   hearkening, than the fat of rams.
> For the diviner's offense is rebellion,   23
>   the transgression of idols—defiance.
> Since you have cast off the word of the LORD,
>   He has cast you aside as king."

---

21. *the troops took.* Once again, Saul shifts the responsibility for the act from
himself to his troops.

22. *Does the LORD delight in burnt-offerings . . .* Samuel caps his prophetic
denunciation with the declamation of a prophetic poem. The theme that God
requires obedience, not rote performance of the cult, is a common one among
the later "literary" prophets, though in their poetry, obedience to God means
refraining from acts of exploitation rather than carrying out a program of exter-
mination.
     listening to the voice of the LORD. The thematic phrase is now placed in the
foreground of the prophetic poem, reinforced by "listening is better than sacrifice" and "hearkening" in the next lines.

23. *the diviner's offense is rebellion.* That is, rebellion is as great a sin as divination or sorcery. The choice of the comparison is not accidental, considering
Saul's repeated futile attempts to divine the future.
     the transgression of idols—defiance. The first phrase in the Hebrew is liter-
ally "transgression and idols," but is readily construed as a hendyadis (two
words for a single concept) without emending the text. The gist of this parallel
verset: defiance is as great a sin as the worship of idols *(teraphim).*

24 And Saul said to Samuel, "I have offended, for I have transgressed the utterance of the LORD, and your word, for I feared the troops and lis-
25 tened to their voice. Now then, forgive, pray, my offense, and turn
26 back with me, that I may bow down before the LORD." And Samuel said to Saul, "I will not turn back with you, for you have cast aside the word of the LORD and He has cast you aside from being king over
27 Israel." And Samuel turned round to go, and Saul grasped the skirt of
28 his cloak, and it tore. And Samuel said to him, "The LORD has torn away the kingship of Israel from you this day and given it to your fel-
29 lowman, who is better than you. And, what's more, Israel's Eternal does not deceive and does not repent, for He is no human to repent."

---

24. *I have transgressed the utterance of the LORD, and your word.* The Hebrew is literally "the mouth of the LORD." There is a kind of hesitation in Saul's words: I have violated God's command, and yours as well. Is there a difference between the two? Though there may well be, Saul is in no position to argue that Samuel's words are not God's.

25. *return with me, that I may bow down.* It would have been Samuel's function to offer the sacrifice. For Samuel not to accompany Saul to the altar would be a manifest public humiliation, a gesture of abandonment.

27. *Saul grasped the skirt of his cloak, and it tore.* The "little cloak" that Hannah would bring each year for the child Samuel has now become the prophet's flowing robe. Samuel, who never misses a cue to express his implacability toward Saul, immediately converts the tearing of the cloak into a dramatic symbol of Saul's lost kingdom. The Saul story, as we shall see, will return to cloaks and to their torn or cut skirts.

29. *Israel's Eternal does not deceive and does not repent.* Samuel's use of the verb "repent" strikes a peculiar dissonance. We in fact have been told that God repented that He made Saul king. What Samuel says here is that God will not change His mind about changing His mind. But might not this verbal contradiction cast some doubt on Samuel's reliability as a source for what God does and doesn't want? There even remains a shadow of a doubt as to whether the election of Saul in the first place was God's, or whether it was merely Samuel's all-too-human mistake.

And Saul said, "I have offended. Now show me honor, pray, before the 30
elders of my people and before Israel, and turn back with me, that I
may bow to the LORD your God. And Samuel turned back from Saul, 31
and Saul bowed to the LORD. And Samuel said, "Bring forth to me 32
Agag king of Amalek!" And Agag went to him with mincing steps, and
he thought, "Ah, death's bitterness is turned away!" And Samuel said, 33

"As your sword has bereaved women,
        more bereaved than all women your mother!"

And Samuel cut him apart before the LORD at Gilgal. And Samuel 34
went to Ramah, while Saul went up to his home in Gibeath-Saul.

---

30. *show me honor*. Saul reverts to the recurrent term *kabed*—"honor" or
"glory" (as in "glory is exiled from Israel"). Knowing that Samuel has rejected
him, he implores the prophet at least to help him save face in offering the sacrifice.

31. *Samuel turned back from Saul*. All English versions render this, erroneously, to indicate that Samuel nevertheless accompanied Saul to the sacrifice. But the expression "turn back with" (*shuv ʿim*), as in verse 30, and "turn
back from [literally, after]" (*shuv ʾaḥarei*) are antonyms, the latter meaning
unambiguously "to abandon." (It is precisely the latter idiom that we see in
God's condemnation of Saul in verse 11.) Samuel is completing his rejection of
Saul here by refusing to accompany him in the cult, shaming him by forcing
him to offer the sacrifice without the officiating of the man of God.

32. *with mincing steps*. The Hebrew adverbial term *maʿadanot* is much disputed. Some interpret it as "stumbling," others, by a reversal of consonants,
read it as "in fetters." But the root of the word seems to point with the least
strain to *ʿ-d-n*—"pleasure," "delicate thing." That makes sense if one construes Agag's words (the meaning of which is also in dispute) as the expression
of a last illusion: I have been spared in the general massacre, and now I am
brought to parlay with the chief holy man of the Hebrews for some important
purpose; so surely they will not kill me.

33. *Samuel cut him apart before the LORD*. There is a long-standing consensus
that the unique verb used here means something to this effect. The ghastly
idea seems to be a kind of ritual butchering.

34. *Ramah . . . Gibeath-Saul*. Each returns to his hometown. Their relationship is to all intents and purposes finished.

35 And Samuel saw Saul no more till his dying day, for Samuel grieved over Saul, and the LORD had repented making Saul king over Israel.

---

35. *Samuel grieved over Saul.* Or is it over the fact that he made the mistake of first choosing Saul? As J. P. Fokkelman notes, this sentence includes both death *(mot)* and grieving or mourning *(hit²abel)*, though Saul is still alive: "we realize that Saul as king is dead; no stronger expression of the termination of his monarchy can be imagined."

CHAPTER 16

And the LORD said to Samuel, "How long are you going to grieve over   1
Saul when I have cast him aside from reigning over Israel? Fill your
horn with oil and go. I am sending you to Jesse the Bethlehemite, for I
have seen Me among his sons a king." And Samuel said, "How can I   2
go? For should Saul hear, he will kill me." And the LORD said, "Take a
heifer with you, and you will say, 'To sacrifice to the LORD I have come.'

---

1. *And the LORD said to Samuel.* In the preceding episodes, the typical form of
divine communication was Samuel's report of what God had said, although at
Samuel's first sighting of Saul, a brief direct message from God is offered. As
we have observed, these reports open up a certain margin of doubt as to
whether the purported divine injunctions are really God's or Samuel's. The
present episode unfolds systematically through repeated dialogue between
God and Samuel, and so God's judgments are rendered with perfect, authoritative transparency. Evidently, the writer (or redactor) felt that the initial election of David had to be entirely unambiguous. As the story continues, God
will no longer play this role of direct intervention.

I have seen Me among his sons a king. The verb "to see" (*ra²ah*) followed by
the preposition lᵉ has the idiomatic sense of "to provide," but it is essential to
preserve the literal meaning because this entire episode is built on the repetition of the thematically weighted word "to see," just as the previous episode
turned on "to listen."

2. *For should Saul hear, he will kill me.* Suddenly, a whole new political perspective is thrown on the estrangement between Samuel and Saul. The
prophet may claim the higher ground of divine authority, but it is the king who
has the armed divisions, and who might be ready to use them if Samuel should
take any active steps to replace him. At this point, Samuel's "grieving" over Saul
begins to look like grieving over the mistake he made in first choosing him.
God, understanding Samuel's political predicament, suggests to him a cover
story for his trip from Ramah to Bethlehem, in the tribal territory of Judah.

3 And you will invite Jesse to the sacrifice. And I Myself shall let you know what you must do, and you will anoint Me the one that I say to
4 you." And Samuel did what the LORD had spoken, and he came to Bethlehem, and the elders of the town came trembling to meet him
5 and they said, "Do you come in peace?" And he said, "In peace! To sacrifice to the LORD I have come. Purify yourselves and come with me to the sacrifice." And Jesse purified his sons and invited them to
6 the sacrifice. And it happened when they came that he saw Eliab and
7 he said, "Ah yes! Before the LORD stands His anointed." And the LORD said to Samuel, "Look not to his appearance and to his lofty stature, for I have cast him aside. For not as man sees does God see. For man sees with the eyes and the LORD sees with the heart."

---

3. *invite Jesse to the sacrifice.* The kind of sacrifice in question, *zevah*, involves both the ritual act and a feast made of the substantial parts of the animal not burned on the altar.

4. *came trembling.* Their reaction is another reflection of the dangerous political situation: the estrangement between Samuel and Saul appears to be generally known, and the elders are terrified at the idea that Samuel may have come to designate a new king, or otherwise subvert the reigning monarch, which could bring royal retribution down on Bethlehem.

and they said, "Do you come in peace?" The Masoretic Text has "he said," but both the Septuagint and the Qumran Samuel scroll show the plural. Both also add "O seer" to the question of the elders.

6. *he saw Eliab.* Nothing could illustrate more vividly Samuel's persistent unreliability as seer (*ro'eh*). Having made a fatal mistake by electing Saul, "head and shoulders taller than all the people," convinced he was directed by God, Samuel is poised to repeat his error in being impressed by the "appearance" and "lofty stature" of Jesse's firstborn. This whole story is also a heightened and stylized playing out of the theme of the reversal of primogeniture that dominates Genesis. Instead of an elder and a younger son, Jesse has the formulaic seven sons, plus an eighth, the youngest of all, who will be chosen.

7. *for I have cast him aside.* The language of rejection links the strapping Eliab with the lofty Saul.

does God see. These words, absent from the Masoretic Text, are supplied by the Septuagint.

the LORD sees with the heart. Some construe this as "into the heart." In any case, the heart is the seat of understanding, or insight, in biblical physiology.

And Jesse called Abinadab and made him pass before Samuel, and he 8
said, "This one, too, the LORD has not chosen." And Jesse made 9
Shammah pass by, and he said, "This one, too, the LORD has not chosen." And Jesse made his seven sons pass before Samuel, and Samuel 10
said to Jesse, "The LORD has not chosen these." And Samuel said to 11
Jesse, "Are there no more lads?" And he said, "The youngest still is left,
and, look, he is tending the flock." And Samuel said to Jesse, "Send and
fetch him, for we shall not sit to eat until he comes here." And he sent 12
and brought him. And he was ruddy, with fine eyes and goodly to look
on. And the LORD said, "Arise, anoint him, for this is the one." And 13
Samuel took the horn of oil and anointed him in the midst of his brothers. And the spirit of the LORD gripped David from that day onward.
And Samuel rose and went to Ramah.

8.–9. The verbatim repetition reflects the stylization of the episode, which is
set off from the surrounding narrative by its formal symmetries. After the first
three named sons, the rest pass by in summary by invocation of a narrative "et
cetera" principle, with the formulaic wrap-up at the end of verse 10, "The
LORD has not chosen these."

11. *he is tending the flock.* By his sheer youth, he has been excluded from consideration, as a kind of male Cinderella left to his domestic chores instead of
being invited to the party. But the tending of flocks will have a symbolic implication for the future leader of Israel, and, in the Goliath story, it will also prove
to have provided him with skills useful in combat.

12. *he was ruddy, with fine eyes and goodly to look on.* David's good looks will
play a crucial role in the magnetic effect he is to have on women and men. But
he is not big, like his brother Eliab, and Samuel has no opportunity to make a
judgment on appearance, for David is brought from the flock sight unseen,
and then God immediately informs Samuel, "this is the one."

13. *anointed him in the midst of his brothers.* The anointment takes place
within the family circle and is a clandestine act.

14 And the spirit of the Lord had turned away from Saul, and an evil
15 spirit from the Lord had struck terror in him. And Saul's servants
    said to him, "Look, pray, an evil spirit from God has stricken terror
16 in you. Let our lord, pray, speak. Your servants are before you—we
    shall seek out a man skilled in playing the lyre, and so, when the
    evil spirit of God is upon you, he will play and it will be well with
17 you." And Saul said to his servants, "See for me, pray, a man who plays
18 well, and bring him to me." And one of the lads answered and said,
    "Look, I have seen a son of Jesse the Bethlehemite, skilled in playing,

---

14. *and the spirit of the Lord turned away from Saul.* In the transfer of election
of monarchs, one gets the picture of a kind of spiritual seesaw. As the spirit of
the Lord descends on, seizes, David, it departs from Saul. That vacuum is
promptly filled by "an evil spirit from the Lord." In the theopsychology of
ancient Israel, extraordinary states were explained as investments by a divine
spirit. The charisma of leadership, now passed to David, was a descent of the
spirit. Saul's psychosis—evidently, fits of depression later accompanied by
paranoia—is possession by another kind of spirit from the Lord.

15. *Saul's servants.* These would be his court officials or attendants.

16. *we shall seek out a man.* The Hebrew is literally "they will seek out a man."
    a man skilled in playing the lyre. In modern terms, what they have in mind
is a kind of music therapist. But David's mastery of the lyre evinces both his
power over the realm of the spirit (or of spirits) and his future association with
song and poetry.

17.–18. *See for me . . . I have seen.* The insistence on this verb picks up the key
word of the preceding episode. Saul first uses it in the sense God did in verse
1, "provide."

18. *Look, I have seen a son of Jesse.* This volunteered information is a bit peculiar because, before any real search is undertaken, one of the young men in
court already has a candidate, and from a different tribal region. Is it possible
that word of David's clandestine anointment has circulated among limited
groups, and that the anonymous "lad" may be a kind of pro-David mole in the
court of Saul? It is also noteworthy that, just as at the beginning of his story, in
his quest for the lost asses, Saul did not know what to do and was dependent
on the counsel of his "lad" (*na‘ar*); here one of his lads (*ne‘arim*) offers the
needed advice for dealing with his melancholia.

a valiant fellow, a warrior, prudent in speech, a good-looking man, and
the LORD is with him." And Saul sent messengers to Jesse and said,   19
"Send me David your son, who is with the flock." And Jesse took a don-   20
key laden with bread and a skin of wine, and a kid, and he sent them by
the hand of David his son to Saul. And David came to Saul and stood   21
in his presence, and Saul loved him greatly, and he became his armor
bearer. And Saul sent to Jesse, saying, "Let him stand, pray, in my pres- 22
ence, for he has found favor in my eyes." And so, when the spirit of   23
God was upon Saul, David would take up the lyre and play, and Saul

---

a valiant fellow, a warrior. These details of the characterization are surprising, for all that should be known about David is that he is a handsome shepherd boy with musical skills. The influence of the subsequent narrative has
clearly made itself felt here, and these epithets may even be an editorial
maneuver to harmonize this episode with the next one, in which David makes
his debut before Saul not as a lyre player but as a military hero.

20. *a donkey laden with bread.* The Hebrew uses what appears to be an ellipsis,
"a donkey of bread."
   bread . . . a skin of wine . . . a kid. As Polzin has shrewdly observed, these
items replicate the items that Samuel told Saul would be carried by the three
men he was to encounter (10:3). David, then, is beginning anew the process
on which Saul launched.

21. *and Saul loved him greatly.* As Fokkelman has noted, Saul is the first of
many people in this narrative reported to love David—the very man who will
become his bitter enemy.
   he became his armor bearer. This is not the position proposed by Saul's
courtiers. Perhaps there was no set position of court lyre player, and so Saul
gives David an appointment that will insure his constant proximity.

22. *Let him stand . . . in my presence.* The Hebrew idiom means to be in someone's service, though it also can suggest being presented to a dignitary, its evident meaning in verse 21.

would find relief, and it would be well with him, and the evil spirit
would turn away from him.

---

23. *would find relief.* The Hebrew employs an untranslatable pun: the verb
"would find relief," *rawah*, is a transparent cognate of *ruah*, "spirit."

the evil spirit would turn away from him. In an elegant verbal symmetry, the
episode that began with the (good) spirit of the LORD turning away from Saul
concludes with the evil spirit turning away from him, thanks to David's musical mastery over the domain of spirits.

CHAPTER 17

And the Philistines gathered their camps for battle, and they gathered at 1
Socoh, which is in Judah, and they encamped between Socoh and
Azekah, at Ephes-dammim. And Saul and the men of Israel had gath- 2
ered and encamped in the Valley of the Terebinth and they deployed to
do battle against the Philistines. The Philistines took their stand on the 3
hill on one side and Israel took its stand on the hill on the other side,
with the ravine between them. And the champion sallied forth from 4
the Philistine camps, Goliath was his name, from Gath, his height was
six cubits and a span. A bronze helmet he had on his head, and in armor 5

---

3. *the hill on one side . . . the hill on the other . . . the ravine between them.* As
we have seen before, this positioning of the opposing armies on opposite hilltops was a characteristic procedure of warfare in the hilly terrain of central
Israel. But the opening verses also set up the strong spatial perspective
through which this episode is organized. The perspective of the previous story
was implicitly vertical: from God above to Samuel below, in the household of
Jesse in Bethlehem. Here, by contrast, is a richly elaborated horizontal
deployment of troops and individuals. God is out of the picture, except for the
invocation through David's words.

4. *the champion.* The literal meaning of the Hebrew is "the man between"—
that is, the man who goes out between the opposed battle lines to fight a
counterpart. That particular Hebrew term thus reinforces the spatial defini-
tion of the story.
    six cubits and a span. This would make him over eight feet tall.

5.–6. *A bronze helmet . . . armor of mail . . . greaves of bronze . . . a spear of
bronze.* This "Homeric" enumeration of armor and weapons is quite untypical
of the Hebrew Bible. The thematic effect is clear: Goliath is represented as a
hulking man of material military impedimenta—everything is given gargan-

of mail he was dressed, and the weight of the armor was five thou-
6 sand bronze shekels. And greaves of bronze were on his legs and a
7 spear of bronze between his shoulder blades. The shaft of his spear
like a weaver's beam, and the blade of his spear six hundred iron
8 shekels. And his shield bearer went before him. And he stood and
called out to the Israelite lines and said to them, "Why should you
come forth to deploy for battle? Am I not the Philistine, and you are
9 slaves to Saul? Choose you a man and let him come down to me! If he
prevail in battle against me and strike me down, we shall be slaves to
you, but if I prevail and strike him down, you will be slaves to us and
10 serve us." And the Philistine said, "I am the one who has insulted the
Israelite lines this day! Give me a man and let us do battle together!"

---

tuan size or weight, again with untypical specification. All this will be counter-
posed to David's declaration on the battlefield that "not by sword and spear
does the LORD deliver."

five thousand bronze shekels. The armor alone is about 125 pounds.

7. *his shield bearer went before him.* For this reason the shield is not included
in the catalogue of Goliath's armor. The gargantuan proportions of his dependence on the material implements of warfare are reinforced by the fact that he
enters the battlefield with a man walking before him carrying his (presumably
massive) shield.

8. *Am I not the Philistine?* Most often in the body of the story he is referred to
as "the Philistine" and not by the name Goliath. This has led many scholars to
infer that a tradition about Goliath was superimposed on an original story fea-
turing an archetypal "Philistine."

9. *we shall be slaves to you.* In the event, this condition is not fulfilled: the
Philistines retreat in disarray, but will later regroup to continue their war
against the Israelites.

10. *I am the one who has insulted the Israelite lines.* Nearly all the English versions render the verb here as "defied," which is one end of the semantic range
of the Hebrew *heref.* But the verb is transparently linked with the noun
herpah—insult, disgrace, shame. By his taunting words, Goliath has laid an
insult on Israel that only a victorious champion can "take away" (see verse 26)

And Saul heard, and all Israel with him, these words of the Philistine, 11
and they were dismayed and very frightened.

And David was the son of this Ephrathite man from Bethlehem in 12
Judah named Jesse, and he had eight sons, and the man in the days of
Saul was old, advanced in years. And the three oldest sons of Jesse 13
went after Saul to the war. And the names of his three sons who went
to the war were Eliab the firstborn and the secondborn Abinadab and
the third Shammah. As for David, he was the youngest, and the three 14
oldest had gone after Saul. And David would go back and forth from 15
Saul's side to tend his father's flock in Bethlehem. And the Philistine 16
came forward morning and evening and took his stand, forty days. And 17
Jesse said to David his son, "Take, pray, to your brothers this ephah of

---

11. *And Saul heard . . . and they were dismayed.* Saul, as the man head and
shoulders taller than all the people, might be thought to be the one Israelite
fighter who stands a chance against Goliath. Instead, he leads his own troops
in fearfulness: the stage is set for his deplacement by David.

12. *David was the son of this Ephrathite man.* The use of the demonstrative pronoun "this" is peculiar. It seems to be the first of several attempts (presumably,
by the redactor) to harmonize this account of David's debut in Saul's court
with the previous one, by referring to Jesse as someone already mentioned.
Polzin has noted that demonstrative pronouns are unusually prominent in this
whole episode: in many instances, they express contempt ("this Philistine"),
but they are also sometimes necessary pointers in the emphatically spatial
organization of the story.

15. *And David would go back and forth from Saul's side.* The last phrase has a
sense close to "from Saul's presence" and is another strategem for harmoniz-
ing the two episodes. It invites us to suppose that David divided his time
between playing the lyre for Saul and tending his father's flocks. The implicit
assumption, however, of the story that unfolds is that David is unknown in the
court of Saul, and that any to-and-fro movement between Bethlehem and the
front would be to bring provisions to his older brothers.

17. *Take, pray, to your brothers . . .* If Saul has organized a standing army, it
seems that his quartermaster corps still leaves something to be desired, and
whatever rations may be provided for the troops need to be supplemented. In
the same connection of skimpy provisions, Jesse sends a gift of ten wedges of
cheese to his sons' commander.

parched grain and these ten loaves of bread and rush them to the camp
18 to your brothers. And these ten wedges of cheese you shall bring to the
captain of the thousand and you shall see if your brothers are well, and
19 you shall take their token. And Saul and they and all the men of Israel
20 are in the Valley of the Terebinth fighting with the Philistines." And
David rose early in the morning and left the flock with a keeper and bore
[the provisions] and went off as Jesse had charged him. And when he
came to the staging ground, the army going out to the lines was shouting
21 the battle cry. And Israel and the Philistines deployed line against line.
22 And David left the gear that was on him with the keeper of the gear and
23 he ran to the lines and came and asked his brothers if they were well. As
he was speaking to them, look, the champion was coming up from the
Philistine lines, Goliath the Philistine from Gath was his name, and he
24 spoke words to the same effect, and David heard. And all the men of
Israel, when they saw the man, fled from him and were very frightened.

25 And a man of Israel said, "Have you seen this man coming up? Why, to
insult Israel he comes up! And the man who strikes him down the king
will enrich with a great fortune, and his daughter he will give him, and

---

18. *take their token.* Jesse expects his sons to send back some object with
David as assurance that they are alive and well.

20. *the staging ground.* The Hebrew is literally "the circle," but the context (and
a few allied ones elsewhere in the Bible) suggests a technical military sense.

22. *David left the gear that was on him with the keeper.* The phrase used precisely echoes his leaving the flock with a keeper. The narrative invokes a series
of divestments by David of impediments for which he has been made responsible—flock, provisions, and then Saul's armor.

25. *the man who strikes him down the king will enrich . . . and his daughter he
will give him.* It is at this point that the folkloric background of the second
story of David's debut becomes particularly clear. The folk-tale pattern is one
that is very familiar from later, European tradition: a community is threatened
by a giant, or ogre, or dragon that nobody can face. The king offers great
wealth, and the hand of his daughter, to the man who can slay the giant. A
young man from the provinces then appears on the scene, who in his youth
and slight stature seems quite unfit for the daunting challenge, but by wit and

his father's household he will make free of levies in Israel." And David   26
said to the men who were standing with him, "What will be done for
the man who strikes down yonder Philistine and takes away insult from
Israel? For who is this uncircumcised Philistine that he should insult
the battle lines of the living God?" And the troops said to him to the   27
same effect, "Thus will be done for the man who strikes him down."
And Eliab his oldest brother heard when he spoke with the men, and   28
Eliab was incensed with David and he said, "Why is it you have come
down, and with whom have you left that bit of flock in the wilderness?

---

resourcefulness, using unexpected means, he conquers the ogre. The appeal
of this archeypal folk tale no doubt made it attractive for inclusion in the
David narrative. What must be emphasized, however, is that the folkloric
materials have been historicized and even to an extent psychologized. The
slaying of the giant becomes an emblem for Israel's prevailing over the numerically superior forces all around it as well as for the resourcefulness of its first
dynastic king in securing power. The dialogue between David and his oldest
brother vividly evokes a thick background of sibling jealousies. And David
appears here—in the first scene in which he is assigned speech in the narrative—as a poised master of rhetoric, who knows how to use publicly enunciated words to achieve political ends.

26. *And David said . . . , "What will be done for the man . . . ?"* These are David's
first recorded words in the narrative—usually, in biblical narrative convention,
a defining moment of characterization. His first words express his wanting to
know what will be gained—implicitly, in political terms—by the man who
defeats Goliath. The inquiry about personal profit is then immediately balanced (or covered up) by the patriotic pronouncement "who is this uncircumcised Philistine that he should insult the battle lines of the living God?" David
has, of course, just heard one of the troops stipulate the reward for vanquishing the Philistine, but he wants to be perfectly sure before he makes his move,
and so he asks for the details to be repeated. One sees how the folk tale has
been artfully historicized, subtly drawn into the realm of politics and individu-
alized character.

28. *that bit of flock.* Eliab prefixes a term of diminution, *me'at,* to "flock" to
express his contempt for David. The demonstrative pronoun, as elsewhere in
the chapter, is also contemptuous, even as it points to the spatial distance
between the battlefield and the pastureland around Bethlehem.

I'm the one who knows your impudence and your wicked impulses, for
29 it's to see the battle that you've come." And David said, "What now
30 have I done? It was only talk." And he turned away from him toward
someone else, and he spoke to the same effect, and the troops
31 answered him with words like the ones before. And the words David
had spoken were heard, and they told them to Saul, and he fetched
32 him. And David said to Saul, "Let no man's heart fail him! Your servant
33 will go and do battle with this Philistine." And Saul said to David, "You
cannot go against this Philistine to do battle with him, for you are a lad
34 and he is a man of war from his youth." And David said to Saul,
"A shepherd has your servant been for his father with the flock. When
the lion or the bear would come and carry off a sheep from the herd,

---

I'm the one who knows. The relative clause here reflects the special emphasis of the Hebrew first-person pronoun *ʾani,* which ordinarily would not be
used because the verb that follows it, *yadʿati,* has a first-person ending. The
same structure occurs in Goliath's boasting speech in verse 10.

your wicked impulses. The literal meaning of the Hebrew is "the wickedness of your heart," the heart being in biblical language the seat of understanding and the place where plans or desires are shaped.

29. *It's only talk.* The translation follows an interpretation that goes back to the
Aramaic Targum of Late Antiquity and to Rashi in the Middle Ages. But the
Hebrew—literally, "Is it not a word?"—is gnomic. The ambiguity is compounded because *davar* can mean "word," "message," "matter," "thing," "mission," and more.

30. *And he turned away from him toward someone else.* Ignoring his brother's
rebuke, David wants to hear the details of the reward a third time.

32. *Let no man's heart fail him.* The Septuagint has "Let not my lord's heart fail
him," but this could easily be an explanatory gloss. David uses a generalizing
phrase because he doesn't want to come out and say directly what all can see,
that the king's heart is failing him (literally, "falling").

34. *A shepherd has your servant been.* David's carefully contrived speech
proclaims his tested courage and strength but, interestingly, is silent about
the shepherd's weapon—the slingshot—that he intends to use against
Goliath.

I would go out after him and strike him down and rescue it from his 35
clutches. And if he would rise against me, I would seize his beard and
strike him and kill him. Both lion and bear your servant has struck 36
down, and this uncircumcised Philistine will be like one of them, for
he has insulted the battle lines of the living God." And David said, 37
"The LORD who has rescued me from the lion and the bear will rescue
me from the hand of this Philistine." And Saul said to David, "Go, and
may the LORD be with you."

And Saul clothed David in his own battle garb and put a bronze helmet 38
on his head and clothed him in armor. And David girded his sword over 39
his garments, but he was unable to walk, for he was unused to it, and

---

35. *from his clutches.* The Hebrew says literally, "from his mouth."

   I would seize his beard. This of course refers only to the lion, not to the bear,
but this sort of focusing of the narrative report on one of its two instances is
perfectly natural in biblical usage, and no emendation of the word for "beard"
is called for.

37. *And David said.* This is a particularly striking instance of the biblical convention that can be schematized as: And X said to Y; [no response from Y]; and
X said to Y, with the intervening silence being dramatically significant. Saul is
nonplussed by these extravagant claims on the part of the young shepherd
from Bethlehem, and he doesn't know what to say. David, observing the skep-
ticism of his interlocutor, now invokes God by way of explanation ("the LORD
who has rescued me from the lion and the bear"). This theological argument
persuades Saul. For another instance of the X said to Y, X said to Y convention,
compare Goliath's boast and Israel's silence in verses 8–10.

38. *his own battle garb.* The Hebrew *madim* is not the ordinary term for "garment" but is most often used either for the special garments worn by men in
battle or by priests in the cult (hence the present translation adds "battle").
The fact that this word is related etymologically to *midah,* proportion or measure, is relevant to the incident as it unfolds, since David is clothed in battle
gear too big for him.

39. *he was unable to walk.* The translation, with the Septuagint, reads *wayil²e,*
instead of the Masoretic *wayo'el* (a simple reversal of letters in the consonantal text), which would yield "he undertook to walk."

David said to Saul, "I cannot walk in these, for I am unused to it." And

40   David removed them. And he took his stick in his hand and chose five smooth stones from the creek and put them in the shepherd's pouch he had, the satchel, and his slingshot was in his hand, and he came for-

41   ward toward the Philistine. And the Philistine was drawing near to

42   David, the man bearing the shield before him. And the Philistine looked and saw David, and he despised him, for he was a lad, and

43   ruddy, with good looks. And the Philistine said to David, "Am I a dog that you should come to me with sticks?" And the Philistine cursed

44   David by his gods. And the Philistine said, "Come to me, that I may give your flesh to the birds of the heavens and the beasts of the

---

I cannot walk in these, for I am unused to it. David states the obvious fact that, as a shepherd boy, he is not used to marching about in heavy armor, with a big sword. What he chooses not to mention is that since this is the armor of the hulking Saul, it is in any case far too big for him. Thematically, heroic fitness will be seen to reside in something other than being head and shoulders taller than all the people, or six cubits tall, like Goliath.

40. *he came forward toward the Philistine . . . the Philistine was drawing near.* The spatial realization of the whole episode is nearing its climax: on the two hilltops, the opposing camps; in front of them, the battle lines; between the hostile lines, David and the Philistine "man between" approaching each other. In a moment, they will be close enough to exchange insults. Goliath will invite David to take the last few steps forward so that they can engage in hand-to-hand combat—"Come to me, that I may give your flesh to the birds of the heavens. . . ." Instead of traversing this final interval of space, David will surprise his adversary by taking him down with a slung stone, accurately aimed at the exposed forehead beneath his huge bronze helmet.

40. *he took his stick.* That is, his shepherd's staff, which he is used to carrying. David evidently does this as a decoy, encouraging Goliath to imagine he will use cudgel against sword (compare verse 43) and thus camouflaging the lethal slingshot.

field!" And David said to the Philistine, "You come to me with sword 45
and spear and javelin, and I come to you with the name of the LORD
of Hosts, God of the battle lines of Israel that you have insulted.
This day shall the LORD give you over into my hand and I will strike 46
you down and take off your head, and I will give your corpse and the
corpses of the Philistine camp this day to the birds of the heavens
and the beasts of the earth, and all the earth shall know that Israel
has a God! And all this assembly shall know that not by sword and 47
by spear does the LORD deliver, for the LORD's is the battle and
he shall give you into our hand!" And it happened as the Philistine 48
arose and was drawing near David that David hastened and ran
out from the lines toward the Philistine. And he reached his hand 49
into the pouch and took from there a stone and slung it and struck
the Philistine in his forehead, and the stone sank into his forehead
and he fell on his face to the ground. And David bested the Philis- 50
tine with sling and stone, and he struck down the Philistine and

---

45. *You come to me with sword and spear and javelin.* This short list of weapons
harks back to the epic catalogue of weapons and armor that introduced
Goliath to the story. David's rejoinder to the Philistine is couched in impecca-
ble terms of standard Israelite belief: as in the Psalms, it is not sword or might
that gives victory but the LORD. David speaks almost as though he expects to
prevail through a miracle of divine intervention ("all the earth shall know that
Israel has a God!"), but in fact his victory depends on his resourcefulness in
exploiting an unconventional weapon, one which he would have learned to
use skillfully as a shepherd.

46. *Your corpse and the corpses.* This is the reading of the Septuagint. The
Masoretic Text lacks "your corpse."

48. *David hastened and ran out from the lines toward the Philistine.* This last
gesture would encourage the Philistine to think David was rushing up for the
awaited hand-to-hand combat. In fact, David is darting in close enough to get
a good shot with his sling. To do this (verse 49), he will break his charge, stop,
and let fly with the sling.

51 killed him, and no sword was in David's hand. And David ran up and stood over the Philistine and took the sword from him and pulled it out of its sheath and finished him off and cut off his head with it.
52 And the Philistines saw that their warrior was dead, and they fled. And the men of Israel and Judah rose and shouted and gave chase to the Philistines until you come to the ravine and until the gates of Ekron, and the Philistine dead fell on the way to Shaaraim and as far as
53 Gath and Ekron. And the Israelites came back from pursuing the
54 Philistines and looted their camps. And David took the Philistine's head and brought it to Jerusalem, but his weapons he put in his tent.

55 And when Saul saw David sallying forth toward the Philistine, he said to Abner the commander, "Whose son is the lad, Abner?" And Abner

---

51. *took the sword . . . and finished him off.* The gigantic Philistine is stunned but perhaps not dead, and so David completes his kill with the sword he takes from the prostrate Goliath.

52. *to the ravine.* The Septuagint corrects *gay*², to *Gath*, with the end of this verse in mind. But there is a ravine between the two hills on which the armies are encamped, and what the narrator may be saying is that the Philistines fled westward by way of the ravine to their own territory.

54. *brought it to Jerusalem.* This notation is problematic because Jerusalem at this point is still a Jebusite city. The report is either proleptic, or simply out of place chronologically. David's bringing the sword into his tent may also be questionable because, as someone who has not been a member of the army, he would have no tent. Some scholars, influenced by the fact that Goliath's sword later appears in the sanctuary at Nob, have proposed reading here "in the tent of the LORD."

55. *Whose son is the lad, Abner?* It is at this point that the evident contradiction between the two stories of David's debut is most striking. If David had been attending Saul in court as his personal music therapist, with Saul having explicitly sent a communication to Jesse regarding David's entering his service, how could he, and Abner as well, now be ignorant of David's identity? Efforts to harmonize the two stories in terms of the logic of later conventions of realism seem unconvincing (e.g., amnesia has been proposed as a symptom of Saul's mental illness, and Abner pretends not to recognize David in defer-

said, "By your life, king, I do not know." And the king said, "Ask you,   56
pray, whose son is the youth?" And when David returned from striking   57
down the Philistine, Abner took him and brought him before Saul, the
Philistine's head in his hand. And Saul said, "Whose son are you, lad?"   58
And David said, "The son of your servant Jesse the Bethlehemite."

---

ence to the ailing king). The prevalent scholarly view that Chapters 16 and 17
represent two different traditions about David's beginnings is persuasive.
What we need to ask, however, is why the redactor set these two stories in
immediate sequence, despite the contradictions that must have been as evident to him as to us. A reasonable conclusion is that for the ancient audience,
and for the redactor, these contradictions would have been inconsequential in
comparison with the advantage gained in providing a double perspective on
David. In the Greek tradition, there were competing versions of the same
myths, but never in a single text. Modern Western narrative generally insists
on verisimilar consistency. In the Bible, however, the variants of a single story
are sometimes placed in a kind of implicit dialogue with one another (compare the two accounts of creation at the beginning of Genesis). Here, in the
first, vertically oriented story, with its explicit instructions from God to man,
David is emphatically elected by God, is associated with the spirit and with
song, and gains entrée in the court of Saul by using song to master the spirit.
In the second story, with its horizontal deployment in space, David makes his
way into Saul's presence through martial prowess, exhibiting shrewdness, calculation, and rhetorical skill. Interestingly, it is this folk-tale version of David's
debut rather than the theological one that will lead directly into the historical
(or at least, historylike) narrative of David's rise and David's reign. But the
redactor must surely have felt that both the "spiritual" and the political-
military sides of the figure of David had to be represented in the account of
his origins. It is also noteworthy that this whole episode, which launches
David on his trajectory to the throne, ends with Saul once more in a state of
ignorance, compelled to ask twice about David's identity, and getting no
answer until David himself speaks out.

CHAPTER 18

1 And it happened as he finished speaking with Saul, that Jonathan's very self became bound up with David's, and Jonathan loved him as himself. And Saul took him on that day and did not let him go back to his 3 father's house. And Jonathan, and David with him, sealed a pact 4 because he loved him like himself. And Jonathan took off the cloak

---

1. *as he finished speaking to Saul.* The speech referred to is the exchange between David and Saul after the vanquishing of Goliath. This is a clear instance in which the (late medieval) chapter division actually interrupts a narrative unit.

Jonathan loved him as himself. No reason is given, so one may infer that Jonathan was smitten by David's personal charm and perhaps by the sheer glamour of his victory, which exceeded even Jonathan's own military exploits. It is noteworthy that throughout this narrative David is repeatedly the object of the verb "to love"—in this chapter, Jonathan, the people, and Michal are all said to love David.

3. *and Jonathan, and David with him, sealed a pact.* This is one of the most significant instances of the expressive grammatical pattern in which there is a plural subject with a singular verb, making the first member of the plural subject the principal agent: the initiative for the pact of friendship is Jonathan's, and David goes along with it.

4. *Jonathan took off the cloak* . . . This gesture strongly invites comparison with Saul's failed effort to dress David in his battle gear in the previous episode. This time David accepts the proffered garments and weapons: practically, they are presumably his own size, but he also is now ready to assume a regular role in the army. The first item Jonathan offers is his cloak, *meʿil,* the very piece of clothing Samuel associated symbolically with kingship. Bearing that in mind, J. P. Fokkelman has proposed that "with his cloak Jonathan is conveying to David the crown prince's rights and claims to the throne." Perhaps one should say that he is conveying these subliminally or proleptically rather than as a fully conscious act.

that was on him and gave it to David, and his battle garb, and even his
sword and his bow and his belt. And David would sally forth, wherever   5
Saul sent him he would succeed. And Saul set him over the men of
war, and it was good in the eyes of the troops and also in the eyes of
Saul's servants. And it happened when they came, when David   6
returned from striking down the Philistine, that the women came out
from all the towns of Israel in song and dance, to greet Saul the king
with timbrels and jubilation and lutes. And the celebrant women   7
called out and said,

> "Saul has struck down his thousands
> and David his tens of thousands!"

And Saul was very incensed, and this thing was evil in his eyes, and   8
he said, "To David they have given tens of thousands and to me
they have given the thousands. The next thing he'll have is the kingship." And Saul kept a suspicious eye on David from that day hence.   9

---

5. *Saul set him over the men of war.* The designation for fighting men is also the
one Saul uses for Goliath. Moshe Garsiel has suggested that this may be a
term for elite troops, and that later, when Saul appoints David captain of a
thousand (verse 13), he is in effect transferring him to the position of an ordinary officer.

6. *lutes.* As is often the case with ancient musical instruments, the precise
identification of the term is in doubt. The Hebrew *shalishim* derives from
sheloshah, three, but it could refer either to a three-stringed lute, which was
fairly common in the ancient Near East, or perhaps to a triangle.

8. *to David . . . tens of thousands, to me the thousands.* It is a fixed rule in biblical poetry that when a number occurs in the first verset, it must be increased
in the parallel verset, often, as here, by going up one decimal place. Saul
shows himself a good reader of biblical poetry: he understands perfectly well
that the convention is a vehicle of meaning, and that the intensification or
magnification characteristic of the second verset is used to set David's triumphs above his own. Saul, who earlier had made the mistake of listening to
the voice of the people, now is enraged by the people's words.

10 And on the next day, an evil spirit of God seized Saul and he went into
a frenzy within the house when David was playing as he was wont to,
11 and the spear was in Saul's hand. And Saul cast the spear, thinking,
"Let me strike through David into the wall." And David eluded him
12 twice. And Saul was afraid of David, for the LORD was with him, but
13 from Saul He had turned away. And Saul removed him from his presence and set him as captain of a thousand, and he led the troops into
14 the fray. And David succeeded in all his ways, and the LORD was
15 with him. And Saul saw that he was very successful, and he dreaded

---

10. *went into a frenzy.* The verb here is the same one that refers to "speaking in
ecstasy" or "prophesying" in the episode of Saul among the prophets, but in
the present context only the connotation of raving and not that of revelation is
relevant.

when David was playing as he was wont to. The present version of the story
at this point seeks to integrate the account of David as victor over Goliath
with the preceding report of David as Saul's personal lyre player. Evidently,
when he is not playing the lyre he is sent out intermittently at the head of the
elite troops. After this incident, Saul removes him entirely from the court by
making him a regular commander. The one thing Saul cannot afford to do is to
dispense with David's brilliant services as a military leader. In the Hebrew,
"was playing" is literally "was playing with his hand," which sets up a neat
antithesis to the spear in Saul's hand ("with" and "in" are represented by the
same particle, *bᵉ* in Hebrew).

11. *let me strike through David.* Saul picks up the verb of striking from the song
of the celebrant women that so galled him.

12. *for the LORD was with him.* This emphatic refrainlike phrase recalls the
Joseph story (see especially Genesis 39), another tale of a handsome shepherd
boy who ascends to regal grandeur. Like Joseph, David is repeatedly said to
"succeed" (though different verbs are used in the two stories.) Allusions to the
Joseph story will turn from this initial consonance to ironic dissonance.

15. *Saul saw . . . and he dreaded him.* Throughout this pivotal episode, Saul's
feelings and motives remain perfectly transparent—here, through the narrator's report of his emotions, and in the next scene, through interior monologue.
At the same time, David is pointedly left opaque. No word of his is reported
when Jonathan gives him his cloak and battle gear. We know that Saul is afraid
of David but not whether David is afraid of Saul, who, after all, has tried to kill
him. And when David speaks in the next scene, it will be manifestly a speech
framed for a public occasion, which leaves his real motives uncertain.

him. But all Israel and Judah loved David, for he led them into the   16
fray.

And Saul said to David, "Here is my eldest daughter, Merab. Her shall   17
I give you as wife, only be a valiant fellow for me and fight the battles of
the LORD." And Saul had thought, "Let not my hand be against him but
let the hand of the Philistines be against him." And David said to Saul,   18
"Who am I and who are my kin, my father's clan in Israel, that I should
be the king's son-in-law?" And it happened at the time for giving Merab   19
the daughter of Saul to David, that she was given to Adriel the Meholathite as wife. And Michal the daughter of Saul loved David, and they   20

---

16. *led them into the fray.* The Hebrew says literally, "was going out and coming
in before them," an idiom that means to lead in battle.

17. *Here is my eldest daughter, Merab.* Only now is the promise of the hand of
the king's daughter for the vanquisher of Goliath implemented. But the fulfillment of that promise, as it turns out, is part of a plan to destroy David.
    Let not my hand be against him. The interior monologue leaves no doubt
about Saul's intentions. Could it be that his very transparency as a political
schemer, manifested in the means of narrative presentation, is a reflection of
his incapacity in the harsh realm of politics? David, by contrast, knows how to
veil his motives and intentions—a veiling replicated in the narrative strategies
used to present him.

18. *Who am I and who are my kin . . .* The translation adopts a scholarly proposal of considerable currency to revocalize the Masoretic *ḥayai*, "my life" as
ḥayi, "my kin," a conjectured term based on the Arabic. David's protestation of
unworthiness recalls Saul's when Samuel hinted he was going to confer the
kingship on him. Perhaps these words are dictated by court etiquette, the
commoner obliged to profess unworthiness when offered the honor of a royal
connection. Perhaps the young David may actually feel unworthy of the
honor. But it is also clearly in his interest to conceal from the jealous king any
desire he may harbor to marry the king's daughter, for such an alliance could
be converted into an implicit claim to be successor to the throne.

20. *and Michal the daughter of Saul loved David.* Not only is she the third party
in this chapter said to love David, but she is also the only woman in the entire
Hebrew Bible explicitly reported to love a man. Nothing is said, by contrast,
about what David feels toward Michal, and as the story of their relationship
sinuously unfolds, his feelings toward her will continue to be left in question.

21 told Saul, and the thing was pleasing in his eyes. And Saul thought, "I
shall give her to him, that she may be a snare to him, and that the hand
of the Philistines may be against him." And Saul said to David,
22 "Through the second one you can be my son-in-law now." And Saul
charged his servants: "Speak to David discreetly, saying, 'Look, the king
desires you, and all his servants love you, and now then, become son-
23 in-law to the king.'" And Saul's servants spoke these words in David's
hearing and David said, "Is it a light thing in your eyes to become son-
24 in-law to the king, and I am a poor man, and lightly esteemed?" And
Saul's servants told him, saying, "Words of this sort David has spoken."
25 And Saul said, "Thus shall you say to David: 'The king has no desire for
any bride price except a hundred Philistine foreskins, to take

---

21. *Through the second one.* The Hebrew is quite cryptic, and the text might be
defective here. Literally, it says, "through two" (*beshtayim*). This has variously
been interpreted to mean: through two daughters (if not one, then the other);
through two conditions (vanquishing the Philistines and bringing back their
foreskins?); for two reasons (perhaps, "the king desires you" and "all his servants love you").

22. *discreetly.* The root of the Hebrew adverb refers to covering up, but the
usual translation of "secretly" is misleading. This is not a clandestine communication but one in which the servants—that is, Saul's court attendants—
must be careful to cover up their master's real intentions.

24. *Words of this sort David has spoken.* Saul may well have counted on the fact
that David would initially demur, perhaps because he was the youngest son of
eight and thus lacked a suitable brideprice for a princess. This refusal would
then set the stage for Saul's extravagant proposal, which he assumed would be
a fatal one, of a hundred dead Philistines.

25. *The king has no desire for any bride price except a hundred Philistine foreskins.* The language Saul directs to David through his attendants—note that
he now has begun to communicate with David only through intermediaries—
makes it sound as though this were a small thing instead of an enormous
thing. Beyond this story, there is no indication that the Israelites had a custom
of collecting the foreskins of the uncircumcised Philistines like scalps.
Fokkelman shrewdly notes that the foreskins are associated with (impure)
sexuality and conjectures that "by this condition Saul really wants to contami-

vengeance against the king's enemies.' " And Saul had devised to make
David fall by the hand of the Philistines. And Saul's servants told these   26
words to David, and the thing was pleasing in David's eyes, to become
son-in-law to the king. And the time was not done, when David arose   27
and went, he and his men, and he struck down among the Philistines
two hundred men, and David brought their foreskins and made a full
count to the king, to become son-in-law to the king, and Saul gave him
Michal his daughter as wife. And Saul saw and marked that the LORD   28
was with David, and Michal the daughter of Saul loved him. And Saul   29
was all the more afraid of David, and Saul became David's constant
enemy. And the Philistine captains sallied forth, and whenever they   30
sallied forth, David succeeded more than all Saul's servants, and his
name became greatly esteemed.

---

nate David"—just as Saul is using his own daughter's sexuality as a lure to
destroy David. "He thinks," Fokkelman goes on to observe, "that this rival has
outdone him amongst the women and now uses woman as a trap."

    Saul had devised to make David fall. The narrator continues his systematic
effort to make Saul's intentions transparent.

26. *And the time was not done.* Literally, "the days were not filled." The pre-
sumable reference is to a period fixed by Saul during which David was to go
out and bring back the grisly trophies. Moshe Garsiel has interestingly proposed that the idiom here deliberately echoes a phrase used in the Jacob story
(Genesis 29:21) and signals a whole network of allusions to the Jacob narrative: in both stories the young man is a candidate to marry two sisters and gets
the one not at first intended; in both stories he must provide a bride price he
cannot pay for from material resources; in both stories he must "count out"
(literally "fill") payment to a devious father-in-law; eventually each man flees
his father-in-law, aided and abetted by his wife; and in each instance, as we
shall see, household idols *(teraphim)* are involved. Later in the David story,
other kinds of parallels with Jacob will be invoked.

28.–30. These verses constitute a formal concluding frame to the whole episode,
much like the concluding verses in Genesis 39, which mirror the opening ones.
Once again, in a pointed repetition of phrases, the following is brought to our
attention: David's success, the fact that the LORD is with him, Saul's fear of
David, Michal's love of David, and David's great reputation. The concluding
words of the chapter, "his name became greatly esteemed" are a pointed antithesis to his protestation of unworthiness, "I am a poor man, and lightly esteemed."

CHAPTER 19

And Saul spoke to Jonathan his son and to all his servants to put David to death, but Jonathan the son of Saul was very fond of David, and Jonathan told David, saying, "Saul my father seeks to put you to death, and so now, be on the watch, pray, in the morning, and stay in a secret place and hide. And I on my part shall come out and stand by my father in the field where you are, and I shall speak of you to my father. And if I see something, I shall tell you." And Jonathan spoke well of David to Saul his father and said to him, "Let not the king offend against his servant David, for he has not offended you, and his deeds have been very good toward you. He took his life in his hands and struck down the Philistine, and the LORD made a great deliverance for all Israel. You saw and rejoiced, and why should you offend with innocent blood to put David to death for no cause?" And Saul heeded Jonathan's voice, and Saul swore, "As the LORD lives, he shall not be put to death."

---

1. *Jonathan his son . . . Jonathan the son of Saul.* In keeping with the biblical practice of using relational epithets to underscore a thematic point, Jonathan is identified as Saul's son at the very moment when he takes David's part against his father.

4. *Let not the king offend.* Saul's royal power is palpable in the dialogue, for his own son is careful to address him by title in the deferential third person.

6. *Saul heeded Jonathan's voice, and . . . swore.* Saul's paranoia and uncontrolled outbursts manifest themselves in an intermittent cycle. He is amenable to the voice of reason and conscience, and vows in presumably good faith not to harm David, but further evidence of David's military brilliance will unleash another round of violent impulses. In consequence, through this sequence of the narrative David oscillates between being a proscribed person and someone Saul expects to be a faithful member of his court.

And Jonathan called to David, and Jonathan told him all these things.   7
And Jonathan brought David to Saul, and he served him as in times
gone by.

And there was still more fighting, and David sallied forth and did battle   8
with the Philistines and struck a great blow against them, and they
fled before him. And an evil spirit of the LORD came upon Saul as he   9
was sitting in his house, his spear in his hand and David playing.
And Saul sought to strike the spear through David into the wall, but   10
he slipped away from Saul, and Saul struck the spear into the
wall. Then David fled and escaped on that night. And Saul sent mes-   11
sengers to David's house to keep watch over him and to put him
to death in the morning. And Michal his wife told David, saying, "If

---

9. *his spear in his hand, and David playing.* As in the previous incident of the
spear cast at David, the Hebrew exhibits the pointed antithesis of "his spear in
his hand [*beyado*]" and David "playing by hand [*beyad*]." Conventional biblical
scholarship explains the repetition of incident, and the other doublets in this
narrative, as an inclusion of two versions of the same event from different
sources. It is at least as plausible to assume that the author of the Saul and
David narrative had a fondness for paired incidents that could be used to good
literary effect. Saul's mental disturbance involves compulsive repetition. He
does his best to be reconciled with David, his soothing lyre player and indispensable military leader, but the recurrent flashes of jealousy drive him again
to the same lethal action. After the second occurrence of spear throwing,
David realizes he must flee the court, but he does not imagine that Saul will
send assassins to surround his house.

10. *he struck . . . David fled.* As several interpreters have noted, these are the
very two verbs used in verse 8 to report David's military triumph over the
Philistines: as David battles Israel's enemies, the distraught king battles David.

11. *Michal his wife.* This is another pointed familial identification. Previously,
she was referred to as Saul's daughter.

12   you do not get yourself away tonight, tomorrow you'll be dead." And
Michal let David down from the window, and he went off and fled and
13   got away. And Michal took the household gods and put them in the
bed, and the twist of goat's hair she put at its head, and covered them
14   with a cloth. And Saul sent messengers to take David, and she said,
15   "He is ill." And Saul sent messengers to see David, saying, "Bring
16   him up to me in the bed, that he may be put to death." And the
messengers came, and, look, the household gods were in the bed and

---

If you do not get yourself away tonight, tomorrow you'll be dead. It is striking
that we are given Michal's urgent dialogue here but not a word of response
from David, only the chain of his rapid actions after she lets him down (by an
improvised rope?) from the window—"he went off and fled and got away."
Perhaps this asymmetrical presentation of the two characters is meant to suggest David's breathless flight, with no time for conversation. In any case, it
continues the pattern of occluding David's inner responses that we observed
in Chapter 18. Michal is risking a great deal in order to save David. We have
no idea about his feelings toward her as she does this.

13. *Michal took the household gods . . . and the twist of goat's hair . . . and covered them with a cloth.* She adopts the familiar trick used by prisoners round
the world of concocting a dummy to mask an escape. But the means she
chooses introduce another elaborate allusion to the Jacob story. The household gods *(teraphim)* are what Rachel stole and hid from her father when
Jacob fled from him. Like Rachel, who pleads her period and does not get up
from the cushions under which the *teraphim* are hidden, Michal also
invokes "illness" (verse 14) to put off the searchers. Both stories feature a
daughter loyal to her husband and rebelling against a hostile father. Michal
puts goat's hair at the head of the bed because, being black or dark brown, it
would look like a man's hair, but goats (and the color of their hair) are also
prominent in the Jacob story. Finally, the cloth or garment *(beged)* used to
cover the dummy recalls the repeated association of garments with deception in the Jacob story. Laban, of course, never finds his *teraphim,* whereas
Saul's emissaries, to their chagrin, find the *teraphim* instead of the man they
are looking for.

15. *Bring him up to me in the bed.* If Michal claims David is ill, Saul will have
him brought up bed and all.

the twist of goat's hair at its head! And Saul said to Michal, "Why have 17
you thus deceived me, and let my enemy go and he got away?" And
Michal said to Saul, "He said to me: 'Let me go. Why should I kill
you?'"

And David had fled and gotten away and had come to Samuel at 18
Ramah and told him all that Saul had done to him. And he, and Samuel
with him, went and stayed at Naioth. And it was told to Saul, saying, 19
"Look, David is at Naioth in Ramah." And Saul sent messengers to take 20
David, and they saw a band of prophets in ecstasy with Samuel standing poised over them, and the spirit of God came upon Saul's messengers and they, too, went into ecstasy. And they told Saul and he 21
sent other messengers and they, too, went into ecstasy. And Saul still
again sent a third set of messengers, and they too, went into ecstasy.

---

17. *Why have you thus deceived me?* These words are close to the ones spoken
by the outraged Laban to Jacob (Genesis 31:26).
   Why should I kill you? This purported death threat by David is of course
pure invention by Michal in order to make it seem that she was forced to help
David flee.

18. *David had fled and gotten away and had come to Samuel.* The twice-
repeated verbs of safe flight are reiterated once more. David takes refuge with
the man who anointed him, though it is not entirely clear whether the
prophet's authority will really protect him, or the prophet.
   Naioth. Some have claimed this is not a place-name but a common noun,
nawot, "oases" (according to one suggestion, a collection of huts where the
prophets resided). But then one would expect a definite article, which does
not occur. Naioth is most plausibly construed as a little village or place of temporary residence in the vicinity of the town Ramah.

20. *Samuel standing poised over them.* The image is implicitly military: the
term for "poised" (*nitsav*) is cognate with the terms for garrison and prefect.
Samuel, like the pope, commands no divisions, but the band of ecstatics are
his troops, and the infectious spirit of God that inhabits them and devastates
Saul's emissaries acts as a defensive perimeter.

22 And he himself went to Ramah, and he came as far as the great cistern which is in Secu, and he asked and said, "Where are Samuel and
23 David?" And someone said, "Here, at Naioth in Ramah." And he went there, to Naioth in Ramah, and the spirit of God came upon him, too, and he walked along speaking in ecstasy until he came to Naioth in
24 Ramah. And he, too, stripped off his clothes, and he, too, went into ecstasy before Samuel and lay naked all that day and all that night. Therefore do they say, "Is Saul, too, among the prophets?"

---

22. *and he himself went.* Again, we have the folk-tale symmetry of three identical repetitions, then a fourth repetition with a crucial change.

Where are Samuel and David? Once more, Saul (*sha'ul*) has to ask (*sha'al*). This particular question recalls his initial question in Chapter 9 about where the seer was.

24. *he . . . stripped off his clothes . . . and lay naked.* In the clash between Saul and Samuel that marked their final estrangement, Samuel had explicitly associated garment with kingship. Now the frenzy that seizes Saul drives him to strip off his garments—implicitly, to divest himself of the kingship, just as the first episode of Saul among the prophets was an investment with kingship. Polzin brilliantly links this moment with Michal's use of a garment and the contrasting narrative presentations of David and Saul: "Whereas Michal covers David's bed with his clothes (v. 13) Saul strips off his clothes and lies naked all day and night (v. 24)—a graphic picture of how the narrator hides David and bares Saul throughout the last two chapters."

Therefore do they say, "Is Saul, too, among the prophets?" This is the same etiological tag as at the end of the first story of Saul among the prophets in Chapter 10. The doublet, far from being a stammer of transmission or inept or automatically inclusive redaction, is vividly purposeful, providing a strong frame for Saul's painful story. Fokkelman states the effect nicely: "The same faculty for the numinous and the same sensitivity for suddenly being lifted into a higher state of consciousness which occurred there [in Chapter 10] under the positive sign of election, appear here under the negative sign of being rejected, and now bring Saul into a lower state of consciousness, a kind of delirium." The conventions of verisimilitude of a later literary tradition would lead one to conclude that this encounter would have to have occurred either at the beginning of Saul's career or at the end, but not twice. To the ancient audience, however, the recurrence would not have seemed a contradiction, and the conflicting valences given to the explanation of the proverbial saying add to the richness of the portrait of Saul, formally framing it at beginning and end.

CHAPTER 20

And David fled from Naioth in Ramah and came and said before ¹
Jonathan: "What have I done? What is my crime and what my offense
before your father that he should seek my life?" And he said to him, ²
"Heaven forbid! You shall not die! Look, my father will do nothing,
whether great or small, without revealing it to me, and why should my
father hide this thing from me? It cannot be!" And David swore again ³

---

1. *David . . . said before Jonathan.* The seeming awkwardness of the preposition
is actually strategically calculated. The normal usage would be "said *to*" (ʾel).
"Before" (*lifney*) is a preposition that commonly designates approach to the
presence of regal or seignorial authority. (Compare its occurrence in David's
words, "What my offense *before* your father.") This speech is a remarkable
instance of the pattern of occluding the personal side of David that we have
been following. Quite strikingly, these are David's first reported words to
Jonathan, though Jonathan's devotion to David and one speech to David
(19:2–3) have been duly recorded. It is noteworthy that this is not a personal
communication to Jonathan but a kind of political statement—a protestation
of innocence cast in patently rhetorical language ("What have I done? What is
my crime . . . ?"). David speaks to Jonathan less as an intimate friend than as a
courtier, later in the dialogue even invoking the deferential self-reference of
"your servant."

2. *why should my father hide this thing from me?* If one considers Saul's previous behavior and his relationship with Jonathan, this faith in his father's openness with him seems singularly misplaced. Throughout, Jonathan remains
well meaning and naive, over against the wary, calculating David.

3. *David swore again.* It is ill advised to emend the verb here, as some scholars
have proposed. In fact, David's first speech ("before" Jonathan) was a kind of
oath of innocence, and now he continues to swear, rather than simply speaking.

and said, "Your father surely knows that I have found favor in your eyes, and he will think, 'Let not Jonathan know this, lest he be pained.' And indeed, as the LORD lives and as you live, there is but a step between

4 me and death." And Jonathan said, "Whatever you desire, I shall do for

5 you." And David said to Jonathan, "Look, it is the new moon tomorrow, and I am supposed to sit with the king to eat. Let me go and I shall

6 hide in the field till the evening of the day after tomorrow. Should your father in fact mark my absence, you shall say, 'David has urgently asked of me that he run to Bethlehem his town, for the seasonal sacrifice is to

7 take place there for the whole clan.' If thus he says, 'Good!', it is well with your servant. But if in fact he is incensed, know that the evil has

8 been resolved by him. And you shall keep faith with your servant, for

---

there is but a step between me and death. This vivid image surely is meant to recall the quick dodging step that twice enabled David to elude Saul's hurled spear.

5. *the new moon.* In early biblical times, this was an important festival. Sacrifices were offered, ceremonial feasts were held, and ordinary business was not transacted.

the day after tomorrow. The Masoretic Text has "the third evening," treating *hashelishit* as an adjective modifying "evening," though it has the wrong gender suffix. It is more likely a noun meaning the day after tomorrow (the day on which one speaks being day one in the sequence of three). One should then read ʿ*erev hashelishit* instead of the Masoretic *haʿerev hashelishit.* In any case, the number three will play an important role as the episode develops.

7. *If thus he says, 'Good!', it is well with your servant.* After Saul's attempts on David's life by the "hand of the Philistines," by the spear in his own hand, and by a team of assassins, can David really believe that any statement by the king of favorable disposition means it will be well with him? Polzin has shrewdly suggested that David's real intention is "to provoke Saul to an angry outburst that would remove Jonathan's misconceptions, not his own."

8. *faith.* The two parties to a pact, contract, or other binding agreement owe each other *ḥesed,* faithful performance of their convenantal obligations.

into a pact of the LORD you have brought your servant with you. And if
there be any crime in me, put me to death yourself, for why should you
bring me to your father?" And Jonathan said, "Heaven forbid you say it! If   9
in fact I learn that the evil has been resolved by my father, would I not tell
it to you?" And David said to Jonathan, "Who will tell me if your father   10
answers you harshly?" And Jonathan said, "Come, let us go out to the   11
field." And the two of them went out to the field. And Jonathan said to   12
David, "Witness the LORD, God of Israel, that I will sound out my father
at this hour tomorrow, [or] the day after, and whether he is well disposed
to David or not, I will send to you and reveal to you. Thus may the LORD   13
do to Jonathan, and even more, if it seems good to my father [to bring]
the evil upon you, I will reveal it to you and I will send you off and you
shall go safely and the LORD shall be with you as He was with my father.

---

into a pact of the LORD you have brought your servant with you. David's formulation of the arrangement is pointed and quite accurate: it was Jonathan
who initiated the pledge of mutual fealty out of his love for David, and who
drew David into the commitment.

9. *Heaven forbid you say it.* The Hebrew has, elliptically, "Heaven forbid you."

10. *Who will tell me . . . ?* David is not questioning Jonathan's good faith but
registering a practical difficulty: if Saul is in fact determined to kill him, how
will Jonathan be able to get word to him?

12. *Witness the LORD.* The word "witness" (*ʿed*) is absent in the Masoretic Text
but is reflected in Josephus and the Peshitta.

    tomorrow, [or] the day after. Again, the time reference in the Hebrew is
somewhat confusing. The text reads literally "tomorrow the third day" or even
"the morrow of the third day."

13. *if it seems good to my father [to bring] the evil.* The ironic antithesis of good
and evil is patent. All ancient versions lack "to bring," which seems required
by the context. The word may have been inadvertently deleted by a scribe
because it closely resembles the preceding word in the text—*ʾavi* (my father),
lehaviʾ (to bring).

    the LORD shall be with you as He was with my father. Here Jonathan explic-
itly recognizes that the persecuted David is to displace Saul, his father.

14 Would that while I am still alive you may keep the LORD's faith with
15 me, that I not die, and that you do not cut off your faithfulness from
my house for all time, not even when the LORD cuts off all David's ene-
16 mies from the face of the earth. For Jonathan has sealed a pact with
the house of David and the LORD shall requite it from the hand of
17 David." And Jonathan once again swore to David in his love for him, for
18 he loved him as he loved himself. And Jonathan said to him, "Tomorrow is the new moon, and your absence will be marked because your
19 place will be vacant. The day after tomorrow you will go all the way
down and come to the place where you hid on the day of the deed and
20 stay by the Ezel stone. As for me, I shall shoot three arrows to the side
21 of it, as though I were aiming at a target. And look, I shall send the lad,
'Go, find the arrows!' If I expressly say to the lad, 'Look, the arrows are
on this side of you, fetch them,' come, for it will be well with you, and

---

14. *Would that.* This translation treats the Hebrew consonants as *welu* instead
of the Masoretic *wel³o* ("and not").

16. *Jonathan has sealed a pact.* The Hebrew idiom is literally "cut" (with "pact"
implied) and so picks up the play of the two different occurrences of "cut off"
in the previous sentence (the same verb in a different conjugation). Jonathan's
insistence that David not cut off Jonathan's descendants once he gains power
will have prominent ramifications later in the story.
   requite it from the hand of David. The Masoretic Text has "from the hand of
the enemies of David," but the substitution of a person's "enemies" for the
person himself is a common Hebrew scribal euphemism (here, so as not to
say something negative about David), as both Rashi and David Kimchi recognized in the Middle Ages.

19. *The day after tomorrow.* The Masoretic vocalization *weshilashta* treats this
as a verb (to do something a third time or in a third instance), but it is more
plausible to vocalize it as a noun, *ushelishit,* "and on the third day." (See the
comment on verse 5.)
   you will go all the way down. The Hebrew, literally "you will go down very
much" (or, "you will wander very much"), is problematic.
   the place where you hid on the day of the deed. The meaning has been disputed, but the most likely reference is to David's hiding, and Jonathan's speaking in his defense, in 19:1–7.

nothing will be the matter, as the LORD lives. But if thus I say to the 22
youth, 'Look, the arrows are on the far side of you,' go, for the LORD will
have sent you away. And as for the matter of which you and I have spo- 23
ken, look, the LORD is witness between you and me for all time."

And David hid in the field, and it was the new moon, and the king 24
sat down to table to eat. And the king sat in his place as he was wont 25
to do, in the seat by the wall, and Jonathan preceded him, and
Abner sat by Saul's side, and David's place was vacant. And Saul 26
spoke no word on that day, for he thought, "It is a mischance. He is
unclean and has not been cleansed." And it happened on the day 27
after the new moon, the second day, that David's place was still
vacant. And Saul said to Jonathan his son, "Why has not the son of
Jesse come to the feast either yesterday or today?" And Jonathan 28
said to Saul, "David has urgently asked of me to go to Bethlehem.

---

23. *the* LORD *is witness.* Again, "witness" is absent from the Masoretic Text but
supplied by the Septuagint.

24. *to table.* The Hebrew is literally "to the bread."

25. *Jonathan preceded him.* This translation reads *weyiqdam* instead of the
Masoretic *wayaqom* ("and he rose"). The seating arrangement remains a little
obscure, but the verb *qadam* cannot mean "to sit opposite," as some scholars
have claimed.

26. *He is unclean.* Since on the new moon celebrants partook of a sacrificial
feast, they would have to be in a state of ritual purity. (A seminal emission, for
example, which might be hinted at in the Hebrew term for "mischance,"
would render a person impure until the evening of the day on which he
cleansed himself by ablution.)

27. *the son of Jesse.* At the end of the Goliath episode, Saul wanted to know
whose son David was. Now he refers to him repeatedly only by patronymic,
which is dismissive, rather like our using a person's last name only. David's status in Saul's eyes is a constant reflex of Saul's acute ambivalence: the king
wants him at court as a royal intimate, or, alternately, as someone under surveillance; yet he makes him flee the court as *persona non grata.*

29 And he said to me, 'Let me go, pray, for we have a clan sacrifice in the town, and my brother has summoned me to it. And so, if I have found favor in your eyes, let me, pray, get away that I may see my brothers.'

30 Therefore has he not come to the king's table." And Saul was incensed with Jonathan and he said to him, "O, son of a perverse wayward woman! Don't I know you have chosen the son of Jesse to your own

31 shame and the shame of your mother's nakedness? For as long as the son of Jesse lives on the earth you and your kingship will not be unshaken! And now, send and fetch him to me, for he is a dead man!"

---

29. *my brother has summoned me.* Jonathan, in playing out the scenario David has dictated to him, improvises one element—that David has gone off to his hometown at the express urging of his brother, and in order to be with his brothers. His evident intention is to provide a palliative to David's absence: he had to go to Bethlehem because of family pressure. But Saul's outraged response suggests that Jonathan's invention has the opposite effect. Saul concludes that David's loyalty to his clan takes precedence over his loyalty to his king, and he may even suspect that David means to use his clan as a power base to challenge the throne.

Let me . . . get away. Jonathan inadvertently substitutes for "run" in David's instructions the very verb of escape repeatedly used when David fled Saul's assassins.

30. *O, son of a perverse wayward woman.* All English translations have treated the last Hebrew term here, *mardut*, as "rebellion," deriving it from the root *m-r-d*, "to rebel." But this form (with the *ut* suffix of abstraction) would be anomalous in the Hebrew, whereas the vocalization in the received text yields a Hebrew word well known in rabbinic Hebrew and meaning "discipline." (The verbal root is *r-d-h*, "to rule sternly.") She is "perverse against discipline"— hence "wayward" in this translation.

the shame of your mother's nakedness. This is quite violent. "Nakedness" refers to the sexual part (as in the idiom for taboo intercourse, "uncovering the nakedness of"), and so it has virtually the force of "your mother's cunt," though the language is not obscene.

31. *he is a dead man.* The Hebrew is literally "son of death," thus playing back on "son of Jesse."

And Jonathan answered Saul his father and said to him, "Why should 32
he be put to death? What has he done?" And Saul cast the spear at him 33
to strike him down, and Jonathan knew that it was resolved by his
father to put David to death. And Jonathan rose from the table in burn- 34
ing anger, and he ate no food on the second day of the new moon
because he was pained for David and because his father had humiliated him.

And it happened in the morning that Jonathan went out to the field 35
for the fixed meeting with David, and a young lad was with him.
And he said to his lad, "Run, find, pray, the arrows that I shoot." 36
The lad ran, and he shot the arrow beyond him. And the lad came to 37
the place of the arrow that Jonathan had shot, and Jonathan called
after the lad and said, "Look, the arrow is on the far side of you."

---

32. *Why should he be put to death? What has he done?* These two questions are
four compact words in the Hebrew.

33. *Saul cast the spear at him to strike him down.* Saul's madness is vividly
reflected in his attempt to kill his own son in the same way that he tried to kill
David—just after he has been urging Jonathan to protect the security of his
own future kingship. The act thus expresses his blind destructive impulse
toward his own dynasty.

34. *because he was pained for David and because his father had humiliated him.*
The Hebrew text does not have "and" but it is clearly implied.

35. *and it happened in the morning.* On the third day there are three figures in
the field and three arrows will be shot. The triangle of two knowing persons
and one ignorant one is an ironic replication of the David-Jonathan-Saul triangle. The lad's running after the arrows may also pick up David's (fictitious)
"running" to Bethlehem.

36. *the arrow.* Some scholars, bothered by the switch from three arrows to one,
have emended the text to reduce all plurals of arrow to a singular. The maneuver is misconceived because, as we have seen before, Hebrew narrative readily switches from multiple instances to a particular case.

37. *Jonathan called after the lad.* Again, the use of the preposition is quite precise because the lad has run on ahead of Jonathan.

38 And Jonathan called after the lad, "Quick, hurry, don't stand still!" And
39 Jonathan's lad gathered up the arrows and came to his master. And the
40 lad knew nothing, but Jonathan and David knew the matter. And
Jonathan gave his gear to his lad and said to him, "Go, bring them to
41 town." Just as the lad came, David arose from by the mound and fell on
his face to the ground and bowed three times, and each man kissed the
42 other and each wept for the other, though David the longer. And
Jonathan said to David, "Go in peace, for the two of us have sworn in
the name of the LORD, saying, 'The LORD is witness between me and
21:1 you, and between my seed and your seed, for all time.'" And Jonathan
arose and came to the town.

---

38. *gathered up the arrows.* The Masoretic Text has "arrow" in the singular at
this point, but the verb "to gather up" *(laqet)* accords much better with collecting several objects, and Jonathan's having shot all three of the arrows earlier mentioned would require more time on the part of the lad and hence
would give Jonathan and David more of an opportunity to talk in confidence.

40. *Jonathan gave his gear to the lad.* Fokkelman reminds us that Jonathan earlier gave his armor and weapons to David, and now "the successor to the
throne indicated by Saul . . . devotes himself defenselessly to the intimate
contact with the man who, according to his father, is his rival."

41. *arose from by the mound.* This follows the Septuagint. The Masoretic Text
has "arose from the south."

42. *The LORD is witness.* As in the previous occurrences in Samuel of this formula of vow taking, the Masoretic Text lacks "witness" but that word is
reflected in the Septuagint. It may well be an idiomatic ellipsis in the original
Hebrew version, but the problem with leaving it that way in the English is that
it could sound as though Jonathan were saying that the LORD will intervene
between him and David ("the LORD will be between me and you"). Polzin contends that the double meaning is intended, but that reading seems a little
strained.

CHAPTER 21

And David came to Nob, to Ahimelech the priest, and Ahimelech trembled to meet David and said to him, "Why are you alone and no one is with you?" And David said to Ahimelech the priest, "The king has charged me with a mission, and said to me, 'Let no one know a thing of the mission on which I send you and with which I charge you.' And the lads I have directed to such and such a place. And now, what do you have at hand, five loaves of bread? Give them to me, or whatever there is." And the priest answered David and said, "I have no common bread at hand, solely consecrated bread, if only the lads have kept themselves from women." And David answered the priest and said to him, "Why,

²

2

3

4

5

6

---

2. *Nob*. This is the very beginning of David's flight after the exchange with Jonathan in the field, and Nob is less than three miles south of Gibeah, his approximate point of departure.

Why are you alone and no one is with you? The doubling of the question (in a pattern that is reminiscent of the parallelism of verse) reflects Ahimelech's astonishment: a prominent commander in Saul's army would not ordinarily go about without his retinue. From his first sight of David, Ahimelech suspects that he may be a fugitive, which is why he "trembles" to meet him—fear of the powerful king's retribution stalks the land.

4. *five loaves of bread*. The number five is sometimes used idiomatically in biblical Hebrew to mean "a few."

5. *if only the lads have kept themselves from women*. Ordinarily, consecrated bread would be eaten only by the priests. Ahimelech is willing to stretch the point if David's "lads"—his fighting men—are not in a state of ritual impurity through sexual intercourse.

women are taboo to us as in times gone by when I sallied forth, and the lads' gear was consecrated, even if it was a common journey, and how

7 much more so now the gear should be consecrated." And the priest gave him what was consecrated, for there was no bread there except the Bread of the Presence that had been removed from before the LORD to be replaced with warm bread when it was taken away.

8 And there a man of Saul's servants that day was detained before the LORD, and his name was Doeg the Edomite, chief of the herdsmen

9 who were Saul's. And David said to Ahimelech, "Don't you have here at hand a spear or a sword? For neither my sword nor my gear have I taken

---

6. *women are taboo to us.* This is the second reference in this narrative to a general practice of refraining from sexual activity during periods of combat.

the lads' gear was consecrated. The term for "gear," the serve-all *kelim,* could equally refer to weapons, clothing, and vessels for containing food. There are no grounds for restricting the meaning here to the last of these three items, as some interpreters have done.

7. *the Bread of the Presence.* This would be twelve loaves laid out in display on a table in the sanctuary. When they were replaced with fresh loaves, the old loaves could be eaten by the priests. Polzin proposes a link between the eating of forbidden food here and in the story of Jonathan and the honey. Death will ensue, though not for the eater.

8. *and there a man of Saul's servants.* This seemingly intrusive notation is a piece of ominous foreshadowing. For the moment, all we can pick up is a certain dissonance in the presence of a foreigner in the sanctuary and the nearness of a high official of Saul's to the fugitive David. The ghastly consequences of David's visit to Nob (Chapter 22) will pivot on Doeg's fatal presence. His identity as Edomite reflects the enlistment of foreign mercenaries in the new royal bureaucracy. It also marks him as a man who will have no inhibitions in what he does to Israelites, even Israelite priests.

detained before the LORD. The verb is derived from the same root (ᶜ-*ts-r*) as the one used for "taboo" in verse 6, but it is unclear whether the reference is to being detained at the sanctuary for some unspecified reason or being detained from participation in the cult.

9. *for neither my sword nor my gear have I taken.* David, of course, has fled weaponless from his encounter with Jonathan in the field. Now he uses the supposed urgency of his royal mission to explain his lack of arms and to ask for a weapon.

with me, for the king's mission was urgent." And the priest said, "The   10
sword of Goliath the Philistine whom you struck down in the Valley of
the Terebinth, here it is, wrapped in a cloak behind the ephod. If this
you would take for yourself, take it, for there is none other but it hereabouts." And David said, "There's none like it. Give it to me."

And David rose on that day and fled from Saul and he came to Achish   11
king of Gath. And the servants of Achish said to him, "Is not this David   12
king of the land? Is it not he for whom they call out in dance, saying,

'Saul has struck down his thousands
and David his tens of thousands.' "

---

10. *If this you would take for yourself, take it, for there is none other but it hereabouts.* The last exchange between Ahimelech and David is a vivid instance
of the biblical use of contrastive dialogue. The priest's language is a wordy
hesitation dance of repetitions and synonymous expressions. David
responds with the most imperative succinctness (just four words in the
Hebrew): "There's none like it. Give it to me." The fact that this huge sword
might be too big for David is submerged by the symbolic notion that it is the
weapon of the Philistine champion he vanquished which he now takes up.
In any case, David is no longer a raw shepherd lad but a battle-hardened
warrior.

11. *he came to Achish king of Gath.* David flees to the southwest to the one
place where he imagines he will be safe from Saul's pursuit—enemy territory.
Such a crossing over to the enemy is a familiar enough move on the part of
political refugees. Gath was the hometown of Goliath, and so one must
assume that David planned to enter the city incognito, as an anonymous
Hebrew fugitive. He would clearly have had to hide the telltale sword before
coming into town.

12. *David king of the land.* The Philistine courtiers, unfortunately, immediately
identify David and can even quote the song sung by the Israelite women after
his victory over Goliath. Their characterization of him as "king of the land" is
no doubt a tribute to his preeminence on the battlefield but also is an inadvertent confirmation of his clandestine election, of his displacing Saul. Appropriately, though, as Fokkelman notes, they use a somewhat vague designation
instead of the more official "king of Israel."

13 And David took these words to heart, and he was very afraid of Achish
14 king of Gath. And he altered his good sense in their eyes and played
the lunatic before them, and he scrabbled on the doors of the gate and
15 drooled onto his beard. And Achish said to his servants, "Look, do you
see this man is raving mad! Why would you bring him to me? Do I lack
madmen that you should bring this one to rave for me? Should this one
come into my house?"

---

13. *he was very afraid of Achish.* He has come unarmed and, evidently, alone,
and now he realizes he has been recognized.

15. *Do I lack madmen that you should bring this one to rave for me?* Achish's
words are a mirror of outrage and disgust. As Shimon Bar-Efrat has nicely
observed, Achish three times uses the root for raving mad (*meshugʿa*), three
times the first person pronoun, and three times the root *b-w-ʾ* ("to bring" or "to
come"). Thus David has succeeded in making himself so revolting that he
arouses in Achish a primitive revulsion from the spectacle of the insane, so
that the king simply wants to get David out of sight rather than have him
killed. This is an extraordinary moment in the story of the founding king of
Israel: David, the glamorous young hero of the preceding episodes, is prepared to do whatever is necessary in order to survive, even if it means making
himself appear to be the most repulsive of humankind. It is an even lowlier
disguise than Odysseus's as beggar, and it is also not the last experience of
humiliation into which David in adversity will willingly plunge. It is noteworthy that David feigns madness in order to survive, in contrast to Saul, whose
genuine madness reflects his loss of control over the kingdom.

CHAPTER 22

A nd David went from there and got away to the Cave of Adullam, and 1
his brothers heard, as well as all his father's household, and they came
down to him there. And every man in straits and every man in debt and 2
every man who was embittered gathered round him, and he became
their captain, and there were about four hundred men with him. And 3
David went from there to Mizpeh of Moab. And he said to the king of

---

1. *Adullam.* The location is in the hilly terrain at the western edge of the tribal
territory of Judah, near the Philistine region.

David's brothers . . . all his father's household. Saul's rage over the notion that
David would have neglected the new moon festivity at the palace to join his
brothers in Bethlehem is given an after-the-fact political confirmation here:
David's brothers and clansmen rally round him, forming a kind of family mili-
tia. But there is a push as well as a pull in their going out to David in the bad-
lands: if they remained in Bethlehem, they would be subject to retribution by
Saul's soldiery. David's decision to move his parents across the border to Moab
(verse 3) is another reflection of fear of royal vengeance against the family.
Jesse, earlier characterized as very aged, would have been too old to join the
fighting men.

2. *every man in straits . . . in debt . . . embittered.* David's guerilla band has a
core drawn from his clan and a rank and file of the dispossessed and malcon-
tent—men with nothing to lose who have been oppressed by the established
order. David's social base as guerilla chieftain is strongly reminiscent of Jephthah's (Judges 11).

3. *Mizpeh of Moab.* The word *mizpeh* (or in some places, *mizpah*) means "outlook" or "vista," and so this particular Mizpeh must be identified as the one in
Moab, east of the Jordan. If the Book of Ruth provides reliable genealogy,
David's great-grandmother Ruth was a Moabite, and so David here may be
calling on a family connection in requesting asylum for his parents.

Moab, "Pray, let my father and my mother come out with you until I
4 know what God will do with me." And he led them into the presence of
the king of Moab and they stayed with him all the time that David was
5 in the stronghold. And Gad the prophet said to David, "You must not
stay in the stronghold. Go, and come you to the territory of Judah." And
David went and came to the forest of Hereth.

6 And Saul heard that David was discovered, and the men who were with
him, and Saul was sitting in Gibeah under the tamarisk on the height,
his spear in his hand and all his servants poised in attendance upon him.

---

4. *all the time that David was in the stronghold.* The identity of the stronghold
has puzzled interpreters, especially because David is said to have set up headquarters in a cave. Some have argued that the two terms refer to the same
place, but the Hebrew for "stronghold," *metsudah,* usually refers to a height.
Others emend "cave," *meʿarah,* to *metsudah.* That proposal is problematic
because Adullam is in the territory of Judah, and in verse 5 David is enjoined
to leave the stronghold and head for the territory of Judah. The most reasonable inference is that after the parlay with the king of Moab, David moves his
fighting men from Adullam at the western border of the territory of Judah to
an unspecified stronghold, probably in the craggy border region between
Moab and Israel.

5. *Gad the prophet.* This figure appears in the story without introduction or
explanation. What is important is that we see David with an open line of communication with the divinity, in sharp contrast to Saul.

6. *Saul heard that David was discovered.* From this point onward, the narrative
will switch back and forth deftly between David and Saul. It now turns to an
ominous piece of unfinished business—Saul's response to the priest of Nob
who helped David in his flight. The specific reference of Saul's hearing "that
David was discovered" could well be intelligence that places David's hideout
at the stronghold. That would explain why Gad urges David to move on from
the stronghold to a forest in Judahite territory.
  his spear in his hand. The same spear in hand with which he sought to kill
David, and then Jonathan. This small detail thus foreshadows the massacre of
an entire town that Saul will order.

And Saul said to his servants poised in attendance upon him, "Listen,   7
pray, you Benjaminites: will the son of Jesse give every one of you fields
and vineyards, will he make every one of you captains of thousands and
captains of hundreds, that all of you should have conspired against me   8
and none revealed to me when my son made a pact with the son of
Jesse, and none of you was troubled for my sake to reveal to me that my
son has set up my servant to lie in wait against me as on this very day?"
And Doeg the Edomite, who was poised in attendance with Saul's ser-   9
vants, spoke out and said, "I saw the son of Jesse coming to Nob to
Ahimelech the son of Ahitub. And he inquired of the LORD, and provi-   10
sions he gave him, and the sword of Goliath the Philistine he gave
him." And the king sent to summon Ahimelech the son of Ahitub and   11
all his father's household, the priests who were in Nob, and they all
came to the king. And Saul said, "Listen, pray, son of Ahitub." And he   12

---

7. *you Benjaminites.* Evidently, the inner circle at the court is enlisted from his
own tribe. The tribal affiliation helps explain the sarcasm of his rhetorical
questions: could they really expect someone from the tribe of Judah to bestow
all these bounties on them?

  fields . . . vineyards . . . captains. As Moshe Garsiel has aptly noted, Saul's
paranoid outburst picks up key terms from Samuel's warning about the "practice of the king" in Chapter 8. It is also noteworthy that Saul's distraught
speech takes the form of one long onrushing sentence (all the way to the end
of verse 8). Once again, Saul refers to David contemptuously by patronymic,
as "the son of Jesse."

8. *none revealed to me.* Once again, Saul's problem, which is also the symptom
of his paranoia, is that he feels essential knowledge is denied him.

10. *he inquired of the LORD.* There was no report in Chapter 21 of Ahimelech's
inquiring of the oracle for David, and it seems unlikely that so essential a fact
would have been simply elided by the narrator. The first item, then, in Doeg's
denunciation of Ahimelech looks like a fabrication—and one that would especially enrage Saul, who has repeatedly had access to divine knowledge
blocked.

12. *son of Ahitub.* It is a shocking piece of rudeness for Saul to address someone invested with the authority of priesthood merely by patronymic.

13 said, "Here I am, my lord." And Saul said, "Why did you conspire
against me, you and the son of Jesse, giving him bread and sword and
inquiring of God for him, so that he set up to lie in wait against me on
14 this very day?" And Ahimelech answered the king and said, "And who
of all your servants is like David, loyal and the king's son-in-law and
15 captain of your palace guard and honored in your house? Did I this day
for the first time inquire for him of God? Far be it from me! Let not the
king impute anything to his servant or to all my father's house, for your
16 servant knew nothing of all this, neither great nor small." And the king
said, "You are doomed to die, Ahimelech, you and all your father's
17 house!" And the king said to the runners poised in attendance on him,
"Turn round and put to death the priests of the LORD, for their hand,
too, is with David, for they knew he was fleeing and did not reveal it to

---

14. *who of all your servants is like David.* Ahimelech may still be laboring under
the delusion that the fugitive David was embarked on a special secret mission
for Saul. His testimony to David's loyalty and eminence will of course stoke
Saul's already blazing anger.

15. *Did I this day for the first time inquire for him of God?* Some interpreters
read this as a declarative sentence, but the context compels one to construe it
as a question: I never previously consulted the oracle for David, and why on
earth would I do it now? (Perhaps he is suggesting that consultation of the
oracle is a service to be offered only to the king.) He is silent, however, about
providing bread and sword, which in fact he has done.

16. *you and all your father's house.* Ahimelech is the great-grandson of Eli. The
slaughter of the entire clan of priests here is the grim fulfillment of the curse
on the house of Eli first enunciated by the man of God in 2:27–36.

17. *for their hand, too, is with David.* The Hebrew adverb *gam*, often a general
term of emphasis, surely has the force of "too" here: the paranoid Saul sees
conspirators on all sides—his son, his Benjaminite court attendants, and now
the priests of Nob.

me!" And the king's servants did not want to reach out their hand to
stab the priests of the LORD. And the king said to Doeg, "You, then,   18
turn round and stab the priests," and Doeg the Edomite turned round
and he it was stabbed the priests and he put to death on that day
eighty-five men who wore the linen ephod. And he struck down Nob   19
the priests' town with the edge of the sword, man and woman, infant
and suckling, ox and donkey and sheep, all by the edge of the sword.

And one son of Ahimelech the son of Ahitub got away, and his name   20
was Abiathar, and he fled after David. And Abiathar told David that   21

---

the king's servants did not want to reach out. Beyond any moral considerations and any concern for the king's sanity, it would be a violation of a taboo to
murder the priests of the LORD.

to stab. The core meaning of the Hebrew verb *pagʿa* is the meeting or inter-
section of two material bodies or human agencies. It can mean "to encounter,"
"to accost," and, by extension, "to entreat," but in contexts of violent action, it
refers to the "encounter" between forged blade and flesh. The verb "to strike
down" (*hikah*, as in verse 19) indicates the consummated act of killing. In
verse 21, the narrator uses *harag*, the unadorned verb that means "to kill."

18. *you, then.* Saul emphatically adds the second person pronoun ʾ*atah* to the
imperative verb: if none of my Israelite subjects will kill the priests, you, then,
as an Edomite, may carry out my orders.

who wore the linen ephod. This is a kind of epic epithet for priests.

19. *man and woman, infant and suckling.* Saul, with the Edomite Doeg as his
catspaw, flings himself into an orgy of mass murder, killing not only the adult
priests but every living creature in Nob. Now he is carrying out the ban he
executed only imperfectly against Amalek (the terms used are virtually identical), but the massacre is directed at his own innocent people. Saul's madness
has become sinister and lethal, like that of Macbeth, who also becomes a
murderer of children—the well-meaning farmer's son who became king has
turned into a bloody tyrant.

all by the edge of the sword. "All" catches the force of the Hebrew preposition ʿ*ad* ("even" or "as far as") reiterated before each term in the catalogue of
the massacre.

20. *and one son of Ahimelech . . . got away.* This sole survivor (his name means
"my father remains") will then be able to provide David with priestly services,
including access to the oracle.

22 Saul had killed the priests of the LORD. And David said to Abiathar, "I knew on that day that Doeg the Edomite was there, that he would surely tell Saul. I am the one who caused the loss of all the lives of your

23 father's house. Stay with me. Do not fear, for whoever seeks my life seeks your life, so you are under my guard."

---

22. *I am the one who caused the loss of all the lives.* The Hebrew uses an ellipsis, "caused all the lives," but the sense is clearly loss of life.

CHAPTER 23

And they told David, saying, "Look, the Philistines are fighting against Keilah and they are looting the threshing floors." And David inquired of the LORD, saying, "Shall I go and strike down these Philistines?" And the LORD said to David, "Go and strike down the Philistines and deliver Keilah." And David's men said to him, "Look, we're afraid here in Judah, and how much more so if we go to Keilah against the Philistine lines!" And David again inquired of the LORD, and the LORD answered him and said, "Rise, go down to Keilah, for I am about to give the Philistines into your hand." And David, and his men with him, went to Keilah and did battle with the Philistines, and he drove off their cattle and struck them a great blow, and David delivered the inhabitants of

---

1. *Keilah.* Keilah is a town on the western perimeter of the territory of Judah, facing the Philistine border. Its vulnerability to Philistine incursions is thus understandable. David's men (verse 3) speak as though Keilah were not part of Judah because as a border town it seems to them much more dangerous than their location deep within their own tribal territory. Some scholars have speculated that Keilah was an independent town without tribal affiliation.

2. *David inquired of the LORD.* The means of inquiry are not specified, but since his questions invite the usual yes-or-no response, it seems likely he is using the ephod and not, as some interpreters have claimed, a more immediate mode of communication with God. The information, then, in verse 6 that the fugitive priest Abiathar has arrived from Nob with the ephod is probably retrospective. The phrase "at Keilah" (one word in Hebrew) in that verse perhaps should be deleted as an inadvertent scribal duplication of "Keilah" at the end of the preceding verse—by the testimony of Chapter 22. Abiathar fled to David when David was in the forest of Hereth in Judah, before he undertook the rescue mission to Keilah.

6   Keilah. And it happened when Abiathar the son of Ahimelech fled to David at Keilah, that the ephod came down in his hand.

7   And it was told to Saul that David had come to Keilah, and Saul said, "God has given him in my hand, for he is closed inside a town with dou-
8   ble gate and bolt." And Saul summoned all the troops for battle to go
9   down to Keilah to lay seige against David and his men. And David knew that Saul was scheming evil against him and he said to Abiathar the
10   priest, "Bring forth the ephod." And David said, "LORD, God of Israel, Your servant has indeed heard that Saul seeks to come to Keilah to
11   destroy the town on my count. Will the notables of Keilah hand me over to him? Will Saul come down, as Your servant has heard? LORD, God of Israel, tell, pray, Your servant." And the LORD said, "He will come
12   down." And David said, "Will the notables of Keilah hand me over, and my men, to Saul?" And the LORD said, "They will hand you over."

---

6. *the ephod came down in his hand.* From the viewpoint of the ancient audience, the ephod would have been indispensable as an instrument of what we would call military intelligence. An ephod, we should recall, is also a priestly garment. At Nob, Saul slaughtered eighty-five priests "who wore the linen ephod." Fokkelman perceptively describes the appearance of the oracular ephod in David's camp as a "countermove by God"—"Saul may bloody the 85 linen priestly garments called the ephod, but the one ephod which acts as a medium for the decisive word of God turns up at the place of the alternative anointed one."

7. *given him in my hand.* The Masoretic Text has *nikar,* "made a stranger," but the Septuagint reflects a verb meaning "sold" or "handed over."

11. *Will the notables . . . hand me over . . . ? Will Saul come down?* Since the binary device of the ephod can only give one answer of yes or no, David receives an answer only to the second question and then is obliged to repeat the first question (verse 12) in order to get a response to it.

12. *They will hand you over.* It may seem base ingratitude on the part of the Keilah notables to betray the man who has just rescued their town from the Philistines. But they must fear Saul's retribution should they collaborate with David at least as much as they fear the Philistines. The political paradox of the situation that has evolved is evident: David has achieved a victory against Israel's principal enemy; Saul now moves to destroy that victor, enlisting the aid of the people David saved.

And David arose, and his men with him, about six hundred men, and 13
they came out from Keilah and moved about wherever they could, and
to Saul it was told that David had gotten away from Keilah, and he
ceased going out.

And David stayed in the wilderness in strongholds, and he stayed in 14
the high country in the wilderness of Ziph. And Saul sought him all the
while but God did not give him into his hand. And David saw that Saul 15
had come out to seek his life, and David was in the wilderness of Ziph
in the forest. And Jonathan the son of Saul arose and went to David in 16
the forest and bade him take heart in the LORD. And he said to him, 17
"Do not fear, for the hand of Saul my father shall not find you, and it is
you who shall reign over Israel, and I on my part will be your viceroy,

---

14. *in the wilderness in strongholds.* Since the Hebrew term for strongholds
(*metsadah* or *metsudah*—attempts to distinguish the two being questionable)
generally occurs in wilderness settings, it seems likely that these are not built-
up structures but rather natural formations that afforded effective defensive
positions, such as promontories surrounded by outcroppings of rock.
    in the wilderness of Ziph. The location is in the tribal territory of Judah,
about five miles southeast of Hebron and about ten miles southeast of Keilah,
where David has just fought the Philistines.

16. *bade him take heart in the LORD.* The literal meaning of the Hebrew idiom
used is "strengthened his hand in the LORD." The Hebrew thus is able to pick
up the word "hand" at the beginning of Jonathan's speech, "the hand of my
father Saul shall not find you."

17. *I on my part will be your viceroy.* For the second time, Jonathan makes a
pact with David in which he concedes that it is David who will inherit the
throne. There is a pattern of incremental repetition here: only now does
Jonathan specify that he will be David's viceroy (literally "second," *mishneh*,
but this is an ellipses for *mishneh lamelekh*, "second to the king"). The faithful
Jonathan persists in his naivete, imagining that he will be able to serve as
viceroy to his dear friend, who is also the man destined to displace the dynasty
Saul would have established. As an alleged doublet, this episode has narrative
plausibility: Jonathan first confirmed a pact with David when he told him he
must flee from Saul; now, no doubt at some risk to himself, he is impelled to
seek out the fugitive and beleaguered David in order to assure him of his continuing loyalty and encourage him in his adversity. Once again, characteristically, David's response to Jonathan is not reported.

18   and even Saul my father knows it." And the two of them sealed a pact before the LORD, and David stayed in the forest but Jonathan went to his house.

19   And Ziphites came up to Saul at Gibeah, saying, "Is not David hiding out among us in the strongholds in the forest on the hill of Hachilah to
20   the south of the wasteland? And so whenever you may desire, O king, to come down, come down, and ours is the part to deliver him into the
21   hand of the king." And Saul said, "Blessed are you to the LORD, for you
22   have shown pity on me. Go, pray, make certain, and mark and see the

---

19. *Ziphites.* Since no definite article is used, this appears to be one group of Ziphites and not a delegation representing the entire clan. The motive for betraying David could equally be desire for a reward and fear of retribution should Saul discover that they had allowed David to hide out in their territory. The ruthless massacre at Nob would have been a grim object lesson duly noted throughout the Israelite populace.

in the strongholds in the forest on the hill of Hachilah to the south of the wasteland. The Ziphite informers want to make their identification of David's whereabouts as precise as possible, hence the unusual string of geographical indications. As it emerges, the intelligence they provide is still not precise enough for the frustrated Saul, as his response ("make certain . . . when you are certain") clearly shows. It should be said that most translators have treated the last geographical term used by the Ziphites, "the wasteland," as a proper noun *(yeshimon)*, but because it bears a definite article, and because *yeshimon* is a well-attested common noun, it is preferable not to construe it as a place-name. This episode uses three different terms for uninhabited terrain— wilderness, wasteland, and desert (or four, if one adds forest)—which has the cumulative effect of emphasizing how David is constrained to take refuge beyond the populated areas of Israel.

21. *you have shown pity on me.* Saul uses the same verb for pity or "sparing" that was prominently deployed in the Amalek story. The idea that the poor king, thwarted by a cunning and malicious David, needs to be shown pity, is surely another manifestation of his paranoia—we might say, of its maudlin side.

place where his foot treads, and who has seen him there, for it has been said to me that he is very cunning. See and mark all the hideouts 23 where he may take cover there and come back to me when you are certain and I shall go with you. And if indeed he is in the land, I shall search for him among all the clans of Judah." And they arose and went 24 to Ziph ahead of Saul, and David and his men were in the wilderness of Maon in the desert south of the wasteland. And Saul went, and his 25 men with him, to seek David. And it was told to David and he went down to the crag and stayed in the wilderness of Maon, and Saul heard, and pursued David into the wilderness of Maon. And Saul went 26 on one side of the mountain and David and his men on the other side of the mountain, and David made haste to go off from before Saul, while Saul and his men were circling the mountain after David and his men to catch them. Just then a messenger came to Saul, 27 saying, "Hurry, and go, for the Philistines have invaded the land!"

---

22. *where his foot treads.* The Hebrew says literally "where his foot is." The focus on David's foot reflects the eye of the pursuer on the track of his elusive prey.

for it has been said to me. The Hebrew reads literally, "for he has said to me," but there is no need to emend the text because biblical Hebrew sometimes uses a third person masculine singular verb with no specified grammatical subject to perform the function of the passive. Notice that Saul claims someone has told him David is very cunning—not, which is the case, that Saul himself has decided that his "enemy" is cunning.

24. *Maon.* This would be roughly three miles due south of the wilderness of Ziph.

26. *Saul and his men were circling the mountain.* Kyle McCarter, Jr. has made the plausible suggestion that what is indicated in this language is a pincer movement: Saul's forces are moving around the circumference of the mountain on two sides in order to trap David between them, who is on the far side of the mountain. He, evidently realizing the nature of Saul's maneuver, scrambles to flee— "David made haste to go off from before Saul"—before the pincer snaps shut.

27. *Hurry, and go, for the Philistines have invaded the land.* This last-minute diversion of course has the effect of rescuing David from Saul, but it also points up the madness of his obsessive pursuit of David: at a time when Israel's major national enemy is repeatedly sending troops against the territory Saul is supposed to be governing and protecting, he is devoting his attention, and his troops, to the pursuit of David.

28   And Saul turned back from pursuing David and went to meet the Philistines. Therefore do they call that place the Crag of the Divide.

24:1   And David went up from there and stayed in the strongholds of En-gedi.

---

28. *the Crag of the Divide.* This etiological notice explains the place-name, *selʿa hamaḥleqot,* as deriving from the "divide" between Saul's forces, which went one way, and David's, which went another. Several commentators have proposed that the name derived not from *maḥloqet,* "division," but from *ḥalaq,* "smooth," and so the original meaning would have been Slippery Crag, or Unforested Crag.

24:1. *the strongholds of En-gedi.* David now flees eastward from the forest area of Ziph, south of Hebron in the central region of Judah's territory, to En-gedi in the rocky heights overlooking the Dead Sea. He would have felt safer in this remote region with its forbidding terrain. But En-gedi is an oasis, which would have provided a water supply and vegetation for him and his troops.

CHAPTER 24

And it happened when Saul turned back from the Philistines that they 2
told him, saying, "Look, David is in the wilderness of En-gedi." And 3
Saul took three thousand picked men from all Israel and he went to
seek David over the rocks of the wild goats. And he came to the sheep- 4
folds along the way, and there was a cave there, and Saul went in
to relieve himself, while David and his men were sitting in the far end
of the cave. And David's men said to him, "Here is the day that 5
the LORD said to you, 'Look, I am about to give your enemy into your
hands and you may do to him whatever seems good in your eyes.'" And
David rose and stealthily cut off the skirt of the cloak that was Saul's.

---

3. *three thousand picked men*. David, it should be recalled, commands a
guerilla band of about six hundred men; so he is outnumbered five to one and
is facing elite troops.

4. *Saul went in to relieve himself . . . David and his men . . . in the far end of the
cave*. The topography is quite realistic, for the cliffs overlooking the Dead Sea
in the region of En-gedi are honeycombed with caves. Power and powerless-
ness are precariously balanced in this episode. David and his men are in all
likelihood hiding in the far end of the cave from Saul's search party. Had a
contingent of soldiers entered the cave, they would have been trapped.
Instead, Saul comes in alone, and he is in a double sense exposed to David
and his men.

5. *Here is the day that the LORD said to you*. David's eager men exhibit a certain
theological presumptuousness. They surely know that their leader has been
secretly anointed to be king, but nothing in the preceding narrative indicates a
divine promise that God would deliver Saul into David's hands.
  do to him whatever seems good in your eyes. They carefully avoid the plain
word "kill."

6   And it happened then that David was smitten with remorse because he
7   had cut off the skirt of the cloak that was Saul's. And he said to his
    men, "The LORD forbid me, that I should have done this thing to my
    master, the LORD's anointed, to reach out my hand against him, for he
8   is the LORD's anointed." And David held back his men with words and
    did not let them rise against Saul, and Saul rose from the cave and
9   went on the way. And David then rose and came out of the cave and
    called after Saul, saying, "My lord, the king!" And Saul looked behind

---

6. *David was smitten with remorse.* The Hebrew is literally "David's heart
smote him."

   he had cut off the skirt of the cloak that was Saul's. Clearly, what David feels
is that he has perpetrated a kind of symbolic mutilation of the king by cutting
off the corner of his garment—not with anything like a scissors, of course, but
surely with his sword, his instrument for killing his enemies. The cloak *(me'il)*
has already been linked emblematically with kingship in the final estrangement between Samuel and Saul, and so David is in symbolic effect "cutting
away" Saul's kingship. For all the remorse he feels, he will continue to make
double use of the corner of the cloak, as we shall see.

7. *that I should have done this thing to my master, the LORD's anointed.* Some
interpreters have read this whole episode as an apology for David's innocence
and piety in relation to Saul. But the very gesture of piety is also self-
interested—David, after all, is conscious that he, too, is the LORD's anointed,
and it is surely in his long-term interest that the reigning king's person should
be held sacred by all his subjects.

8. *David held back his men.* The meaning of the verb *shise'a* is disputed, but it
is most plausibly linked with the noun *shes'a,* a split or cleft. The sense here
would then be: he "split off" his men from Saul, using his words to interpose a
kind of barrier between them and the king. In any case, the first clause of this
verse appears to respond to the men's initial inclination to kill Saul (verse 5)
rather than following from David's remorse over the cutting of the garment—a
chronological displacement noted as early as Rashi.

9. *David . . . came out of the cave and called after Saul.* David is taking a calculated risk. Saul could, after all, order his troops to attack David and the men
behind him in the cave. David first throws Saul off his guard by paying obeisance
to him as king and prostrating himself—hardly what one would expect of a fugitive or rebel. He then counts on the persuasive power of his own rhetoric, and on
the tell-tale scrap of the king's cloak that he clutches, to deflect Saul from his
lethal intentions. David is cannily self-protective but he is also a gambler.

him, and David knelt, his face to the ground, and bowed down. And   10
David said to Saul, "Why should you listen to people's words, saying,
'Look, David seeks to harm you'? Look, this day your eyes have seen   11
that the LORD has given you into my hand in the cave, and they said to
kill you, and I had compassion for you and said, 'I will not reach out my
hand against my master, for he is the LORD's anointed.' And, my father,   12
see, yes, see the skirt of your cloak in my hand, for when I cut off
the skirt of your cloak and did not kill you, mark and see that there
was no evil or crime in my hand and I did not offend you, yet you stalk
me to take my life. Let the LORD judge between me and you, and   13
the LORD will avenge me of you, but my hand will not be against you.

10.–11. *Why should you listen to people's words? . . . this day your eyes have seen.*
Instead of rumor heard about David's harmful intentions, here is ocular evidence of his innocence—and of God's having devised to give David the upper
hand over Saul.

11. *and they said to kill you.* The Masoretic Text has "he said," which may be
either corrected to a plural, as some of the ancient versions do, or construed
as "someone said."

12. *my father see, yes, see the skirt of your cloak in my hand.* It is, appropriately,
ambiguous whether "my father" is a form of respectful address to an authority or an attempt to reach back to the moment of affectionate intimacy in
their relationship. We may note that David, for all the remorse he felt over
having cut off the skirt of Saul's garment, makes great display of it now as
evidence of having had Saul entirely at his mercy. The proof of his innocence is thus inseparable from the reminder of the power he had over his
rival.

13. *Let the LORD judge between me and you . . . the LORD will avenge me of you.*
David's great protestation of innocence and his purported gesture of reconciliation move toward a barely veiled threat: you are the one who has wronged
me, and vengeance will be exacted, but by God, not by me.

14   As the proverb of the ancients says, 'From wicked men does wicked-
15   ness come forth.' But my hand will not be against you. After whom has
the king of Israel come forth, after whom are you chasing? After a dead
16   dog, after a single flea? The LORD will be arbiter and judge between me
and you, that He may see and plead my case and judge me against
17   you." And it happened when David had finished speaking these words
to Saul, that Saul said, "Is this your voice, my son, David?" And Saul

---

14. *The proverb of the ancients.* The Masoretic Text has "ancient," in the singular, but the Qumran Samuel scroll, more plausibly, shows the plural form.

From wicked men does wickedness come forth. The gnomic saying—only
three words in the Hebrew!—that David chooses to cite is archly double
edged: Wicked acts are perpetrated only by the wicked, so I won't be the one
to touch you. But there is also the distinct hint that the wicked person in
question could be Saul himself. Though David cannot know this, Saul will die
by his own hand.

But my hand will not be against you. The words that the writer attributes to
David ironically echo the words of Saul's first murderous plot against David,
conveyed in interior monologue, when Saul said, "Let not my hand be against
him but let the hand of the Philistines be against him" (18:17).

15. *has the king of Israel come forth.* The very verb attached to the wicked in the
proverb!

After a dead dog, after a single flea. In his peroration, David outdoes himself
in professing his humble station. A dead dog was proverbial in ancient Israel
as a contemptible, worthless thing, but David goes the idiom one better by
saying he is scarcely more important than a single flea on the dead dog's car-
cass—a brilliant adaptation to prose of the logic of intensification of biblical
poetry, in which a term introduced in the first part of the line is raised to the
second power semantically in the parallel second half.

16. *judge me against you.* The Hebrew is literally "judge me from your hand,"
that is, judge me favorably and rescue me from your hand. The term thus
picks up the insistence on "hand" throughout David's speech.

17. *Is this your voice, my son, David?* These first words of Saul's response to
David are one of the most breathtaking instances of the biblical technique of
contrastive dialogue. David's speech had been, by biblical standards, quite
lengthy, and very much a speech—a beautifully crafted piece of rhetoric, with
complex political aims in mind. Saul responds with four choked Hebrew
words, *haqolkha zeh beni Dawid?* His designation of David as "my son" is free

raised his voice and wept. And he said to David, "You are more in the · 18
right than I, for it is you who requited me good whereas I requited you
evil. And you told today how you wrought good with me, when the · 19
LORD delivered me into your hand and you did not kill me. For if a man · 20
finds his enemy, does he send him off on a good way? The LORD will
repay you with good for what you have done for me this day. And so, · 21
look, I know that you will surely be king and that the kingship of Israel
will stay in your hands. And now, swear to me by the LORD, that you · 22
shall not cut off my seed after me and that you shall not blot out my
name from my father's house." And David swore to Saul, and Saul went · 23
home while David and his men went up to the stronghold.

---

of the ambiguity attached to David's calling him "my father." This is one of
those extraordinary reversals that make biblical narrative such a probing representation of the oscillations and the unpredictabilities of human nature:
David's words have cut to the quick of the king's conscience, and suddenly the
obsessive pursuer feels an access of paternal affection, intertwined with
remorse, for his imagined enemy. Saul asks his question because he has to
shake himself to believe his enemy is his friend, because he stands at a certain
distance from David (who has called out "after" Saul), and also because his
eyes are blinded with tears. He is thus reminiscent of the blind father Isaac
who was able to make out the voice, but not the identity, of his son Jacob, and
from whom a blessing was wrested.

18. *You are more in the right than I.* These words echo the ones pronounced by
Judah, referring to his vindicated daughter-in-law Tamar, who will become the
progenitrix of David's line.
    you . . . requited me good . . . I requited you evil. The antithesis of good and
evil is played on through the next three verses and should not be sacrificed in
the English for the sake of imagined idiomatic fluency.

21. *I know that you will surely be king.* This marks Saul's first open admission
that David is the "fellowman who is better than you" of whom Samuel spoke.
He has been doubly convinced—by God's having put him at David's mercy
and by David's refusal to harm him, a kingly act and not the act of a rebel and
usurper.

CHAPTER 25

Ind Samuel died, and all Israel gathered and mourned him, and they buried him at his home in Ramah. And David arose and went down to the wilderness of Paran.

2 And there was a man in Maon, whose stock was in Carmel, and the man was very great; he had three thousand sheep and a thousand goats. And it happened when he was shearing his sheep in Carmel—
3 and the man's name was Nabal and his wife's name was Abigail, and the woman had a good mind and lovely looks, but the man was hard

---

1. *the wilderness of Paran.* This geographical indication is puzzling because, unless there is some other place called Paran, it would refer to the Sinai desert, where it would make no sense for David to go and where he could scarcely be if he and his men are engaged with Nabal's shepherds in Judea. The Septuagint reads "wilderness of Maon."

2. *Maon . . . Carmel.* Both places are in the tribal territory of Judah, in the vicinity of Hebron, and just a few miles apart.

3. *the man's name was Nabal.* On the face of it, this is an improbable name because *nabal* in Hebrew plainly means "base fellow," "churl," or "fool," as Abigail (verse 25) will point out. In all likelihood, the name is not originally Hebrew, and various meanings drawn from other ancient Near Eastern languages have been proposed for it, such as "archer" and "chosen one of the god."
   a good mind and lovely looks. As yet, we do not know why this characterization will be important. Her shrewd intelligence will be vividly demonstrated in her brilliant speech to David, and her physical attractiveness will stir his matrimonial interest in her.

and evil in deeds, and a Calebite—David heard in the wilderness 4
that Nabal was shearing his sheep. And David sent ten lads, and David 5
said to the lads, "Go up to Carmel, and come to Nabal and ask him
in my name how he fares. And say, 'Thus may it be this time next 6
year, that you fare well, and your house fare well, and all that is
yours fare well. And so, I have heard that they are doing your shearing. 7
Now, the shepherds who belong to you were with us—we did not
humiliate them and nothing of theirs was missing the whole time
they were at Carmel. Ask your lads and they will tell you! And may 8
our lads find favor in your eyes, for we have come on a festive day. Give,

---

and a Calebite. The Calebites were non-Israelites who in effect joined the
tribe of Judah. Several medieval Hebrew commentators detected a double
meaning because *kalibi* could also be construed as "doglike."

6. *Thus may it be this time next year.* The compact Hebrew phrase *koh leḥay*
occurs only here, and its meaning has been disputed. This translation adopts
an interpretation that goes back to Rashi, which is based on the similarity to a
well-known idiom, *kaʿet ḥayah.* That would make sense in terms of the narrative situation: the prosperous Nabal is obviously "faring well" at the moment,
and David's greeting of peace (to fare well in the Hebrew idiom is to possess
shalom) contains a veiled threat—let us hope that you continue to fare well a
year from now.

7. *we did not humiliate them.* This is the same verb used for Jonathan's sense
of his father's treatment of him (20:34), though here it has the meaning of
"molest."

nothing of theirs was missing. The message is that David's men did not permit themselves to take any of Nabal's flock, and perhaps also that as armed
men they defended Nabal's people against marauders (compare verse 16,
"They were a wall around us both night and day."). But there is a certain ambiguity as to whether David was providing protection out of sheer good will or
conducting a protection racket in order to get the necessary provisions for his
guerilla band.

8. *our lads.* The Hebrew says "the lads"—"our" is added for the sake of clarity,
to distinguish David's retainers from Nabal's.

for we have come on a festive day. The time of sheep shearing was a sort of
holiday, with feasting and drinking. Nabal's own feast back home at Maon
(verse 36) may have been encouraged by the festivities in which he joined
with his shearers out in the field.

pray, whatever you can to your servants and to your son, to David.' "
9 And David's lads came and spoke to Nabal all these words in David's
10 name, and they paused. And Nabal answered David's servants and said,
"Who is David and who is the son of Jesse? These days many are the
11 slaves breaking away from their masters. And shall I take my bread and
my water and my meat that I slaughtered for my shearers and give it to
12 men who come from I know not where?" And David's lads whirled
round on their way and went back and told him all these words.

Give, pray, whatever you can to your servants. The request for a payoff is
politely worded, and no quantities are specified.

to your son, to David. This is an expression of deference or humility to the
powerful and presumably older Nabal. It also strikes an ironic note of correspondence with the language of David's encounter with Saul at the cave near
En-gedi in the previous episode. There, David addressed Saul as "my father,"
and the king, in an access of feeling, called David "my son."

10. *Who is David and who is the son of Jesse?* This sarcastic question, in verselike parallelism, picks up another ironic correspondence with Saul, who after
the vanquishing of Goliath asked whose son this was. In Nabal's case, of
course, the question expresses the contempt of a rich landowner for David
and his ragtag band of dispossessed men and malcontents ("men who come
from I know not where").

many are the slaves breaking away from their masters. On the surface, these
words reflect the disdain of a propertied man (who would also be a slave-
holder) for all landless rebels that threaten the established social hierarchy.
But there is also a barbed hint that David himself is a slave or subject (the
same word in Hebrew) who has rebelled against his master, Saul.

11. *shall I take my bread and my water.* The Septuagint has "wine" instead of
"water." In any case, Nabal's harsh and contemptuous response to David's
men vividly illustrates that he is a "hard" man, and a churlish one. His outrage
over the notion of parting with any of his possessions is nicely indicated, as
Shimon Bar-Efrat has noted, by the fact that there are eight grammatical
expressions of the first person singular in this one sentence.

12. *Every man, gird his sword.* The angry David wastes no words: he merely
gives the urgent command to take up weapons and move out for the kill.

And David said to his men, "Every man, gird his sword!" And every man   13
girded his sword, and David, too, girded his sword. And about four hundred men went up after David, while two hundred stayed with the gear.

And to Abigail the wife of Nabal one of the lads told, saying, "Look,   14
David sent messengers from the wilderness to greet our master, and he
pounced on them. And the men have been very good to us and we were   15
not humiliated and we missed nothing the whole time we went about
with them, when we were out in the field. They were a wall around us   16
both night and day the whole time we were with them tending the
sheep. And now, mark and see what you must do, for the evil is resolved   17
against our master and against all his house, and he is such a scoundrel
no one can speak to him." And Abigail hurried and fetched two hundred   18
loaves of bread and two jugs of wine and five dressed sheep and five
seahs of parched grain and a hundred raisin cakes and two hundred fig
cakes, and she put them on the donkeys. And she said to her lads, "Pass   19
on ahead of me and I'll be coming right after you." But her husband she
did not tell. And so she was riding on the donkey coming down under   20
the cover of the mountain and, look, David and his men were coming

---

15. *And they have been very good to us.* In keeping with the general practice of
biblical dialogue, the servant recycles the language of David's message to
Nabal—"we were not humiliated and we missed nothing the whole time"—
but amplifies it by adding this clause as well as the image in the next verse,
"They were a wall around us both night and day." He thus makes emphatically
clear that David's men really provided protection faithfully, whether in the
simple sense or in the racketeering sense.

17. *And now, mark and see what you must do.* Unlike the "lads" who address
Saul, this one offers no specific advice to Abigail, for she is more than clever
enough to figure out what steps she must immediately take.

20. *And so she was riding on the donkey coming down under the cover of the
mountain and, look, David and his men were coming.* The two parties moving
toward each other introduce a moment of suspense, for David, after all, as the
next verse (with a pluperfect verb) makes utterly clear, is armed and angry.
The "look" *(hineh)* is used in characteristic fashion to indicate Abigail's visual
perspective: he at first doesn't see her because she is coming down the shel-
tered slope of the mountain but she sees him and his men with their swords
girded ready for battle.

21 down toward her, and she met them. And David had said, "All in vain did I guard everything that belonged to this fellow in the wilderness, and nothing was missing from all that was his, and he paid me back
22 evil for good! Thus may God do to David and even more, if I leave from
23 all that is his until morning a single pisser against the wall!" And Abigail saw David and hurried and got down from the donkey and flung herself
24 on her face before David and bowed to the ground. And she flung herself at his feet and said, "Mine, my lord, is the blame! But let your ser-
25 vant speak in your ears, and hear the words of your servant. Pray, let not my lord pay mind to this scoundrel of a man, to Nabal, for just like his name he is, his name means Base and baseness is with him. And as for me, your servant, I never saw my lord's lads whom you sent.

---

22. *a single pisser against the wall*. The literal meaning of the Hebrew is properly followed in the King James Version, as it is in this translation. The phrase, of course, is a rough and vivid epithet for "male," and one that occurs only in curses. Its edge of vulgarity seems perfectly right for David's anger.

23.–24. *flung herself on her face . . . bowed to the ground . . . flung herself at his feet*. In a world where an angry king could massacre every man, woman, and child in Nob, Abigail has no way of knowing whether David will have an impulse to kill her on the spot. (She has not heard the words that limit the threat of slaughter to the males.) Thus, her first move in this highly dangerous situation, before she speaks a word, is to demonstrate her absolute submission to David through these extravagant gestures of obeisance.

24. *Mine*. The shrewdness of her extraordinary speech begins with the very first syllable she utters. She immediately takes all the blame on herself, though in the next breath she will be sure to transfer it heartily to her contemptible husband. At the same time, she exploits a momentary pun, for the word *bi* ("mine," "in me") in other contexts can mean "I beseech you," so she initiates her address to David with what sounds like a term of imploring.

25. *this scoundrel of a man . . . his name means Base . . . And as for me . . .* It is hard to think of another instance in literature in which a wife so quickly and so devastatingly interposes distance between herself and her husband. She rapidly denounces her spouse and then counterposes herself ("And as for me," *waʾani*) as a person who had no part in the rude rejection of David's emissaries. Abigail of course wants to save her own neck, but she clearly has been chafing over her marriage with a boorish, unpleasant, and probably older man, and she sees an opportunity here.

And now, my lord, as the LORD lives and as you live—the LORD   26
Who kept you from coming into blood guilt with your own hand
delivering you—and now, like Nabal may your enemies be who seek
evil against my lord. And now, this blessing that your servant has   27
brought to my lord, let it be given to the lads who go about in the
footsteps of my lord. Forgive, pray, the crime of your servant, for the   28
LORD will surely make for my lord a stalwart house, for he fights
the battles of the LORD and no evil will be found in you all your days.

---

26. *Who kept you from coming into blood guilt.* Abigail is no doubt speaking
in general, but the reader can scarcely forget the immediately preceding
episode, in which David refused to harm Saul when he had him in his
power.

27. *this blessing that your servant has brought.* The obvious sense of "blessing"
(berakhah) in context is "gift," but the primary meaning of the word is worth
preserving for two reasons. First, it is clearly intended to answer to David's
reiterated use of "blessed" in his response to Abigail. Then, as Moshe Garsiel has aptly observed, it is a key term in a network of allusions to the
moment in Genesis 33 when Jacob is reunited with his brother Esau: Esau,
too, approaches dauntingly with four hundred armed men; Jacob, like Abigail, prostrates himself before the figure he fears; and he, too, has brought
with him generous tribute to be offered in conciliation, which he refers to
not as a "gift" *(minhah)* but as a "blessing." And in Genesis 33, that term
plays back against the fraught meanings of "blessing" in the larger Jacob-
Esau narrative.

28. *Forgive, pray, the crime of your servant.* "Servant" is in the feminine, but the
conventional "handmaiden" sounds too fussy. By way of deference, Abigail
once again speaks as though the fault were hers, though she has made it quite
clear that her husband alone is the guilty one.
   a stalwart house. A stalwart, or enduring, house is precisely what was
promised the priestly line that was to replace the house of Eli (2:35).
   no evil will be found in you all your days. Abigail exploits the temporal ambiguity of the Hebrew imperfective verb to make a statement that is both
descriptive of the way David has conducted himself and predictive of the way
he will, or should, conduct himself.

29 And when a person rises to pursue you, to seek your life, my lord's life will be bound in the bundle of the living with the LORD your God, and the lives of your enemies He will sling from the hollow of 30 the sling. And so, when the LORD does for my lord all the good that He has spoken about you and He appoints you prince over Israel, 31 this will not be a stumbling and a trepidation of the heart to my lord, to have shed blood for no cause and for my lord to have carried out his own deliverance, then will the LORD do well with my lord, and

---

29. *when a person rises to pursue you.* The generality of "a person" (*ʾadam*) picks up David's use of the same word in the preceding episode when he addresses Saul ("Why should you listen to people's words" [*divrey ʾadam*]), and even more pointedly, recalls his very first speech to Saul in 17:32, "Let no man's heart [*lev ʾadam*] fail him," where the term seems to refer to Saul himself, who may be the hidden referent here.

bound in the bundle of the living. Although Kyle McCarter, Jr., following Tur-Sinai, has claimed that "bundle" (*tsror*) actually means document or book, a more plausible identification is the pouch in which little stones keeping a tally of live sheep were placed. Thus both this positive image and the negative one of the slingshot would be associated with sheepherding. And as Shimon Bar-Efrat has nicely observed, *tsror* in biblical Hebrew also means "stone," the object that would normally be placed in the hollow of the sling; so there is a punning cross-link between the two images.

will sling from the hollow of the sling. Instead of being bound up and safely kept, their lives will be flung out into the void of extinction. (The literal sense of the preposition attached to "hollow" in the Hebrew is "in.") Abigail has chosen her metaphor shrewdly because it would be general knowledge that David used his sling to destroy a formidable enemy.

30.–31. *when the LORD . . . appoints you prince over Israel, this will not be a stumbling and a trepidation of the heart to my lord.* Abigail deftly pitches her argument to David's political self-interest. Once he makes the move from guerilla chieftain to monarch, he will not want his record stained by blood he has spilled. It is therefore more prudent to let God take care of his enemies— "the LORD" in biblical parlance being the piously proper way to talk about the cause of events, but its pragmatic equivalent being "other people" or "circumstances."

you will remember your servant." And David said to Abigail, "Blessed is   32
the LORD, God of Israel, Who has sent you this day to meet me. And   33
blessed is your good sense and blessed are you, for this day you held
me back from coming into blood guilt with my own hand delivering
me. And yet, as the LORD, God of Israel, lives, Who kept me from   34
harming you, had you not hurried and come to meet me, there would
not have been left to Nabal by morning's light a single pisser against
the wall!" And David took from her hand what she had brought him,   35
and to her he said, "Go up in peace to your house. See, I have heeded
your voice and granted your petition."

And Abigail came to Nabal, and, look, he was having himself a feast in   36
his house like a king's feast, and Nabal's heart was of good cheer, and
he was exceedingly drunk. And she told him nothing, neither great nor
small. And it happened in the morning when the wine was gone out of   37

---

31. *and you will remember your servant.* These final words of Abigail's lengthy
and carefully calculated speech are strategically chosen, and discreet. What,
in fact, does she have in mind? The Israeli novelist, Meir Shalev, in a perceptive and lively essay on this story, makes a bold and, to my mind, persuasive
proposal. Abigail has matrimony in view, once her cantankerous old husband
is out of the way, but why does she think she will deserve so signal an honor, or
reward, from David? Shalev argues that when Abigail dissuades David from
killing Nabal, repeatedly assuring him that the LORD will pay off David's
scores against him, she is really suggesting herself as the agency for "the
LORD." She is, in other words, proposing to David that she carry out a kind of
contract killing of her husband, with the payoff that she will become the wife
of the handsome young warrior and future king.

32.–34. David, though persuaded by Abigail's prudent advice, cannot resist
one last reminder that he was indeed about to cut down every pisser against
the wall in the house of Nabal.

36. *and she told him nothing.* Abigail again makes a careful calculation: she
does not want to convey the scary news to him while he is enveloped in an
alcoholic haze.

37. *in the morning when the wine was gone out of him.* She catches him cold
sober, and perhaps even with a painful hangover.

Nabal that his wife told him these things and his heart died within him
38   and he became like a stone. And it happened after about ten days that
the LORD smote Nabal and he died.

39   And David heard that Nabal had died, and he said, "Blessed is the
LORD Who has taken up my cause of insult against Nabal, and His servant He has withheld from evil, and Nabal's evil the LORD has brought
down on his own head." And David sent and spoke out for Abigail to
40   take her as wife. And David's servants came to Abigail at Carmel and
spoke to her, saying, "David sent us to you to take you to him as wife."
41   And she arose and bowed, her face to the ground, and said, "Look,
your servant is but a slavegirl to wash the feet of my lord's servants."

---

his heart died within him and he became like a stone. The terrifying information that David had been on his way—or did she say, was still on his
way?—with four hundred armed men intent on mayhem triggers a paralyz-
ing heart attack, or, perhaps, a stroke (the biblical understanding of physiology not being ours). Abigail gives the distinct appearance of counting on her
husband's cowardice and on a bad heart she might have been aware of from
previous manifestations of ill health. If this assumption is correct, she
would be using her knowledge of his physical frailty to carry out the tacit
contract on his life—bloodlessly, with God Himself left to do the deed
(compare the end of verse 38). Polzin perceptively notes that the figurative
use of the stone for paralysis cinches a circle of images: the enemies flung
from the hollow of the sling and the smooth stone with which David killed
Goliath.

39. *David . . . spoke out for Abigail.* In biblical idiom, the verb "to speak" followed by the preposition *b^e* instead of the usual *ʾel* ("to") means to enter into
discussion about a betrothal. David, losing no time, has certainly grasped the
veiled implication of Abigail's last words to him.

41. *your servant is but a slavegirl to wash the feet of my lord's servants.* In one last
flourish of the etiquette of humility, she professes herself unworthy of so great
an honor as to become David's wife. But perhaps this is just what she has
been aiming to become, and so, once again "hurrying," she sets off to join her
new husband. She then vanishes from the subsequent narrative.

And Abigail hurried and rose and rode on the donkey, her five young   42
women walking behind her, and she went after David's messengers,
and she became his wife. And Ahinoam David had taken from Jezreel,   43
and both of them became his wives. And Saul had given Michal his   44
daughter, David's wife, to Palti son of Laish, who was from Gallim.

---

44. *And Saul had given Michal his daughter, David's wife, to Palti.* The legality
of this act is questionable. David's having taken two wives—of Ahinoam all we
know is her place of origin—while hiding out from Saul is no justification
because, given the practice of polygamy, he could have done that even if he
were living under the same roof with Michal. Saul's motive is political, to
deprive David of one claim to the throne by removing the connection through
marriage with the royal family. But that connection has already been established, as the narrator's identification of Michal as "David's wife" is meant to
remind us. We can only guess what Michal, who we know loved David, feels
about being passed around in this fashion, or what she feels about the man
her father has imposed on her. Later, we will be accorded a brief but unforget-
table glimpse into Palti's feelings for Michal.

CHAPTER 26

1 And the Ziphites came to Saul at Gibeah, saying, "Is not David hiding
2 out at the hill of Hachilah facing the wasteland?" And Saul arose and
went down to the wilderness of Ziph, and with him three thousand
3 picked men of Israel, to seek David in the wilderness of Ziph. And Saul
camped at the hill of Hachilah which is facing the wasteland, along the

---

1. *And the Ziphites came to Saul at Gibeah.* This verse, echoing much of the
language of 23:19, announces the beginning of the last of the elaborately
paired episodes that structure the story of David and Saul. Scholarly consensus assumes that these doublets reflect different sources or traditions
bearing on the same events, though the possibility cannot be rejected out of
hand that the original writer may have deliberately composed his story with
paired incidents. In any case, the pairings need to be read as part of the purposeful compositional design of the redacted version of the narrative that
we have. As the Russian Formalist critic Viktor Shklovsky observed long ago,
every parallelism in a literary text serves to point up a certain semantic difference. Here, we note at the outset that the elaborately detailed intelligence about David's whereabouts provided by the Ziphites in 23:19 is largely
absent from this briefer account: this story will prove to be an *inversion* of
the earlier one, David discovering Saul instead of the other way around.
Another indication that the doublet is manipulated as an element of purposeful design is the fact that this episode simultaneously repeats *two different* previous episodes—not only the earlier story of Saul's pursuit of David
into the wilderness of Ziph but also the encounter between David and Saul
at the cave near En-gedi (Chapter 24). There, just as here, David refused to
kill Saul when he, or one of his men, could have done so, and there he pro-
fessed his innocence to a remorseful Saul who called him as he does here,
"my son, David."

way; and David was staying in the wilderness, and he saw that Saul had come after him into the wilderness. And David sent spies and he knew 4 with certainty that Saul had come. And David arose and came to the 5 place where Saul had camped. And David saw the place where Saul lay, and Abner son of Ner and Saul were lying within the staging ground, and the troops were encamped around him. And David spoke 6 up and said to Ahimelech the Hittite and to Abishai son of Zeruiah, saying, "Who will come down with me to Saul, to the camp?" And Abishai said, "I on my part shall go down with you." And David came, 7 and Abishai, to the troops by night, and, look, Saul was lying asleep

---

3. *he saw that Saul had come after him.* The placement of this second account of pursuit in the wilderness of Ziph after Saul's solemn pledge in Chapter 24 not to harm David underlines the compulsive character of his obsession with David. Whatever his avowed good intentions, Saul cannot restrain his impulse to destroy his rival. There is thus strong narrative logic in the recurrence: after this last encounter with Saul, David will sensibly conclude that he can no longer trust the king's professions of good faith, and he will take flight beyond the borders of Israel.

4. *David sent spies and he knew with certainty.* In contrast to the episode in Chapter 23, it is David here who commands military intelligence. The writer makes this point neatly by using the same (relatively unusual) phrase, *ʾel nakhon,* "with certainty," which in Chapter 23 was spoken by Saul, referring to the information about David he expected to get from the Ziphites.

6. *Ahimelech the Hittite.* In biblical usage, "Hittite" is a loose designation for Canaanite peoples and does not necessarily refer to the Indo-European group that originated in Anatolia. The presence of a foreigner in David's inner circle of warriors suggests an openness of his band of disaffected men to adventure seekers, freebooters, and other mobile types in the Canaanite population. Ahimelech is nowhere else mentioned in the biblical record, which has led some scholars to infer that the mention of this foreigner may be an authentic early notice of a historical personage. The name itself is Hebrew.

Abishai son of Zeruiah. If the report in Chronicles is reliable, Zeruiah was David's sister—hence the unusual matronymic instead of a patronymic. David the warrior chieftain is surrounded by his three nephews, the three bloody-minded sons of Zeruiah: two of them impetuous (Abishai and Asahel), the third, who is David's commander, ruthlessly calculating (Joab).

within the staging ground, his spear thrust into the ground at his head,
8   and Abner and the troops were lying around him. And Abishai said to
David, "God has this day delivered your enemy into your hand, and
now, let me, pray, strike him through with the spear into the ground
9   just once, I will need no second blow." And David said to Abishai,
"Do no violence to him! For who can reach out his hand against the
10 LORD's anointed and be guiltless?" And David said, "As the LORD
lives, the LORD will smite him, or his day will come and he will die, or
11 in battle he will go down and perish. The LORD forbid that I should
reach out my hand against the LORD's anointed! And so now, take, pray,
the spear which is at his head and the water jug and let us go off."

---

8. *God has this day delivered your enemy into your hand.* These words explicitly
echo the words of David's men when they discover Saul unawares in the cave.
   strike him through with the spear . . . just once, I will need no second blow.
This bit of warrior's bravado helps us make an important connection, as J. P.
Fokkelman has nicely observed: twice Saul hurled this same spear at David,
who eluded him. Abishai on his part vows he will deliver one swift, lethal blow.

9. *Do no violence to him.* Instead of one of three expected verbs, "to strike
down," "to kill," "to put to death," David uses the verb *hishḥit,* which basically
means "to destroy," but which can carry the association, as Kyle McCarter, Jr.
rightly observes, of mutilation or defacement, the taboo acts that should not
be perpetrated on the person of the king.

10. *And David said.* Abishai, dumbfounded, offers no response to David's forbidding him to harm this archenemy, and so David has to explain that God
will settle accounts with Saul in His own good time.

11. *take . . . the spear.* In the episode at the cave, David carried away the cut-off
corner of Saul's garment, which had been symbolically linked with kingship.
The spear is an alternative image of kingship, obviously more directly associated with martial potency, and so this version conveys a greater sense that
David is depriving Saul of something essential in the token of kingship he
bears off. Again, the placement of this version of the paired episodes is telling,
for the next time we see Saul in the narrative he will be undone on the battlefield by the Philistines and will turn his own weapon against himself.
   and the water jug. The spear protects life by destroying; the water jug sustains life for the warrior in battle under the hot sun.

And David took the spear and the water jug at Saul's head, and they 12
went off, with no one seeing and no one knowing and no one waking,
for they were all asleep, for the LORD's deep slumber had fallen upon
them. And David crossed over to the opposite slope and stood on the 13
mountaintop from afar, great was the distance between them. And 14
David called out to the troops and to Abner son of Ner, saying, "Will
you not answer, Abner?" And Abner answered and said, "Who are
you, that you have called out to the king?" And David said to Abner, 15
"Are you not a man, and who is like you in Israel, and why have
you not guarded your lord the king? For one of the troops has come
to do violence to the king your lord. It is not good, this thing that 16
you have done, as the LORD lives, for you all deserve death, because
you did not guard your master, the LORD's anointed. And now, see,
where are the king's spear and the water jug that were at his head?"

---

12. *And David took the spear and the water jug.* David takes them himself,
after having ordered Abishai to do it. The medieval Hebrew exegete David
Kimchi offers a shrewd explanation: "He changed his mind and didn't want
Abishai to approach the king, lest he prove unable to restrain himself and
kill Saul."

14. *Who are you, that you have called out to the king?* Some ancient versions
omit "to the king" because David has called out to Abner, not to Saul. David's
shouting from the prominence, however, occurs in the middle of the night,
and it clearly has awakened Saul, which seems to be what is bothering Abner.
David has chosen Saul's commander as his first interlocutor in order to stress
the sacred responsibility of those around the king to protect his person. His
noble words are not devoid of self-interest because David is clearly conscious
of the fact that he is the future king.

15. *one of the troops has come to do violence to the king.* Although this could
refer to Abishai, the essential referent is David himself—something he does
not want to say in so many words.

16. *you all deserve death.* "All" is supplied in the translation in order to convey
the fact that here the pronoun "you" is a plural in the Hebrew. This death sentence pronounced on Saul's entire entourage is extravagant, but Abner at least
will die a violent death.

17 And Saul recognized David's voice and he said, "Is this your voice, my son,
18 David?" And David said, "It is my voice, my lord the king." And he said,
"Why is it that my lord chases after his servant, for what have I done, and
19 what evil is in my hand? And now, let my lord the king hear, pray, the
words of his servant. If the LORD has incited you against me, let Him be
appeased by an offering, and if it be men, cursed are they before the
LORD, for they have banished me today from joining the LORD's inheri-
20 tance, saying, 'Go, serve other gods.' And now, let not my blood fall to the
ground away from the LORD's presence, for the king of Israel has come
forth to seek a single flea, as he would chase a partridge in the mountains."

---

17. *Is this your voice, my son, David?* These are the identical words he pronounces outside the cave near En-gedi. Here, he "recognizes" the voice—as,
symbolically, in this remission of his madness, he recognizes his paternal bond
with David—but he is not entirely sure because of the darkness, and so he asks.

18. *What evil is in my hand?* As elsewhere, "hand" and "in my hand" have multiple valences. What David literally has in his hand as he speaks is the king's
spear!

19. *let Him be appeased by an offering.* The Hebrew says literally, "let Him
smell [the fragrant odor of] an offering."
　If the LORD has incited . . . if it be men. These two alternatives are a kind of
diplomatic maneuver. David doesn't want to put the blame squarely on Saul,
so he proposes that the king either was "incited" by God for some mysterious
reason or by malicious people.
　banished me . . . from . . . the LORD's inheritance. The LORD's inheritance
clearly refers to the land of Israel. Since every national region had its own cult,
David is saying that to be excluded from his own national borders is tanta-
mount to being obliged to worship other gods. In fact, his flight from Saul has
been mostly within Israelite territory, but he seems to be anticipating that his
next move, for his own safety, will have to be into Philistine country.

20. *to seek a single flea, as he would chase a partridge in the mountains.* The language of the entire clause recycles the words David used to conclude his
speech outside the cave. But the dead dog has been deleted and a partridge
has been introduced instead. This image is less forceful, but its attraction in
the Hebrew, as several commentators have noted, is a witty pun: partridge
(*qor̄e*) is a homonym for "he who calls out." David (verse 14) was identified by
Abner as the one who called out to the king—a caller out on the mountain, a
partridge pursued on the mountains.

And Saul said, "I have offended. Come back, my son, David, for I will 21
not harm you again inasmuch as my life was precious in your eyes this
day. I have played the fool and have erred gravely." And David answered 22
and said, "Here is the king's spear. Let one of the lads cross over and
take it. And the LORD will pay back to a man his right actions and his 23
loyalty, for the LORD gave you today into my hand and I did not want to
reach out my hand against the LORD's anointed. And, look, just as I val- 24
ued your life highly today, may the LORD value my life highly and may
He save me from every strait." And Saul said to David, "Blessed are 25
you, my son, David. You shall surely do much and you shall surely win
out." And David went on his way, but Saul returned to his place.

---

22. *And David answered and said, "Here is the king's spear."* It is noteworthy that
David does not immediately respond to Saul's renewed profession of regret
and good faith. (The Masoretic consonantal text, the *ketiv*, tries to rescue this
lapse by representing these words as a vocative, "Here is the spear, king," but
the *qeri*, or pronounced Masoretic version, properly renders it as *hanit
hamelekh*, "the king's spear.") In the encounter at the cave, David vowed he
would not harm Saul's descendants, though his actual words were not
reported. Here, he first gives an impersonal order to have the spear brought
back to Saul. It is only when he goes on to recapitulate his profession of innocence that he again addresses Saul. By this point, he no longer trusts any
promises Saul may make not to harm him but hopes that God will note his
own proper conduct and therefore protect him (verse 24).

24. *I valued your life highly.* The literal Hebrew idiom is "your life was great in
my eyes."

25. *Blessed are you, my son, David.* These words of fatherly blessing are the last
ones Saul speaks to David: the two never meet again. It is notable that in their
previous encounter, Saul explicitly conceded that David would replace him as
king, whereas here he merely says in general language, "You shall surely do
much and you shall surely win out."
    David went on his way but Saul returned to his place. This is a biblical for-
mula for marking the end of a narrative unit, but it also nicely distinguishes
between the two men: David continues on the move while Saul goes back to
his set place of residence.

CHAPTER 27

¹ And David said in his heart, "Now, I shall perish one day by the hand of Saul. There is nothing better for me than to make certain I get away to Philistine country. Then Saul will despair of seeking me anymore through all the territory of Israel, and I shall get away from him." And ² David arose, and he crossed over, he and the six hundred men who ³ were with him, to Achish son of Maoch, king of Gath. And David stayed with Achish in Gath, he and his men, each man with his household, David with his two wives, Ahinoam the Jezreelite and Abigail

---

1. *And David said in his heart.* This is the first actual interior monologue given for David. The decision to "cross over" (verse 2) to the enemy is a momentous one, and the writer wants to make it perfectly clear that David had definitively realized Saul was bound to kill him sooner or later ("I shall perish one day by the hand of Saul") unless he moved to the safety of enemy territory.

2. *he crossed over . . . to Achish . . . king of Gath.* For those scholars who have argued that David is no more a historical figure than King Arthur, this whole episode constitutes a problem: why would a much later, legendary, and supposedly glorifying tradition attribute this act of national treachery to David? (It would be rather like the invention of a story that Winston Churchill spent 1917–1918 in Berlin, currying the favor of the kaiser.) The compelling inference is that the writer had authentic knowledge of a period when David collaborated with the Philistines; he was unwilling to omit this uncomfortable information, though he did try to mitigate it.

3. *David stayed with Achish in Gath . . . each man with his household.* The circumstances have changed drastically since David arrived in Gath alone and was obliged to play the madman. Now he comes with six hundred men under his command, a fighting unit that could be of great use to Achish, and essentially offers to become Achish's vassal. The notice about the households sets the stage for the Amalekite raid on Ziklag in Chapter 29, for we now become aware that David's guerilla band carries in its train a sizable group of wives and children.

wife of Nabal the Carmelite. And it was told to Saul that David had 4
fled to Gath, and he no longer sought after him.

And David said to Achish, "If, pray, I have found favor in your eyes, let 5
them give me a place in one of the outlying towns that I may dwell
there. For why should your servant dwell in the royal town with you?"
And Achish gave him Ziklag on that day. Therefore has Ziklag belonged 6
to the kings of Judah until this day. And the span of time that David 7
dwelled in Philistine country was a year and four months.

And David went up, and his men with him, and they raided the Geshu- 8
rite and the Gerizite and the Amalekite, for they were the inhabitants of the land of old, till you come to Shur and to the land of Egypt.

---

5. *For why should your servant dwell in the royal town with you?* On his part,
David would like to establish his own headquarters and enjoy much greater
freedom of movement. But given that his six hundred men with multiple
wives and children could easily have made up a group of two or three thousand people, they would have in fact been a rather burdensome presence in a
modest-sized Philistine city.

6. *Ziklag.* The best archeological guess is that this is a site a few miles to the
northwest of Beersheba, in an area under Philistine jurisdiction but facing the
border with Israel

Therefore has Ziklag belonged to the kings of Judah. This seemingly technical geopolitical notice serves a function of historical foreshadowing, as
Fokkelman observes: David, the Philistine vassal and fugitive from Saul, is
destined to found a lasting dynasty, "the kings of Judah."

8. *for they were the inhabitants of the land of old till you come to Shur.* There
might be a textual distortion here: several versions of the Septuagint read
"the inhabited land from Telem to Shur." But the Masoretic version has a
certain logic: what David sets out to do is to attack the age-old inhabitants
of the land, who are Israel's staunch enemies, throughout this southern
region. In doing this, he is also serving Achish's purposes, for these peoples
are also hostile to the Philistines (like the Israelites, latecomer interlopers in
Canaan).

9 And David struck the land, and he left not a man or woman alive, and he took sheep and cattle and donkeys and camels and clothes, and he

10 returned and came to Achish. And Achish said, "Where were you raiding now?" And David said, "The Negeb of Judah and the Negeb of the

11 Jerhahmeelite and the Negeb of the Kenite." And neither man nor woman did David leave alive to bring to Gath, thinking, "Lest they tell about us saying, 'Thus did David do.'" And such was his practice all

12 the time he dwelled in Philistine country. And Achish trusted David, saying, "He has surely become repugnant to Israel and he will be my perpetual vassal."

---

9. *he left not a man or woman alive.* The narrator offers no indication of whether he thinks these massacres are morally objectionable or merely what Israel's traditional enemies deserve. A pragmatic reason for the butchery will be given in verse 11. It should be noted that David is not carrying out a "ban" (*ḥerem*) against these groups because he keeps all the livestock as booty, thus palpably building up a base of wealth for himself and his followers.

10. *Where were you raiding now?* Achish of course wants to know about the military activities of his vassal. David answers with a flat lie, claiming he has been conducting raids against his own tribe, Judah, and against two ethnic groups more or less attached to Judah. In fact, he has been attacking only non-Israelite groups.

the Negeb. The term Negeb means "dry land" and refers to the desert stretching across southern Israel from near the Dead Sea to near the coastal plain. Its subregions are then identified by the tribe or ethnic group that inhabits each.

11. *Lest they tell about us, saying, 'Thus did David do.'* David wipes out all these populations because he wants no one surviving to bring word back to Gath that he has restricted his attacks entirely to Canaanite and related peoples, and also that he has been enriching himself with more booty than he has been sharing with Achish his overlord by way of tribute. David is clearly a man who will do anything to survive. His words here will come back in a surprising new context in his elegy for Saul and Jonathan, when he says, "Tell it not in Gath."

12. *Achish trusted David.* He believes the lie, or so it seems.

my perpetual vassal. The Hebrew *ʿeved* has the general meaning of "slave" or "servant," but the present episode makes the sense of "vassal" compelling.

And it happened at that time that the Philistines had gathered their   28:1
ranks for the army to do battle with Israel, and Achish said to David,
"You surely know that with me you must sally forth in the ranks, both
you and your men." And David said, "Then you yourself know what   2
your servant will do." And Achish said to David, "Then I shall make you
my bodyguard for life."

28:1. *You surely know that with me you must sally forth.* Despite the just
reported "trust" in David, Achish appears to harbor a lingering doubt (hence
the coercive edge of "you surely know") as to whether David will actually fight
against his fellow Israelites, something that, to Achish's knowledge, David has
only claimed to do (27:10).

2. *you yourself know what your servant will do.* This is an artful dodge: it could
be construed, as David means it to be construed, as "yes, of course, I'll do it,"
but the language evasively does not repeat Achish's words about sallying forth
(against Israel).

   I shall make you my bodyguard for life. As befits a ruler addressing a former
enemy with whom he is in uneasy alliance, Achish's gesture is a studied ambiguity—either he is rewarding David for his loyalty by making him a permanent
bodyguard, or he is seeking to maintain surveillance over David by an appointment that would keep him close to the court.

CHAPTER 28

3 And Samuel had died, and all Israel mourned him, and they buried him in Ramah, in his town. And Saul had taken away the ghosts and the familiar spirits from the land.

4 And the Philistines gathered and came and camped at Shunem. And
5 Saul gathered all Israel and they camped at Gilboa. And Saul saw the Philistine camp, and he was afraid, and his heart trembled greatly.

---

3. *And Samuel had died.* This second obituary notice for Samuel, with a pluperfect verb, is introduced in order to set the stage for the conjuration of Samuel's ghost.

4. *Saul had taken away the ghosts and the familiar spirits from the land.* The two Hebrew terms, ʾovot and yidʿonim, are generally paired, and both refer to the spirits of the dead. (The latter is derived from the verbal root y-d-ʿ, "to know," and so prepares the way for the reappearance of the theme of [withheld] knowledge that has been stalking Saul from the beginning of his story.) The ghosts and familiar spirits are linked metonymically with the necromancers who call them up—it is the latter who of course would have been the actual object of Saul's purge—but the terms themselves primarily designate the spirits. Biblical views about post-mortem existence tend to fluctuate. Often, the dead are thought to be swallowed up in "the Pit" (*sheʾol*) where they are simply silenced, extinguished forever. Sometimes, the dead are imagined as continuing a kind of shadowy afterlife in the underworld, rather like the spirits of the dead in Book 11 of the Odyssey. Following on this latter view, necromancy in the ancient Hebrew world is conceived not as mere hocus pocus but as a potentially efficacious technology of the realm of spirits which, however, has been prohibited by God, Who wants no human experts interfering in this realm. Saul, then, has been properly upholding monotheistic law—reflected in Leviticus—in proscribing necromancy, but in his desperation, he is now about to violate his own prohibition.

And Saul inquired of the LORD, and the LORD did not answer him, 6
neither by dreams nor by the Urim nor by prophets. And Saul said 7
to his servants, "Seek me out a ghostwife, that I may go to her
and inquire through her." And his servants said to him, "There is a
ghostwife at En-dor." And Saul disguised himself and put on differ- 8
ent clothes, and he went—he together with two men—and they
came to the woman by night, and he said, "Conjure me, pray, a ghost,
and summon up the one I say to you." And the woman said to him, 9
"Look, you yourself know what Saul did, that he cut off the ghosts
and the familiar spirits from the land, and why do you entrap me
to have me put to death?" And Saul swore to her by the LORD, say- 10
ing, "As the LORD lives, no blame will befall you through this thing."

---

6. *the* LORD *did not answer.* One last time, Saul is excluded from divine knowledge, all the accepted channels for its conveyance being enumerated here—
dream interpretation, oracular device, prophecy.

8. *Saul disguised himself and put on different clothes.* The narrative motivation
is obvious: as the very ruler who has made necromancy a capital crime (see
verse 9), Saul can scarcely come to engage the services of a necromancer
unless he is disguised as a commoner. But his disguise also is the penultimate
instance of the motif of royal divestment. As we have seen, clothing is associated with Saul's kingship—the torn or cut garment is the tearing of his kingship, and among the ecstatics surrounding Samuel, Saul stripped himself
naked. Now, in an unwitting symbolic gesture, he divests himself of his royal
garments before going to learn of his own impending death.

9. *you yourself know.* An ironically emphatic use of "to know" to the man who
never knows what he needs to.
    he cut off the ghosts. In place of the more abstract term, "to take away," used
by the narrator in verse 3, she, from her perspective as a threatened practi-
tioner, chooses the violent verb, "to cut off."
    why do you entrap me. She uses the verb of entrapment with neat precision,
for she fears that the stranger who has come to her may be an undercover
agent for Saul's necromancy enforcement authority.

10. *Saul swore to her by the* LORD. The irony of Saul's doing this in a negotiation with a conjurer of spirits is vividly caught by the Midrash: "Whom did
Saul resemble at that moment? A woman who is with her lover and swears by
the life of her husband" (Yalkut Shimoni 2:247:139).

11 And the woman said, "Whom shall I summon up for you?" And he
12 said, "Samuel summon up for me." And the woman saw Samuel and
 she screamed in a loud voice, and the woman said to Saul, "Why did
13 you deceive me, when you are Saul?" And the king said to her, "Do not
 fear. But what do you see?" And the woman said to Saul, "A god do I
14 see rising up from the earth." And he said to her, "What does he look

---

12. *the woman saw Samuel and she screamed in a loud voice.* What terrifies her
is not the apparition of Samuel but the sudden realization of the identity of
her nocturnal visitor. How does she know it is Saul? The most persuasive
explanation has been offered by Moshe Garsiel. As other biblical references
to conjuration of the dead suggest, the usual method would be for the necromancer to listen to and interpret the supposed "chirping" (*tsiftsuf*) or murmuring sounds made by shadows or wispy wraiths believed to be the presences of
the dead. (There is scant biblical evidence for the claim that the necromancer
was a medium from whose throat the ghost spoke.) In this case, however, the
spirit appears not as a murmuring wisp or shadow but as the distinctly defined
image of Samuel, in his prophet's cloak (see verses 13–14), and the woman of
En-dor immediately realizes that it is only for the king that the prophet
Samuel would have thus risen from the underworld in full-body image. It is
noteworthy that the narrator is discreetly silent about the actual mechanics of
the conjuration procedure, perhaps out of a kind of monotheistic reticence.

13. *Do not fear. But what did you see?* Saul assures her that even though he is
the very king who prohibited necromancy, he will stand by his vow that no
blame will be attached to her. What he urgently wants to know is the identity
of the conjured presence—she can see the spirit, but he cannot, so once more
Saul needs some mediation for the knowledge he seeks.
 A god do I see rising up from the earth. The Hebrew balances precariously
on a linguistic ambiguity that has no happy English equivalent. The word for
"god" here is *ʾelohim*, which when treated gramatically as a singular (it has a
plural ending) usually means God. In the plural, it often refers to "gods" in the
polytheistic sense. It also occasionally means "angel" or "divine being," and
there are a few usages in which it evidently refers to a judge. A further complication here is that the ghostwife uses *ʾelohim* with a plural participle (and
hence the King James Version renders it as "gods"). It seems likely that the
grammatical crossover we have just reviewed encouraged a fluidity of usage in
which the plural might sometimes be employed with a singular sense, even
when the referent was not the one God. In the immediately following question and response between Saul and the woman, it is presupposed that she
has seen only one male figure, and the narrator has already told us she has

like?" And she said, "An old man rises up, and he is wrapped in a cloak." And Saul knew that it was Samuel, and he bowed to the ground and did obeisance. And Samuel said, "Why have you troubled me to summon me up?" And Saul said, "I am in dire straits, and the Philistines are fighting against me and God has turned away from me and no longer answers me, neither through prophets nor dreams, and I called to you to let me know what I should do." And Samuel said, "And why do you ask me, when the LORD has turned away from you and

15

16

---

seen Samuel. When she says she sees ˀelohim rising up, she probably means an imposing figure like unto a god or an angel, or perhaps she is using it as a term for "spirit."

14. *wrapped in a cloak.* It is the cloak, meˁil, that clinches the identification for Saul—the same prophet's cloak that he clung to and tore. From childhood, when Samuel's mother would make him a new meˁil each year, to the grave, Samuel is associated with this garment.

15. *Why have you troubled me . . . ?* In perfect character, Samuel begins by addressing an angry question to Saul, using a verb that refers to disturbing a person from sleep, or from the sleep of death. In divergence from the usual necromantic procedure, the ghost of Samuel speaks directly to Saul, who in turn questions Samuel himself. In fact, the ghostwife appears to have absented herself at this point, for the indication in verse 21, "And the woman came to Saul and saw that he was very distraught," is that she is returning to the room—or perhaps to an outdoor location alongside the house—after having left it.

I am in dire straits, and the Philistines are fighting . . . and God has turned away . . . and I called you. The desperate Saul spills out all the causes for his desperation in one breathless run-on sentence, which this translation tries to reproduce.

neither through prophets nor dreams. Addressing a prophet, Saul makes prophecy the first item. He deletes the Urim—perhaps, it has been suggested, because of his guilty recollection of his massacre of the priests at Nob.

16. *Why do you ask me . . . ?* Once again, in this case sardonically, there is a play on Saul's name (Shaˀul) and the verb "to ask" (shaˀal).

17 become your foe? And the LORD has done to you as He spoke through me, and the LORD has torn the kingship from your hand and given it to
18 your fellowman, to David. Inasmuch as you did not heed the voice of the LORD and you did not carry out His burning wrath against Amalek,
19 therefore has the LORD done this thing to you this day! And the LORD shall give Israel, too, together with you, into the hands of the Philistines. And tomorrow—you and your sons are with me. The camp of Israel, too, shall the LORD give into the hand of the Philistines."

---

17. *the LORD has torn the kingdom from your hand.* As this particular clause highlights, Samuel's entire speech is a recapitulation of the denunciatory speech he made to Saul at the end of the Amalek episode (Chapter 15). The tearing of the kingdom "from your hand" visually recalls Saul's hand grasping the torn skirt of Samuel's cloak. There, Samuel had said God would give the throne to "your fellowman, who is better than you." Now, of course, he can spell out the name David.

18. *you did not heed the voice of the LORD.* The phrasal motif of "heeding the voice" from Chapter 15 is again invoked. After Samuel's return to the underworld, the woman of En-dor, on a purely mundane plane, will speak twice about heeding voices (verses 21–22).

19. *and tomorrow—you and your sons are with me.* Saul, having come to seek advice on the eve of a great battle, is given a denunciation concluding with a death sentence, conveyed in these words with spooky immediacy, as the ghost of Samuel beckons Saul and his sons down into the underworld. This entire scene is conceivably one of the inspirations for Macbeth's encounter with the three witches, though the biblical writer, in contrast to Shakespeare, places it at the penultimate moment of his doomed king's story.

   The camp of Israel, too . . . There is no need to perform textual surgery on this sentence simply because it repeats the burden of the first sentence of the verse. It would be perfectly in character for Samuel to rub in the news of the imminent catastrophe: not only will you and your sons perish, but, as I have said, all your forces will be defeated by the Philistines, your kingship ending in wholesale failure.

And Saul hastened and flung himself full length on the ground   20
and was very frightened by Samuel's words. Neither did he have
strength, for he had eaten no food all day and all night. And the   21
woman came to Saul and saw that he was very distraught, and she
said to him, "Look, your servant has heeded your voice, and I took my
life in my hands and heeded your words that you spoke to me.
And now, you on your part, pray heed the voice of your servant, and I   22
shall put before you a morsel of bread, and eat, that you may have
strength when you go on the way." And he refused and said, "I will not   23
eat." And his servants pressed him, and the woman as well, and he
heeded their voice and arose from the ground and sat upon the couch.

---

20. *Saul hastened and flung himself full length on the ground.* Most translators
have interpreted the second verb here as an involuntary one ("fell"). But the
verb "to hasten" *(miher)* is generally part of a sequence of voluntary actions, as
its use in verse 24 ("and she hastened and butchered it and took") neatly illustrates. Saul, in his terror and despair, flings himself to the ground, and then
scarcely has the strength to get up. The Hebrew for "full length" includes the
component *qomah*, "stature," and so is a reminder that the man of majestic
stature is now cast to the ground in final defeat.

21. *for he had eaten no food.* There is no convincing evidence to support the
claim of some scholars that a person had to fast before seeing a necromancer.
Perhaps Saul's fasting is a reflex of his distraught condition, but he may well
be fasting because he is about to enter into battle. (It appears that his two
bodyguards have also not eaten.) This would invite a connection, which has
been made by both Fokkelman and Garsiel, with the vow of abstinence from
food that Saul earlier imposed on his troops (Chapter 14). There, he was ready
to put Jonathan to death for having tasted a bit of honey; here, he will end by
partaking of a feast.

22. *a morsel of bread.* She says this to play down what she will serve him, which
is a hearty dinner, with a main course of veal.

24 And the woman had a stall-fed calf in the house. And she hastened and butchered it and took flour and kneaded it and baked it into flat bread,
25 and set it before Saul and before his servants, and they ate, and they arose and went off on that night.

---

24. *the woman had a stall-fed calf.* It would have taken several of hours to accomplish this slaughtering and cooking and baking. One must imagine Saul sitting in the house at En-dor, brooding or darkly baffled or perhaps a little catatonic. It is an odd and eerie juncture of the story. David has already twice been saved, from death and then from blood guilt, by women. Saul is now given sustaining nurture by a woman—but only to regain the strength needed to go out to the battlefield where he will die.

CHAPTER 29

And the Philistines gathered all their camps at Aphek, while Israel 1
was encamped by the spring in Jezreel. And the Philistine 2
overlords were advancing with hundreds and with thousands,
and David and his men were advancing at the rear with Achish.

---

1. *the Philistines gathered all their camps at Aphek.* The "all" stresses that this is
a massing of the entire Philistine army, not merely a division or two, for a decisive confrontation with the Israelites. As Polzin notes, the first major clash
with the Philistines in 1 Samuel began with the Philistines' camping at Aphek
(4:1), so the mention of their encampment here at the same site creates a kind
of symmetrical frame for the book. Aphek is roughly forty miles south of
Jezreel, not far from Philistine territory, and would have served as a general
staging ground. The Philistine army then advances northward to camp at
Shunem (27:4), just opposite Saul's forces at the spring of Jezreel and near
Mount Gilboa.

2. *David and his men were advancing at the rear with Achish.* Given David's
double role as Achish's vassal and as his special bodyguard, his position in battle would have been alongside Achish. Until this mention of David, we might
have imagined that the report of the deployment of forces was a direct continuation of the account of Saul's seance at En-dor on the night before the battle.
Now it rapidly becomes clear that the narrative has again switched tracks
from Saul to David, suspending the fulfillment of Saul's dire fate in order to
follow the movement of his successor, who approaches the very same battlefield as part of the enemy forces, only to be turned away. The switch in narrative focus also involves backtracking in time: we left Saul in the dark of the
night (also a symbolic darkness for him); the deployment of armies and the
Philistine dialogues take place on the previous day; David's early departure,
"just when it is brightening" (an antithesis to Saul in the dark, as Fokkelman
notes), will be on the morning of the battle.

3 And the Philistine captains said, "Who are these Hebrews?" And
Achish said to the Philistine captains, "Is this not David, servant of
Saul king of Israel, who has been with me these many days or years,
and I have found nothing amiss in him from the day he fell in with me
4 until this day." And the Philistine captains were enraged with him, and
the Philistine captains said to him, "Send the man back and let him go
back to his place that you set aside for him there, and let him not come
down with us into battle, so that he become not our adversary in battle.
For how would this fellow be reconciled with his master—would it not
5 be with the heads of our men? Is this not David for whom they sing out
in the dances, saying,

'Saul has struck down his thousands,
    and David his tens of thousands'?"

---

3. *the Philistine captains.* These are the military commanders, *sarim,* and they
should not be thought of as synonymous with the overlords (*seranim*) of the
five Philistine cities. It is the military men who, understandably, fear a serious
security risk in the presence of a Hebrew contingent in their ranks.

Who are these Hebrews? The Hebrew is literally "What are these
Hebrews?", which many translations interpret as "What are these Hebrews
doing here?" Again, "Hebrews" is the term used by foreigners for the Israelites.

David, servant of Saul king of Israel. Achish means to stress that Saul's former courtier and commander has defected to the Philistine side, but his
choice of words inadvertently reminds the Philistine captains that David may
still be loyal to Saul.

these many days or years. Some scholars suspect that these two terms reflect
a conflated text, and that one should simply read "these many days." It could,
however, make sense for Achish to be a little vague about the time and to
exaggerate it in order to emphasize David's loyalty—in fact, David has been
with him one year and two months.

fell in with me. Kyle McCarter, Jr. proposes that the verb has the sense of
"to defect."

4. *would it not be with the heads of our men?* They actually use a euphemism,
"the heads of these men," in order to avoid pronouncing a terrible fate on
themselves. Perhaps another euphemism is involved, through upward displacement, since in Chapter 18 it was a different part of the anatomy of the
slain Philistines that David brought back to Saul.

And Achish called to David and said to him, "As the LORD lives, you 6
are upright, and your going into the fray with the camp has been good
in my eyes, for I have found no evil in you from the day you came to me
until this day. But in the eyes of the Philistine overlords you are
not good. And so now, return, and go in peace, and you shall do no 7
evil in the eyes of the Philistine overlords." And David said to 8
Achish, "But what have I done, and what have you found in your servant from the day I appeared in your presence until this day, that I
should not come and do battle with the enemies of my lord the king?"

---

6. *as the* LORD *lives.* It is curious that a Philistine should be swearing by the
LORD, unless, as has been argued, he is leaning over backward to adopt
David's perspective.

you are upright. In fact, David has been lying to Achish about the object of
his raids (27:8–11).

good in my eyes . . . I have found no evil in you. This entire exchange turns
on the neat antithesis between good and evil, rather like the exchange
between Saul and David outside the cave near En-gedi. Achish will go on to
say, quite extravagantly, that David is "as good in my eyes as a messenger of
God" (verse 9). The reader, however, may well wonder whether David is in
fact so unambiguously good.

in the eyes of the Philistine overlords you are not good. Some scholars, following the Septuagint, read here "you are good," contending that Achish claims a
difference of opinion between the overlords and the captains. It makes better
sense simply to assume that he is referring the negative view of David to the
highest echelon of authority, though in fact the complaint came from the field
commanders.

8. *from the day I appeared in your presence.* The idiomatic force of the phrase
is, "from the day I entered your service." Achish had simply said, "from the day
you came to me."

*what have I done . . . that I should not . . . do battle with the enemies of my
lord the king.* Continuing to play the role of the perfect Philistine vassal,
David protests his eagerness to fight the Israelites, though in point of fact he
must be immensely relieved to escape from the intolerable position of battling
against his own people. As several interpreters have noticed, the words he
archly chooses have a double edge because "my lord the king" could be a
covert reference to Saul, in which case the "enemies" would be the armies of
Achish and his confederates. Whether David, lacking this providential way
out, would really have pitted himself against his own people is another imponderable in the character of this elusive figure.

9 And Achish answered and said to David, "I know that you are as good in my eyes as a messenger of God. But the Philistine captains have
10 said, 'He shall not go up with us to battle.' And so now, rise early in the morning, you and the servants of your lord who have come with you,
11 and rise early in the morning when it is just brightening, and go." And David rose early, he and his men, to go in the morning to return to Philistine country, while the Philistines went up to Jezreel.

---

10. *you and the servants of your lord.* The translation follows the reading in the Septuagint. The Masoretic Text, a little less coherently, lacks "you."

11. *to Philistine country.* They are in fact headed to the place Achish has "set aside" for them at the eastern border of Philistine country—the town of Ziklag. Disaster awaits them there.

CHAPTER 30

And it happened when David and his men came to Ziklag on the third day, that the Amalekites had raided the Negeb, and Ziklag, and they had struck Ziklag and burned it to the ground. And they had taken the women captive, from the youngest to the oldest, they put no one to death.

---

1. *on the third day.* If, as seems plausible, David and his men were sent away from the Philistine ranks just before the engagement with the Israelites, the battle, ending in the catastrophic defeat of Saul's forces, took place while David was traveling southward. The writer, it seems, wants to get David as far away as he can from the battlefield in the Valley of Jezreel, perhaps to remove him from any possible implication in Saul's death. But an indirect question lurks in the margin of the narrative, for we are left to wonder what would have been the outcome of the battle had David turned against his Philistine allies, as their field commanders feared he would.

the Amalekites had raided the Negeb and Ziklag. David must initially confront a military disaster on his own home front that mirrors the disaster which, unknown to him, has unfolded in the north. His habitual enemies, the Amalekites, have of course exploited the absence of the fighting men at Ziklag.

burned it to the ground. The Hebrew is literally "burned it in fire." "In fire" is quite frequently attached to the verb "to burn" in biblical usage—the apparent nuance of meaning is to indicate that the object of the burning is entirely consumed.

2. *they put no one to death.* At first blush this notice casts a favorable light on the Amalekites in comparison to David, whose practice as a raider has been general massacre of the conquered population. What becomes clear, however, is that the Amalekites (who do not have David's motive of secrecy) consider the women and children to be part of the booty and have carried them off in order to exploit them as slaves. The appearance of the Egyptian man (verse 11) serves as a reminder of the Amalekites' role as slaveholders, and of how inhumanely they treat their slaves.

3 And they drove them off and went on their way. And David, and his
men with him, came to the town, and, look, it was burned to the
ground, and their wives and their sons and their daughters were taken

4 captive. And David, and the troops who were with him, raised their

5 voices and wept until there was no strength left in them to weep. And
David's two wives were taken captive, Ahinoam the Jezreelite and Abi-

6 gail wife of Nabal the Carmelite. And David was in dire straits, for the
troops thought to stone him, for all the troops were embittered, every
man over his sons and his daughters. And David took strength in the

7 LORD his God. And David said to Abiathar the priest, son of Ahimelech, "Bring forth, pray, the ephod." And Abiathar brought forth the

---

they drove them off. This rather brutal verb is typically used for driving
animals, as in verse 20, and so highlights the rapaciousness of the Amalekites.

6. *And David was in dire straits, for the troops thought to stone him.* The initial
phrase might momentarily be construed as referring to David's feelings ("and
he felt very distressed"), but it is immediately made clear that the reference is
to the practical predicament in which he suddenly finds himself in relation to
his men. As before, David's real emotions remain opaque—we know only of
his participation in the public orgy of weeping. This moment is also a vivid
reminder, as are others in the Saul-David story, of how precarious political
power is: David, the charismatic and brilliant commander who has led his
men through a host of dangers, suddenly discovers that these hard-bitten warriors are ready to kill him because of the disastrous turn of events. It was he,
after all, who drew them to the north with the Philistine army, leaving Ziklag
exposed.

David took strength in the LORD his God. He finds encouragement in the
face of mortal despair—specifically, as the next verse explains, by calling
for the oracle. In this fashion, he staves off the assault his men are contem-
plating by dramatically showing that they still have means of redress
against the Amalekites, and that he has a special channel of communication with God.

7. *Bring forth, pray, the ephod.* As several interpreters have observed, there is
an antithetical contrast here between David, who has priest and ephod to
convey to him God's oracular counsel, and Saul, who, frustrated in all his
attempts to discover God's intentions, resorts to forbidden necromancy.

ephod to David. And David inquired of the LORD, saying, "Shall I pursue   8
this raiding party? Shall I overtake it?" And He said, "Pursue, for you will
surely overtake it, and you will surely rescue." And David went, he and   9
the six hundred men who were with him, and they came to the Wadi
Besor, and those to be left stayed behind. And David continued the pur-   10
suit, he and four hundred men, and the two hundred men who were too
exhausted to cross the Wadi Besor stayed behind. And they found an   11
Egyptian man in the field and took him to David, and they gave him
bread and he ate, and they gave him water. And they gave him a slice of   12
pressed figs and two raisin cakes. And he ate, and his spirits revived, for
he had eaten no bread and drunk no water three days and three nights.

---

8. *you will surely rescue.* The ephod, as we have noted before, can yield only a
binary yes-or-no answer, so the gist of the oracle is that David should pursue
the raiding party. But rescuing the captives, which is surely paramount in the
minds of the embittered guerilla fighters, was not an explicit part of David's
inquiry of the oracle—perhaps because he was afraid to presume so much.
The "yes" from the oracle is now taken to imply that David and his men will
both overtake the raiders and rescue their dear ones.

9. *those to be left stayed behind.* The first phrase (literally, "the ones being left")
has bothered some commentators, but it is in keeping with occasional biblical
usage to introduce this sort of proleptic reference, creating what from a modern point of view is a redundancy between the first and second phrases.

10. *were . . . exhausted.* The verb *piger* may be related to the noun *peger,*
corpse, and so would have the sense of "dead tired." It should be kept in mind
that David and his men had been traveling three days from the Philistine
camp, and now they have had to continue on into the desert at top speed in
order to overtake the raiding party.

11. *they found an Egyptian man in the field.* This is the first of three memorable
instances in the David story in which a foreigner brings intelligence of a dire
event, although in this case the subject of the intelligence is not the event
itself but the whereabouts of the perpetrators.

12. *for he had eaten no bread and drunk no water.* The act of abandoning a sick
slave in the desert to perish of thirst and hunger dispels any illusions we may
have harbored about the humanity of the Amalekites. Fokkelman has proposed a correspondence (in his calculation, also a synchronicity) between the
starving Egyptian and the fasting Saul at En-dor.

13 And David said to him, "To whom do you belong, and where are you from?" And he said, "I am an Egyptian lad, the slave of an Amalekite man, and my master abandoned me, for I have been sick now three

14 days. We on our part had raided the Negeb of the Cherethites and that of Judah and the Negeb of Caleb, and Ziklag we burned to the

15 ground." And David said to him, "Will you lead me down to this raiding party?" And he said, "Swear to me by God that you will not put me to death and that you will not hand me over to my master. Then I shall

16 lead you down to this raiding party." And he led him down, and, look, they were sprawled out all over the ground eating and drinking and reveling with all the vast booty they had taken from the land of the

17 Philistines and the land of Judah. And David struck them from daybreak till the evening of the next day, and not a man of them got away

18 except for four hundred lads who rode off on camels and fled. And David rescued all that the Amalekites had taken, and his own two

19 wives David rescued. And nothing of theirs was missing, from the youngest to the oldest, from sons to daughters to booty, all that they

---

13. *I am an Egyptian lad.* The term "lad" (*naᶜar*) does not necessarily indicate chronological age here but rather subservient status, a decorous synonym for "slave," which the Egyptian proceeds to use.

16. *and, look, they were sprawled out.* The presentative "look" (*hineh*) as an indicator of transition from the narrator's overview to the character's point of view has particular tactical importance here. The Amalekites, as we can infer from the fact that four hundred escape the general slaughter, must number well over a thousand. David arrives with only four hundred men. But he finds the raiders entirely vulnerable to a surprise attack—drunk, sated, and sleeping (rather like the Hessian mercenaries whom Washington caught unawares by the Delaware after their Christmas feast). The term rendered as "sprawled out" (*netushim*) derives from a verbal root that means to abandon or cast away, and so in this context suggests some kind of dissipation. The people who left the Egyptian to starve to death in the desert are now exposed to destruction through their unrestrained indulgence in food and drink.

17. *four hundred lads.* Again, the versatile *naᶜar* is not an indication of chronological age but is used in its military sense, which appears to be something like "elite troops," or perhaps simply "fighting men."

had taken for themselves, David restored it all. And David took all the   20
sheep and the cattle. They drove before them that livestock and said,
"This is David's booty."

And David came to the two hundred men who had been too exhausted   21
to go with David, so he had them stay at the Wadi Besor. And they
came out to greet David and to greet the troops who were with him,
and David approached with the troops and asked how they fared. And   22
every wicked and worthless man of the men who had gone with David
spoke up and said, "Inasmuch as they did not go with us, we will give
them nothing from the booty that we rescued, only each man his wife
and his children, that they may drive them off and go." And David said,   23
"You must not do so, my brothers, with what the LORD has given us.

---

20. *They drove before them that livestock.* The Masoretic Text has the syntactically problematic "before that livestock" (*lifney hamiqneh hahu³*). This translation is based on a small emendation, *lifneyhem* ("before them"), assuming a
haplography—an inadvertent scribal deletion of repeated letters, since the
last two letters of *lifneyhem* (*heh* and *mem*) are also the first two letters of
hamiqneh.

   This is David's booty. Since the Amalekites had been raiding throughout the
Negeb, both in Judahite and Philistine territory, they would have assembled a
very large collection of plundered flocks. Thus David has abundant livestock
to distribute as "gifts"—the word also means "blessing" or "greeting"—to the
sundry elders of Judah.

21. *he had them stay.* The Masoretic Text has "they had them stay" (a difference
of one vowel). The Septuagint has the singular subject.

22. *that they may drive them off.* The coarseness of the ill-spirited men is
reflected in the verb they use for taking away the wives and children, *nahag,*
which, as we have noted, usually means to drive cattle. (Compare the irate
Lot's use of the same verb in reference to Jacob's treatment of Rachel and
Leah, Genesis 31:26.)

23. *with what the LORD has given us.* The syntactical link of this clause with
what precedes is not entirely clear. Given the ideology of victory that David
assumes—all triumph and all spoils of war come from God—it is best to construe the particle *³et* that introduces the clause not as a sign of the accusative
but as "with."

For He has guarded us and has given into our hands the raiding party
24 that came against us. And who would listen to you in this matter?
Rather, as the share of him who goes down into battle is the share of
25 him who stays with the gear—together shall they share." And so from
26 that day hence it became a set practice in Israel until this day. And
David came to Ziklag and he sent from the booty to the elders of Judah,
to his friends, saying, "Here is a gift for you from the booty of the
27 LORD's enemies." to those in Bethel, and to those in Ramoth-negeb,
28 and to those in Jattir, and to those in Aroer, and to those in Siphmoth,
29 and to those in Eshtomea, and to those in Racal, and to those in the
30 towns of the Jerahmeelite, and to those in the towns of the Kenite, and
to those in Hormah, and to those in Bor-ashan, and to those in Athach,
31 and to those in Hebron and in all the places where David, with his
men, had moved about.

---

24. *who stays with the gear.* There is an implicit rationale for giving an equal
share to those who remain behind—beyond the consideration of exhaustion,
they have played a role in guarding the gear, thus enabling the other fighting
men to proceed to battle with a lightened load. It is for this reason that David
"had them stay" (or "posted them") at the ford of the wadi. In all respects, this
episode is meant to demonstrate David's attributes as leader: he finds strength
in the face of disaster, consults God's oracle, intrepidly leads his troops in a
counterattack, and now makes the most equitable arrangement for the division of spoils.

26. *he sent from the booty to the elders of Judah, to his friends.* This act shows
David the consummate political man, shoring up support among the sundry
leaders of his home tribe of Judah (hence the catalogue of place-names), and
preparing for himself a base in Hebron (at the end of the catalogue), the principal town of Judah, where he will soon be proclaimed king. Some scholars
have been troubled by "to his friends" (*lereïeihu,* which would normally mean
"to his friend") and have sought to emend it. Kimchi, however, persuasively
argues that the ostensibly singular noun can be legitimately read as a plural on
the basis of other biblical precedents, and that the reference to "friends" makes
good political sense: these are the same elders of Judah who provided cover for
David during the period when he was hiding out from Saul in his own tribal
territory. The verb "move about" (*hithalekh*) in the wrap-up verse of this section
is an allusion to precisely this period, for it recalls David's flight with his men
from Saul at Keilah in 23:13—"and they moved about wherever they could."

CHAPTER 31

And meanwhile the Philistines were battling against Israel, and the men 1
of Israel fled before the Philistines, and they fell slain on Mount
Gilboa. And the Philistines followed hard upon Saul and his sons, and 2
the Philistines struck down Jonathan and Abinadav and Malkishua, the
sons of Saul. And the battle went heavy against Saul, and the archers, 3
the bowmen, found him, and he quaked with fear of the archers.

---

1. *and meanwhile the Philistines were battling.* The Hebrew does not explicitly
say "meanwhile," but it is implied by the unusual use of the participial form of
the verb (literally, "are battling") to begin the narrative unit. Rashi neatly catches
the effect: "As when a person says, 'Let us return to the previous subject.'"

3. *the archers, the bowmen.* It has been argued that the duplication reflects a
conflation of two textual variants, but it may be that the writer intended to
highlight the use of the bow, in contrast to other weapons. In characteristic
biblical fashion, the narrative offers no details of the battle, but the following
broad outline can be reconstructed: The major engagement of forces takes
place in the Jezreel Valley, to the northwest of Mount Gilboa. The level
ground of the valley would have given the Philistines the opportunity to
deploy their iron chariots, one of their great strategic advantages over the
Israelites. In the rout of the Israelites that ensues, Saul's forces retreat to the
high ground of Mount Gilboa, where the Philistine chariots would have
greater difficulty maneuvering. But the Philistines send contingents of
archers—the bow being the ideal weapon to use against an army in flight—
who exact heavy casualties from the Israelite forces.

he quaked with fear. A revocalization of the verb favored by many scholars
yields "he was badly wounded." But there is much to be said for the Masoretic
vocalization: Saul's fear has been a recurring theme in the narrative; here it
would be matched by the armor bearer's great fear of violating the king; and it
is far from clear that Saul is seriously wounded when he decides to commit
suicide (if he were, would he have the strength to fling himself on his sword?).

4 And Saul said to his armor bearer, "Draw your sword and run me through with it, lest these uncircumcised come and run me through and abuse me." But the armor bearer did not want to do it because he 5 was very frightened, and Saul took the sword and fell upon it. And the armor bearer saw that Saul was dead, and he, too, fell upon his sword, 6 and he died with him. And Saul died, and his three sons and his armor 7 bearer, and all his men as well, together on that day. And the men of Israel who were on the other side of the valley and on the other side of the Jordan saw that the men of Israel had fled and that Saul and his sons were dead, and they abandoned the towns and fled, and the Philistines came and occupied them.

8 And it happened the next day that the Philistines came to strip the slain, and they found Saul and his three sons fallen on Mount 9 Gilboa. And they cut off his head and stripped him of his armor, and they

---

4. *and abuse me.* Like the urgent request of the dying Abimelech in Judges 9, with whom the dying Saul has sometimes been compared, Saul's last wish will be denied him—the Philistines, though deprived of the opportunity to kill him, will decapitate his body and defile it by hammering it up on the wall of Beth-shan.

6. *and all his men as well.* The parallel texts in both 1 Chronicles 10 and in the Septuagint lack this phrase. The argument for it is that it reinforces the image of martial solidarity in defeat: Saul, his sons, his armor bearer, his men, all perish "together" (*yaḥdaw*).

7. *they abandoned the towns . . . and the Philistines came and occupied them.* After this major victory, the Philistines manage to cut the Israelite settlement in two by establishing a sedentary presence across the lower Galilee from the coastal plain to the Jordan, separating the tribes in the far north from Benjamin and Judah to the south.

9. *they cut off his head and stripped him of his armor.* Saul's successor David had marked his entry on the scene by cutting off the head of a Philistine; now they cut off Saul's head. The stripping of the armor—and the all-purpose Hebrew *kelim* could also include his clothing—is the final divestment of Saul, who is stripped before the prophets, stripped of his royal garments at En-dor, and now lies naked on the battlefield in ultimate defeat.

sent throughout the Philistine country to bring the tidings to the temples of their idols and to the people. And they put his armor in the temple of   10
Ashtaroth, and his body they impaled on the wall of Beth-shan. And   11
the inhabitants of Jabesh-gilead heard what the Philistines had done to Saul. And every valiant fellow arose, and they went all night long, and   12
they took Saul's corpse, and the corpses of his sons from the wall of Beth-shan, and they came back to Jabesh and burned them there.

---

they sent throughout the Philistine Country. There is some grammatical ambiguity as to whether they simply sent tidings, or Saul's armor as visible token of the victory. The parallel verse in Chronicles lacks "temples of."

10. *his body they impaled on the wall of Beth-shan.* Throughout the ancient Mediterranean world, there was a horror about leaving a corpse unburied (compare, for example, the potency of this question in Sophocles' *Antigone*). Saul's corpse, moreover, is disfigured through decapitation. Beth-shan (or, Beth-sheʾan) is a town about eleven miles to the southwest of Mount Gilboa, near the Jordan.

11. *the inhabitants of Jabesh-gilead.* This settlement is roughly another twelve miles to the southwest of Beth-shan, on the eastern side of the Jordan, and hence just beyond the perimeter of the new Philistine occupation. It was Jabesh-gilead that Saul rescued from Nahash the Ammonite (Chapter 11) to inaugurate his career as king and general, and there are kinship bonds between Jabesh-gilead and Saul's tribe of Benjamin.

12. *every valiant fellow arose.* It would have been a very dangerous exploit to sneak into the territory now controlled by the Philistines and, under the cover of night, to make off with the corpses.
   the corpses of his sons. This is an amplification of the Philistine atrocity, since we were not previously informed that the bodies of the sons were impaled along with Saul's.
   and burned them there. Cremation was not the usual Israelite practice, but it may be, as Kimchi has proposed, that in this case the bodies were burned because the flesh had already begun to rot.

13   And they took their bones and buried them under the tamarisk in
Jabesh, and they fasted seven days.

---

13. *and they fasted seven days.* This, too, is an unusual practice as a mourning
rite. Perhaps it merely reflects the grievousness of the loss that the men of
Jabesh-gilead have experienced, though Fokkelman makes the interesting
proposal that the seven days of fasting are a counterpart to the seven days
Nahash the Ammonite allowed Jabesh-gilead for a deliverer (who turned out
to be Saul) to appear.

2 SAMUEL

CHAPTER 1

And it happened after the death of Saul, when David had returned from
striking down Amalek, that David stayed in Ziklag two days. And it
happened on the third day that, look, a man was coming from the
camp, from Saul, his clothes torn and earth on his head. And it happened when he came to David, that he fell to the ground and did obeisance. And David said to him, "From where do you come?" And he
said, "From the camp of Israel I have gotten away." And David said to
him "What has happened? Pray, tell me." And he said, "The troops fled
from the battle, and also many of the troops have fallen and died, and
also Saul and Jonathan his son died." And David said to the lad who
was telling him, "How do you know that Saul died, and Jonathan his

1

2

3

4

5

---

1. *after the death of Saul . . . David had returned from striking down Amalek.* As
the story unfolds, an odd symmetry emerges: David has just struck down
Amalek; an Amalekite says he has struck down Saul; David has this Amalekite
put to death.

2. *look, a man was coming . . . his clothes torn and earth on his head.* The "look"
signals the visual perspective of David and his entourage: what they see is a man
who has adopted the most visible signs of conventional mourning. The
Amalekite wants to make it clear that he regards Saul's death, and the defeat, as
a catastrophe, though, as we shall see, he really has another purpose in mind.

4. *What has happened?* The words he uses, *meh hayah hudavar,* are identical
with those spoken to the messenger who brings the news of the disastrous
defeat to Eli in 1 Samuel 4:16. There are several other echoes here of that earlier scene.

5. *the lad who was telling him.* The triple repetition of this phrase, as Fokkelman has noted, calls attention to the act of telling and by underlining that act
may make us wonder whether this is an authentic report or a fabrication.

6 son?" And the lad who was telling him said, "I just chanced to be on
Mount Gilboa, and, look, Saul was leaning on his spear, and, look,
7 chariots and horsemen had overtaken him. And he turned round
8 behind him and saw me and called to me, and I said 'Here I am.'
And he said to me, 'Who are you?' And I said to him, "I am an
9 Amalekite.' And he said to me, "Pray, stand over me and finish me off,
for the fainting spell has seized me, for while life is still within me. . . .'

---

6. *I just chanced to be on Mount Gilboa.* Does one accidentally stumble onto
a battlefield while the killing is still going on? A more likely scenario is that
the Amalekite came onto the battlefield immediately after the fighting as a
scavenger, found Saul's corpse before the Philistines did, and removed the
regalia.

Saul was leaning on his spear. From Saul's words in verse 9, what this
means is not that he was resting but that he was entirely spent, barely able to
stand.

8. *I am an Amalekite.* Only now, in the middle of the story, is the national
identity of the messenger revealed. The fact that he was an Amalekite
means he would have felt no recoil of taboo about doing violence to the
king of Israel—something Saul appears to grasp at once. (Compare Doeg
the Edomite's slaughter of the priests of Nob in 1 Samuel 22.) But there is
also dramatic irony here: Saul lost his hold on the kingship when he failed
to kill the Amalekite king; now he begs an Amalekite to kill him, the king of
Israel.

9. *Pray, stand over me and finish me off.* "Stand over" suggests that Saul himself
is barely standing, that he is collapsed against the support of his spear—the
very spear that has been associated with his kingship and with his outbursts of
rage. "Finish me off" is somewhat inelegant as English diction, but the nuance
of the Hebrew (the *polel* conjugation of the verbal stem that means "to die") is
essential to the story: Saul feels he is dying, and he asks the Amalekite lad not
to kill him but to finish him off before the Philistines can get to him. The
Amalekite and David concur in this indication of what the Amalekite does to
Saul.

The fainting spell. The Hebrew noun appears only here. It may be related
to a root that suggests "confusion," or, alternately, "weakness."

for while life is still within me. . . . This clause, which has vexed some critics
and has led to emendations, is most simply construed as a broken-off sentence that the failing Saul does not have the strength to complete.

And I stood over him and finished him off, for I knew that he could not   10
live after having fallen. And I took the diadem that was on his head and
the band that was on his arm, and I have brought them here to my
lord." And David took hold of his garments and tore them, and all the   11
men who were with him did so, too. And they keened and they wept   12
and they fasted till evening for Saul and for Jonathan his son and for
the LORD's people and for the house of Israel because they had fallen
by the sword. And David said to the lad who had told him, "From   13
where are you?" And he said, "The son of an Amalekite sojourner am I."
And David said to him, "How were you not afraid to reach out your   14
hand to do violence to the LORD's anointed?" And David called to one   15
of the lads and said, "Come forward, stab him." And he struck him
down, and he died. And David said to him, "Your blood is on your own   16

---

10. *I stood over him and finished him off.* This whole story obviously contradicts the account of Saul's death by his own hand in 1 Samuel 31. Predictably,
this has led many critics to imagine two conflicting "sources." It is reassuring
that more recent scholarly consensus has come to the sensible conclusion
that the Amalekite lad is lying. Having come upon Saul's body, he sees a great
opportunity for himself: he will bring Saul's regalia to David, claim personally
to have finished off the man known to be David's archenemy and rival, and
thereby overcome his marginality as resident alien ("sojourner," *ger*) by
receiving a benefaction from the new king—perhaps a portion of land at
David's disposal. Fokkelman shrewdly notes that the Amalekite, instead of
removing the diadem and armband from Saul's body, might better have
buried the body or dragged it off and so saved it from desecration by the
Philistines.

   for I knew that he could not live after having fallen. The Amalekite sees
Saul's condition "leaning" on his spear to be equivalent to having fallen ("for
the fainting spell has seized me") and assumes, as does Saul himself in this
account, that in any case the king will not survive.

14. *How were you not afraid . . . to do violence to the LORD's anointed?* Though
the Israelite piety of David's statement is noteworthy, his words, as in the previous episodes in which he warned against harming Saul, are also politically
self-interested because he, too, is the LORD's anointed. In fact, now with
Saul's death, he alone is the LORD's anointed.

head, for your mouth bore witness against you, saying, 'I was the one
17 who finished off the LORD's anointed.'" And David sang this lament for
18 Saul and for Jonathan, and he said to teach hard things to the sons of
Judah—look, it is written down in the Book of Jashar:

19   "The splendor, O Israel, on your heights lies slain,
How have the warriors fallen!

---

16. *your mouth bore witness against you.* There is no way of knowing whether
David actually believes the Amalekite's story, but it is certainly convenient for
him to be able to point an accusing finger at someone with whom he has had
nothing to do as the person responsible for Saul's death, and then to order
immediate punishment.

   the LORD's *anointed.* At the end of the episode, David makes a point of
using the epithet of divinely grounded royal status instead of simply calling his
predecessor "Saul," as the Amalekite (who never even refers to him as "king")
had done.

17. *And David sang this lament.* We have been aware since 1 Samuel 16 of
David's gift as a lyre player and (presumably) as a singer. Only now do we hear
him in action as a singer-poet. This grandly resonant lament, cast in archaic
epic diction, marks a great moment of transition in the larger narrative, as the
David-Saul story becomes the David story. It is also another public utterance
of David's that beautifully serves his political purposes, celebrating his dead
rival as it mourns his loss and thus testifying that David could never have
desired Saul's death.

18. *to teach hard things.* The Masoretic Text has "to teach the bow"—a problematic reading because the lament scarcely provides instruction in the arts of
war. Some critics delete "bow" (*qeshet*), following the Septuagint. The present
translation revocalizes *qeshet* as *qashot*, with Fokkelman.

   look, it is written down in the Book of Jashar. This lost work, mentioned elsewhere in the Bible, was obviously familiar to the ancient audience. The title
probably means "Book of the Upright," though another reading of *yashar,* as a
verb rather than as a noun, yields "Book of Songs." It might have been an
anthology of archaic Hebrew poems.

Tell it not in Gath,   20
   proclaim not in Ashkelon's streets.
Lest the Philistine daughters rejoice,
   lest the daughters of the uncircumcised gloat.
O hills of Gilboa—no dew!   21
   and no rain upon you, O lofty fields.
For there the warriors' shield was besmirched,
   the shield of Saul unburnished with oil.
From the blood of the slain,   22
   from the warriors' fat—

---

20. *Tell it not in Gath.* There is an ironic echo here of the account of David's activities as vassal to the king of Gath, activities that he did not want told in Gath (see 1 Samuel 27:11).

Lest the Philistine daughters rejoice. In this martial culture, the young women had the role of celebrating the victors ("Saul has struck down his thousands. . . ."), gloating over the defeated enemy, and enjoying the spoils the men brought back from their conquests (compare verse 24).

21. *O hills of Gilboa.* As Shimon Bar-Efrat has observed, apostrophe is the dominant form of address throughout the elegy. David first turns, in a plural verb, to Israel at large ("Tell it not in Gath"), then to the hills of Gilboa, then to Saul and Jonathan, then to the daughters of Israel, then to Jonathan alone. The apostrophe is a form of address that underscores the actual absence of the person or object addressed and so is especially apt for an elegy.

lofty fields. The Hebrew *usedeh terumot* is a little obscure. The simplest solution is to treat the initial particle *u* as an excrescence and to read the phrase as a poetic inversion of the similar *meromey sadeh* in Judges 5:18. In the parallelism here, "lofty fields" would be an epithet for "hills of Gilboa."

unburnished with oil. The shields were made of leather, often studded with metal plates. Rubbing them with oil before battle would have made their outer surface slippery and thus would have enhanced their effectiveness in deflecting weapons. But the Hebrew for "unburnished," *beli mashiah*, is a pun—it means "unanointed" or "messiah-less," a haunting intimation that the LORD's anointed is no more. Clearly, the image of the royal shield lying befouled in the dust is a powerful metonymy for Saul himself.

Jonathan's bow did not retreat,
and the sword of Saul never turned away empty.

23   Saul and Jonathan, beloved and dear,
in their life and their death they were not parted.
They were swifter than eagles,
and stronger than lions.

24   O daughters of Israel, weep over Saul,
who clothed you in scarlet and bangles,
who studded your garments with jewelry of gold.

25   How have the warriors fallen
in the midst of the battle.
Jonathan, upon your heights slain!

26   I grieve for you, my brother, Jonathan.
Very dear you were to me.
More wondrous your love to me
than the love of women.

---

22. *Jonathan's bow . . . the sword of Saul.* After the image of the implement of defense, the shield, lying cast aside, we get a retrospective picture of these two offensive weapons destroying the enemy. The idea of the sword or the bow consuming flesh and blood is conventional in ancient Near Eastern martial poetry.

23. *in their life and their death they were not parted.* This is, of course, an extravagant idealization on the part of the elegist since father and son were almost estranged and twice Saul was on the point of killing Jonathan.

24. *O daughters of Israel, weep.* The invocation of the daughters of Israel to weep over the king who brought them precious booty is a symmetrical antithesis to the initial warning to keep the news away from the daughters of the Philistines, who would rejoice.

26. *I grieve for you, my brother, Jonathan.* Jonathan several times proclaimed his love for David. It is only in Jonathan's death, and at the distance of apostrophe, that David calls him "my brother" and says that Jonathan was dear to him.
      More wondrous . . . than the love of women. Repeated, unconvincing attempts have been made to read a homoerotic implication into these words. The reported details of the David story suggest that his various attachments to women are motivated by pragmatic rather than emotional concerns—and in one instance, by lust. This disposition, however, tells us little about David's

How have the warriors fallen, 27
and the gear of battle is lost."

---

sexual orientation. The bond between men in this warrior culture could easily be stronger than the bond between men and women.

27. *How have the warriors fallen, / and the gear of battle is lost.* The first clause here echoes the second verset of the opening line of the poem and so closes the elegy in a ringing envelope structure. The second clause beautifully picks up the image of the castoff shield lying in the dust, and of the relentless bow and sword that will never more be borne into battle. It is misguided to render the verb at the end as "perished" (King James Version, New JPS) because that presupposes that "gear of battle" is actually an epithet for Saul and Jonathan. Far more effectively, the lament concludes with a concrete image of shield and sword and bow abandoned, and by a simple process of metonymy we vividly understand the fate of the two men who once wielded them.

CHAPTER 2

1   And it happened afterward that David inquired of the LORD, saying, "Shall I go up into one of the towns of Judah?" And the LORD said to him, "Go up." And David said, "Where shall I go up?" And He said, "To 2 Hebron." And David went up there, and his two wives as well, Ahi- 3 noam the Jezreelite and Abigail wife of Nabal the Carmelite. And his men who were with him David brought up, each man and his house- 4a hold, and they settled in Hebron. And the men of Judah came and anointed David there as king over the house of Judah.

---

1. *David inquired of the* LORD. In keeping with the repeated emphasis of the preceding narrative, David, at each crucial juncture, solicits guidance from God's oracle before he makes his move.

go up into one of the towns of Judah. The preposition is used with precision: David does not want to "go up to one of the towns" but "into one of the towns"—that is, to set up headquarters in the town, leaving Ziklag at the edge of Philistine territory.

Where shall I go up? Given the binary character of the oracle's response, the actual form of the question would have been, "Shall I go up to Hebron?" But the question is recast in its present form to emphasize that God has picked out Hebron from all the towns of Judah.

4. *king over the house of Judah.* It is a little odd for a single tribe to have a "king," but the act is deliberately presumptive on David's part—first the king of Judah, eventually of all the tribes. Saul's son Ish-bosheth, by contrast, becomes king of an alliance of northern tribes. The text is silent on the Philistines' view of David's move to kingship in Hebron, but one can assume they countenanced it as a reasonable act on the part of their vassal opposing the house of Saul.

And they told David, saying, "It was the men of Jabesh-gilead who   4b
buried Saul." And David sent messengers to the men of Jabesh-gilead   5
and said to them, "Blessed are you to the LORD, that you have done this
kindness with your lord, with Saul, and have buried him. And now, may   6
the LORD show faithful kindness to you, and I on my part as well shall
do this bounty for you because you have done this thing. And now, may   7
your hands be strengthened and be you men of valor, for your lord Saul
is dead, and it is I whom the house of Judah has anointed as king over
them."

And Abner son of Ner commander of Saul's army had taken Ish-bosheth   8
son of Saul and brought him over to Mahanaim and made him king over   9
Gilead and over the Asherite and over Jezreel and over Ephraim and over

---

5. *David sent messengers to the men of Iabesh-gilead.* This is another shrewd
political maneuver. The men of Jabesh-gilead had been closely allied with
Saul. David, seizing the occasion of their act of bravery, summons them,
praises their burying of Saul, and offers them an unspecified "bounty" (or
"benefice"—literally, "good thing").

7. *for your lord Saul is dead, and it is I whom the house of Judah has anointed as
king over them.* David finesses Saul's hostility toward him and presents himself as the legitimate successor: just as the men of Jabesh-gilead have been
valorous in burying Saul, they should now show valor in following the newly
anointed David.

8. *Abner . . . had taken Ish-bosheth.* Abner the commander in chief is clearly the
real power here, and this surviving son of Saul is little more than a puppet king.
The original name (reflected in Chronicles) was Ish baal, with the "baal" component being a general epithet for God (or god), not necessarily referring to the
Canaanite deity. But because of its pagan associations, the sternly monotheistic
later editors systematically substituted *boshet* for *baʿal, boshet* meaning "shame."
    Mahanaim. The location is to the east of the Jordan and hence outside the
new area of Philistine conquest.

9. *Asherite.* The Masoretic Text reads "Ashurite," which would be, implausi-
bly, a non-Israelite people. Some critics emend to "Geshurite," but that is a
Canaanite group, and so the emendation perpetuates the problem. It is simplest to read this word as a reference to the northern tribe of Asher.

10   Benjamin and over Israel altogether. Forty years old was Ish-bosheth
     when he became king over Israel, and two years did he reign. But the
11   house of Judah followed David. And the span of time that David was
     king in Hebron over the house of Judah was seven years and six months.

12   And Abner son of Ner with the servants of Ish-bosheth sallied forth
13   from Mahanaim to Gibeon. And Joab son of Zeruiah and the servants
     of David had sallied forth, and they met each other by the pool of
14   Gibeon, and they took up their positions on either side of the pool. And
     Abner said to Joab, "Pray, let the lads arise and play before us." And
15   Joab said, "Let them arise." And they arose and crossed over—twelve
     in number for Benjamin and for Ish-bosheth son of Saul and twelve

---

and over Israel altogether. Shimon Bar-Efrat has made the plausible proposal that this final phrase is not a summary of the preceding list but the last
stage in a chronological process: Ish-bosheth extended his rule gradually,
beginning with Gilead in Transjordan and moving westward into the territory
the Philistines had conquered. It was only after a time that he actually ruled
"over Israel altogether."

10. *two years did he reign.* At first thought, his reign should have been nearly as
long as David's seven and a half years in Hebron. But if it took him five years
to consolidate his control over the northern tribes, the reign of two years
would make perfect sense.

12. *Abner . . . sallied forth from Mahanaim to Gibeon.* The reason for this expedition may have been David's attaching the men of Jabesh-gilead, who had
clearly been in Saul's camp, to himself. Gibeon is in the territory of Benjamin,
just a few miles northwest of Jerusalem.

14. *let the lads arise and play before us.* The "lads" (*neʿarim*) are elite warriors.
The verb "play" clearly indicates gladitorial, or representative, combat.
(Goliath calling for an Israelite champion to fight him is another instance of
combat through designated representative.) It is, however, deadly combat and
not just a form of jousting, as the details of the fighting make clear.

15. *twelve in number.* Throughout this strange episode, as Polzin has aptly
observed, there is an "extended ritualization of action as it is described
through extensive stylization of language." The ritual combat is virtually an
allegory of the civil war that it inaugurates. (Polzin reads it as an allegory of
Israelite monarchy.) The twelve champions on each side recall the twelve

from the servants of David. And each man grasped the head of the 16
other with his sword at the side of the other, and they fell together. And
they called that place the Field of Flints, which is in Gibeon. And the 17
fighting was very fierce on that day, and Abner with the men of Israel
were routed by the servants of David. And the three sons of Zeruiah 18
were there, Joab and Abishai and Asahel. And Asahel was as swift
footed as one of the gazelles of the open field. And Asahel chased after 19
Abner, and he swerved not to the right or left in going after Abner. And 20
Abner turned round and said, "Are you Asahel?" And he said, "I am."

---

tribes of Israel—an image of a nation destructively divided against itself. (The
number of fallen soldiers on Abner's side will be 360—thirty times twelve—
and on Joab's side twenty, an eighteenth part of the other side's casualties.)
The implausibility of the account of combat, then, would have been overriden
for the writer by the neatness of its symbolic function.

16. *each man grasped the head of the other with his sword at the other's side.* The
evidence of artifacts from the ancient world suggests that precisely this mode
of ritualized combat was quite widespread. A bas-relief found in Syria, roughly
contemporaneous with our story, an Egyptian carving, archaic Greek vase
paintings, and a Roman sculpture all show warriors in precisely this posture.

they fell together. All twenty-four warriors were killed—hardly a surprising
outcome if each man was free to wield a sword against his adversary's side.
Because there can be no decisive outcome in this encompassing mutual
slaughter, general fighting then breaks out.

the Field of Flints. It is not clear whether they were fighting with flint
weapons (perhaps because these were archaic and part of the ritualized combat), or whether the old term had become a general designation for knives or
swords.

17. *Abner with the men of Israel were routed.* Given the relatively low number
of casualties, it seems likely that less than a thousand on each side were
engaged. In such limited combat, the veterans of David's battle-hardened
guerilla band of six hundred might have had a distinct advantage.

20. *Are you Asahel?* Abner, who surely would not have had any compunction
about killing some other Judahite, realizes, quite accurately, that it will mean
trouble for him to kill one of the sons of Zeruiah. Asahel, the ace sprinter,
sounds very much like the youngest of the three, although we are not told
specifically about the order of their birth.

21 And Abner said to him, "Swerve you to your right or your left and seize
for yourself one of the lads, and take you his tunic." But Asahel did not
22 want to turn away from him. And Abner once more said to Asahel, "Turn
you away from me. Why should I strike you to the ground, and how
23 would I show my face to Joab your brother?" And he refused to turn
aside, and Abner struck him in the belly with the butt of the spear and
the spear came out behind him, and he fell there and died on the spot.
And it happened that whoever came to the place where Asahel fell and
24 died, stood still. And Joab and Abishai chased after Abner, and as the
sun was setting, they had come to the hill of Ammah, which faces Giah
25 on the way to the wilderness of Gibeon. And the Benjaminites gathered
behind Abner and formed a single band, and they took a stance on the
26 top of a certain hill. And Abner called out to Joab and said, "Must the

---

22. *Why should I strike you to the ground . . . ?* Abner, the seasoned warrior, is
coolly confident that if necessary he has the skill and the combat experience
to kill this impetuous young man.

How would I show my face to Joab your brother? The literal wording of the
Hebrew is "lift up my face." What is at stake here is not merely a question of
diplomatic relations with the opposing commander but vendetta justice
(Hebrew, *geʾulat hadam*, "redemption of the blood"): if Abner sheds the blood
of Joab's brother, Joab will feel honor bound to shed the blood of the killer in
return.

23. *struck him in the belly with the butt of the spear.* Asahel is pursuing Abner
at top speed. Abner, to save his own life, uses an old soldier's trick: he suddenly stops short and thrusts his spear backward, under his pursuer's shield
(if Asahel is carrying one) and into the soft belly. The momentum of Asahel's
rapid running would have contributed to the penetrating force of the spear's
butt.

24. *Ammah . . . Giah.* The first name means "conduit," the second "gushing,"
and so both may be related to an aquaduct system linked to the pool at
Gibeon.

sword devour forever? You surely know that it will be bitterness in the
end. And how long will you not say to the troops to turn back from their
brothers?" And Joab said, "As God lives, had you but spoken, from this   27
morning the troops would have given up pursuit of their brothers." And   28
Joab sounded the ram's horn, and all the troops halted, and they no
longer chased after Israel, and they fought no more. And Abner and his   29
men went all that night through the Arabah, and they crossed the Jordan
and went all the way through the ravine and came to Mahanaim. And   30
Joab had turned back from pursuing Abner, and he gathered together all
the troops, and nineteen of David's servants were missing, and Asahel.
And David's servants had struck down from Benjamin and from Abner's   31
men three hundred and sixty men. And they bore away Asahel and   32
buried him in his father's grave, which is in Bethlehem, and Joab and his
men went all night long, and day brightened for them in Hebron.

---

26. *You surely know that it will be bitterness in the end.* This grim prognostication hovers over not only the continuing civil war but over the entire David
story. In the previous verse, Abner's forces were reported regrouping and taking up a defensive position on the hilltop, so they are now, after the rout, in a
state to inflict serious casualties on their adversaries if Joab persists. Therefore he agrees to the truce, though he surely has vendetta on his mind.

27. *had you but spoken.* The Masoretic Text has "had you not spoken." This has
led some interpreters to construe "morning" as "tomorrow morning" (i e., the
troops would have gone on pursuing you all night long had you not spoken up
now). But this is strained because the Hebrew *ʾaz mehaboker* (literally, "then
from the morning") idiomatically refers to the morning of the day on which
one is speaking. One should either emend "had not" (*luleiʾ*) to "had" (*lu*) or, as
Rashi proposed long ago, construe the former in the sense of the latter.

29. *the Arabah.* This is a north-south depression running from the Sea of
Galilee all the way to the Gulf of Aqabah.
　　the ravine. The Hebrew term *bitron* might conceivably be a place-name.
The root means to cleave or split and occurs in the Song of Songs collocated
with "mountains," yielding something like "mountains of the divide." The
scholarly proposal that this word means "middle of the morning" has no warrant in ancient Hebrew usage.

32. *all night long.* Perhaps the reason for this forced march through the night
is that Joab's troops want to get safely out of Benjaminite territory, not entirely
trusting the truce.

CHAPTER 3

1   And the fighting between the house of Saul and the house of David went on a long time, and David grew stronger and stronger and the house of Saul weaker and weaker.

2   And sons were born to David in Hebron. And his firstborn was Amnon,
3   by Ahinoam the Jezreelite. And the second was Chileab, by Abigail wife of Nabal the Carmelite. And the third was Absalom son of
4   Maacah daughter of Talmai king of Geshur. And the fourth was Adoni-

---

1. *And the fighting . . .* This summary notice at the head of the chapter follows directly from the story of the battle at Gibeon that precedes it: the truce on that day is only temporary, and a drawn-out civil war ensues.

2. *And sons were born to David.* The insertion of this genealogical list here may be motivated by the fact that the northern tribes, brought round by Abner, are about to cast their lot with David, making him monarch of the entire nation and thus a properly dynastic king. But succession to the throne is not simple, and the list bristles with future disasters: Amnon, who will rape his half sister and will be murdered by her brother; Absalom, who will usurp the throne; Adonijah, who will proclaim himself king while the infirm, aged David lies in bed unawares.

3. *Chileab.* The Septuagint and the Qumran Samuel fragment have a different name, Daluiah. In any case, this son plays no role in the ensuing narrative, nor do Shephatiah and Ithream.
   Maacah daughter of Talmai king of Geshur. Geshur is a small Transjordanian kingdom at the foot of the Golan. The marriage is clearly a political act through which David establishes an alliance in the north, outflanking the house of Saul. It is conceivable that Absalom's later aspiration to the throne may be influenced by his awareness that, alone of David's sons, he is grandson of a king. After the killing of Amnon, he will take refuge in Geshur.

jah son of Haggith. And the fifth was Shephatiah son of Abital. And the   5
sixth was Ithream, by Eglah wife of David. These were born to David in
Hebron.

And it happened during the fighting between the house of Saul and the   6
house of David that Abner kept growing in strength in the house of
Saul. And Saul had a concubine named Rizpah daughter of Aiah. And   7
Ish-bosheth said to Abner, "Why did you come to bed with my father's
concubine?" And Abner was very incensed over the words of Ish-   8
bosheth, and he said, "Am I a dog's head attached to Judah? Today I

---

5. *Eglah wife of David.* It is a little odd that only she is so designated. This
might be because she stands at the end of the list, or because there was
knowledge of another Eglah who was not David's wife. In all this, one notes
that David the guerilla leader with his two wives has now become David the
king with a whole royal harem.

6. *Abner kept growing in strength.* This is the same verb, in a different conjugation, as in the opening verse of the chapter, which reported David's growing
strength and the weakening of the house of Saul. As the Saulide forces are
progressively harder pressed in the continuing war, the nominal king becomes
more and more dependent on his military commander; and Abner, while not
actually pretending to the throne, arrogates more and more power to himself.

7. *Why did you come to bed with my father's concubine?* This crucial act is
elided in the narrative report and revealed only in Ish-bosheth's indignant
question. To take sexual possession of a king's consort was to make an implicit
claim to the power he exercised, as we shall see again when Absalom publicly
cohabits with David's concubines. "To come to bed with"—literally, "to come
into"—is an idiom for sexual intercourse that generally indicates sexual possession of a woman with whom a man has not been previously intimate. (I
explain the semantic logic of the idiom in my commentary on Genesis.)

8. *Am I a dog's head attached to Judah?* The dog in biblical idiom regularly figures as a contemptible beast—the antonym of the fierce and regal lion. The
phrase "attached to Judah" is lacking in the Septuagint, and some critics have
inferred that it is a scribal interpolation. It might make sense, however, as a
compounding of the insult because Judah is the despised enemy of Benjamin,
the tribe of Saul.

have kept faith with the house of Saul your father, with his kinsmen and his companions, in not handing you over to David, and you dare

9 reproach me with guilt over the woman today? Thus may God do to Abner, and even more, for as the LORD has sworn to David, just so will

10 I do for him—to transfer the kingship from the house of Saul and to set up the throne of David over Israel and over Judah from Dan to Beer-

11 sheba!" And he could say back not a word more to Abner in his fear of him.

12 And Abner sent messengers to David in his stead, saying, "To whom should the land belong? Make a pact with me and, look, my hand will

13 be with you to bring round to you all Israel." And he said, "Good. I shall make a pact with you. But one thing do I ask of you, namely, you shall not see my face until you bring Michal daughter of Saul when you

---

you dare reproach me with guilt over the woman. Abner's angry protest has a nice double edge. You are entirely dependent on my loyal support, he tells Ish-bosheth, so how could you dare object to so trivial a thing as my taking a particular woman as sexual partner? Alternately, the implication could be: you are entirely dependent on me, so how could you object to my taking possession of this sexual symbol of political power? You should have been content that I left you nominally on the throne.

9. *for as the* LORD *has sworn to David.* Ish-bosheth's protest about Rizpah drives Abner, David's military adversary, to embrace the notion that God has promised the throne to David. Rather than continue to serve a carping, pusillanimous man like Ish-bosheth, who neither fully accepts Abner's power nor knows how to exercise power on his own, Abner now is ready to throw his weight with a truly kingly leader and to help him become king over all the nation's tribes (verse 10).

11. *he could say back not a word.* The contrast between the angry Abner and the quaking Ish-bosheth is all the stronger because the puppet king's fearful silence is set against what is by biblical standards a rather long speech—one continuous outburst.

13. *see my face.* An idiom used for coming into the presence of royalty.
Michal daughter of Saul. The first marriage buttresses David's claim to reign over all Israel, including the tribe of Benjamin. That is why he identifies Michal to Abner as Saul's daughter. There is no indication that he has a personal motive as well as a political one in wanting Michal back.

come to see my face." And David sent messengers to Ish-bosheth son   14
of Saul, saying, "Give back my wife, Michal, whom I betrothed with a
hundred Philistine foreskins." And Ish-bosheth sent and took her from   15
her husband, from Paltiel son of Laish. And her husband went with   16
her, weeping as he went after her, as far as Bahurim. And Abner said to
him, "Go back!" And he went back.

And Abner parlayed with the elders of Israel, saying, "Time and again in   17
the past you sought to have David become king over you. And now, act,   18

---

14. *sent messengers to Ish-bosheth.* It is to be inferred that Abner has made clear
to Ish-bosheth that he must accede to this demand.

my wife Michal, whom I betrothed with a hundred Philistine foreskins. In
turning to the man who has jurisdiction over Michal (and her second husband), David makes clear now that she is his wife, whom he legitimately
acquired by providing the bride price of a hundred Philistine foreskins stipulated by her father, Saul.

15. *from her husband.* The Masoretic Text has "a husband" (or, "a man"), but
the possessive pronoun is supplied in the Septuagint and the Vulgate as well
as in at least two Hebrew manuscripts.

16. *weeping as he went.* There is scarcely a more striking instance of the evoca-
tive compactness of biblical narrative. We know almost nothing about Paltiel.
He speaks not a word of dialogue. Yet his walking after Michal, weeping all
the while, intimates a devoted love that stands in contrast to David's relationship with her. Paltiel is a man whose fate is imposed on him. Michal was given
to him by Saul, evidently without his initiative. He came to love her. Now he
must give her up, and confronted by Saul's strongman with the peremptory
order to go back, he has no choice but to go back.

17. *Time and again in the past.* The idiom for "times gone by," *temol shilshom*
(literally, "yesterday and the day before") is reinforced by the emphatic adverb
gam, repeated before each of the two components of the idiom, probably as an
indication of repeated acts in time past. Most commentators refer the idea of
Israel's wanting David as king to his immense popularity during his early military successes (1 Samuel 18). But there was no intimation then that the people
wanted to replace Saul with David on the throne. The suggestion of repeated
popular support for David's claims might well point to an otherwise unre-
ported undercurrent of dissatisfaction with the house of Saul and an interest
in going over to David as a result of the losing civil war, if it is not Abner's own
diplomatic invention.

for the LORD has said, 'By the hand of David My servant will I deliver
My people Israel from the hand of the Philistines and from the hand of
19   all their enemies.' " And Abner spoke as well in the hearing of Benjamin, and Abner went as well to speak in David's hearing in Hebron all
20   that was good in the eyes of Israel and in the eyes of Benjamin. And
Abner came to David in Hebron, and with him were twenty men. And
David made a feast for Abner and for the men who were with him. And
21   Abner said to David, "Let me rise and go and gather to my lord the king
all Israel, that they may make a pact with you, and you shall reign over
all your heart desires." And David sent Abner off, and he went in peace.
22   And look, David's servants and Joab had come from a raid, and abundant booty they brought with them, and Abner was not with David in
23   Hebron, for he had sent him off, and he went in peace. And Joab and all
the force that was with him had come, and they told Joab, saying,
"Abner son of Ner has come to the king, and he sent him off, and he
24   went in peace." And Joab came to the king and said, "What have you

---

21. *And David sent Abner off, and he went in peace.* The going in peace befits
the feast of reconciliation and the agreed-on pact. The writer contrives to
repeat this sentence verbatim three times (here, verse 22, verse 23). But when
Joab refers to this very same departure of Abner from Hebron in verse 24, he
substitutes for "in peace" *(beshalom)* the emphatic infinitive *halokh* ("going
off"). This ominous substitution, as I put it in *The Art of Biblical Narrative,*
"falls like the clatter of a dagger after the ringing of bells"—especially because
"to go" sometimes occurs in the Bible as a euphemism for dying (see Job 27:21
and Jeremiah 22:10). Polzin has noted that this entire episode is a crowded
juncture of comings and goings. The least complicated inference to be drawn
from that fact is that this is a crucial moment of *transition* in the David story:
the house of Saul comes to treat with the house of David; the long conflict
with Saul, culminating in civil war, comes to an end; David is about to become
king of the whole Israelite nation; a new line of division now emerges between
David and his chief henchman, Joab. All this flurry of transition and realign-
ment is nicely caught in the multiple comings and goings of Abner and Joab
and the troops.

done? Look, Abner has come to you! Why did you send him off, and he
went, going off? You know that Abner son of Ner to dupe you has come   25
and to learn your comings and goings and to learn all that you do." And
Joab went out from David's presence and sent messengers after Abner,   26
and they brought him back from the cistern of Sirah, and David did not
know. And Abner came back to Hebron, and Joab drew him aside into   27
the gate to speak with him deceptively, and he struck him there in the
belly, and he died for the blood of Asahel, Joab's brother. And David   28
heard afterward and said, "Innocent am I, and my kingship, before the

---

24. *Look, Abner has come to you.* The simple idiom for arrival (*bᵃ ᵓel*) ironically
echoes Ish-bosheth's use of the very same idiom in its sexual sense ("come
into," "come to bed with") in his complaint to Abner. The sexual undertone is
sustained in the next verse because the prominent verb "to dupe" (*pitah*) has
the primary meaning of "seduce."

26. *the cistern of Sirah.* The actual location has not been identified but it
would have to be in the general vicinity of Hebron.
    and David did not know. The narrator takes pains to underscore David's
innocence of involvement in Joab's scheme of murder. David on his part will
take extravagant steps to declare his innocence.

27. *deceptively.* The Hebrew adverb *besheli* occurs only here. It derives either
from the root *sh-l-h,* "to delude," or from the root *sh-l-w,* "to be quiet." Those
who favor the latter root render it, with a small leap of semantic inference, as
"privately."
    he struck him there in the belly. Although this is the same part of the body
in which the now avenged Asahel received his fatal wound from Abner,
there is a world of difference between the two killings. Abner struck down
Asahel in a deft maneuver as Asahel was pursuing him on the battlefield
with intent to kill. Joab draws Abner aside into the gate under the pretence
of speaking confidentially with him, and, catching him unawares, stabs him
in the belly.
    for the blood of Asahel. Joab's vendetta is accomplished. But it has not
escaped notice that he is also eliminating a rival for the position of commander in the new united monarchy.

28. *Innocent am I.* David's first eminently political reflex is to dissociate himself categorically from the killing.

29 LORD for all time of the blood of Abner son of Ner! May the blood guilt come down on the head of Joab and all his father's house, and may there never lack in the house of Joab a sufferer of discharge from his member and running sores on his skin and a man clutching the woman's spindle, and one falling by the sword and one wanting for 30 bread!" And Joab and Abishai his brother had lain in wait for Abner because he put to death Asahel their brother in Gibeon in the battle. 31 And David said to Joab and to all the troops who were with him, "Tear your garments and gird on sackcloth and keen for Abner." And King

---

of the blood of Abner son of Ner. The Qumran Samuel text puts a full stop after "before the LORD for all time," then makes this phrase the subject of the next clause: "May the blood of Abner son of Ner come down on the head of Joab." The Masoretic Text has simply "May it come down on the head of Joab," and this translation supplies "blood guilt" (plural of *dam,* blood) for the sake of clarity.

29. *discharge from his member.* The single Hebrew word *zav* refers to a man suffering from diseased discharge from the male organ.

running sores on his skin. This is again one word in the Hebrew, *metsora,* rendered as "leper" in the older translations but now generally thought to indicate a different skin disease.

a man clutching the woman's spindle. Some prefer to interpret the Hebrew term as "crutch," thus linking it with the two preceding images of disease. This noun, *pelekh,* occurs quite infrequently, but there is scant indication in the biblical corpus that as a wooden implement it meant anything but "spindle." The word "woman's" is added in the translation to catch the nuance of scorn in a man's being reduced to woman's work. All in all, David puts together a first-class curse to emphasize the distance between him and Abner's killer. This blood guilt, many times compounded, will indeed come down on Joab's head, but not till the end of David's life.

30. *had lain in wait for Abner.* The Masoretic Text reads "had killed Abner" (*hargu leʾavner*). There are two problems with that reading. It is a flat repetition of what has already been reported more vividly (only adding the information that Abishai was complicit in the act), and the use of the particle *leʾ* (as a preposition, it means "to" or "for") to indicate the direct object of a verb is an Aramaicism generally restricted to late biblical Hebrew. The Qumran Samuel scroll has a different verb, evidently (the first consonant is not visible on the parchment) *tsafnu,* "to lie in wait," "to hide."

David was walking behind the bier. And they buried Abner in Hebron. 32
And the king raised his voice and wept over the grave of Abner, and all
the people wept. And the king lamented over Abner and said, 33

> "Like the death of the base
>   should Abner have died?
> Your hands—never bound, 34
>   your feet never placed in fetters!
> As one falls before scoundrels you fell."

And all the people continued to weep over him. And all the people 35
came to give David bread to eat while it was still day, and David
swore, saying, "Thus and more may God do to me, if before the sun
sets I taste bread or anything at all." And all the people took note and 36
it was good in their eyes, all that the king had done was good in the

---

33. *lamented.* This is David's second poetic lament (*qinah*) in quick sequence
in the text. It is much briefer than the lament over Jonathan and Saul and
derives its power from the lapidary character of its language.

the death of the base. The term for "base fellow," *naval,* is the one encountered in 1 Samuel 25 as an explanation for the name of Nabal, Abigail's husband. A *naval* is someone who, as Kyle McCarter, Jr. rightly observes,
perpetrates *nevalah,* a contemptible or scandalous act. It is an outrage, David
says, that a noble figure such as Abner should have been cut down in stealth
as some scoundrel might perish at the hands of hired assassins.

34. *Your hands—never bound, / Your feet never placed in fetters.* The elliptical
nature of the language has led to some dispute over interpretation. It is most
plausibly understood as a brief retrospection on Abner's glory days as a martial
hero: no one ever succeeded in taking him captive, in putting him in a pris-
oner's humiliating fetters.

As one falls before scoundrels you fell. But now the noble Abner has been
undone by treachery. In all the grandeur of the poetry, the sharp rebuke to the
sons of Zeruiah, who figure as vulgar cutthroats, is clear.

37 eyes of the people. And all the people and all Israel knew on that day that it had not been from the king to put to death Abner son of Ner.
38 And the king said to his servants, "You must know that a commander
39 and a great man has fallen this day in Israel. And I am gentle, and just anointed king, and these sons of Zeruiah are too hard for me. May the LORD pay back the evildoer according to his evil!"

37.–38. The vehemence with which David here is repeatedly dissociated from the killing of Abner leads one to suspect that, beyond his desire to exculpate himself on the spot, there may have been a lingering shadow of suspicion that he ordered the killing, a suspicion that the writer takes pains to dispel.

39. *I am gentle, and just anointed king.* David's plight as a self-proclaimed "gentle" or "tender" man *(rakh)* vis-à-vis the "hard" sons of Zeruiah will continue to play a crucial role in the story. But although he dissociates himself from Joab and Abishai and goes so far as to pronounce a scathing curse on them and their descendants, he makes no move to get rid of them, and continues to depend on their activity as strongmen. And what of Joab's reaction to all this bitter denunciation? Is it possible that he prudently understands it is politic for the king to dissociate himself from the killing by denouncing the killers in poetry and prose? There is also a question here about the relation between the two phrases David uses. Many translations explain the link as "though anointed king." That construction is possible, though it would be an unusual use of the Hebrew particle *v^e* ("and"). The present translation adds "just," on the assumption that David is dramatizing his predicament as a gentle person on whom the kingship has been newly thrust and who must contend with these hard sons of Zeruiah. In point of fact, he was anointed in Hebron several years earlier, but this might be either rhetorical exaggeration or a reference to his brand-new condition of king of the nation, not just of the tribe of Judah.

CHAPTER 4

And the son of Saul heard that Abner had died in Hebron, and he was 1
utterly shaken, and all Israel was dismayed. And the son of Saul had 2
two men, commanders of raiding parties, the name of the one was
Baanah and of the other Rechab, sons of Rimmon the Beerothite, who
was of the Benjaminites, for Beeroth, too, was reckoned with Benjamin. And the Beerothites fled to Gittaim and have been sojourners 3
there till this day.

---

1. *the son of Saul.* The son in question is Ish-bosheth. Both the Septuagint and
the Qumran Samuel scroll read, erroneously, "Mephibosheth." It has been
surmised that scribes deleted the mistaken name without replacing it by the
correct one.

was utterly shaken. The Hebrew says literally "his hands grew weak," the
hands being an idiomatic token of strength or courage. The force of the idiom
is a little like the colloquial English "lost his grip."

2. *sons of Rimmon the Beerothite, who was of the Benjaminites.* The Beerothites
are an originally non-Israelite group who have become what we might call naturalized Benjaminites. The two brothers are considered sufficiently Benjaminite to have been entrusted with positions as the commanders of raiding
parties—also making them experienced killers—and so we are meant to
understand that the pusillanimous Ish-bosheth is betrayed by his own tribes-
men. At the same time, the foreign origin of Baanah and Rechab participates
in the recurring pattern of the foreign messenger bringing news of a disaster to
David. Finally, the treacherous killing of the king by two brothers echoes the
immediately preceding episode, in which two brothers, Joab and Abishai, are
said to lie in wait for and kill Abner.

4 And Jonathan son of Saul had a lame son, five years old he was when the news of Saul and Jonathan came from Jezreel. And his nurse bore him off and fled, and it happened in her haste to flee that he fell and 5 was crippled. And his name was Mephibosheth. And the sons of Rimmon the Beerothite, Rechab and Baanah went and came in the heat of the day to the house of Ish-bosheth as he was taking his midday rest. 6 And, look, the woman who kept the gate had been gleaning wheat, and 7 nodded and fell asleep. And they came into the house as he was lying in his bed in his bedchamber, and they struck him and killed him and cut off his head and took his head and went off through the Arabah all 8 night long. And they brought Ish-bosheth's head to David in Hebron and said to the king, "Here is the head of Ish-bosheth son of Saul your

---

4. *Jonathan . . . had a lame son.* The notice is inserted here to make clear that after the murder of Ish-bosheth, there will be no fit heir left from the house of Saul, for Saul's one surviving grandson is crippled.

Mephibosheth. As with Ish-bosheth / Ish-baal, the original form of the name was Mephibaal, a component meaning "shame" substituted for the theophoric *ba'al* with its pagan associations.

6. *And, look, the woman who kept the gate. . . .* The translation of this entire verse follows the text reflected in the Septuagint—reluctantly, out of sense that the received text at this point is simply not viable. The Masoretic Text is problematic as idiomatic Hebrew usage, includes one entirely unintelligible phrase, and is redundant with the narrative report of the next verse. It reads: "and they [feminine pronoun!] came into the midst of the house, taking wheat [?], and they struck him in the belly, and Rechab and Baanah his brother got away."

gleaning wheat. This odd little domestic detail suggests that Ish-bosheth does not inhabit a grand palace with royal guards but lives in modest homey circumstances.

nodded and fell asleep. Both the king and the gatekeeper are asleep when the assassins arrive, so they can slip by her and easily dispatch him.

7. *as he was lying in his bed in his bedchamber.* This twice-asserted detail underlines the scurrilousness of the act of assassination. The next time we encounter a king taking his siesta, it will be David before he rises to behold Bathsheba. Again, murder will ensue, though the king himself will be the perpetrator.

8. *Ish-bosheth son of Saul your enemy, who sought your life.* The two sons of Rimmon make exactly the same misguided calculation as the Amalekite messenger in Chapter 1, imagining that David will be delighted to hear of the destruction of anyone associated with Saul and will reward the bearers of the news.

enemy, who sought your life. The LORD has granted my lord the king
vengeance this day against Saul and his seed." And David answered   9
Rechab and Baanah his brother, the sons of Rimmon the Beerothite,
and he said to them, "As the LORD lives, Who saved my life from every
strait, he who told me, saying 'Look, Saul is dead,' and thought he was   10
a bearer of good tidings, I seized him and killed him in Ziklag instead of
giving him something for his tidings. How much more so when wicked   11
men have killed an innocent man in his house in his bed, and so, will I
not requite his blood from you and rid the land of you?" And David   12
commanded the lads, and they killed them and chopped off their
hands and feet and hung them by the pool in Hebron. And Ish-
bosheth's head they took and buried in the grave of Abner in Hebron.

---

11. *when wicked men have killed an innocent man in his bed in his house.* Either
this detail has been elided in the dialogue reported for Baanah and Rechab
when they come before David, or he has received advance word of the killing
and its circumstances from another source. In all this, the common scholarly
view is that the narrative is framed as an apology for David, taking pains to
clear him of any complicity in the deaths, first of Saul, then of Abner, and now
of Ish-bosheth. But it is still more plausible that the writer is continuing his
representation of David as the consummately politic man: whether he really
feels moral revulsion against these assassins we have no way of knowing, but
he surely is aware, as he was after the murder of Abner, that it is in his political
interest to put the greatest possible distance between himself and the killers of
Saul's son, and what better way to do this than to have them executed on the
spot? David is nevertheless a beneficiary of the murder, for now there is no
claimant to the throne whom the northern tribes might follow instead of him.

12. *chopped off their hands and feet.* The dismembering of malefactors or prisoners was a common ancient Near Eastern practice, as we have seen before
(and compare the first chapter of Judges). Here the corpses are defiled by cutting off the hands that did the killing and the feet that carried the killers into
the victim's bedchamber. The whole episode ends in a strange image cluster
of detached body parts: the hands and feet of the two executed assassins and
the head of their victim. Even as David is about to assume control of a united
monarchy, we have an intimation of mayhem and dismemberment that is an
apt thematic prelude to the story of David's reign.

CHAPTER 5

¹And all the tribes of Israel came to David in Hebron, and they said, ²"Here we are, your bone and your flesh are we. Time and again in the past when Saul was king over us you were the one who led Israel into the fray, and the LORD said to you,

'It is you who will shepherd My people Israel
    and it is you who will be prince over Israel.' "

³And all the elders of Israel came to the king in Hebron, and King David made a pact with them in Hebron before the LORD, and they anointed

---

1. *all the tribes of Israel came to David.* "The tribes of Israel," in keeping with the consistent usage of the preceding narrative, refers to the northern tribes that had been loyal to the house of Saul. With the assassination of Abner and then of Ish-bosheth, they understandably now turn to David.

2. *you were the one . . . It is you.* The language of the tribal representatives puts considerable emphasis on the second-person pronoun: you are the one that we, and God, have chosen. The divine declaration of David's legitimacy as ruler, quoted by the tribal spokesmen, is appropriately given the elevated status of poetry.

3. *all the elders of Israel came to the king.* This is not a duplication of the report in verse 1 from another source, as is often claimed. The convention used here is the well-attested one of "resumptive repetition": when an interrupted narrative strand is resumed, a phrase from the point of interruption is repeated verbatim to mark the return to the main line. Here, the move to confirm David as king of Israel, with which the episode began, after the insertion of the tribes' dialogue (verses 1 and 2), is carried forward. It is the role of the tribal rank and file to proclaim fealty, but of the elders to sign a pact and anoint David, and so

David as king over Israel. Thirty years old was David when he became 4
king, forty years he was king. In Hebron he was king over Judah seven 5
years and six months, and in Jerusalem he was king thirty-three years
over all Israel and Judah.

And the king went, and his men with him, to Jerusalem, to the 6
Jebusite, the inhabitant of the land, and he said to David, saying, "You
shall not enter here unless you can remove the blind and the lame,"

"elders" is now strategically substituted for "tribes" of the first verse. One
should note that the tribes come "to David" whereas the elders come "to the
king," for they are about to consummate the official business of kingmaking.

4. *forty years he was king.* In biblical usage, this is a formulaic number—in
Judges often used to indicate a full term of governing. But the specificity of
"seven years and six months" in Hebron has the look of a real number,
whether or not it is historically precise.

6. *the king went . . . to Jerusalem.* The chronological link between this action
and what precedes, as well as the chronology of the subsequent events in the
chapter, is not clear. The principle of organization appears to be thematic or
ideological rather than temporal. What we have here is a catalogue of salient
actions by which David consolidates his new monarchy: the conquest of a
capital city in the center of the north-south axis of the country that does not
belong to any tribal territory (the same logic that led to the creation of Washington as capital in the District of Columbia, not part of any state); the construction of a palace with the assistance of a Phoenician alliance; the
begetting of many offspring, including the future heir to the throne, Solomon;
the defeat of the Philistines. The birth of Solomon is the clearest indication
that these notices do not follow the chronology of the preceding narrative.
    the blind and the lame. This puzzling phrase, together with its even more
enigmatic occurrence in verse 8, is a notorious crux. The most disparate theo-
ries have been proposed for how to read the words of the text and how to
reconstruct what is said to go on in the conquest of the city. The Qumran
Samuel scroll for this verse reads: "You shall not enter here, for the blind and
the lame have incited [*hesitu* for Masoretic *hesirkha*], saying, 'David shall not
enter here.'" This variant has the advantage of fluency, but one suspects it
may have been invented to make a difficult traditional text more intelligible.
The explanation proposed by Yigael Yadin is probably the most plausible: he
points to a Hittite text for the swearing in of troops in which a blind woman

7 which is to say, "David shall not enter here!" And David captured the
8 stronghold of Zion, which is the City of David. And David said on that
day, "Whoever strikes down the Jebusite and reaches the conduit, and
the lame and the blind utterly despised by David . . ." Therefore do
9 they say, "No blind man nor lame shall enter the House." And David
stayed in the stronghold and called it the City of David, and David
10 built round the rampart and within. And David grew greater and
greater, and the LORD God of Hosts was with him.

---

and a lame man are set before the men with the monitory imprecation that
their fate will be like that of those wretches if they fail in their duty. The
Jebusites, then, might have displayed the lame and the blind on the ramparts
with an analogous curse against those who would presume to attack the city.
This taunting curse would explain why these maimed figures are "despised by
David."

8. *whoever strikes down the Jebusite and reaches the conduit.* These words are
the other salient element of the crux, with debate still raging over the meaning of "conduit" *(tsinor)*. Some scholars have claimed it refers here to the
windpipe, or a lower part of the anatomy, of the Jebusites who are to be
struck down, but there is no Hebrew evidence for *tsinor* as anything but a
water channel or tube, and the argument from the analogy of shape is a weak
one. Moreover, the verb used here, *nagʿa,* means primarily "to touch," and in
some biblical contexts, "to reach" or "take charge of" but not "to strike." The
most likely reference, then, is to a daring route of surprise access into the
city. A frequently proposed candidate is Warren's Shaft, discovered in 1867,
an underground tunnel feeding in from the Gihon Spring on a slope outside
the wall to the east. Though everything about this report remains uncertain,
David may be saying that whoever manages to crawl through the tunnel,
make his way up the vertical shaft that transects it, and cut down the
Jebusites within the town together with their loathsome display of lame and
blind, will be given a great reward. (The reward clause is missing; one is supplied in the parallel verse in Chronicles—"will become a chief and commander.")
    No blind man nor lame shall enter the house. The story is thus given an etio-
logical turn as an explanation for a known taboo, evidently pertaining to the
Temple but perhaps to David's "house" (i.e., the palace). One wonders
whether there is an invitation here to think of Jonathan's lame son—which
would be another gesture for denying the Saulides all future claim to the
throne.

And Hiram king of Tyre sent messengers to David with cedar wood   11
and carpenters and stonemasons, and they built a house for David.
And David knew that the LORD had set him up unshaken as king over   12
Israel and had exalted his kingship for the sake of His people Israel.

And David took other concubines and wives from Jerusalem after com-   13
ing from Hebron, and other sons and daughters were born to David.
And these are the names of those born to him in Jerusalem: Shammua   14
and Shobab and Nathan and Solomon, and Ibhar and Elishua and   15
Nepheg and Japhia,and Elishama and Eliada and Eliphelet.   16

And the Philistines heard that David had been anointed as king over   17
Israel, and all the Philistines came up to seek David. And David heard
and went down to the stronghold. The Philistines had come and   18
deployed in the Valley of Rephaim. And David inquired of the LORD,   19
saying, "Shall I go up against the Philistines? Will you give them into

---

11. *Hiram king of Tyre.* Hiram as a provider of timber and artisans points forward to Solomon's construction of the Temple. If this is the Hiram with
whom Solomon had dealings, David's palace building would have been
undertaken rather late in his own reign in order to coincide with Hiram's
regnal span.

13. *from Jerusalem.* Some Septuagint versions read "in Jerusalem."

17. *the Philistines heard.* David's assumption of the throne of all the tribes of
Israel means that he has decisively cast aside his vassal status, and so the
Philistines, who all along have been warring with the northern tribes,
assemble their united forces ("all the Philistines") to suppress the new
monarchy.
    the stronghold. The claim often made that this refers to the stronghold at
Adullam (compare 1 Samuel 22) is unlikely because the battle here is entirely
in the immediate vicinity of Jerusalem. This would have to be the stronghold
within the city, referred to in verse 9. David can "go down" to it because his
residence in Jerusalem could be topographically above the stronghold.

18. *the valley of Rephaim.* The location is outside the walls of the Jebusite city,
a couple of miles to the west.

20 my hand?" And the LORD said, "Go up, for I will surely give the Philistines into your hand." And David came into Baal-perazim, and David struck them down there, and he said, "The LORD has burst through my enemies before me like a bursting of water!" Therefore did 21 he call the name of that place Baal-perazim. And they abandoned their 22 idols there, and David with his men bore them off. And once more the 23 Philistines came up and deployed in the Valley of Rephaim. And David inquired of the LORD, and He said, "You shall not go up. Turn round 24 behind them and come at them from opposite the willows. And as soon as you hear the sound of marching in the tops of the willows, then you must move boldly, for then shall the LORD go out before you to strike 25 down the camp of the Philistines." And David did just as the LORD had commanded him, and he struck down the Philistines from Geba till you come to Gezer.

---

20. *burst through my enemies like a bursting of water.* The existing place-name is etiologically reinscribed to fit the military victory. Baal-perazim may mean "god of earthquakes." The image of bursting through—the Hebrew term means "breach"—could suggest that David's forces have succeeded in punching a hole in the Philistine lines rather than in producing a general rout.

23. *opposite the willows.* The Hebrew *bekha'im* resists botanic identification—mulberry tree, pear tree, mastic bush, and others have been proposed. Some think it is a place-name, but the next verse makes that unlikely.

24. *the sound of marching in the tops of the willows.* Presumably, this is the wind. But it gives a sense that mysterious unseen agents of the LORD are advancing against the Philistines. More practically, some interpreters have proposed that the sound of the wind in the branches provided a cover for the sound of David's troops stealthily advancing for their surprise attack from the rear.

25. *from Geba till you come to Gezer.* Unlike the first victory, David now inflicts a general defeat on the Philistine forces, driving them back from the territory in central Palestine that they had occupied after triumphing over Saul at Gilboa. David has now completed the consolidation of his rule over all the land, and his real troubles are about to begin.

CHAPTER 6

A nd David gathered again all the picked men of Israel, thirty thousand. 1
And David arose and went, and all the troops who were with him, to 2
Baalah in Judah to bring up from there the Ark of God, over which the
name of the LORD of Hosts enthroned on the cherubim is called. And 3
they mounted the Ark of God on a new cart and carried it off from the
house of Abinadab, which is on the Hill, and Uzzah and Ahio, the sons
of Abinadab, were driving the cart, and Ahio was walking before the 4

---

1. *thirty thousand.* Some modern commentators understand ʾalafim, "thousands," as "military contingents," and thus reduce the number of troops to a
few hundred elite soldiers. But ʾalafim in a non-numerical sense refers to
clans, not military units; and as we have abundantly seen, exaggerated numbers are common in these stories. Polzin, moreover, has aptly observed that
thirty thousand is precisely the number of Israelites slain when the Ark was
captured by the Philistines (1 Samuel 4)

2. *to Baalah in Judah.* This place-name is a synonym for the Kiriath-jearim of 1
Samuel 7:1—see, for example Joshua 15:9. The Qumran Samuel scroll in fact
reads here: "Baalah, which is Kiriath-jearim in Judah." The Masoretic Text
reads baʿaley yehudah. Because this erroneous phrase was construed to mean
"the notables of Judah," a *mem* prefix ("from") was added to it to yield "from
the notables of Judah." But David is clearly going *to* the place Baalah.

3. *A new cart.* The new cart is a vehicle unpolluted by any previous secular use.

4. The Masoretic Text begins this verse with a whole clause that is a scribal
duplication (dittography) of the first half of verse 3: "And they carried it off
from the house of Abinadab which is on the Hill." This clause is not present in
the Qumran Samuel, in the Septuagint, or in the parallel verse in 1 Chronicles
13:7. The Masoretic Text also repeats the adjective "new" (ḥadashah) at the
end of verse 3, a repetition not reflected in the other ancient versions.

5   Ark. And David and the whole house of Israel were playing before the
LORD with all their might in song on lyres and tambourines and cas-
6   tanets and cymbals. And they came to the threshing floor of Nacon,
and Uzzah reached out to the Ark of God and took hold of it, for the
7   oxen had slipped. And the LORD's wrath flared up against Uzzah, and
God struck him down there for reaching out his hand to the Ark, and
8   he died there by the Ark of God. And David was incensed because the
LORD had burst out against Uzzah. And that place has been called
9   Perez-uzzah to this day. And David was afraid of the LORD on that day
10 and he said, "How can the Ark of the LORD come to me?" And David
did not want to remove the Ark of the LORD to himself in the City of
David, and David had it turned aside to the house of Obed-edom the

---

5. *with all their might in song.* The translation reads here *bekhol ʿoz uveshirim*
with 1 Chronicles 13:8. The Masoretic Text has *bekhol ʿatsey beroshim,* "with
all cypress woods," which only by a long interpretive stretch has been made to
refer to percussion instruments.

6. *the threshing floor of Nacon.* The proper name here is in question. The
Qumran Samuel reads "Nadon."

7. *the LORD's wrath flared up . . . and God struck him down.* This is an archaic
story that defies later ethical categories: The Ark, as God's terrestrial throne, is
invested with awesome divine power (compare 1 Samuel 6). To touch it, even
in an effort to keep it from slipping off the cart, is to risk being consumed by
its indwelling mana, as when one comes in contact with a high-voltage elec-
tric core. God's wrath against Uzzah triggers an answering wrath (the same
verb in the Hebrew) on the part of David, frustrated in his purposes and now
wondering whether he will ever manage to bring this symbol and earthly focus
of God's power to his newly conquered capital.
    for reaching out his hand to the Ark. The translation follows the parallel ver-
sion in 1 Chronicles 13:10. The Masoretic Text here has a single incomprehen-
sible word, *shal,* which might be simply two consonants from the initial words
of the lost clause recorded in Chronicles.

8. *Perez-uzzah.* The Hebrew is construed to mean "bursting out against
Uzzah." The naming story forms an antithetical symmetry with the story in 2
Samuel 5 of Baal-perazim, there associated with God's "bursting through" the
Philistine ranks.

Gittite. And the Ark of the LORD remained in the house of Obed-edom   11
three months and the LORD blessed Obed-edom and all his house. And   12
it was told to King David saying, "The LORD has blessed the house of
Obed-edom and all that he has on account of the Ark of God." And
David went and brought up the Ark of God from the house of Obed-
edom to the City of David with rejoicing.

  13

And it happened when the bearers of the Ark of the LORD had taken six   14
steps that he sacrificed a fatted bull. And David was whirling with all   15
his might before the LORD, girt in a linen ephod. And David and the
whole house of Israel were bringing up the Ark of the LORD in shouts   16
and with the sound of the ram's horn. And as the Ark of the LORD came

---

11. *Obed-edom the Gittite.* He is a foreigner, perhaps (though this is not certain) from Philistine Gath—conceivably someone who had attached himself
to David during his sojourn there.

13. *when the bearers of the Ark of the LORD had taken six steps.* Some construe
this as an imperfect verb: with every six steps David would sacrifice a bull.
Apart from the difficulty that these constant sacrifices would make the procession interminable and require scores of thousands of bulls, the imperfect
would require the verb "to be" at the beginning of the sentence to appear in
the suffix conjugation *wehayah,* instead of the way it is, in the prefix conjugation, *wayehi,* which implies a singulative, not an iterative, tense for the
verb.

14. *girt in a linen ephod.* The wearing of the ephod surely underscores the fact
that in the procession of the Ark into Jerusalem David is playing the roles of
both priest and king—a double service not unknown in the ancient Near East
(compare Melchisedek in Genesis 14). The ephod was probably a short garment tied around the hips or waist, and so David whirling and leaping might
easily have exposed himself, as Michal will bitterly observe.

into the City of David, Michal daughter of Saul looked out through the window and saw King David leaping and whirling before the LORD, and

17 she scorned him in her heart. And they brought the Ark of the LORD and set it up in its place within the tent that David had pitched for it, and David offered up burnt offerings before the LORD and communion

18 sacrifices. And David finished offering up the burnt offering and the communion sacrifices, and he blessed the people in the name of the

19 LORD of Hosts. And he shared out to all the people, to all the multitude of Israel, every man and woman, one loaf of bread and one date cake and one raisin cake, and every one of the people went to his home.

20 And David turned back to bless his house. And Michal daughter of Saul came out to meet David, and she said, "How honored today is the

---

16. *Michal daughter of Saul looked out through the window and saw King David.* The preceding verse reports the shouts of jubilation and the shrill blasts of the ram's horn: first she hears the procession approaching from the distance, then she looks out and sees David dancing. Strategically, her repeated epithet in this episode of final estrangement is "daughter of Saul," not "wife of David," and the figure she sees is not "David her husband" but "King David." Shimon Bar-Efrat neatly observes that at the beginning of their story a loving Michal helped David escape "through the window" from her father's henchmen while now she looks at him from a distance "through the window," in seething contempt.

17.–20. Instead of proceeding directly to the confrontation between Michal and David, as we might expect, the narrative lingers for a long moment over David's cultic ministrations and royal benefactions to the people. One can imagine that Michal continues to watch from the window at David, performing his role as the people's darling, and that she continues to simmer.

19. *date cake.* The Hebrew *ʾeshpar* appears nowhere else and so it is only a guess as to what sort of delicacy it might be. Some traditional commentators construe it as a portion of meat.

20. *How honored today is the king of Israel.* Astoundingly, until this climactic moment, there has been no dialogue between Michal and David—only her urgent instructions for him to flee in 1 Samuel 19 and his silent flight. We can only guess what she may have felt all those years he was away from her, acquiring power and wives, or during the civil war with her father's family. We are equally ignorant of her feelings toward her devoted second husband, Paltiel son of Laish. Now the royal couple are finally represented meeting, and

king of Israel who has exposed himself today to the eyes of his servants'
slavegirls as some scurrilous fellow would expose himself!" And David   21
said to Michal, "Before the LORD, Who chose me instead of your
father and instead of all his house, to appoint me prince over the
LORD's people, over Israel, I will play before the LORD! And I will be   22
dishonored still more than this and will be debased in my own eyes!

---

when Michal speaks out, it is in an explosion of angry sarcasm. Her first significant word "honored" (balanced in David's rejoinder by two antonyms, "dishonored" and "debased") is a complex satellite to the story of the grand entry
of the Ark with which it is linked. When the Ark was lost to the Philistines (1
Samuel 4), the great cry was that "glory [or, honor, *kavod*—the same verbal
root Michal uses here] was exiled from Israel." Now glory/honor splendidly
returns to Israel, but the actual invocation of the term is a sarcastic one, bitterly directed at David, who will then hurl back two antonyms and try to rede-
fine both honor and dishonor to his wife. The logic of the larger story's moral
and historical realism requires that no triumph should be simple and unambiguous, that strife and accusation pursue even the fulfillment of national
destiny. One should also note here that Michal speaks to her husband in the
third person, not deferentially but angrily, and refers to him by public title, not
in any personal relation to her.

who has exposed himself today to the eyes of his servants' slavegirls. The verb
"to expose" is clearly used in the sexual sense. The proud Michal's reference
to the lowly slavegirls' enjoying the sight of David's nakedness probably suggests an edge of sexual jealousy as well as political resentment in her rage
against him. He has, after all, assembled a harem during their years apart, and
there is no indication that he has resumed sexual relations with her after having her brought back to him forcibly for obviously political motives.

as some scurrilous fellow would expose himself. The social thrust of the comparison is evident: she is a king's daughter, whereas he has now demonstrated
that he is no more than riffraff.

21. *Before the LORD.* Isaac Abravanel, the Hebrew commentator who was also
Ferdinand and Isabella's financial advisor until the expulsion of 1492, aptly
explains this: "Had he danced before some person to honor him, it would have
been a contemptible act, for his status was higher than any other person's. But
in his leaping before the LORD there is no cause for contempt." Thus David
can go on to say that he will perform ostensibly debasing acts, even debasing
in his own eyes (emending this to "His eyes" only clouds matters), acts which
in paradoxical fact are the opposite of debasement.

But with the slavegirls about whom you spoke, with them let me be
23 honored!" And Michal daughter of Saul had no child till her dying day.

---

22. *with the slavegirls . . . with them let me be honored.* David flings back
Michal's sarcastic "how honored," suggesting that, unlike Michal, the simple
slavegirls will understand that his gyrations before the Ark are an act of reverence and will honor him for it. And there may also be a sexual edge in his
rejoinder: I will display myself to whomever I please, and it is I who will
decide whether it is honorable or not.

23. *And Michal daughter of Saul had no child till her dying day.* The whole story
of David and Michal concludes on a poised ambiguity through the suppression of causal explanation: Is this a punishment from God, or simply a refusal
by David to share her bed, or is the latter to be understood as the agency for
the former?

CHAPTER 7

And it happened when the king was dwelling in his house and the LORD 1
had granted him respite all around from his enemies, that the king said 2
to Nathan the prophet, "See, pray, I dwell in a cedarwood house while
the Ark of God dwells within curtains." And Nathan said to the king, 3

---

1. *And it happened when the king was dwelling in his house.* This transitional
note establishes a link with the previous episode, in which David brought the
Ark into Jerusalem and had his final confrontation with Michal, which in a
sense was the final blow to the house of Saul. What follows is a major cesura in
the David story—a long pause marked by ideological reflections on the future,
before David must deal once again with external enemies and then be engulfed
by internecine strife in his court. The language of both Nathan's night vision
and David's prayer is strikingly different from that of the surrounding narrative—more hortatory, more formulaic, more reminiscent of the Deuteronomistic school that would come to dominate Israel's national literature nearly
four centuries after the reign of David. The literary archeology that has been
performed on these two long passages remains in contention, some scholars
claiming these are late compositions of a Deuteronomistic writer, others argu-
ing that two or more authentically old literary strata have been joined together
and framed by a later editor. These are not issues that it will be useful to
attempt to resolve here. What is worth noting is the deliberate structural separation effected by these two passages between everything that precedes the
ensconcing of throne and Ark in Jerusalem and everything that follows.

respite . . . from his enemies. The respite is partial, and temporary, because
the subsequent chapters report further military campaigns.

2. *Nathan the prophet.* Not previously mentioned, and of unspecified background, he will play an important role in what follows.

a cedarwood house. The palace would have been a stone structure with cedar
panelling within. Cedar was an expensive import item brought from Lebanon.
(See 5:11.)

curtains. The term is an obvious synecdoche for tent (compare 6:17).

4 "Whatever is in your heart, go, do, for the LORD is with you." And it
happened on that night, that the word of the LORD came to Nathan,
5 saying, "Go, say to My servant, to David, 'Thus says the LORD: Is it you
6 who would build Me a house for Me to dwell in? For I have dwelt in no
house from the day I brought up the Israelites out of Egypt until this
7 day, but I have gone about in tent and tabernacle. Wherever I went
about among all the Israelites, did I speak a word with any of the tribal
chiefs of Israel whom I charged to shepherd My people Israel, saying,
8 Why did you not build me a cedarwood house? And now, thus shall you

---

3. *Whatever is in your heart, go, do.* Nathan's response to the brilliantly successful king, who has demonstrated through his triumphs that God is with
him, is perfectly reasonable. But in the night vision God will give different
directions.

5. *Thus says the* LORD. The "messenger formula" signals the beginning of
explicit prophetic discourse. God's address to Nathan as a whole emphasizes
the act of speech, being constructed as an elaborate nesting of quoted speech
within quoted speech.

6. *I have dwelt in no house.* This is not, as some interpreters have claimed, the
expression of a pre-Solomonic antitemple ideology. The author of this episode
is faced with the difficulty of explaining a historical fact, that David did not
build the temple, as we might have expected, but rather it was his son
Solomon who carried out the construction. The probable historical reason
was that David was too preoccupied with the struggles within his own court
and family. In Chronicles, the reason given is that he had shed blood. Here,
the argument God makes is that it is an act of presumption for a mere mortal
to build a temple for the unhoused God of Israelite history. But this line of
reasoning actually enhances the theological importance of Solomon's temple,
for it suggests that God Himself will build a house when He is good and ready,
using the human agency He chooses. Thus the temple that is to be raised up
by David's seed will have a more than human importance, being at once a
token of God's indwelling among His people Israel and a divine underwriting
of the Davidic dynasty.
    in tent and tabernacle. The latter was a portable shrine made of boards and
curtains. Presumably, local sanctuaries such as the one at Shiloh are assimi-
lated into the archetype of tabernacle, being neither cultic centers for the
entire nation nor grand edifices like the Solomonic temple.

say to My servant, to David, Thus says the LORD of Hosts: I Myself took you from the pasture, from following the flocks, to be prince over My people, over Israel. And I have been with you wherever you have 9 gone, and I have cut down your enemies before you. And I will make you a great name, like the name of the great of the earth. And I will set 10 aside a place for My people, for Israel, and plant them, and they shall abide there and no longer quake, and the wicked shall no more afflict them as before, from the day that I appointed judges over My people 11 Israel. And I will grant you respite from all your enemies, and the LORD declares that it is He Who will make you a house. When your days are 12 full and you lie with your fathers, I will raise up your seed after you, who will issue from your loins, and I will make his kingship unshaken. He it is who will build a house for My name and I will make the throne 13 of his kingship unshaken forever. I will be a father to him and he will 14 be a son to me, so should he do wrong, I will chastise him with the rod men use and with the afflictions of humankind. But My loyalty shall 15 not swerve from him as I made it swerve from Saul whom I removed from before you. And your house and your kingship shall be steadfast 16

10.–11. *no more afflict them as before, from the day I appointed judges.* Though the judges succeeded in temporarily driving off Israel's sundry oppressors, the period as a whole was one of instability and recurrent harrassment by enemy peoples.

11. *it is He Who will make you a house.* Both in this prophecy and in David's prayer the double meaning of "house" is repeatedly exploited. God will grant David a house—that is, a continuing dynasty, and then will have David's son build Him a house—that is, a temple. The house in which David dwells in the opening verse of this chapter is of course his palace in Jerusalem.

14. *the rod men use   the afflictions of humankind.* God will discipline the future king as a father disciplines his son, and with familiar human tribulations, not with supernatural bolts from the heavens.

15. *my loyalty.* The Hebrew *hesed* is the faithfulness and goodwill that one party of a pact owes to the other.
whom I removed. The Hebrew uses the same verb that is rendered here in the immediately preceding phrase as "made it swerve."

17 forever, your throne unshaken forever.' " In accordance with all these
words and in accordance with all this vision, so did Nathan speak to
David.

18 And King David came and sat before the LORD and said, "Who am I,
LORD God, and what is my house, that you have brought me this far?
19 And even this is too little in Your eyes, LORD God, for You have also
spoken of Your servant's house in distant time, and this is a man's
20 instruction, LORD God. And how can David speak more to You, when
21 You know Your servant, LORD God? For the sake of Your word, and
according to Your heart You have done all these great things, to make
22 known to Your servant. Therefore are You great, O LORD God, for there
is none like You and there is no god beside You, in all we have heard
23 with our own ears. And who is like Your people Israel, a unique nation

---

18. *David came and sat before the* LORD. David comes into the tent in which
the Ark has been placed. The verb "sat," *yashav,* is identical with the verb at
the beginning of the chapter that also means "dwell," and thus establishes a
structural parallel between the passage on the postponed building of the temple and David's prayer.

19. *You have also spoken of Your servant's house in a distant time.* These
words refer directly to the prophecy conveyed to Nathan in verses 12–16,
and thus undermine the claim of some scholars that David's prayer was originally part of the story of the introduction of the Ark to Jerusalem (Chapter
6), from which it was supposedly separated by the insertion of Nathan's
prophecy.
    this is a man's instruction. That is, he would scarcely think himself worthy
of all this divine bounty about which God has just instructed him. But this is
no more than an interpretive guess, for the meaning of the Hebrew—*zᵓot torat
haᵓadam*—is obscure.

22. *Therefore are You great, O* LORD *God. . . .* Although the thread of piety in
David's complex and contradictory character could be perfectly authentic, he
does not elsewhere speak in this elevated, liturgical, celebratory style, and so
the inference of the presence of another writer in this passage might be plausible. Yet it is at least conceivable that the writer has introduced this celebratory rhetoric to punctuate David's moment of respite in the story.

upon earth, whom a god has gone out to redeem as a people to make
Him a name and to do great and awesome things for them, to drive out
from before Your people whom You redeemed from Egypt, nations with
their gods? And you made them Your own people Israel unshaken for-   24
ever, and You, O LORD, became their God. And now LORD God, the   25
word that You have spoken to Your servant concerning his house—
make it stand forever and do as You have spoken. And may Your name   26
be great forever, so it be said, 'The LORD of Hosts is God over Israel,
and the house of David Your servant shall be unshaken before You.' For   27
You, O LORD of Hosts, God of Israel, have revealed to Your servant,
saying, 'A house will I build you.' Therefore has Your servant found the
heart to pray to you this prayer. And now, O LORD God, You are God   28
and Your words must be truth, You have spoken of this bounty to Your
servant. And now, have the goodness to bless the house of Your servant   29
to be before You forever, for it is You, LORD God, Who have spoken,
and with Your blessings may Your servant's house be blessed forever."

---

23. *for them.* The Masoretic Text, at several points in these verses problematic,
has "for you" (plural). The Qumran Samuel and the Septuagint have no pronoun.

to drive out. The Masoretic Text is syntactically odd and semantically
obscure. The parallel verse in Chronicles omits "for your land" and adds "to
drive out," as does this translation.

25. *the word that You have spoken to Your servant concerning his house.* This
word has just been conveyed to David through Nathan as God's intermediary.
It is humanly understandable that David should now fervently pray to God
that the grand promise of the night vision be fulfilled in time to come.

29. *it is You, LORD God, Who have spoken, and with Your blessings may Your servant's house be blessed forever.* The fondness of biblical prose for thematic key
words is especially prominent in the grand theological performance that is
David's prayer, in which the key words function as formal rhetorical motifs.
The salient repeated terms are "speak" (the act of God's promise and continuing revelation), "house" (dynasty and palace but, in this speech, not temple),
"blessing" (in the final sentence it occurs three times in three different forms),
and "forever" (the adverbial index of the permanence of God's promise).

CHAPTER 8

1   And it happened thereafter that David struck down the Philistines and subjugated them, and David took Metheg-ammah from the hand of the Philistines. And he struck down Moab, and measured them out with a line, making them lie on the ground, and he measured two lengths of a line to put to death and one full length to keep alive. And

3   Moab became tribute-bearing vassals to David. And David struck

---

1. *And it happened thereafter.* This characteristically vague temporal reference actually reflects the achronological arrangement of the narrative material at this point. Chapter 7 was a long pause in the progress of the larger story that was devoted to the theological grounds for the postponement of building a temple and to the promise of a perpetual Davidic dynasty. Chapter 8 offers a summary of David's conquests (which in historical fact would have spanned at least several years) resulting in the establishment of a small empire. We then revert to the intimate story of David.

David struck down the Philistines and subjugated them. Neither the Hebrew terms of the text nor the scant extrabiblical evidence allow one to conclude whether David actually occupied the Philistine cities on the coastal plain or merely reduced them to vassal status. In any case, he put an end to the Philistine military threat and was free to turn his attention to adversaries east of the Jordan.

Metheg-ammah. There are differences of opinion as to whether this is an otherwise unknown place-name or the designation of some precious trophy (*meteg* is an equestrian bit, ʾ*amah* is a watercourse) taken from the Philistines.

2. *Moab.* It should be recalled that Moab, with whom David is linked by ancestry, provided refuge for his parents from Saul. Perhaps now that David has consolidated an Israelite monarchy, each side views the other as a threat. Or perhaps Moab has been compelled by proximity to join forces with the anti-Israelite kingdoms east of the Jordan.

and measured them out with a line. This procedure is not otherwise known.

down Hadadezer son of Rehob, king of Zobah, as he went to restore his
monument by the Euphrates River. And David captured from him one 4
thousand seven hundred horsemen and twenty thousand foot soldiers,
and David hamstrung all the chariot horses, leaving aside a hundred of
them. And the Arameans of Damascus came to aid Hadadezer, king of 5
Zobah, and David struck down twenty-two thousand men from among
the Arameans. And David set up prefects in Aram-Damascus, and the 6
Arameans became tribute-bearing vassals to David, and the LORD
made David victorious wherever he went. And David took the golden 7
quivers that had belonged to the servants of Hadadezer and brought
them to Jerusalem. And from Betah and from Berothai, the towns of 8
Hadadezer, King David took a great abundance of bronze.

---

3. *Zobah.* Aram-Zobah was at this point the large dominant kingdom of
Mesopotamia, to the north and east of biblical Israel.

as he went to restore his monument. Presumably, the absence of the king
from the Aramean heartland exposed it to David's attack. The term *yad* here
(usually "hand") is construed in its occasional sense of monument or stele,
though the idiom *heshiv yad* (literally, "to bring back the hand") also has the
sense of "strike." Were that the case here, however, one would probably
expect an object to the striking ("brought his hand back against X.").

4. *one thousand seven hundred horsemen . . .* The numbers reflected in Chronicles and in the Septuagint as well as in the Qumran Samuel scroll are "one
thousand chariots and seven thousand horsemen."

David hamstrung all the horses. The most likely explanation for this cruel
act is that the Israelites, who initially fought in mountainous terrain, as yet
made no significant use of cavalry, and so David's only concern would be to
disable the horses in order that they could not be used against him in the
future. The hundred horses left unmaimed might perhaps be for use as a
small experiment with cavalry, or as draft animals.

7. *the golden quivers.* The relatively rare Hebrew term *shelitim* has often been
understood as "shields," but most of the other biblical occurrences encourage
the notion of something that contains arrows, as Rashi observed, and this
sense is supported by cognates in Babylonian and Aramaic.

9 And Toi king of Hammath heard that David had struck down all the
10 forces of Hadadezer. And Toi sent Joram his son to King David to ask
after his well-being and to salute him for having done battle with
Hadadezer and for striking him down, as Hadadezer was Toi's adversary.
And in Joram's hand there were vessels of silver and vessels of gold and
11 vessels of bronze. These, too, did King David consecrate to the LORD,
together with the silver and the gold that he consecrated from all the
12 nations he had conquered: from Edom and from Moab and from the
Ammonites and from the Philistines and from Amalek and from the
13 plunder of Hadadezer son of Rehob, king of Zobah. And David made a
name when he came back from striking down the Edomites in the Val-
14 ley of Salt—eighteen thousand of them. And he set up prefects in
Edom, throughout Edom he set up prefects and all Edom became vassals to David, and the LORD made David victorious wherever he went.

15 And David was king over all Israel, and it was David's practice to mete
16 out true justice to all his people. And Joab son of Zeruiah was over the

---

9. *Toi king of Hammath*. Hammath lay to the northwest of the kingdom of
Aram-Zobah, in present-day Syria. It was a neo-Hittite state.

10. *And Toi sent Joram his son to King David*. Sending the prince as emissary is
a token of the importance that the king attaches to the mission. The vessels of
precious metals are a peace offering to David or, from another perspective, an
advance payment of tribute. Toi, as a king who has been threatened by the
Arameans, has good reason to pledge fealty to David, but he surely also wants
to ward off any possible military thrust of the expansionist Israelites against
his own kingdom.

12. *from Edom*. The Masoretic Text has "from Aram," but Chronicles, the Septuagint, and the Peshitta all have Edom, a kingdom contiguous with Moab,
which immediately follows. Aram (Zobah) is mentioned at the end of the verse.

13. *from striking the Edomites*. Again, the Maoretic Text has "Aram" in contradiction to several other ancient versions. Since the Valley of Salt was most
probably in the vicinity of the Dead Sea, it would have been Edomite, not
Aramean, territory.

15. *And David was king over all Israel*. The chronicle of David's conquests is
followed by a kind of epilogue—a notice of the royal bureaucracy.

army, and Jehoshaphat son of Ahilud was recorder. And Zadok son of   17
Ahitub and Abiathar son of Ahimelech were priests, and Seraiah was
scribe. And Benaiah son of Jehoidah was over the Cherethites and the   18
Pelethites, and David's sons served as priests.

---

16. *recorder.* The Hebrew term *mazkir* could also be represented as "remem-
brancer." It is not entirely clear what his duties were, though they obviously
went far beyond being a mere clerk. He may have been in control of the royal
archives. It has been proposed that he was also chief of protocol in the palace.

17. *Abiathar son of Ahimelech.* The Masoretic Text makes Ahimelech the son
and Abiathar the father, in flat contradiction to the occurrences of these two
figures both earlier and later in the narrative.
   scribe. As with "recorder," the responsibilities were more than those of an
amanuensis. They might have included diplomatic translation and even coun-
seling in affairs of state.

18. *the Cherethites and the Pelethites.* There is debate over the national identity
of the latter but consensus that the former are people of Cretan origins, part
of the wave of so-called Sea Peoples who immigrated to Palestine from the
Aegean toward the beginning of the eleventh century. David has taken care to
set up a special palace guard of foreign mercenaries on whose loyalty he can
rely, in contrast to Israelites who might have motives of tribal allegiance or
support for some pretender to the throne to attempt to displace him.
   and David's sons served as priests. This curious detail is probably parallel to
the report of a palace guard of foreign origins: just as David creates an elite
military contingent outside the framework of the Israelite troops, he invests
his own sons with sacerdotal duties within the circle of the court, outside the
framework of the hereditary priesthood that controlled the public cult.

CHAPTER 9

nd David said, "Is there anyone who is still left from the house of Saul, that I may keep faith with him for the sake of Jonathan?" And there was a servant of the house of Saul named Ziba, and they called him to David, and the king said to him, "Are you Ziba?" And he said, "Your servant." And the king said, "Is there anyone at all left from the house of Saul, that I might keep God's faith with him?" And Ziba said to the

---

1. *And David said.* We are immediately alerted to the fact that we are returning from the chronicle summary of Chapter 8 (where there is no dialogue) and from the long set speeches of Chapter 7 to the main body of the David story because once again the narrative is carried forward to a large extent by dialogue. We are again plunged into a world of personal and political transactions engaged through exchanges of spoken language.

Is there anyone who is still left from the house of Saul? The added emphasis of "still," *ʿod* (compare the analogous emphatic phrase in verse 3) reflects David's genuine uncertainty as to whether, after all the deaths of the Saulides previously reported, there are in fact any surviving descendants of Saul. The courtiers who are queried evidently don't know, so they propose summoning a retainer of Saul's in order to put the question to him. The fact that David is later complicit in the execution of seven men of the house of Saul (Chapter 21) has led many analysts to conclude that the original place of that episode was before the present chapter. Polzin, on the other hand, argues that the postponement of the report in Chapter 21 is deliberately delayed exposition, meant to reveal another troubling facet of David near the end of his story.

3. *keep God's faith.* The "faith" in question (*ḥesed*) is not credal but faithful performance of one's obligation in a covenant, a term that also has the connotation of "kindness." "God" here has the force of an intensifier. The covenant that is explicitly alluded to is the one between Jonathan and David (1 Samuel 20:42). That tight link is one of several arguments against the view widely held ever since the 1926 study of Leonhard Rost that this episode marks the beginning of a wholly independent Succession Narrative which continues till 1 Kings 2.

king, "There is yet a son of Jonathan's, who is crippled." And the king   4
said, "Where is he?" And Ziba said, "Why, he is in the house of Machir
son of Amiel from Lo-debar." And King David sent and fetched him   5
from the house of Amiel son of Machir from Lo-debar. And Mephi-   6
bosheth son of Jonathan son of Saul came to David and flung himself
on his face and prostrated himself. And David said, "Mephibosheth!"
And he said, "Your servant here." And David said to him, "Fear not, for   7
I will surely keep faith with you for the sake of Jonathan your father,
and I will give back to you all the land of Saul your grandfather, and as
for you, you shall eat bread at my table always." And he prostrated him-   8
self and said, "What is your servant that you should have turned to a

---

who is crippled. Ziba's mention of the surviving Saulide's handicap is probably intended to assure David that Mephibosheth will not pose any challenge
to the throne.

4. *Lo-debar.* Mephibosheth was evidently taken to this northern Transjordanian town because it was a place of refuge. It is in the general vicinity of
Jabesh-gilead, the town inhabited by Saul's allies and perhaps kinsmen.
Mephibosheth, it will be recalled, was five years old when he was dropped by
his nurse and crippled in the flight after the defeat at Gilboa. Since it seems
implausible that more than fifteen or so years would have passed since that
moment, one may surmise that he is now a man in his twenties.

6. *Mephibosheth . . . flung himself on his face and prostrated himself.* These gestures of abasement may have been standard etiquette in approaching a
monarch, but Ziba is not reported making them. Mephibosheth is clearly terrified that the king may have summoned him in order to have him put to
death—David's possible complicity in the deaths of other figures associated
with the house of Saul might well have been a matter of continuing speculation in Benjaminite circles. As Fokkelman aptly notes, it would have been a
particularly painful business for a man crippled in both legs to fling himself
down in this fashion.

7. *I will give back to you all the land of Saul.* With the descendants of Saul fled
or dead, the king had expropriated Saul's ancestral land around Gibeah.

9   dead dog like me?" And the king called to Ziba, Saul's lad, and said to
    him, "All that was Saul's and his whole household's I give to your mas-
10 ter's son. And you shall work the soil for him, you and your sons and
    your slaves, and you shall bring food to your master's house and they
    will eat. But Mephibosheth will always eat bread at my table."
11 And Ziba had fifteen sons and twenty slaves. And Ziba said to the
    king, "Whatever my lord the king commands his servant, thus will
    his servant do." And Mephibosheth ate at David's table like one of
12 the king's sons. And Mephibosheth had a little son named Micha,
    and all who dwelled in Ziba's house were servants to Mephibosheth.

---

9. *Saul's lad.* The Hebrew *na'ar* denotes subservience, but it is unclear
whether, as some have claimed, it indicates Ziba's role as majordomo (the
philological grounds for that construction are shaky) or rather his subaltern
status in the house of Saul.

10. *your slaves.* The Hebrew term *'eved* straddles the sense of freeborn
underling and slave. Ziba evidently belongs to the former category, and so
the designation *'eved* is rendered as "servant" when it is attached to him. It
seems likely that the underlings of a prosperous servant would be slaves.
Polzin has noted that different forms of this verbal stem occur ten times in
the chapter, which is all about establishing lines of dominance and subservience.

   and you shall bring food for your master's house and they will eat. The translation here follows the text of the Septuagint. The Masoretic Text reads: "and
you shall bring and it will be food for your master's son and he will eat it." That
version can be maintained only with strain, for the very next clause informs us
that Mephibosheth was not dependent on the yield of his own land but
resided in Jerusalem, sustained at the royal table.

11. *And Mephibosheth ate at David's table.* Again, the translation follows the
Septuagint. The Masoretic Text has "And Mephibosheth is eating at my
table," but the Bible never gives reported speech without an explicit introduction ("and David said").

And Mephibosheth dwelled in Jerusalem, for at the king's table he   13
would always eat. And he was lame in both his feet.

---

13. *for at the king's table he would always eat.* The refrainlike repetition of this
clause should give us pause. David is indeed treating Jonathan's crippled son
like one of his own sons, "keeping faith" or "showing kindness" to the offspring
of his dead comrade, as he had pledged. He surely means his benefaction to
be publicly perceived. At the same time, it is clearly in David's interest to keep
the only conceivable Saulide pretender to the throne close at hand, under
easy scrutiny. Mephibosheth's condition is ostensibly that of an unofficially
adopted son, but with an uneasy suspicion that it is really a kind of luxurious
house arrest.

And he was lame in both his feet. This emphatic concluding reiteration of
his physical impairment might be intended, as some commentators have proposed, to explain why he could not travel back and forth between his estate
and Jerusalem. But it surely also strikes a plaintive note at the end, underscor-
ing the vulnerability of Mephibosheth, whether cosseted or held under surveillance in the Jerusalem court. As the court becomes more and more the
arena of plots and murderous conflict, Mephibosheth will be victimized by
someone close to him. This notice at the end about Mephibosheth's lameness
also underscores the continuing antithesis between the fates of the house of
Saul and the house of David: King David came into Jerusalem whirling and
dancing before the LORD; the surviving Saulide limps into Jerusalem, crippled
in both legs.

CHAPTER 10

1 And it happened thereafter that the king of the Ammonites died and
2 Hanun his son was king in his stead. And David said, "Let me keep
faith with Hanun son of Nahash as his father kept faith with me." And
David sent his servants in order to console him for his father, and
3 David's servants came to the land of the Ammonites. And the
Ammonite commanders said to Hanun their lord, "Do you imagine
David is honoring your father in sending you consolers? Is it not in

---

1. *And it happened thereafter.* Once again this vague temporal formula reflects
the achronological ordering of the text. Since the Aramean king Hadadezer is
reported in 8:3–7 to have been decisively defeated by David and to have
become David's vassal, the campaign that is represented here, in which
Hadadezer musters Aramean forces east of the Euphrates in order to confront
David, must have taken place as part of David's victorious struggle with Aram
Zobah registered in the summary of Chapter 8. This whole account of military
operations—given its rather dry technical style, it may well have been drawn
from Davidic annals—is meant to establish the facts of continuing armed
conflict with the Ammonites, which is the crucial background for the story of
David and Bathsheba in the next chapter.

2. *Let me keep faith with Hanun son of Nahash as his father kept faith with me.*
This chapter, like the preceding one, opens with a declaration of David's
desire to keep faith with, or do kindness to, the son of a father toward whom
he feels some prior obligation. There is no notice in the previous narrative of
Nahash's having done favors for David, but several scholars have surmised
that Nahash's enmity toward Saul (see 1 Samuel:11) might have led him to
provide refuge or logistical support to David and his men when they were
being hunted down by Saul.

order to search out the city and to spy on it and to overthrow it that
David has sent his servants to you?" And Hanun took David's servants   4
and shaved off half the beard of each and cut off half their diplomat's
garb down to their buttocks, and sent them off. And they told David,   5
and he sent to meet them, for the men were very humiliated, and the
king said, "Stay here in Jericho until your beards grow back and you
can return."

And the Ammonites saw that they had become repugnant to David,   6
and the Ammonites sent and hired Arameans from Beth-rehob and
Arameans from Zobah, twenty thousand foot soldiers, and King

---

3. *to search out the city.* As Moshe Garsiel notes, the walled cities of the ancient
Near East often had tunnels, underground conduits, or other points of vulnerability that could provide access to the enemy in a seige. David's forces may
have broken into Jerusalem in this fashion. (See the comment on 5:8).

4. *Shaved off half the beard of each and cut off their diplomats' garb.* Shaving the
beard is an insult to the masculinity of the ambassadors, all the more so
because it is done in a disfiguring way, with half the beard left uncut. The
exposure of one buttock, by cutting away half the garment vertically, is simula-
rly shaming, perhaps sexually shaming. The garments in question, moreover,
are not ordinary clothes, *begadim,* but *madim,* garb worn in the performance
of an official function (compare the "battle garb," *madim,* that Saul gives to
David in 1:17:38). The Ammonites thus are not merely insulting the ambassadors personally but provocatively violating their diplomatic privilege. In all
this, we observe an extravagant reflection of the symbolic violation of Saul by
David when he cut off a corner of the king's robe.

5. *Stay here in Jericho.* The town of Jericho is in the Jordan Valley just west of
the Jordan, and is plausibly the first place of habitation that the ambassadors
would come to on crossing back from Ammonite territory.

6. *And the Ammonites saw.* Shimon Bar Efrat observes that this narrative
sequence is formally structured by the "seeing" of David's Transjordanian
adversaries (here, verse 14, verse 15, verse 19), in counterpoint to David's
"hearing." The latter implies receiving word at a distance, as does the associated locution, "it was told to David," whereas the former signifies immediate
observation. Thus Joab, making out the deployment of hostile forces on the
battlefield, is also said to see.

Maacah with a thousand men, and the men of Tob, twelve thousand
7 men. And David heard and sent out Joab together with the whole army
8 of warriors. And the Ammonites sallied forth and drew up for battle at
the entrance to the gate, and Aram Zobah and Rehob and the men of
9 Tob were apart in the field. And Joab saw that there was a battle line
against him in front and behind, and he chose from all the picked men
10 of Israel and drew them up to meet the Arameans. And the rest of the
troops he gave into the hand of Abishai his brother, and he drew them
11 up to meet the Ammonites. And he said, "If the Arameans prove too
strong for me, you will rescue me, and if the Ammonites prove too

---

7. *David heard and sent out Joab.* Throughout this chapter and the next, the
verb "to send" is repeatedly linked with David: for the first time, he plays the
role not of martial leader but of sedentary king, delegating the military task to
his commander. This new state of affairs will have major implications in the
Bathsheba story.

the whole army of warriors. This is a slight variant, supported by three
ancient versions, of the Masoretic Text, which reads "the whole army, the warriors."

9. *there was a battle line against him in front and behind.* The Israelite forces
are in danger of being caught in the pincer movement between the Aramean
mercenaries advancing on them from the northeast and the Ammonites, presumably to the south. Joab rapidly improvises a counterstrategy, selecting a
corp of elite troops to assault the larger force of Arameans and sending his
brother Abishai with the rest of the troops against the Ammonites. Such
attention to military detail is quite untypical of biblical narrative, as is the
rousing battlefield exhortation (verse 12) with which Joab concludes his
instructions. The point of such detail is surely to show Joab as a superbly com-
petent and resolute field commander, just before the great pivotal episode in
the next chapter in which Joab maintains the seige against Rabbath-Ammon
while his commander in chief slumbers, and lusts, in Jerusalem.

10. *the rest of the troops he gave.* Polzin observes, with puzzlement, that this
story proceeds by dividing things in half: beards, clothing, anti-Israelite
forces, Israelite troops. One wonders whether this narrative dynamic of mito-
sis, even though it is a saving strategy in Joab's case, might be a thematic introduction to all the inner divisions in court and nation, the fractures in the
house of David, that take up the rest of the narrative.

strong for you, I shall come to rescue you. Be strong, and let us find   12
strength for the sake of our people and for the sake of the cities of our
God, and the LORD will do what is good in His eyes!" And Joab   13
advanced, and the troops who were with him, to battle against the
Arameans, and they fled before him. And the Ammonites saw that   14
the Arameans had fled, and they fled from Abishai and went into the
city, and Joab turned back from the Ammonites and came to
Jerusalem.

And the Arameans saw that they had been routed by Israel, and   15
they reassembled. And Hadadezer sent and brought out the   16
Arameans who were beyond the Euphrates, and their forces came
with Shobach the commander of Hadadezer's army at their
head. And it was told to David, and he gathered all Israel and   17
crossed the Jordan, and they came to Helam. And the Arameans   18
drew up their lines against David and did battle with him. And the
Arameans fled before Israel, and David killed seven hundred chario-
teers of the Arameans and forty thousand horsemen, and Shobach,
the commander of their army, he struck down, and he died there.

---

13. *and they went into the city.* The city into which they withdraw under pressure from Abishai's troops is not named. It could be the capital, Rabbath-
Ammon (present-day Amman), though some analysts have wondered
whether Hanun would be so unwise as to wait till the Israelites were at the
gates of his own city before taking a decisive stand. Another candidate that
has been proposed is Medbah, an Ammonite city considerably farther to the
south.

15. *they reassembled.* This major regrouping for a second campaign against the
Israelites involves the enlisting of greater numbers of troops from the
Arameans east of the Euphrates, ethnic kin and in all likelihood political vas-
sals to the people of Aram Zobah.

17. *he gathered all Israel.* Alerted to the augmented size of the Transjordanian
forces, David musters his entire national army and this time elects to command it himself.

19 And all the kings who were vassals to Hadadezer saw that they had been routed by Israel, and they made peace with Israel and became its vassals, and the Arameans were afraid to rescue the Ammonites again.

---

19. *And all the kings who were vassals . . . made peace with Israel.* Seeing who has the military upper hand, they take a small and logical step in exchanging vassal status under Hadadezer for vassal status under David. It should be noted that this whole annalistic prelude to the story of David and Bathsheba concludes with an invocation of "all the kings." The immediately following episode begins by mentioning "the time the kings sally forth"—though, as we shall see, the noun itself there is pointedly ambiguous—and the tale that unfolds will powerfully raise the question of what constitutes kingly behavior.

CHAPTER 11

And it happened at the turn of the year, at the time the kings sally forth,   1
that David sent out Joab and his servants with him and all Israel, and

---

Chapters 11 and 12, the story of David and Bathsheba and its immediate after-
math, are the great turning point of the whole David story, as both Sternberg
and Polzin have duly observed; and it seems as though the writer has pulled out
all the stops of his remarkable narrative art in order to achieve a brilliant realization of this crucially pivotal episode. The deployment of thematic key words,
the shifting play of dialogue, the intricate relation between instructions and
their execution, the cultivated ambiguities of motive, are orchestrated with a
richness that scarcely has an equal in ancient narrative. Though the analytic
scholars have variously sought to break up these chapters into editorial frame
and Succession Narrative, Prophetic composition and old source, emending
patches of the text as they proceed, such efforts are best passed over in silence,
for the powerful literary integrity of the text speaks for itself.

1. *at the turn of the year.* The most plausible meaning is the beginning of the
spring, when the end of the heavy winter rains makes military action feasible.
at the time when the kings sally forth. There is a cunning ambiguity here in
the Hebrew text. The received consonantal text reads *mal'akhim,* "messengers," though many manuscripts show *melakhim,* "kings." As Polzin observes,
the verb "to sally forth" (or, in nonmilitary contexts, "to go forth") is often
attached to kings and never to messengers, so "kings" is definitely the more
likely reading, though the ghost of "messengers" shows through in the letters
of the text. Polzin beautifully describes this double take: "the verse clearly
doubles back on itself in a marvelous display of narrative virtuosity: at a time
when kings go forth, David did not, making it a time, therefore, when messengers must go forth; at a time when messengers go forth, David, remaining in
Jerusalem, sent Joab, his servants and all Israel to ravage Ammon."
David sent out Joab. The verb "to send"—the right verb for "messengers"—
occurs eleven times in this chapter, framing the beginning and the end. This
episode is not a moral parable but a story anchored in the realities of political
history. It is concerned with the institutionalization of the monarchy. David,

they ravaged the Ammonites and besieged Rabbah. And David was sitting in Jerusalem.

2 And it happened at eventide that David arose from his bed and walked about on the roof of the king's house, and he saw from
3 the roof a woman bathing, and the woman was very beautiful. And David sent and inquired after the woman, and the one he sent said, "Why, this is Bathsheba daughter of Eliam wife of Uriah the Hittite."

---

now a sedentary king removed from the field of action and endowed with a dangerous amount of leisure, is seen constantly operating through the agency of others, sending messengers within Jerusalem and out to Ammonite territory. Working through intermediaries, as the story will abundantly show, creates a whole new order of complications and unanticipated consequences.

And David was sitting in Jerusalem. The verb for "sitting" also means "to stay" (compare verse 12), but it is best to preserve the literal sense here because of the pointed sequence: sitting, lying, rising, and because in biblical usage "to sit" is also an antonym of "to go out" (or sally forth).

2. *at eventide.* The Hebrew term, *lᵉet ʿerev,* echoes ironically with the phrase *lᵉet tsᵉet,* "at the time of sallying forth" in the previous verse. A siesta on a hot spring day would begin not long after noon, so this recumbent king has been in bed an inordinately long time.

he saw from the roof. The palace is situated on a height, so David can look down on the naked Bathsheba bathing, presumably on her own rooftop. This situation of the palace also explains why David tells Uriah to "go down" to his house. Later in the story, archers deal destruction from the heights of the city wall, the Hebrew using the same preposition, *meʿal,* to convey the sense of "from above."

3. *the one he sent said.* The Hebrew uses an unspecified "he said."

Bathsheba daughter of Eliam wife of Uriah the Hittite. It is unusual to identify a woman by both father and husband. The reason may be, as Bar-Efrat suggests, that both men are members of David's elite corps of warriors. Although Uriah's designation as Hittite has led some interpreters to think of him as a foreign mercenary, the fact that he has a pious Israelite name ("the LORD is my light") suggests that he is rather a native or at least a naturalized Israelite of Hittite extraction. In any case, there is obvious irony in the fact that the man of foreign origins is the perfect Good Soldier of Israel, whereas the Israelite king betrays and murders him.

And David sent messengers and fetched her and she came to him and   4
he lay with her, she having just cleansed herself of her impurity, and
she returned to her house. And the woman became pregnant and sent   5
and told David and said, "I am pregnant." And David sent to Joab: 6
"Send me Uriah the Hittite." And Joab sent Uriah the Hittite to David.

And Uriah came to him, and David asked how Joab fared and how the   7
troops fared and how the fighting fared. And David said to Uriah, "Go   8
down to your house and bathe your feet." And Uriah went out from the

---

4. *David sent . . . and fetched her and she came to him and he lay with her.* It is
not uncommon for biblical narrative to use a chain of verbs in this fashion to
indicate rapid, single-minded action. What is unusual is that one verb in the
middle of this sequence switches grammatical subject—from David to
Bathsheba. When the verb "come to" or "come into" has a masculine subject
and "into" is followed by a feminine object, it designates a first act of sexual
intercourse. One wonders whether the writer is boldly toying with this double
meaning, intimating an element of active participation by Bathsheba in David's
sexual summons. The text is otherwise entirely silent on her feelings, giving the
impression that she is passive as others act on her. But her later behavior in the
matter of her son's succession to the throne (1 Kings 1–2) suggests a woman
who has her eye on the main chance, and it is possible that opportunism, not
merely passive submission, explains her behavior here as well. In all of this,
David's sending messengers first to ask about Bathsheba and then to call her to
his bed means that the adultery can scarcely be a secret within the court.

cleansed herself of her impurity. The reference is to the ritually required
bath after the end of menstruation. This explains Bathsheba's bathing on the
roof and also makes it clear that she could not be pregnant by her husband.

5. *I am pregnant.* Astonishingly, these are the only words Bathsheba speaks in
this story. In keeping with the stringent efficiency of biblical narrative, the
story leaps forward from the sexual act to the discovery of pregnancy.

8. *Go down to your house and bathe your feet.* Some interpreters have made this
more heavy handed than it is by construing the final phrase as a euphemism
for sex (because "feet" in the Bible is occasionally a euphemism for the male
genitals). But in the biblical world, bathing the feet is something travelers regularly do when they come from the dusty road. This bathing of the feet stands
in a kind of synecdochic relation to Bathsheba's bathing of her whole body,
discreetly suggesting that after the bathing of the feet other refreshments of
the body will ensue.

9 king's house and the king's provisions came out after him. And Uriah
lay at the entrance to the king's house with all the servants of his mas-
10 ter, and he went not down to his house. And they told David, saying,
"Uriah did not go down to his house." And David said to Uriah, "Look,
you have come from a journey. Why have you not gone down to your
11 house?" And Uriah said to David, "The Ark and Israel and Judah are
sitting in huts, and my master Joab and my master's servants are
encamped in the open field, and shall I then come to my house to eat
and to drink and to lie with my wife? By your life, by your very life, I

---

the king's provisions. David has not explicitly mentioned food or wine, but
he sends a kind of catered dinner after Uriah, hoping that the feast with
Bathsheba will get husband and wife into the desired amorous mood.

9. *And Uriah lay at the entrance of the king's house.* The verb "to lie," according
to David's expectations, should have been followed by "with his wife." Instead,
we have not sex but a soldier's sleeping with his comrades, who are guarding
the king. It should be remembered (compare 1 Samuel:21) that soldiers in
combat generally practiced sexual abstinence.

11. *sitting in huts.* Some construe *sukot,* "huts," as a place-name, the city of
Succoth a little east of the Jordan. But if the Ark is sent out of Jerusalem to
the front, it would make no sense to detain it at a logistics center only halfway
to the battlefield, and Uriah's point is that neither the Ark nor the troops enjoy
proper shelter (while David is "sitting in Jerusalem").

shall I then come to my house to eat and to drink and to lie with my wife?
Uriah now spells out all that David left unsaid when he urged him to go down
to his house. The crucial detail of sleeping with Bathsheba comes at the very
end. Menakhem Perry and Meir Sternberg, in a pioneering Hebrew article in
1968 (revised by Sternberg for his English book of 1985), raised the provoca-
tive issue of deliberate ambiguity (comparing the strategy of this story with
the two mutually exclusive readings possible for Henry James's short story
"The Turn of the Screw"). In their view, there are two equally viable readings.
If Uriah does *not* know that David has cuckolded him, he is the instrument of
dramatic irony—the perfect soldier vis-à-vis the treacherous king who is desperately trying to manipulate him so that the husband will unwittingly cover
the traces of his wife's sexual betrayal. If Uriah *does* know of the adultery, he is
a rather different character—not naive but shrewdly aware, playing a dangerous game of hints in which he deliberately pricks the conscience of the king,
cognizant, and perhaps not caring, that his own life may soon be forfeit. More

will not do this thing." And David said to Uriah, "Stay here today as 12
well, and tomorrow I shall send you off." And Uriah stayed in
Jerusalem that day and the next. And David called him, and he ate 13
before him and drank, and David made him drunk. And he went out in
the evening to lie in the place where he lay with the servants of his
master, but to his house he did not go down. And it happened in the 14
morning that David wrote a letter to Joab and sent it by the hand of
Uriah. And he wrote in the letter, saying, "Put Uriah in the face of the 15
fiercest battling and draw back, so that he will be struck down and die."

---

recently, Moshe Garsiel has proposed a reconciliation of these two readings:
when Uriah first arrives from the front, he is unaware of what has occurred;
after the first night with his comrades at the palace gate, he has been duly
informed of the sexual betrayal, so that in his second dialogue with the king,
he cultivates a rhetoric of implicit accusation. Garsiel observes that when
Uriah swears emphatically by David's life (verse 11), he does not add the deferential "my lord the king."

13. *David called him.* The verb here has the idiomatic sense of "invite."
    he ate before him. The preposition is an indication of hierarchical distance
between subject and king.
    David made him drunk. "David" has been added for clarity. The Hebrew
says only "he made him drunk." Plying Uriah with wine is a last desperate
attempt, and a rather crude one, to get him to have sex with his wife.

14. *sent it by the hand of Uriah.* The letter would be in the form of a small scroll
with either a seal or threads around it. David is counting on the fact that
Uriah as a loyal soldier will not dream of opening the letter. If he does not
know of the adultery, he has in any case no personal motive to look at the letter. If he does know, he is accepting his fate with grim resignation, bitterly
conscious that his wife has betrayed him and that the king is too powerful for
him to contend with.

15. *so that he will be struck down and die.* With no possibility of making Uriah
seem responsible for Bathsheba's pregnancy, David now gravely compounds
the original crime of adultery by plotting to get Uriah out of the way entirely
by having him killed. What follows in the story makes it clear that bloodshed,
far more than adultery, is David's indelible transgression.

16 And it happened, as Joab was keeping watch on the city, that he placed
17 Uriah in the place where he knew there were valiant men. And the
men of the city sallied forth and did battle with Joab, and some of the
troops, some of David's servants, fell, and Uriah the Hittite also died.
18, 19 And Joab sent and told David all the details of the battle. And Joab
charged the messenger, saying, "When you finish reporting all the
20 details of the battle to the king, if it should happen that the king's
wrath is roused and he says to you, 'Why did you approach the city to
21 fight? Did you not know they would shoot from the wall? Who struck
down Abimelech son of Jerubbesheth? Did not a woman fling down on
him an upper millstone from the wall, and he died in Thebez? Why did
you approach the wall?' Then shall you say, 'Your servant Uriah the Hit-

---

17. *some of the troops . . . fell, and Uriah the Hittite also died.* As Perry and
Sternberg have keenly observed, one of the salient features of this story is
the repeated alteration of instructions by those who carry them out. It is,
indeed, a vivid demonstration of the ambiguous effecting of ends through
the agency of others which is one of the great political themes of the story.
The canny Joab immediately sees that David's orders are impossibly clumsy
(perhaps an indication that the Machiavellian David has suddenly lost his
manipulative coolness): if the men around Uriah were to draw back all at
once, leaving him alone exposed, it would be entirely transparent that there
was a plot to get him killed. Joab, then, coldly recognizes that in order to
give David's plan some credibility, it will be necessary to send a whole contingent into a dangerous place and for many others beside Uriah to die. In
this fashion, the circle of lethal consequences of David's initial act spreads
wider and wider.

21. *Did not a woman fling down on him an upper millstone . . . ?* The specificity
of the prospective dialogue that Joab invents for a wrathful David may at first
seem surprising. The story of the ignominious death of Abimelech at the hand
of a woman (Judges 9: 52–54) may have become a kind of object lesson in
seige strategy for professional soldiers—when you are laying seige against a
city, above all beware of coming too close to the wall. One suspects also that
Joab's emphasis on a woman's dealing death to the warrior—Abimelech had
asked his armor bearer to run him through so that it would *not* be said he was
killed by a woman!—points back to Bathsheba as the ultimate source of this
chain of disasters. (This would be Joab's soldierly judgment, not necessarily
the author's.)

tite also died.' " And the messenger went and came and told David all   22
that Joab had sent him for. And the messenger said to David, "The men   23
overpowered us and sallied forth against us into the field, and then we
were upon them back to the entrance of the gate. And they shot at your   24
servants from the wall, and some of the king's servants died, and your
servant Uriah the Hittite also died." And the king said to the messen-   25
ger, "Thus shall you say to Joab, 'Let this thing not seem evil in your
eyes, for the sword devours sometimes one way and sometimes

Your servant Uriah the Hittite also died. Joab obviously knows that this is the
message for which David is waiting. By placing it in the anticipatory "script"
that he dictates to the messenger, he is of course giving away the secret, more
or less, to the messenger. Might this, too, be calculated, as an oblique dissem-
ination of David's complicity in Uriah's death, perhaps to be used at some
future point by Joab against the king? In any case, given David's track record
in killing messengers who bear tidings not to his liking, Joab may want to be
sure that this messenger has the means to fend off any violent reaction from
the king, who would not have been expecting a report of many casualties.

23. *and then we were upon them back to the entrance of the gate.* The astute messenger offers a circumstantial account that justifies the mistake of approaching
too close to the wall: the Ammonites came out after the Israelites in hot pursuit; then the Israelites, turning the tide of battle, were drawn after the fleeing
Ammonites and so were tricked into coming right up to the gates of the city.

24. *and your servant Uriah the Hittite also died.* The messenger has divined the
real point of Joab's instructions all too well. He realizes that what David above
all wants to hear is the news of Uriah's death, and rather than risk the whole
outburst, indicated by the prospective dialogue invented by Joab with the reference to the woman who killed Abimelech, the messenger hastens to conclude his report, before the king can react, by mentioning Uriah's death. Thus
the narrative makes palpable the inexorable public knowledge of David's
crime.

25. *the sword devours sometimes one way and sometimes another.* The king
responds by directing to Joab what sounds like an old soldier's cliché (on the
order of "every bullet has its billet"). These vapid words of consolation to the
field commander are an implicit admission that Joab's revision of David's
orders was necessary: David concedes that many a good man had to die in
order to cover up his murder by proxy of Uriah.

another. Battle all the more fiercely against the city and destroy it.' And
so rouse his spirits."

26 And Uriah's wife heard that Uriah her man was dead, and she keened
27 over her husband. And when the mourning was over, David sent and
gathered her into his house and she became his wife. And she bore him
a son, and the thing that David had done was evil in the eyes of the
LORD.

---

battle all the more fiercely. The Hebrew is literally "make fierce [or,
strengthen] your battle." The phrase is an emphatic formal echo of "the
fiercest battling" in verse 15.

and so rouse his spirits. Literally, "and strengthen him," that is, Joab. Some
read this as part of the message to Joab, construing it as "strengthen it [i.e.,
the battle]," though the verb has a masculine pronominal object and the word
for battle is feminine.

27. *when the mourning was over.* Normally, the mourning period would be
seven days. Bathsheba, then, is even more precipitous than Gertrude after the
death of Hamlet the elder in hastening to the bed of a new husband. She
does, of course, want to become David's wife before her big belly shows.

David sent and gathered her into his house and she became his wife. Throughout this story, David is never seen anywhere but in his house. This sentence at
the end strongly echoes verse 4: "David sent . . . and fetched her and she came
to him and he lay with her."

the thing that David had done was evil in the eyes of the LORD. Only now,
after the adultery, the murder, the remarriage, and the birth of the son, does
the narrator make an explicit moral judgment of David's actions. The invocation of God's judgment is the introduction to the appearance of Nathan the
prophet, delivering first a moral parable "wherein to catch the conscience of
the king" and then God's grim curse on David and his house.

CHAPTER 12

And the LORD sent Nathan to David, and he came to him and said to him: "Two men there were in a single town, one was rich and the other   1

---

1. *And the LORD sent.* The second stage of the story of David and Bathsheba—the phase of accusation and retribution—begins with a virtual pun on a prominent thematic word of the first half of the story. David was seen repeatedly "sending" messengers, arranging for the satisfaction of his lust and the murder of his mistress's husband through the agency of others. By contrast, God here "sends" his prophet to David—not an act of bureaucratic manipulation but the use of a human vehicle to convey a divine message of conscience.

Two men there were . . . Nathan's parable, from its very first syllables, makes clear its own status as a traditional tale and a poetic construction. The way one begins a storyteller's tale in the Bible is with the formula "there was a man"—compare the beginning of Job, or the beginning of the story of Hannah and Elkanah in 1 Samuel 1. The Hebrew prose of the parable also is set off strongly from the language of the surrounding narrative by its emphatically rhythmic character, with a fondness for parallel pairs of terms—an effect this translation tries to reproduce. The vocabulary, moreover, includes several terms that are relatively rare in biblical prose narrative: *kivsah* (ewe), *ra'sh* (poor), *helekh* (wayfarer), *'oreaḥ* (traveler). Finally the two "men" of the opening formula are at the end separated out into "rich man," "poor man," and "the man who had come" (in each of these cases, Hebrew *'ish* is used). This formal repetition prepares the way, almost musically, for Nathan's two-word accusatory explosion, *'atah ha'ish*, "You are the man!" Given the patently literary character of Nathan's tale, which would have been transparent to anyone native to ancient Hebrew culture, it is a little puzzling that David should so precipitously take the tale as a report of fact requiring judicial action. Nathan may be counting on the possibility that the obverse side of guilty conscience in a man like David is the anxious desire to do the right thing. As king, his first obligation is to protect his subjects and to dispense justice, especially to the disadvantaged. In the affair of Bathsheba and Uriah, he has done precisely the opposite. Now, as he listens to Nathan's tale, David's compensatory zeal to be a champion of justice overrides any awareness he might have of the evident artifice of the story.

2 poor. The rich man had sheep and cattle, in great abundance. And the
3 poor man had nothing save one little ewe that he had bought. And he
nurtured her and raised her with him together with his sons. From his
crust she would eat and from his cup she would drink and in his lap
4 she would lie, and she was to him like a daughter. And a wayfarer came
to the rich man, and it seemed a pity to him to take from his own sheep
and cattle to prepare for the traveler who had come to him, and he
took the poor man's ewe and prepared it for the man who had come to
5 him." And David's anger flared hot against the man, and he said to
Nathan, "As the LORD lives, doomed is the man who has done this!

---

3. *eat . . . drink . . . lie.* As Polzin observes, these terms effect full contact with
the story of David and Bathsheba, being the three activities David sought to
engage Uriah in with his wife (compare Uriah's words in 11:11). The parable
begins to become a little fantastic here in the interest of drawing close to the
relationships of conjugal intimacy and adultery to which it refers: the little lamb
eats from her master's crust, drinks from his cup, and lies in his lap ("lap" as a
biblical idiom has connotations not merely of parental sheltering but also of
sexual intimacy: compare verse 8, "I gave . . . your master's wives in your lap").

4. *it seemed a pity to him.* The Hebrew uses an active verb, "he pitied," preparing for a literal ironic reversal in verse 6, "he had no pity"—or, "he did not pity."
    to prepare. The Hebrew is literally "to do" or "to make." When the verb has
as its direct object a live edible animal, it means to slaughter and cook.

5. *David's anger flared hot against the man.* Nathan's rhetorical trap has now
snapped shut. David, by his access of anger, condemns himself, and he is now
the helpless target of the denunciation that Nathan will unleash.
    Doomed is the man. Actually, according to biblical law someone who has
illegally taken another's property would be subject to fourfold restitution
(verse 6), not to the death penalty. (The Hebrew phrase is literally "son of
death"—that is, deserving death, just as in 1 Samuel 26:16.) David pronounces
this death sentence in his outburst of moral indignation, but it also reflects
the way that the parable conflates the sexual "taking" of Bathsheba with the
murder of Uriah: the addition of Bathsheba to the royal harem could have
been intimated simply by the rich man's placing the ewe in his flock, but as
the parable is told, the ewe must be slaughtered, blood must be shed. David
himself will not be condemned to die, but death will hang over his house. As
the Talmud (Yoma 22B) notes, the fourfold retribution for Uriah's death will
be worked out in the death or violent fate of four of David's children: the
unnamed infant son of Bathsheba, Tamar, Amnon, and Absalom.

And the poor man's ewe he shall pay back fourfold, in as much as he 6
has done this thing, and because he had no pity!" And Nathan said to 7
David, "You are the man! Thus says the LORD God of Israel: 'It is I who
anointed you king over Israel and it is I Who saved you from the hand
of Saul. And I gave you your master's house and your master's wives in 8
your lap, and I gave you the house of Israel and of Judah. And if that be
too little, I would give you even as much again. Why did you despise 9
the word of the LORD, to do what is evil in His eyes? Uriah the Hittite
you struck down with the sword, and his wife you took for yourself as
wife, and him you have killed by the sword of the Ammonites! And so 10
now, the sword shall not swerve from your house evermore, seeing you

---

7. *Thus says the LORD God of Israel.* After the direct knife thrust of "You are the
man!", Nathan hastens to produce the prophetic messenger formula in its
extended form, in this way proclaiming divine authorization for the dire
imprecation he pronounces against David and his house.

7.–8. *It is I who anointed you. . . . And if that be too little, I would give you even
as much again.* In the first part of this speech, there are several ironic echoes
of David's prayer in Chapter 7, in which David thanks God for all His benefactions and professes himself unworthy of them.

8. *and your master's wives in your lap.* At least in the account passed down to
us, there is no mention elsewhere of David's having taken sexual possession of
his predecessor's consorts, though this was a practice useful for its symbolic
force in a transfer of power, as Absalom will later realize.

9. *Uriah the Hittite you struck down with the sword.* The obliquity of working
through agents at a distance, as David did in contriving the murder of Uriah,
is exploded by the brutal directness of the language: it is as though David himself had wielded the sword. Only at the end of the sentence are we given the
explanatory qualification "by the sword of the Ammonites."

10. *the sword shall not swerve from your house evermore.* As Bar-Efrat notes,
David's rather callous message to Joab, "the sword sometimes consumes one
way and sometimes another," is now thrown back in his face. The story of
David's sons, not to speak of his descendants in later generations, will in fact
turn out to be a long tale of conspiracy, internecine struggle, and murder. One
of the most extraordinary features of the whole David narrative is that this
story of the founding of the great dynasty of Judah is, paradoxically, already a
tale of the fall of the house of David. Once again, no one has grasped this

have despised Me and have taken the wife of Uriah the Hittite to be
11 your wife.' Thus says the LORD, 'I am about to raise up evil against you
from your own house, and I will take your wives before your eyes and
give them to your fellowman, and he shall lie with your wives in the
12 sight of this sun. For you did it in secret but I will do this thing before
13 all Israel and before the sun.' " And David said to Nathan, "I have
offended against the LORD." And Nathan said to David, "The LORD has
14 also remitted your offense—you shall not die. But since you surely
spurned the LORD in this thing, the son born to you is doomed to die."

15 And Nathan went to his house, and the LORD afflicted the child whom
Bathsheba wife of Uriah the Hittite had born David, and he fell gravely
16 ill. And David implored God for the sake of the lad, and David fasted,

---

tragic paradox more profoundly than William Faulkner in his recasting of the
story in *Absalom, Absalom!* The author of the David story continually exercises
an unblinking vision of David and the institution of the monarchy that
exposes their terrible flaws even as he accepts their divinely authorized legitimacy.

11. *I am about to raise up evil against you from your own house.* As befits a predictive curse, the agents of the evil are left unnamed. The disaster announced
is clearly the rebellion of Absalom—as the reference to public cohabitation
with David's wives makes clear—and the rape of Tamar and the murder of
Amnon that lead up to it. But further "evil" from the house of David will persist to his deathbed, as Absalom's rebellion is followed by Adonijah's usurpation.

12. *For you did it in secret but I will do this thing before all Israel.* The calami-
tous misjudgments that defined David's dealings with Bathsheba and Uriah
were a chain of bungled efforts at concealment. Now, in the retribution, all
his crimes are to be revealed.

14. *spurned the LORD.* The Masoretic Text has "spurned the enemies of the
LORD," a scribal euphemism to avoid making God the object of a harsh negative verb.

15. *Bathsheba wife of Uriah the Hittite.* At this point, she is still identified as
wife of the husband she betrayed in conceiving this child.

and he came and spent the night lying on the ground. And the elders of 17
his house rose over him to rouse him up from the ground, but he would
not, nor did he partake of food with them. And it happened on the sev- 18
enth day that the child died, and David's servants were afraid to tell
him that the child was dead, for they said, "Look, while the child was
alive, we spoke to him and he did not heed our voice, and how can
we say to him, the child is dead? He will do some harm." And David 19
saw that his servants were whispering to each other and David understood that the child was dead. And David said to his servants, "Is the
child dead?" And they said, "He is dead." And David rose from the 20
ground and bathed and rubbed himself with oil and changed his garments and came into the house of the LORD and worshiped and came
back to his house and asked that food be set out for him, and he ate.

---

17. *fasted . . . and spent the night lying on the ground.* David's acts pointedly
replicate those of the man he murdered, who refused to go home and eat but
instead spent the night lying on the ground with the palace guard.

18. *on the seventh day.* Seven days were the customary period of mourning. In
this instance, David enacts a regimen of mourning, in an effort to placate
God, before the fact of death.

   He will do some harm. Presumably, the courtiers fear that David will do
harm to himself in a frenzy of grief.

19. *He is dead.* In Hebrew, this is a single syllable, *met* "dead"—a response corresponding to idiomatic usage because there is no word for "yes" in biblical
Hebrew, and so the person questioned must respond by affirming the key
term of the question. It should be noted, however, that the writer has contrived to repeat "dead" five times, together with one use of the verb "died," in
these two verses: the ineluctable bleak fact of death is hammered home to us,
just before David's grim acceptance of it.

20. *David rose . . . bathed . . . rubbed himself with oil . . . changed his garments
. . . worshiped . . . ate.* This uninterrupted chain of verbs signifies David's brisk
resumption of the activities of normal life, evidently without speech and certainly without explanation, as the courtiers' puzzlement makes clear. The
entire episode powerfully manifests that human capacity for surprise, and for
paradoxical behavior, that is one of the hallmarks of the great biblical characters. David here acts in a way that neither his courtiers nor the audience of
the story could have anticipated.

21 And his servants said to him, "What is this thing that you have done?
For the sake of the living child you fasted and wept, and when the
22 child was dead, you arose and ate food?" And he said, "While the child
was still alive I fasted and wept, for I thought, 'Who knows, the LORD
23 may favor me and the child will live.' And now that he is dead, why
should I fast? Can I bring him back again? I am going to him and he
will not come back to me."

24 And David consoled Bathsheba his wife, and he came to her and lay
with her, and she bore a son and called his name Solomon, and the

---

23. *Can I bring him back again? I am going to him and he will not come back to
me.* If the episode of Bathsheba and Uriah is the great turning point of the
David story, these haunting words are the pivotal moment in the turning
point. As we have repeatedly seen, every instance of David's speech in the preceding narrative has been crafted to serve political ends, much of it evincing
elaborately artful rhetoric. Now, after the dire curse pronounced by Nathan,
the first stage of which is fulfilled in the death of the child, David speaks for
the first time not out of political need but in his existential nakedness. The
words he utters have a stark simplicity—there are no elegies now—and his
recognition of the irreversibility of his son's death also makes him think of his
own mortality. In place of David the seeker and wielder of power, we now see
a vulnerable David, and this is how he will chiefly appear through the last half
of his story.

24. *David consoled Bathsheba his wife.* Now, after the terrible price of the
child's life has been paid for the murder of her husband, the narrator refers to
her as David's wife, not Uriah's. A specific lapse of time is not mentioned, but
one must assume that at least two or three months have passed, during which
she recovers from the first childbirth.
   she . . . called his name Solomon, and the LORD loved him. As a rule, it was
the mother who exercised the privilege of naming the child. Despite some
scholarly efforts to construe the name differently, its most plausible etymology
remains the one that links it with the word for "peace" (the Hebrew term
Shelomoh might simply mean "His peace"). The LORD's loving Solomon, who
will disappear from the narrative until the struggle for the throne in 1 Kings 1,
foreshadows his eventual destiny, and also harmonizes this name giving with
the child's second name, Jedidiah, which means "God's friend."

LORD loved him. And He sent by the hand of Nathan the prophet and   25
called his name Jedidiah, by the grace of the LORD.

And Joab battled against Rabbah of the Ammonites and he captured   26
the royal city. And Joab sent messengers to David and said,   27

> "I have battled against Rabbah,
>   Yes, I captured the Citadel of Waters.

And so now, assemble the rest of the troops and encamp against the   28
city and capture it, lest it be I who capture the city and my name be

---

25. *Jedidiah, by the grace of the* LORD. For the last phrase, this translation
adopts a proposal by Kyle McCarter, Jr. The usual meaning of the preposition
used, *ba'avur*, is "for the sake of." It remains something of a puzzlement that
the child should be given two names, one by his mother and the other by God
through His prophet. One common suggestion is that Jedidiah was Solomon's
official throne name. But perhaps the second name, indicating special access
to divine favor, reflects a political calculation on the part of Nathan: he is
already aligning himself with Solomon (and with Bathsheba), figuring that in
the long run it will be best to have a successor to David under some obligation
to him. In the event, Nathan's intervention will prove crucial in securing the
throne for Solomon.

26. *Joab battled against Rabbah.* It is possible, as many scholars have claimed,
that the conquest of Rabbah, in the seige of which Uriah had perished, in fact
occurs before the birth of Solomon, though sieges lasting two or more years
were not unknown in the ancient world.

27. *I have battled against Rabbah.* . . . Joab is actually sending David a double
message. As dutiful field commander, he urges David (verse 28) to hasten to
the front so that the conquest of the Ammonite capital will be attributed to
him. And yet, he proclaims the conquest in the triumphal formality of a little
victory poem (one line, two parallel versets) in which it is he who figures
unambiguously as conqueror. This coy and dangerous game Joab plays with
David about who has the real power will persist in the story.
   the Citadel of Waters. The reference is not entirely clear, but the narrative
context indicates that Joab has occupied one vital part of the city—evidently,
where the water supply is—while the rest of the town has not yet been taken.

29 called upon it." And David assembled all the troops and went to Rab-
30 bah and battled against it and captured it. And he took the crown of
their king from his head, and its weight was a talent of gold, with precious stones, and it was set on David's head. And the booty of the city
31 he brought out in great abundance. And the people that were in it, he
brought out and set them to work with saws and iron threshing boards
and iron axes, and he put them to the brick mold. Thus did he do to all
the Ammonite towns. And David, and all the troops with him, returned
to Jerusalem.

---

30. *the crown of their king.* The Septuagint reads "Milcom" (the Ammonite
deity) instead of *malkam,* "their king."

31. *set them to work with saws and iron threshing boards and iron axes* . . . The
meaning of this entire sentence is a little uncertain, but the most plausible
reading is that David impressed the male Ammonites into corvée labor. Some
have suggested that the Ammonites were forced to tear down the walls of
their own cities with the cutting tools listed in the catalogue here, though the
reference to the brick mold at the end indicates some sort of construction, not
just demolition.

CHAPTER 13

And it happened thereafter—Absalom, David's son, had a beautiful sis- 1
ter named Tamar, and Amnon, David's son, loved her. And Amnon was 2
so distressed that he fell sick over Tamar his sister, for she was a virgin
and it seemed beyond Amnon to do anything to her. And Amnon had a 3
companion named Jonadab son of Shimeah brother of David, and Jon-

---

1. *a beautiful sister.* The catastrophic turn in David's fortune began when he
saw a beautiful woman and lusted after her. Now, the curse pronounced by
Nathan on the house of David begins to unfold through the very same mechanism: a sexual transgression within the royal quarters resulting in an act of
murder elsewhere. Several important terms and gestures here reinforce this
link with the story of David and Bathsheba.

Amnon . . . loved her. The love in question will be revealed by the ensuing
events as an erotic obsession—what the early rabbis aptly characterized as
"love dependent upon a [material] thing."

2. *she was a virgin and it seemed beyond Amnon to do anything to her.* The last
phrase here has a definite negative connotation (rather like the British "to
interfere with her") and makes clear the narrow carnal nature of Amnon's
"love" for Tamar. Sexual tampering with a virgin had particularly stringent consequences in biblical law.

3. *companion.* The Hebrew *reʿa* could simply indicate a friend, though in royal
contexts it is also the title of someone who played an official role as the king's,
or the prince's, companion and counselor. The emphasis on Jonadab's "wisdom"—in biblical usage, often a morally neutral term suggesting mastery of
know-how in a particular activity—makes the technical sense of counselor
more likely.

4 adab was a very wise man. And he said to him, "Why are you so poorly,
prince, morning after morning? Will you not tell me?" And Amnon said
5 to him, "Tamar the sister of Absalom my brother I do love." And Jonadab said to him, "Lie in your bed and play sick, and when your father
comes to see you, say to him, 'Let Tamar my sister, pray, come and
nourish me with food and prepare the nourishment before my eyes, so
6 that I may see and eat from her hand.'" And Amnon lay down and

---

4. *And he said to him.* Shimon Bar-Efrat has aptly observed that the whole
story of the rape of Tamar is constructed out of seven interlocking scenes with
two characters in each, one of whom appears in the next scene. (The story of
the stealing of Isaac's blessing in Genesis 27 has the same structure.) The
sequence is: (1) Jonadab-Amnon, (2) Amnon-David, (3) David-Tamar, (4)
Tamar-Amnon, (5) Amnon-attendant, (6) attendant-Tamar, (7) Tamar-
Absalom. J. P. Fokkelman adds to this observation that the spatial and structural center of this design is the bed in Amnon's inner chamber (4), where the
rape is perpetrated.

Tamar the sister of Absalom my brother . . . Kyle McCarter, Jr. vividly notes
that Amnon's speech with its alliterated initial aspirants in the Hebrew "is a
series of gasping sighs" (ʾet-tamar ʾaḥot ʾavshalom ʾaḥi ʾani ʾohev).

5. *Lie in your bed and play sick.* David at the beginning of the Bathsheba story
was first seen lying in bed, and then he arranged to have the desired woman
brought to his chamber. Jonadab on his part observes that Amnon already
looks ill (verse 2) and so suggests that he play up this condition by pretending
to be dangerously ill and in need of special ministrations.

nourish me. The Hebrew verbal root b-r-h and the cognate noun *biryah*
("nourishment") denote not eating in general but the kind of eating that is sustaining or restoring to a person who is weak or failing. When you eat a *biryah*
you become *barʾi,* healthy or fat, the opposite of "poorly," *dal.* The distinction
is crucial to this story.

so that I may see and eat from her hand. Perhaps Amnon is encouraged to say
this because, as a person supposed to be gravely ill, he would want to see with
his own eyes that the vital nourishment is prepared exactly as it should be.
The writer is clearly playing with the equivalence between eating and sex, but
it remains ambiguous whether Jonadab has in mind the facilitating of a rape,
or merely creating the possibility of an intimate meeting between Amnon and
Tamar.

played sick, and the king came to see him, and Amnon said to the king,
"Let Tamar my sister, pray, come, and shape a couple of heart-shaped
dumplings before my eyes, that I may take nourishment from her
hand." And David sent to Tamar at home, saying, "Go, pray, to the   7
house of Amnon your brother, and prepare nourishment for him." And   8
Tamar went to the house of Amnon her brother—he lying down—and
she took the dough and kneaded it and shaped it into hearts before his
eyes and cooked the dumplings. And she took the pan and set it before   9
him, and he refused to eat. And Amnon said, "Clear out everyone
around me!" and everyone around him cleared out. And Amnon said to   10
Tamar, "Bring the nourishment into the inner chamber, that I may take
nourishment from your hand." And Tamar took the dumplings that she
had made and brought them to Amnon her brother within the chamber. And she offered them to him to eat, and he seized her and said to   11

---

6. *the king came to see him.* In Jonadab's original scenario, it was to be Absalom
who played this role. As the events work out, David, who sinned through lust,
inadvertently acts as Amnon's pimp for his own daughter.

   shape a couple of heart-shaped dumplings. The verb and its object are both
transparently cognate with *lev* (or *levav*), "heart." The term could refer to the
shape of the dumplings, or to their function of "strengthening the heart"
(idiomatic in biblical Hebrew for sustaining or encouraging). In the Song of
Songs, this same verb is associated with the idea of sexual arousal.

9. *Clear out everyone around me!* The identical words are pronounced by
another princelike figure, Joseph, just before he reveals his true identity to his
brothers (Genesis 45:1). In Genesis, these words preface the great moment of
reconciliation between long-estranged brothers. Here they are a prelude to a
tale of fraternal rape that leads to fratricide. The story of the rape of Tamar
continues to allude to the Joseph story, in reverse chronological order and
with pointed thematic reversal. The moment before the rape echoes the
encounter between Joseph and Potiphar's wife (Genesis 39) in the middle of
the Joseph story, and the attention drawn to the ornamented tunic that the
violated Tamar tears takes us back to Joseph's ornamented tunic at the beginning of his story (Genesis 37). From such purposeful deployment of allusion,
the inference is inevitable that the author of the David story was familiar at
least with the J strand of the Joseph story in a textual version very like the one
that has come down to us.

12 her, "Come lie with me, my sister." And she said to him, "Don't, my
brother, don't abuse me, for it should not be done thus in Israel,
13 don't do this scurrilous thing. And I, where would I carry my
shame? And you, you would be like one of the scurrilous fellows
in Israel. And so, speak, pray, to the king, for he will not withhold
14 me from you." And Amnon did not want to heed her voice, and

---

11. *Come lie with me, my sister.* The core of this abrupt command is a citation
of the words of Potiphar's wife to Joseph, "Lie with me." Perhaps, as some
have suggested, "Come" has a slight softening effect. The addition of "my
sister" of course highlights the fact that *this* sexual assault is also incestu-
ous.

12. *Don't, my brother* . . . Tamar's response constitutes a *structural* allusion
to Joseph and Potiphar's wife, for he, when confronted by the sexual
brusqueness of her terse "lie with me," also responds, in contrastive dialogue, with a nervous volubility in a relatively lengthy series of breathless
objections.

    it should not be done thus in Israel . . . this scurrilous thing. The language
here echoes that of another sexual episode in Genesis, the rape of Dinah
(Genesis 34). Again, the divergence in the parallel is significant, for Dinah's
rapist comes to love her after violating her and wants to make things good by
marriage, whereas Amnon despises Tamar after he possesses her, and drives
her away. The rape in both stories leads to murderous fraternal vengeance.
But our writer's brilliant game of literary allusion does not end here, for, as
Robert Polzin has pointed out, Tamar's words are also a precise echo of the
plea of the Ephraimite in Gibeah to the mob of rapists: "Don't, my brothers
. . . don't do this scurrilous thing" (Judges 19:23). That story ended in the
woman's being gang raped to death, an act which in turn led to bloody civil
war—as Tamar's rape will lead to fratricide and, eventually, rebellion and
civil war.

13. *speak, pray, to the king, for he will not withhold me from you.* Marriage
between a half brother and a half sister is explicitly banned by biblical law.
Perhaps, it has been suggested, this prohibition was not yet held to be binding
in the early tenth century, or in the royal circle in Jerusalem. But it is at least
as plausible that the desperate Tamar is grasping at any possibility to buy time
and deflect her sexual assailant: why do this vile thing and take me by force
when you can enjoy me legitimately?

he overpowered her and abused her and bedded her. And Amnon hated   15
her with a very great hatred, for greater was the hatred with which he
hated her than the love with which he had loved her. And Amnon said,
"Get up, go!" And she said to him, "Don't!—this wrong is greater than   16
the other you did me, to send me away now." And he did not want to

---

14. *he overpowered her and abused her and bedded her.* The three transitive
verbs in quick sequence reflect the single-minded assertion of male physical
force. In the analagous story of Joseph and the Egyptian woman, because the
gender roles are reversed, the sexually assaulted male is strong enough to
break free from the woman's grasp and flee. Here, the assaulted woman cannot break her assailant's grip (verse 11), and so she now succumbs to brute
force. The verb represented as "bedded" *(shakhav)* is the same one used by
Jonadab in verse 5 ("Lie in your bed," *shekhav ʿal-mishkavkha*) and in Amnon's
"lie with me." But when it has a direct feminine object (instead of "lie *with*"),
it suggests sexual violation, and a transitive verb is called for in the English.

15. *greater was the hatred with which he hated her than the love with which he
had loved her.* The psychological insight of this writer is remarkable throughout the story. Amnon has fulfilled his desire for this beautiful young woman—
or, given the fact that she is a bitterly resistant virgin, perhaps it has hardly
been the fulfillment he dreamed of. In any case, he now has to face the possibly dire consequences to himself from her brother Absalom, or from David.
The result is an access of revulsion against Tamar, a blaming of the victim for
luring him with her charms into all this trouble.
    Get up, go! The brutality of these imperative verbs is evident. They are also,
as Bar-Efrat neatly observes, exact antonyms, in reverse order, of the two
imperative verbs of sexual invitation he used before, "Come, lie."

16. *Don't!—this wrong is greater* . . . There is a textual problem here in the
Hebrew, which seems to say, "Don't—about this wrong . . ." (*ʿal-ʾodot haraʿah*).
Some versions of the Septuagint read here "Don't, my brother" (*ʾal ʾaḥi*), as in
verse 12, but this could reflect an attempt to straighten out a difficult text
rather than a better Hebrew version used by the ancient Greek translators.
    to send me away now. "Now" is added in the translation in order to remove
an ambiguity as to when the sending away is done. "Sending away" is an idiom
that also has the sense of "divorce"—precisely what the rapist of a virgin is not
allowed to do in biblical law. If some modern readers may wonder why being
banished seems to Tamar worse than being raped, one must say that for biblical women the social consequence of pariah status, when the law offered the
remedy of marriage to the rapist, might well seem even more horrible than the

17 heed her. And he called his lad, his attendant, and said, "Send this
18 creature, pray, away from me, and bolt the door behind her!" And she
had on an ornamented tunic, for the virgin princesses did wear such
robes. And his attendant took her outside and bolted the door behind
19 her. And Tamar put ashes on her head, and the ornamented tunic that
she had on she tore, and she put her hand on her head and walked
20 away screaming as she went. And Absalom her brother said to her,
"Has Amnon your brother been with you? For now, my sister, hold your

---

physical violation. Rape was a dire fate, but one which could be compensated
for by marriage, whereas the violated virgin rejected and abandoned by her
violator was an unmarriageable outcast, condemned to a lifetime of "desola-
tion" (verse 20).

17. *Send this creature, pray, away from me.* "This creature" reflects the sting-
ingly contemptuous monosyllabic feminine demonstrative pronoun, *zᵓot* ("this
one"). Note that at the same time that Amnon speaks brutally to Tamar, he is
polite to his servant, using the particle of entreaty *nᵓa* ("pray").
  and bolt the door behind her. Having devised such an elaborate strategy for
drawing Tamar into the inner chamber where he can have his way with her, he
now has her thrust out into the open square, with the door bolted against her
as though she were some insatiable, clinging thing against which he had to set
up a barricade.

18. *ornamented tunic.* The translation for this term follows a suggestion of E.
A. Speiser. (The famous KJV rendering in Genesis is "coat of many colors.")
Others interpret this as a garment reaching the ankles. In any case, Tamar and
Joseph are the only two figures in the Bible said to wear this particular garment. Joseph's, too, will be torn, by his brothers, after they strip him of it and
toss him into the pit, and they will then soak it in kid's blood. Tamar's ornamented tunic may well be blood stained, too, if one considers what has just
been done to her.

19. *put her hand on her head.* This is a conventional gesture of mourning, like
the rending of the garment and the sprinkling of ashes on the head.

20. *Has Amnon your brother been with you?* Absalom, addressing his screaming, tear-stained, disheveled sister, exercises a kind of delicacy of feeling in
using this oblique euphemism for rape.

peace. He is your brother. Do not take this matter to heart." And Tamar
stayed, desolate, in the house of Absalom her brother. And King David   21
had heard all these things, and he was greatly incensed. And Absalom   22
did not speak with Amnon either evil or good, for Absalom hated
Amnon for having abused Tamar his sister.

And it happened after two years that Absalom had a sheep shearing at   23
Baal-hazor, which is near Ephraim, and Absalom invited all the king's
sons. And Absalom came to the king and said, "Look, pray, your servant   24

He is your brother. This identification, which plays back against the heavily
fraught, often ironic uses of "brother" and "sister" throughout the story,
would hardly be a consolation. What Absalom may be suggesting is that,
were it any other man, I would avenge your honor at once, but since he is
your brother, and mine, I must bide my time (*"For now,* my sister, hold your
peace.")

Do not take this matter to heart. The idiom he uses echoes ironically against
the making of heart-shaped dumplings to which Amnon enjoined her.

21. *King David had heard all these things, and he was greatly incensed.* The
Qumran Samuel and the Septuagint add here: "but he did not vex the spirit of
Amnon his son, for he loved him, since he was his firstborn." But this looks
suspiciously like an explanatory gloss, an effort to make sense of David's
silence. That imponderable silence is the key to the mounting avalanche of
disaster in the house of David. Where we might expect some after-the-fact
defense of his violated daughter, some rebuke or punishment of his rapist son,
he hears, is angry, but says nothing and does nothing, leaving the field open for
Absalom's murder of his brother. In all this, the rape of Tamar plays exactly
the same pivotal role in the story of David as does the rape of Dinah in the
story of Jacob. Jacob, too, "hears" of the violation and does nothing, setting the
stage for the bloody act of vengeance carried out by his sons Simeon and Levi.
By the end of the episode, Jacob is seen at the mercy of his intransigent sons,
and that is how this once-powerful figure will appear through the rest of his
story. An analogous fate, as we shall abundantly see, awaits David from this
moment on.

23. *a sheep shearing.* The sheep shearing is a grand occasion for feasting and
drinking (compare 1 Samuel 25. 2–0), and so it is proper to speak of "having" a
sheep shearing as one would have a celebration.

25 has a sheep shearing. Let the king, pray, go, and his servants, with your
servant." And the king said to Absalom, "No, my son, we shall not all of
us go, and we shall not burden you." And he pressed him but he did not
26 want to go, and he bade him farewell. And Absalom said to him, "If not,
pray, let Amnon my brother go with us." And the king said to him,
27 "Why should he go with you?" And Absalom pressed him, and he sent
28 Amnon with him, together with all the king's sons. And Absalom
charged his lads, saying, "See, pray, when Amnon's heart is merry with
wine and I say to you, 'Strike down Amnon,' you shall put him to death,
fear not, for is it not I who charge you? Be strong, and act as valiant
29 men." And Absalom's lads did to Amnon as Absalom had charged them,
and all the king's sons arose and rode away each on his mule and fled.
30 And as they were on the way, the rumor reached David, saying, "Absalom has struck down all the king's sons, and not one of them remains."

---

24. *Let the king, pray, go.* Given David's increasingly sedentary habits, Absalom appears to count on the fact that his father will refuse the invitation,
and this refusal will then give greater urgency to his invitation of Amnon.
Had Absalom begun by asking David to help him persuade Amnon to go the
festivities, David might have been suspicious about Absalom's motives,
since the grudge he bore his half brother would scarcely have been a secret.
In any case, Absalom is making David his go-between to lure Amnon to his
death, just as Amnon made David his go-between to lure Tamar to her violation.

27. *with all the king's sons.* This phrase recurs like a refrain from this point on:
David is haunted by the specter of the ultimate catastrophe, that "all the
king's sons" have perished, a specter that will cast a shadow over the subsequent events of the story as well. The man promised an everlasting house is
threatened with the prospect (like his avatar, Faulkner's Sutpen, in *Absalom,
Absalom!*) of being cut off without surviving progeny.

28. *When Amnon's heart is merry with wine.* The heart that lusted after Tamar
and asked her to make heart-shaped dumplings will now be fuddled with wine
to set up the murder.

29. *each on his mule.* In this period in ancient Israel, the mule was the customary mount for royal personages.

And the king arose and tore his garments and lay on the ground, with 31
all his servants standing in attendance in torn garments. And Jonadab 32
son of Shimeah brother of David spoke up and said, "Let not my lord
think, 'All the lads, the king's sons, they have put to death,' for Amnon
alone is dead, for it was fixed upon by Absalom from the day he abused
Tamar his sister. And now, let not my lord the king take the matter to 33
heart, saying, 'All the king's sons have died,' but Amnon alone is dead."

And Absalom fled. And the lookout lad raised his eyes and saw and, 34
look, a great crowd was going round the side of the mountain from the
road behind it. And Jonadab said to the king, "Look, the king's sons 35
have come, as your servant has spoken, so it has come about." And just 36
as he finished speaking, look, the king's sons came, and they raised
their voices and wept, and the king, too, and all his servants wept very
grievously.

---

31. *the king arose and tore his garments and lay on the ground.* These acts of
mourning are reminiscent of Tamar's, and of David's own when his infant son
by Bathsheba was deathly ill. Again there is a resemblance to Jacob, who
flings himself into extravagant mourning over a son supposed to be dead who
is actually alive (Genesis 37).

32. *they have put to death.* Jonadab, exercising his "wisdom," is careful not to
condemn Absalom immediately, but instead first uses a plural verb with an
unspecified agent. Then he introduces Absalom as the source of the determination to kill Amnon, choosing a verb, "abused," that concedes the crime of
rape. Whether or not this was a possibility he had in mind when he offered
counsel to Amnon, he now implicitly distances himself from Amnon's act.

33. *let not my lord the king take the matter to heart.* This is virtually the same
idiom Absalom used to Tamar in consoling her after the rape.

34. *going round the side of the mountain from the road behind it.* The Hebrew
has "the road behind it" before "the side of the mountain," such proleptic use
of pronominal reference sometimes occuring in biblical Hebrew. The Septuagint reads "from the Horonim road" (*miderekh horonim*) instead of "from the
road behind it" (*miderekh aharaw*).

36. *wept very grievously.* The literal Hebrew phrasing is "wept a very great
weeping."

37 And Absalom had fled, and he went to Talmai son of Amihur king of
38 Geshur. And David mourned for his son all the while. And Absalom
39 had fled and gone to Geshur, and he was there three years. And David's
urge to sally forth against Absalom was spent, for he was consoled over
Amnon, who was dead.

---

37. *Talmi son of Amihur king of Geshur.* Absalom takes refuge in the court of
his maternal grandfather in Geshur, to the north and east of the Jordan, outside David's jurisdiction.

   David mourned for his son all the while. As verse 39, which will mark the
beginning of a new narrative episode, makes clear, the son he is mourning is
the dead Amnon, not the absent Absalom.

39. *David's urge to sally forth against Absalom was spent.* The received text is
either defective or elliptical at this point. The verb, *watekhal*, is feminine,
though there is no feminine noun in the clause. Many have construed it as the
predicate of an omitted noun, *nefesh*, which coupled with this verb would
yield idiomatically "David pined after Absalom." Such paternal longings
scarcely accord with David's refusal to see his son once he has returned to
Jerusalem, or with the very necessity of elaborate manipulation in order to get
him to agree to rescind Absalom's banishment. The Qumran Samuel scroll,
though incomplete at this point, appears to have the feminine noun *ruah*—
"spirit," "impulse," "urge,"—as the subject of the verb. An abatement of hostility against Absalom rather than a longing for him makes much more sense in
terms of what follows.

CHAPTER 14

And Joab son of Zeruiah knew that the king's mind was on Absalom. 1 And Joab sent to Tekoa and fetched a wise woman from there and said 2 to her, "Take up mourning, pray, and, pray, don mourning garments, and do not rub yourself with oil, and you shall be like a woman a long while mourning over a dead one. And you shall come to the king and 3

---

1. *the king's mind was on Absalom.* The preposition ʿal is ambiguous, and it could also mean "against."

2. *Joab sent to Tekoa.* Tekoa is a village about ten miles north of Jerusalem. Why does Joab contrive to make David agree to Absalom's return? Given his relentlessly political character, it seems likely that Joab perceives Absalom's continuing banishment as a potential source of rebellion against the throne, and concludes that the safest course is to reconcile the king with his son. This calculation will prove to be gravely misguided because Joab does not reckon with David's ambivalence toward his fratricidal son (see verse 24) or with the impulse to usurpation which that ambivalence will encourage in Absalom.

a wise woman. It should be noted that the whole David story, seemingly dominated by powerful martial men, pivots at several crucial junctures on the intervention of enterprising "wise women." The first of these is Abigail, though, unlike two of the others, she is not assigned the epithet "wise woman" as a kind of professional title. Later, a resourceful woman hides the two spies who are bringing intelligence of Absalom to David in Transjordan. In the subsequent rebellion of Sheba son of Bichri, another wise woman prevents Joab's massacre of the besieged town of Abel of Bethmaacah.

like a woman a long while mourning over a dead one. The phrasing here pointedly echoes "David mourned for his son all the while" in 13:37.

speak to him in this manner—" and Joab put the words in her mouth.
4 And the Tekoite woman said to the king, and she flung herself on her
5 face to the ground and bowed down, and she said, "Help, O king!" And
the king said to her, "What troubles you?" And she said, "Alas, I am a
6 widow woman, my husband died. And your servant had two sons, and
they quarreled in the field, and there was no one to part them, and one
7 struck down the other and caused his death. And, look, the whole clan
rose against your servant and said, 'Give over the one who struck down
his brother, that we may put him to death for the life of his brother
whom he killed, and let us destroy the heir as well.' And they would
have quenched my last remaining ember, leaving my husband no name
8 or remnant on the face of the earth." And the king said to the woman,
"Go to your house and I myself shall issue a charge concerning you."

---

3. *Joab put words in her mouth.* As Polzin observes, the entire episode turns on manipulation of people through language, with abundant repetition of the verb "speak." In contrast to the common practice elsewhere in biblical narrative, we are not given the actual script that Joab dictates to the woman, which she will then repeat to David. This omission heightens the sense that, using a general outline provided by Joab, the woman is in fact brilliantly improvising—which in some ways she would have to do, given the fact that she is not reciting an uninterrupted speech but responding to David's declarations, picking up clues from the way he reacts.

4. *Help, O king!* This is a formulaic plea used by petitioners for royal justice.

6. *they quarreled in the field . . . and one struck down the other.* As several commentators have noted, her formulation aligns the story with the archetypal tale of Cain and Abel. The fratricidal Cain is banished, but also given a sign to protect him from blood vengeance.

7. *and let us destroy the heir as well.* Although it is unlikely that the clansmen would have actually said these words, there is no need to tamper with the text. The wise woman, in reporting the dialogue, insinuates her own anxious maternal perspective into this last clause. The implication is that the members of the clan would like to kill the remaining son not only to execute justice but in order to get his inheritance.

8. *I myself shall issue a charge concerning you.* Although David emphatically announces (by adding the first-person pronoun ʾ*ani*) that he himself will take up the case, his language remains vague ("issue a charge"), and the Tekoite woman's response in the next verse clearly indicates that she requires something further of him.

And the Tekoite woman said to the king, "Upon me, my lord the king,   9
and upon my father's house, let the guilt be, and the king and his
throne shall be blameless." And the king said, "The man who dares   10
speak to you I will have brought to me, and he will not touch you any
more." And she said, "May the king, pray, keep in mind the LORD your   11
God, that the blood avenger should not savage this much and let them
not destroy my son." And he said, "As the LORD lives, not a single hair
of your son's shall fall to the ground!" And the woman said, "Let your   12
servant, pray, speak a word to my lord the king." And he said, "Speak."
And the woman said, "Why did you devise in this fashion against God's   13

---

9. *Upon me . . . the guilt . . . and the king and his throne shall be blameless.* The
legal issue involved is blood guilt. From David's vagueness, she infers that he
is loath to intervene on behalf of the fratricide because by so doing he, and his
throne, would take on the guilt of allowing the killing to go unavenged.

10. *The man who dares speak to you I will have brought to me.* Her declaration
that she and her father's house will bear the guilt for allowing the killer to
live—evidently construed by David as a performative speech act, efficacious
once uttered—encourages the king to declare that he will absolutely protect
her against the vengeful kinsmen who are seeking out her son.

11. *let them not destroy my son.* The woman is still not satisfied, for David's
pledge to safeguard her did not mention her son: she wants to extract an
explicit declaration from David that he will protect the life of her son.
    not a single hair of your son's shall fall to the ground. Now she has what she
has been after, with David's hyperbolic declaration about guarding the well-
being of the fratricidal son, she is prepared to snap shut the trap of the fiction,
linking it to David's life, just as Nathan did with the parable of the poor man's
ewe. We should note that not a single hair of the fictitious son is to fall to the
ground, whereas the extravagantly abundant hair of his real-life referent,
Absalom, will be cut annually in a kind of public ceremony.

12. *Let your servant, pray, speak.* She uses these words of entreaty to preface
the transition to the real subject, David and Absalom.

13. *against God's people.* The implicit key concept here is "inheritance," which
links her fiction to the national political situation. She may be hinting that
Absalom is the appropriate heir to the throne. In any case, his banishment is
potentially divisive to the kingdom.

14 people? And in speaking this thing, the king is as though guilty for the king's not having brought back his own banished one. For we surely will die, like water spilled to the ground, which cannot be gathered again. And God will not bear off the life of him who devises that no one 15 of his be banished. And so now, the reason I have come to speak this thing to the king my lord is that the people have made me afraid, and your servant thought, 'Let me but speak to the king. Perhaps the king

---

in speaking this thing, the king is as though guilty . . . The Hebrew of this whole sentence is rather crabbed, an effect reproduced in the translation. Rather than reflecting difficulties in textual transmission, her language probably expresses her sense of awkwardness in virtually indicting the king: he is "as though guilty," for "in speaking this thing," in declaring his resolution to protect the fratricidal son, he has condemned his own antithetical behavior in the case of Absalom. But the woman is careful not to mention Absalom explicitly by name—she struggles verbally in the crossover from fiction to life, knowing she is treading on dangerous ground.

14. *we surely will die, like water spilled to the ground.* Moving beyond Absalom to a wise woman's pronouncement on human fate, she breaks free of her verbal stumbling and becomes eloquent. The spilled water as an image of irreversible mortality is an obvious and effective counterpoint to her previous image of the ember that should not be quenched. It also picks up thematically David's own bleak reflection on the irreversibility of death after his infant son expires (Chapter 12).

God will not bear off the life of him who devises that no one of his be banished. As the wise woman switches back from philosophic statement to the juridical issue confronting David, her language again becomes knotty and oblique. What she is saying is that God will scarcely want to punish the father who brings back his banished son, even though blood guilt remains unavenged.

15. *the reason I have come to speak this thing to the king* . . . The Tekoite woman, having nervously broached the issue of David and Absalom, now hastily retreats to the relative safety of her invented story about two sons, as though that were the real reason for her appearance before the king. The dramatic and psychological logic of this entire speech argues against scholarly attempts to make it more "coherent" by moving around whole swatches of it.

will do what his servant asks. For the king would pay heed to save his 16
servant from the hand of the person bent on destroying me and my son
together from God's heritage.' And your servant thought, 'May the word 17
of my lord the king, pray, be a respite, for like a messenger of God, so is
my lord the king, understanding good and evil.' And may the LORD your
God be with you." And the king said to the woman, "Pray, do not con- 18
ceal from me the thing that I ask you." And the woman said, "Let my
lord the king speak, pray." And the king said, "Is the hand of Joab with 19
you in all this?" And the woman answered and said, "By your life, my
lord the king, there is no turning right or left from all that my lord the
king has spoken! For your servant Joab, he it was who charged me, and
he it was who put in your servant's mouth all these words. In order to 20
turn the thing round your servant Joab has done this thing. And my
lord is wise, as with the wisdom of a messenger of God, to know every-

---

17. *respite.* The king's word will give her respite from her persecutors, the
would-be killers of her son. The Hebrew term, *menuhah,* also points to a
bound locution, *menuhah wenahalah,* "respite and inheritance," the very thing
the kinsmen would take from her.

19. *Is the hand of Joab with you in all this?* David rightly infers that a village
wise woman would have no motive of her own for undertaking this elaborate
stratagem, and so someone in court with political aims must be behind her.
Polzin shrewdly proposes that Joab may actually have wanted David to detect
him at the bottom of the scheme: "The woman's eventual admission that she
has been sent by Joab (vv. 19–20) may itself be part of Joab's indirect message
to David—something like, 'Bring Absalom back or I may side with him against
you.' "

   there is no turning right or left from all that my lord the king has spoken. She
is saying two things at once—that the king has hit the target in saying that
Joab is behind her, and that, having committed himself by his own speech to
protect the fratricidal son, he cannot now permit himself to continue Absalom's banishment.

20. *my lord is wise, as with the wisdom of a messenger of God.* It is of course she
who has been demonstrably wise. David will soon show unwisdom by bringing
Absalom back while resisting real reconciliation, and his subsequent blindness to Absalom's demagogic activities within a stone's throw of the court indicates that there is much in the land about which he knows nothing.

21 thing in the land." And the king said to Joab, "Look, pray, I have done
22 this thing. Go and bring back the lad Absalom." And Joab flung himself
on his face to the ground and bowed down. And he blessed the king,
and Joab said, "Your servant knows that I have found favor in the eyes
23 of my lord the king, for the king has done what his servant asked." And
Joab rose and went to Geshur and he brought Absalom to Jerusalem.
24 And the king said, "Let him turn round to his house, and my face he
shall not see." And Absalom turned round to his house, and the king's
face he did not see.

25 And there was no man so highly praised for beauty as Absalom in all
Israel—from the sole of his foot to the crown of his head, there was no
26 blemish in him. And when he cut his hair, for from one year's end
till the next he would cut it, as it grew heavy upon him, he would
weigh the hair of his head, two hundred shekels by the royal weight.

---

21. *bring back the lad Absalom.* Momentarily, David refers to Absalom by a
term *(naʿar)* that is generally an expression of paternal affection. He will use
the same word repeatedly during Absalom's rebellion to stress his concern for
Absalom's safety.

25. *there was no man so highly praised for beauty.* Both Absalom and his sister
Tamar are remarkable for their beauty (as was the young David). For Absalom, this will become an asset he trades on in his appeal for popular support.

26. *he would cut his hair . . . he would weigh the hair of his head.* There is
clearly something narcissistic about this preoccupation with his luxuriant hair.
It is of course a foreshadowing of the bizarre circumstances of Absalom's
death (Chapter 18:9–15). Beyond that, the spectacular growth of hair invokes
a comparison with Samson, who never cut his hair until the cutting of the hair
against his will led to his undoing. The parallel with Samson is extended in the
burning of Joab's field, which recalls the foxes with torches tied to their tails
used by Samson to set fire to the fields of the Philistines. Perhaps the parallel
with Samson is meant to foreshadow Absalom's fate as a powerful leader
whose imprudence brings him to an early death.

And three sons were born to Absalom and a daughter named Tamar, 27
she was a beautiful woman. And Absalom lived in Jerusalem two 28
years, but the king's face he did not see. And Absalom sent to Joab in 29
order to send him to the king, but he did not want to come to him
and he sent still a second time, but he did not want to come. And he 30
said to his servants, "See Joab's field next to mine, in which he has
barley—go set it on fire!" And Absalom's servants set fire to the field.
And Joab rose and came to Absalom's house and said to him, "Why 31
did your servants set fire to the field that belongs to me?" And 32
Absalom said to Joab, "Look, I sent to you, saying, 'Come here that I
may send you to the king, saying, Why did I come from Geshur? It
would be better for me were I still there. And now, let me see the face
of the king, and if there be guilt in me, let him put me to death.' "

---

27. *and three sons were born to Absalom, and a daughter named Tamar, she was a beautiful woman.* Later, we are informed (18:18) that Absalom was childless. The two reports can be harmonized only with considerable strain, and it is best to view them as contradictory traditions incorporated in the final text. But it is noteworthy that, against patriarchal practice, the sons are left unnamed here, and only the daughter, named after Absalom's raped sister, is not anonymous. It is unnecessary to assume that this second beautiful Tamar was born after the violation of her aunt by Amnon: here she is represented as a woman, and it seems unlikely that so many years would have passed from the time of Tamar's rape until Absalom's resumption of residence in Jerusalem.

29. *he did not want to come.* Throughout this story, there is a precarious game of power going on. Joab has manipulated David to effect Absalom's return, but seeing that the king remains estranged from Absalom, Joab does not want to push his luck by interceding at court on Absalom's behalf. The power of the king may be qualified, but he remains the king.

30. *set it on fire.* Absalom's Samson-like burning of the field is a strong indication that he is a man prepared to use violence to achieve his ends: Mafia style, he presents Joab with an offer he can't refuse.

32. *if there be guilt in me, let him put me to death.* Absalom of course knows he is responsible for the killing of Amnon, but he construes that act as something other than "guilt" because it was done to avenge the violation of Tamar—a crime David left unpunished.

33 And Joab came to the king and told him. And he called to Absalom and he came to the king and bowed down to him, his face to the ground before the king, and the king kissed Absalom.

---

33. *he bowed to him, his face to the ground.* Fokkelman notes that there is a series of three acts of prostration before the king—first the Tekoite woman, then Joab, and now Absalom, the third bowing down ostensibly consummating the reconciliation of father and son toward which all three acts are directed.

and the king kissed Absalom. The noun used (rather than "David") may suggest that this is more a royal, or official, kiss than a paternal one. It clearly gives Absalom no satisfaction, as his initiative of usurpation in the next episode strongly argues.

CHAPTER 15

And it happened thereafter that Absalom made himself a chariot with 1
horses and fifty men running before him. And Absalom would rise early 2
and stand by the gate road, and so, to every man who had a suit to
appear in judgment before the king, Absalom would call and say, "From
what town are you?" And he would say, "From one of the tribes of Israel
is your servant." And Absalom would say to him, "See, your words are 3
good and right, but you have no one to listen to you from the king."

---

1. *A chariot with horses and fifty men running before him.* All this vehicular
pomp and circumstance, as other biblical references to chariots, horses, and
runners in conjunction with kings suggest, is a claim to royal status. The gestures of usurpation are undertaken in Jerusalem, under David's nose, yet the
king, who has been described by the Tekoite woman as "knowing everything
in the land," does nothing.

2.–5. This whole tableau of Absalom standing at the gate to the city, accosting
each newcomer, professing sympathy for his cause, and announcing that were
he the supreme judicial authority, he would rule in the man's favor, is a stylized representation of the operation of a demagogue. It is hard to imagine realistically that Absalom would tell each person so flatly that, whatever the legal
case, he would declare in his favor, but the point of the stylization is clear: the
demagogue enlists support by flattering people's special interests, leading
them to believe that he will champion their cause, cut their taxes, increase
their social security benefits, and so forth.

3. *you have no one to listen to you from the king.* The heart of Absalom's demagogic pitch is his exploiting what must have been widespread dissatisfaction
over the new centralized monarchic bureaucracy with its imposition of taxes
and corvées and military conscription: there is no one in this impersonal
palace to listen to you with a sympathetic ear, as I do.

4   And Absalom would say, "Would that I were made judge in the land, and to me every man would come who had a suit in justice, and I

5   would declare in his favor." And so, when a man would draw near to bow down to him, he would reach out his hand and take hold of him

6   and kiss him. And Absalom would act in this fashion to all the Israelites who appeared in judgment before the king, and Absalom stole the hearts of the men of Israel.

7   And it happened at the end of four years that Absalom said to the king, "Let me go, pray, and pay my vow that I pledged to the LORD in

8   Hebron. For your servant made a vow when I was staying in Geshur in Aram, saying, "If the LORD indeed brings me back to Jerusalem, I shall

9   worship the LORD." And the king said to him, "Go in peace to Hebron."

10   And he arose and went to Hebron. And Absalom sent agents through

---

5. *he would reach out his hand and take hold of him and kiss him.* The odd "rhyming" of Absalom's kiss to each man he seduces and David's kiss to Absalom at the end of the immediately preceding chapter is obvious. Could it suggest, retrospectively, that David's kiss has an element of falseness that recurs, grossly magnified, in Absalom's kiss? It should also be noted that Absalom's gesture of "taking hold" of each of his political victims is verbally identical with Amnon's "taking hold" of Tamar before the rape.

7. *at the end of four years.* The Masoretic Text has "forty years," an untenable number in this narrative context, but four different ancient versions show "four years."

    pay my vow that I pledged to the LORD in Hebron. Haim Gevaryahu proposes that the vow is to offer an exculpatory sacrifice for the crime of manslaughter. With three years in Geshur and another four in Jerusalem, Absalom would have come to the end of the period of seven years of penance that, according to some ancient parallels, might have applied to such crimes. Absalom of course wants to go off to Hebron—David's first capital city—in order to proclaim himself king at a certain distance from his father's palace. It also appears that he feels he can call on a base of support from Judah, his father's tribe. But why is not David suspicious when his son proposes to pay his cultic vow in Hebron rather than in Jerusalem? Gevaryahu, citing Greek analogues, makes the interesting suggestion that a fratricide who had not yet atoned for his crime was not permitted to worship in the same sanctuary as his father and brothers.

all the tribes of Israel, saying, "When you hear the sound of the ram's horn, you shall say, 'Absalom has become king in Hebron.'" And with 11 Absalom two hundred men went from Jerusalem, invited guests going in all innocence, and they knew nothing. And Absalom sent Ahitophel 12 the Gilonite, David's counselor, from his town, from Giloh, while he was offering the sacrifices, and the conspiracy was strong, and the people with Absalom were growing in number. And the informant came to 13 David saying, "The hearts of the men of Israel are following Absalom." And David said to all his servants who were with him in Jerusalem, 14 "Rise and let us flee or none of us will escape from Absalom. Hurry and go, lest he hurry and overtake us and bring down evil upon us and strike the city with the edge of the sword." And the king's servants said 15 to the king, "Whatever my lord the king chooses, look, we are your servants." And the king went out, and all his household with him, on 16 foot, and the king left his ten concubines to watch over the house.

---

11. *invited guests going in all innocence*. In a shrewd maneuver, Absalom takes with him a large contingent of people not known to be his partisans, and not willing participants in the conspiracy, and in this way he wards off suspicion about the aim of his expedition. Once in Hebron, the two hundred men would presumably be caught up in the tide of insurrection.

14. *Rise and let us flee*. Suddenly, under the pressure of crisis, with intelligence that Absalom has overwhelming support, David shakes himself from his slumber of passivity, realizing he must move at once if he is to have any chance of surviving. Against superior forces, the walled city of Jerusalem would be a death trap. As Fokkelman aptly puts it, "Once again he is in contact with his old self. . . . Once again men seek his death and he enters the wilderness both figuratively and literally."

15. *Whatever my lord the king chooses, we are your servants*. As the episode unfolds, there is a constant counterpoint between those who reveal their unswerving loyalty to David no matter how grim the outlook and the betrayal of David by his son and all those who have rallied to the usurper.

16. *the king left his ten concubines to watch over the house*. This gesture sounds as though it might be an expression of hope that David will return to Jerusalem. In the event, it produces a disastrous consequence that fulfills one of the dire terms of Nathan's curse in Chapter 12.

17 And the king, and all the people with him, went out on foot, and they
18 stopped by the outlying house. And all his servants were crossing over
alongside him, and all the Cherethites and the Pelethites and all the
Githites, six hundred men who had come at his heels from Gath, were
19 crossing over before the king. And the king said to Ittai the Gittite,

---

17. *the king, and all the people with him, went out on foot.* This restatement of
the first clause of the previous verse reflects the device that biblical scholars
call "resumptive repetition": after an interruption of the narrative line—here,
the introduction of the information about the concubines—the words just
before the interruption are repeated as the main line of the narrative resumes.
Moreover, the emphasis through repetition on going by foot suggests how
David and his entourage have been reduced from royal dignity in this abrupt
flight.

the outlying house. The literal meaning of the Hebrew is "the house of distance." It clearly means the last house in the settled area beyond the walls of
the city.

18. *all his servants were crossing over.* The verb "to cross over" (*ʿavar*), abundantly repeated, is a thematic focus of the episode. David and his followers
are crossing over eastward from Jerusalem, headed first up the Mount of
Olives and then down the long declivity to the Jordan, which they will
cross (the verb *ʿavar* is often used for Jordan crossing) in their flight. The
entire episode is unusual in the leisurely panoramic view it provides of the
eastward march from the city. Instead of the preterite verb form ordinarily
used for narration, participial forms ("were crossing over") predominate,
imparting a sense of something like a present tense to the report of the
action.

Cherethites . . . Pelethites . . . Githites. This elite palace guard, which we
have encountered before, are Philistine warriors who became David's followers when he was residing in Gath. Ittai's expression of loyalty suggests that
they were more than mere mercenaries.

19. *Ittai.* His name is close to the preposition *ʾiti*, "with me." Both Moshe Garsiel and Robert Polzin have proposed that the name has a symbolic function:
Ittai is the loyalist who insists on remaining with David. Polzin notes that this
preposition is constantly reiterated in the episode, rather than its synonym
ʿim: David, for example, says to Ittai, "Why should you, too, go with us
[*ʾitanu*]?"

"Why should you too go with us? Go back, stay with the king. For you
are a foreigner, and you are also in exile from your own place. Just yes-   20
terday you came, and today should I make you wander with us, when I
myself am going to wherever I may go. Turn back, and bring back your
brothers. Steadfast kindness to you!" And Ittai answered the king and   21
said, "As the LORD lives, and as my lord the king lives, whatever place
that my lord the king may be, whether for death or for life, there your
servant will be." And David said, "Go and cross over." And Ittai crossed   22
over, and all his men and all the children who were with him. And all   23
the land was weeping loudly and all the people were crossing over, and
the king was crossing over the Wadi Kidron, and all the people were
crossing over along the road to the wilderness. And, look, Zadok and all   24
the Levites were also with him, bearing the Ark of the Covenant of
God, and they set down the Ark of God, and Abiathar came up, until
all the people had finished crossing over from the city. And the king   25
said to Zadok, "Bring back the Ark of God to the city. Should I find

---

Stay with the king. This designation of the usurping son would be especially painful for David to pronounce. He does it in order to try to persuade
Ittai that he should cast his fate with the person exercising the power of king.

20. *Steadfast kindness to you!* The translation reproduces the elliptical character of the Masoretic Text at this point. The Septuagint has an easier reading:
"May the LORD show steadfast kindness to you."

21. *whether for death or for life.* Given the grim circumstances, this loyal soldier
unflinchingly puts death before life in the two alternatives he contemplates.

23. *and the king was crossing over the Wadi Kidron.* In the slow-motion report
of the flight, reinforced by the participial verbs, David is now crossing the
Kidron brook at the foot of the slope descending eastward from the walled
city. He will then make his way up the Mount of Olives.

25. *Bring back the Ark of God to the city.* Given the difficulties David encountered in bringing the Ark to Jerusalem in the first place, and given the disastrous consequences at the time of Eli in carrying it out to the battlefield, it is
understandable that he should want the Ark left in Jerusalem. He makes this
act a token of his reiterated fatalism about his predicament.

favor in the eyes of the LORD, He will bring me back and let me see it
26 and its abode. And should He say thus, 'I want no part of you,' let Him
27 do to me what is good in His eyes." And the king said to Zadok the
priest, "Do you see? Go back to the city in peace, and Ahimaaz your
28 son and Jonathan son of Abiathar—your two sons with you. See, I shall
be tarrying in the steppes of the wilderness until word from you
29 reaches me to inform me.'" And Zadok, and Abiathar with him,
brought back the Ark of God to Jerusalem, and they stayed there.
30 And David was going up the Slope of Olives, going up weeping,
his head uncovered and he walking barefoot, and all the people
who were with him, everyone with his head uncovered, went on up
31 weeping the while. And to David it was told, saying, "Ahitophel is
among the conspirators with Absalom." And David said, "Thwart,
32 pray, the counsel of Ahitophel, O LORD." And David had come to

---

27. *and the king said to Zadok the priest.* Again we see the distinctive biblical
convention in the deployment of dialogue: when the first party speaks and
the second party does not respond, and a second speech of the first party is
introduced, there is an intimation of some sort of failure of response. Zadok
is nonplussed by David's instructions to return the Ark and also by David's
fatalism. Now, in his second speech, David provides a practical, strategic
rationale for Zadok's going back to the city with the Ark—he and his two
acolytes will then be able to act as spies for David (see the end of his speech
in verse 28).

30. *his head uncovered.* There is a difference of philological opinion as to
whether the verb here means covered or uncovered. The usual meaning of the
root is "to cover," but an uncovered head is more likely as a gesture of mourning—which is clearly intended—and this could be an instance of the same
term denoting antonyms, like the English verb "cleave."

31. *and to David it was told.* The Masoretic Text reads, "And David told," but
both the Qumran Samuel and the Septuagint reflect the more likely idea—a
difference of one Hebrew letter—that someone told David.

the summit, where one would bow down to God, and, look, coming
toward him was Hushai the Archite, his tunic torn and earth on his
head. And David said, "If you cross over with me, you will be a burden   33
to me." But if you go back to the city and say to Absalom, 'Your servant,   34
O king, I will be. Your father's servant I always was, and now I am your
servant,' you shall overturn Ahitophel's counsel for me. And are not   35
Zadok and Abiathar the priests there with you? And so, whatever you
hear from the king's house you shall tell to Zadok and to Abiathar the
priests. Look, there with them are their two sons, Ahimaaz, who is   36
Zadok's, and Jonathan, who is Abiathar's, and you shall send by their
hand to me whatever you hear." And Hushai, David's friend, came to   37
the city, as Absalom was coming into Jerusalem.

---

32. *the summit, where one would bow down to God, and look, coming toward
him was Hushai.* This crucial moment in the story is an especially deft manifestation of the system of double causation that Gerhard von Rad and others
after him have attributed to the David narrative: everything in the story is
determined by its human actors, according to the stringent dictates of political realism; yet, simultaneously, everything is determined by God, according
to a divine plan in history. David, informed that his own shrewd political advisor Ahitophel is part of Absalom's conspiracy, urgently and breathlessly
invokes God, "Thwart, pray, the counsel of Ahitophel, O LORD." Then he
reaches a holy site, an altar on the crest of the Mount of Olives ("where one
would bow down to God"), and here he sees Hushai, his loyalty betokened by
the trappings of mourning he has assumed, coming toward him. Theologically,
Hushai is the immediate answer to David's prayer. Politically, David seizes
upon Hushai as the perfect instrument to thwart Ahitophel's counsel, so from
a certain point of view David is really answering his own prayer through his
human initiative. Yet the encounter with Hushai at a place of worship leaves
the lingering intimation that Hushai has been sent by God to David.

34. *say to Absalom, 'Your servant, O king, I will be. . . .'* David, passive to a fault
in the preceding episodes, now improvises in the moment of crisis a detailed
plan for subverting Absalom, even dictating to Hushai the exact script he is to
use when he comes before the usurper.

35. *are not Zadok and Abiathar the priests there with you?* David is both offering
encouragement to Hushai, assuring him that he will not be the sole, isolated
undercover agent in Jerusalem, and indicating to him what every spy needs to
know, that there will be a reliable network for transmitting intelligence to the
command center for which the spy is working.

CHAPTER 16

¹ nd when David had crossed over a little beyond the summit, look, Ziba, Mephibosheth's lad, was there to meet him, with a yoke of saddled donkeys and on them two hundred loaves of bread and a hundred
² raisin cakes and a hundred of summer fruit and a jug of wine. And the king said to Ziba, "What would you with these things?" And Ziba said, "The donkeys are for the king's household to ride upon, and the bread

---

1. *David crossed over.* The verbal motif of "crossing over," which virtually defines David's flight eastward from Jerusalem to Transjordan, is continued here. It will be given another odd turn in verse 17 when the bloody-minded Abishai volunteers to "cross over" and lop off Shimei's head.

a little beyond the summit. The summit in question is of course the top of the Mount of Olives, where David has just encountered Hushai and sent him off to Jerusalem as an undercover agent. Polzin acutely observes that the two low points of David's abasement—his humiliation by Shimei and the sexual possession of his concubines by his son—both take place on an elevation: near the summit and on the palace roof. The Hebrew term for summit used here is *roʾsh*, which is the ordinary word for "head," and as Polzin goes on to note, "head" is an organizing image of the entire episode: David goes up the mountainside with his head uncovered in sign of mourning, as do the people with him. Hushai puts dirt on his head as a related expression of mourning. Both Hushai and Ziba are encountered on or near the head of the mountain. Abishai is prepared to cut off Shimei's head. And, as in other languages, head also designates political leader—an ironic verbal background to this moment when the head of all Israel has been displaced. Finally, Absalom's usurpation will come to a violent end when his head—the narrator does not say hair—is caught in the branches of a tree.

2. *for the king's household.* That is, for a couple of members of the king's immediate family. David, it should be recalled, has set off on foot.

and the summer fruit for the lads to eat, and the wine for the exhausted to drink in the wilderness." And the king said, "And where is ₃ your master's son?" And Ziba said to the king, "Why, he is staying in Jerusalem, for he has said, 'Today the house of Israel will give back to me my father's kingdom.' " And the king said to Ziba, "Look, everything ₄ of Mephibosheth's is yours!" And Ziba said, "I am prostrate! May I find favor in your eyes, my lord the king."

And King David came as far as Bahurim, and, look, from there out ₅ came a man from the clan of the house of Saul, Shimei son of Gera was his name, and he came cursing. And he hurled stones at David and ₆

---

the exhausted. The Hebrew term *ya ͨef*—also, by metathesis, *ͨayef,* as in verse 14—straddles the two meanings of exhausted and famished.

3. *and where is your master's son?* Mephibosheth, who is crippled in both legs, would scarcely have been up to joining the flight from Jerusalem. But David, overwhelmed by betrayals from within his own court, is suspicious of Mephibosheth's absence, and it is clear that Ziba has been counting on this suspicion in his scheme to discredit Mephibosheth and take over his property. It is noteworthy that, at this late date, David still refers to Mephibosheth as "your master's son," still thinks of the long-dead Jonathan as Ziba's real master.

Today the house of Israel will give back to me my father's kingdom. There is no corroborating evidence in the story that Mephibosheth actually said these words. What in fact seems to be happening is that Ziba is flatly lying about his master in order to make himself appear to be the only loyal subject worthy of David's benefactions, and of title to Saul's property. The notion Ziba puts forth that Absalom would have turned over the throne to the surviving Saulide is highly improbable, but what he proposes to David is that the purportedly treacherous Mephibosheth sees in the general political upheaval of the rebellion an opportunity to reinstate the house of Saul.

5. *as far as Bahurim.* This is a village in the vicinity of Jerusalem on the eastern slope of the Mount of Olives.

7
8
at all King David's servants, and all the troops and all the warriors were
at his right and at his left. And thus said Shimei as he cursed, "Get out,
get out, you man of blood, you worthless fellow! The LORD has brought
back upon you all the blood of the house of Saul, in whose place you
became king, and the LORD has given the kingship into the hand of
Absalom your son, and here you are, because of your evil, for you are a

9
man of blood." And Abishai son of Zeruiah said to the king, "Why
should this dead dog curse my lord the king? Let me, pray, cross over

---

6. *and all the troops and all the warriors were at his right and at his left.* Perhaps
Shimei is counting on the abject mood of David and his men to guarantee his
safety in this act of extreme provocation. Yet he is clearly playing a very dangerous game—the history of David's warriors and of the sons of Zeruiah in
particular as ruthless and implacable enemies is well known to him, as the
very language of his words of revilement attest. Only a great, pent-up rage
against David, joined now with gloating over David's being thrust from power,
could explain Shimei's act.

7. *Get out, get out, you man of blood, you worthless fellow.* The blood that,
according to the narrative itself, David has on his hands, is that of Uriah the
Hittite, and of the fighting men of Israel who perished at Rabbath Ammon
with Uriah. But the Benjaminite Shimei clearly believes what David himself,
and the narrative with him, has taken pains to refute—that the blood of the
house of Saul is on David's hands: Abner, Ish-bosheth, and perhaps even Saul
and Jonathan (for David was collaborating with the Philistine Achish when
they fell at Gilboa). Hence the phrase Shimei hurls at David in his next sentence, "all the blood of the house of Saul, in whose place you became king,"
suggesting a conjunction of murder and usurpation.

8. *and here you are, because of your evil.* Most translations understand the last
phrase (a single word in the Hebrew) to mean "You are in evil circumstances,"
but the prefix *bet,* which can mean "in," also has a *causal* meaning, and that
makes more sense here: David has come into dire straits, losing the throne,
displaced by his own son, because of his own evil actions.

9. *Why should this dead dog curse my lord the king?* We have seen previously
the idiomatic use of "dead dog" to mean the lowest of the low, David applying
this designation to himself in his speech to Saul at En-gedi. Here the polar
contrast between "dead dog" and "my lord the king" is striking. But Abishai is
also reviving the literal force of the idiom, since he proposes to deal swift
death to the snarling Shimei. This is not the first time that Abishai has been

and take off his head." And the king said, "What do I have to do with 10
you, O sons of Zeruiah? If he curses, it is because the LORD has said to
him, 'Curse David,' and who can say, 'Why have you done this?'" And 11
David said to Abishai and to all his servants, "Look—my son, the issue
of my loins, seeks my life. How much more so, then, this Benjaminite.
Leave him be and let him curse, for the LORD has told him. Perhaps 12
the LORD will see my affliction and the LORD may requite me good for
his cursing this day." And David, and his men with him, went off on the 13
way, and Shimei was walking round the side of the mountain alongside
him, cursing and hurling stones at him and flinging dirt. And the king 14
came, and all the troops who were with him, exhausted, and they took

---

prepared to kill someone on the spot: when he accompanied David into Saul's
camp (1 Samuel 26:8), he had to be restrained from his impulse to dispatch
Saul with a single thrust of the spear.

10. *If he curses, it is because the LORD has said to him, 'Curse David.'* This is one
of the most astonishing turning points in this story that abounds in human sur-
prises. The proud, canny, often implacable David here resigns himself to
accepting the most stinging humiliation from a person he could easily have his
men kill. David's abasement is not a disguise, like Odysseus's when he takes on
the appearance of a beggar, but a real change in condition—from which, however, he will emerge in more than one surprising way. The acceptance of humiliation is a kind of fatalism: if someone commits such a sacrilegious act against
the man who is God's anointed king, it must be because God has decreed it.
Behind that fatalism may be a sense of guilt: I am suffering all this because of
what I have done, for taking Bathsheba and murdering her husband, for my
inaction in Amnon's rape of Tamar and Absalom's murder of Amnon. The guilt
is coupled with despair: as David goes on to say, When my own son is trying to
kill me, what difference could it make if this man of a rival tribe, who at least
has political grounds for hostility toward me, should revile me?

13. *cursing and hurling stones at him and flinging dirt.* It is with this image that
the episode concludes—Shimei walking along, angrily persisting in his
insults, the dirt flung a material equivalent of the words uttered.

14. *came.* Some indication of where he came seems to be required. One version of the Septuagint supplies "to the Jordan" as the answer. That would be a
plausible stopping place.

15   a breathing stop there. And Absalom and all the troops, the men of
     Israel, had come to Jerusalem, and Ahithophel was with him.

16   And it happened when Hushai the Archite, David's friend, came to
17   Absalom, that Hushai said, "Long live the king, long live the king!" And
     Absalom said to Hushai, "Is this your loyalty to your friend? Why did
18   you not go with your friend?" And Hushai said to Absalom, "On the
     contrary! Whom the LORD has chosen, and this people and every man
19   of Israel—his I will be and with him I will stay. And, besides, whom
     should I serve? Should it not be his son? As I served your father, so will
20   I be in your service." And Absalom said to Ahitophel, "Give you counsel:

---

15. *and Absalom . . . had come to Jerusalem, and Ahitophel was with him.* This
brief switch of narrative tracks, in a pluperfect verbal form, lays the ground for
the fateful clash of counsels between Ahitophel and Hushai and also provides
the necessary indication that David and his people have succeeded in fleeing
a good many miles to the east by the time Absalom's forces enter the city.

16. *David's friend.* As we have noted, *reʿa,* "friend" or "companion," is a court
title, but when Absalom uses it, he leans on the ordinary sense of friendship.
    Long live the king. Fokkelman nicely observes that "what he particularly
does not say is 'long live King Absalom.' " Thus, in a dramatic irony evident to
the audience of the story and of course concealed from Absalom, Hushai is
really wishing long life to *his* king—David. And again in his response to Absalom's question about his disloyalty to David, he avoids the use of Absalom's
name in a sentence that he secretly applies to David: "Whom the LORD has
chosen . . . his I will be and with him I will stay."

19. *And, besides, whom should I serve? Should it not be his son?* Only now does
Hushai invoke the line of explanation that David instructed him to use when
he came before Absalom.

20. *Give you counsel.* Both the verb and the ethical dative "you" are in the
plural, though Absalom is said to be speaking to Ahitophel. Shimon Bar-Efrat
proposes that the language implies Absalom is addressing both Ahitophel and
Hushai, though it is from Ahitophel as his official advisor that he expects to
receive counsel. The plural forms, then, suggest that Absalom has been persuaded by Hushai and has accepted him into his circle of court counselors.
That inference helps make sense of the immediately following encounter in
which both men appear as members of Absalom's national security council.

what shall we do?" And Ahitophel said to Absalom, "Come to bed with 21
your father's concubines whom he left to watch over the house, and let
all Israel hear that you have become repugnant to your father, and the
hand of all who are with you will be strengthened." And they pitched a 22
tent for Absalom on the roof, and he came to bed with his father's concubines before the eyes of all Israel. And the counsel of Ahitophel that 23
he would give in those days was as one would inquire of an oracle of
God, even so was every counsel of Ahitophel, for David and for Absalom as well.

---

21. *Come to bed with your father's concubines . . .* Cohabiting with the sexual
consorts of a ruler is an assertion of having taken over all his prerogatives of
dominion. Ahitophel's shrewd counsel especially addresses the effect on public opinion of the action proposed: after it, no one will be able to imagine a
reconciliation between Absalom and his father ("let all Israel hear that you
have become repugnant to your father"), and so the hand of Absalom's supporters will be strengthened, for no one will hedge his support, thinking that
David and Absalom will somehow come to terms.

22. *he came to bed with his father's concubines before the eyes of all Israel.* The
tent on the roof ensures sexual privacy, but Absalom's entering into it with
each of the women is a public display of the act of cohabitation. Either this is
to be accepted as an unrealistic event, given that there are ten concubines, or
Absalom is supposed to be not only beautiful and hirsute but also a sexual ath-
lete. His act, of course, is a fulfillment of Nathan's dire curse in Chapter 12.
As several commentators have noted, the usurper's sexual transgression of
David's women takes place on the very palace roof from which his father first
looked lustfully at Bathsheba.

23. *the counsel of Ahitophel . . . was as one would inquire of an oracle of God.*
This quasi-religious trust in Ahitophel's counsel is obviously from the point of
view of those who seek it, there being a sour irony in likening the sordid, if
pragmatic, counsel to have sex with the king's concubines to a divine oracle.
In any event, this observation throws a retrospective light on David's disturbance over the news that Ahitophel was among the conspirators and his
prayer to God to confound Ahitophel's counsel (15:31). Ahitophel, it seems, is
a kind of Israelite Metternich or Bismarck, and David fears that in losing him
he has lost a vital strategic resource. The canniness of Ahitophel's military
advice will be evident in his clash with Hushai.

CHAPTER 17

₁ And Ahitophel said to Absalom, "Let me pick, pray, twelve thousand men,
₂ and let me rise and pursue David tonight. And let me come upon him
when he is tired and slack handed, and I shall panic him, and all the
troops who are with him will flee, and I shall strike down the king alone.
₃ And let me turn back all the troops to you, for it is one man you seek,

---

1. *Let me pick . . . twelve thousand men . . . and pursue David tonight.* Ahitophel
not only offers counsel but proposes to undertake the command of the expedition himself, in striking contrast to Hushai, who begins with a lengthy
descriptive statement and then uses a third-person verbal form (verse 11, "let
all Israel gather round you") to express his recommended course of action. It
seems as though the urgent Ahitophel has taken on the attribute of his rival's
name, which carries the verb *ḥush*, "hurry."

2. *let me come upon him when he is tired and slack handed.* This is, of course,
very sound advice: David and his men are in fact fatigued from their flight to
the banks of the Jordan (16:14), and are likely to be vulnerable to a surprise
attack.
    I shall strike down the king alone. Ahitophel seeks to avoid a protracted civil
war: if he can panic David's forces into a general retreat, the death of David
will then put an end to the opposition and his troops are likely to transfer their
loyalty to Absalom. The image of one man struck down as the troops flee may
ironically echo David's plan for doing away with Uriah.

3. *for it is one man you seek.* The Masoretic Text has three simple Hebrew
words here that make no sense as a syntactic sequence: *keshuv hakol ha²ish*
("as-return all the-man"). Many modern interpreters follow the Septuagint,
which rearranges the Hebrew letters to read *keshuv kalah l²ishah*, "as a bride
returns to her husband." But, as Bar-Efrat contends, this would be a strange
image for the movement of troops to the opposite side and it would violate
the pointedly unmetaphoric, businesslike character of Ahitophel's language,

and all the troops will be at peace." And the thing seemed right in the   4
eyes of Absalom and in the eyes of all the elders of Israel. And Absalom   5
said, "Call, pray, to Hushai the Archite, too, and let us hear what he,
too, has to say." And Hushai came to Absalom and Absalom said to   6
him, saying, "In the following manner Ahitophel has spoken. Shall we
act on his word? If not, you must speak." And Hushai said to Absalom,   7
"The counsel that Ahitophel has given is not good this time."
And Hushai said, "You yourself know of your father and his men   8
that they are warriors and that they are bitter men, like a bear in the
field bereaved of its young. And your father is a seasoned fighter and

---

which stands in sharp contrast to Hushai's elaborately figurative rhetoric of
persuasion. This translation therefore adopts Bar-Efrat's proposal that *keshuv
hakol* is an inadvertent scribal repetition of *weᵓashiva kol* ("let me turn back
all") at the beginning of the verse; that phrase is omitted here, and *ᵓish ᵓeḥad*,
"one man," is presumed instead of *haᵓish ᵓasher*, "the man who."

4. *the elders of Israel*. This term clearly designates an official group, a kind of
royal council. Ahitophel, addressing this group, acts as national security advisor.

5. *Hushai the Archite, too*. Although Hushai does not have Ahitophel's official
standing, he has sufficiently won Absalom's trust that the usurper is at least
curious to see whether Hushai will concur with Ahitophel. This will prove to
be a fatal error.

7. *not good this time*. Shrewdly, Hushai begins by implicitly conceding that as a
rule Ahitophel's counsel is good—but in this specific instance, the trusty advi
sor has exhibited a lapse in judgment.

8. *and Hushai said*. Absalom is silent, astounded that anyone should deny the
self-evident rightness of Ahitophel's counsel. So the formula for introducing
direct discourse, according to the biblical convention, must be repeated, and
now Hushai launches upon his cunningly devised argument.

You yourself know. Hushai's opening rhetorical move is to flatter his interlocutor: I hardly have to tell you what you yourself well know, that your father
is a very dangerous adversary who cannot be attacked impulsively, without
proper preparation.

warriors . . . bitter men . . . like a bear in the field . . . a seasoned fighter.
Hushai uses language which, as Bar-Efrat and others have noted, recapitu-
lates a series of moments from the earlier story of David. What he is doing in
effect is invoking the legend of the heroic David, who as a boy slew bear and
lion (compare the lion simile in verse 10), and who gathered round him bitter
men, warriors, seasoned fighters.

9 he will not spend the night with the troops. Look, he will now be
hiding in some hollow or some other place, and it will happen
when they fall from the very first that he who hears of it will say,
10 'There's a rout among the troops who follow Absalom.' And though he
be a valiant fellow whose heart is like the heart of a lion, he will surely
quail, for all Israel knows that your father is a warrior and valiant
11 men are those who are with him. And so I counsel you—let all
Israel gather round you, from Dan to Beersheba, multitudinous as the
sand that is on the seashore, and you in person will go forward into bat-
12 tle. And we shall come upon him in whatever place that he may
be, and we shall light upon him as the dew falls upon the ground, and

---

he will not spend the night with the troops. This image of David as the constantly wakeful, elusive guerilla leader scarcely accords with the figure David
has cut in the last several years of reported narrative—sleeping through the
long afternoon while his army fights in Ammon, sedentary in his palace while
internecine struggle goes on between his own children.

9. *he will now be hiding in some hollow or some other place.* Hushai's rather
vague language once again evokes the time when David was a fugitive from
Saul, hiding in caves and wildernesses.

when they fall from the first. The unspecified subject of the verb—actually
emended by some as "the troops"—clearly refers to Absalom's forces:
ambushed by the wily David, they will quickly panic.

10. *he will surely quail.* The literal meaning of the Hebrew is "he will surely
melt."

11. *multitudinous as the sand . . . on the seashore.* This traditional simile is used
to convey the idea that only overwhelmingly superior numbers, achieved
through a general (and time-consuming!) conscription, can prevail against so
formidable a foe as David.

12. *we shall light upon him as the dew falls upon the ground.* Hushai, as Fokkelman has observed, pairs the traditional simile of the sands of the seashore
with a more innovative, yet related simile of dew on the field. The dew falls
silently, effortlessly, and this is how this huge army will "light upon" David's
forces. Dew, elsewhere an image of peacetime blessing, is here associated
with destruction.

not a single one will be left of all the men who are with him. And 13
should he withdraw into a town, all Israel will bear ropes to the town
and haul it away to the wadi until not a stone remains there." And 14
Absalom said, and every man of Israel with him, "The counsel of
Hushai the Archite is better than the counsel of Ahitophel." And the
LORD had ordained to overturn Ahitophel's good counsel in order for
the LORD to bring evil upon Absalom.

And Hushai said to Zadok and to Abiathar the priests, "Such and such 15
did Ahitophel counsel Absalom and the elders of Israel, and such and
such I on my part counseled. And now, send quickly and inform David, 16

---

not a single one will be left of all the men who are with him. Ahitophel proposed a strategy through which it might be possible to kill David alone and then to enlist the support of his followers. Hushai's counsel is to annihilate David's forces, a much more violent means of preventing civil war. The bloodthirsty alternative evidently appeals to something in Absalom, who is unwilling to trust the future loyalty of the troops that have remained with David.

13. *should he withdraw into a town.* This little addendum to Hushai's scenario is intended to anticipate an obvious objection to it: the recommended course of action would give David time to pull back his forces to a strong defensive position in a fortified town. Hushai's counterargument is that with so huge an army, Absalom's people could easily take down the walls of the town stone by stone.

14. *the counsel of Hushai . . . is better than the counsel of Ahitophel.* This entire episode turns on an ingenious reversal of values. The straight-talking, clear-seeing advisor is defeated by the lying secret agent who musters the resources of a figurative, psychologically manipulative rhetoric to achieve his ends. Yet it is the master of deception who serves the forces of legitimacy while the plain dealer looks out for the interests of a usurper and would-be parricide.

the LORD had ordained to overturn Ahitophel's good counsel. This theological explanation can be viewed as adding an overarching perspective, or as merely secondary, to the thoroughly human machinations of Hushai, instigated by David.

16. *and now, send quickly and inform David.* Although Zadok and Abiathar presumably know that Absalom has chosen to follow Hushai's counsel, they appear to be nervous that he may change his mind and implement Ahitophel's strategy, for they urge David not to waste a moment but to flee eastward across the Jordan.

saying, 'Spend not the night in the steppes of the wilderness, but rather cross over onward, lest disaster engulf the king and all the troops
17 who are with him.' " And Jonathan and Ahimaaz were stationed at En-rogel, and the slavegirl would go and inform them and they would go and inform King David, for they could not be seen coming into the city.
18 And a lad saw them and informed Absalom, and the two of them went quickly and came to the house of a man in Bahurim who had a well in
19 his courtyard, and they went down into it. And the woman took a cloth and stretched it over the mouth of the well and spread groats on top of
20 it, so that nothing could be noticed. And Absalom's servants came to the woman in the house and said, "Where are Ahimaaz and Jonathan?" And she said to them, "They've crossed over past the water reservoir." And they searched and they found nothing and they went back to

---

17. *En-rogel.* The site of this village has not been confidently identified, but it would have to be near Jerusalem to the east.

the house of a man in Bahurim. This village on the eastern slope of the Mount of Olives is the hometown of Shimei, who cursed David. What appears to be reflected is a political reality in which the populace is divided between loyalists and supporters of the usurper.

19. *and the woman took a cloth.* The woman is evidently the wife of the man from Bahurim (the same Hebrew word means both "woman" and "wife," like *femme* in French and *Frau* in German). This is still another instance in the David story in which the enterprising intervention of a shrewd woman saves the day. As has often been noted, this moment alludes to the story told in Joshua 2 of Rahab the harlot, who hides the two spies sent out to Jericho by Joshua. In Joshua, the spies are hidden up above, in the roof thatch; here they hide below in the well. There may be a certain agricultural affinity between the covering of thatch and the cloth covered with groats (if that is what the anomalous Hebrew *rifot* means) under which the pairs of spies hide. In any case, the destruction of all the men of Jericho who sought Joshua's spies foreshadows the destruction of Absalom's army.

20. *They've crossed over past the water reservoir.* Rahab, too, gives the pursuers false directions about where the spies have gone. Here, the thematically crucial "cross over" is again invoked. The meaning of *mikhal,* the word rendered here as "reservoir" is a little doubtful, though it could be derived from a verbal root that means "to contain."

Jerusalem. And it happened after they had gone that Ahimaaz and   21
Jonathan came up from the well and went and informed King David,
and they said to David, "Rise and cross over the water quickly, for thus
has Ahitophel counseled against you." And David rose, and all the   22
troops with him, and they crossed over the Jordan. By the light of
morning not a single one was missing who had not crossed over the Jordan.

And Ahitophel saw that his counsel was not acted on, and he saddled   23
his donkey and arose and went to his home to his town, and he left a
charge for his household, and he hanged himself and died. And he was
buried in the tomb of his father. And David had come to Mahanaim   24
when Absalom crossed over the Jordan, he and every man of Israel
with him. And Absalom had placed Amasa instead of Joab over the   25
army, and Amasa was the son of a man named Ithra the Ishmaelite,

---

21. *cross over the water quickly, for thus has Ahitophel counseled against you.*
The two couriers now assume the worst-case scenario, that Ahitophel's counsel will after all be followed. The reference to crossing over the water is a clear
indication that David is encamped on the west bank of the Jordan.

23. *he saddled his donkey and arose and went to his home to his town, and he left a
charge for his household, and he hanged himself.* This haunting notice of Ahitophel's suicide shows him a deliberate, practical man to the very end, making
all the necessary arrangements for his family and being sure to do away with
himself in his hometown, where he knows he will be readily buried in the ancestral tomb. Ahitophel kills himself not only because, in quasi-Japanese fashion,
he has lost face, but also out of sober calculation: he realizes that Hushai's counsel will enable David to defeat Absalom, and with the old king returned to the
throne, an archtraitor like Ahitophel will surely face death. Thus, in tying the
noose around his own neck, he anticipates the executioner's sword.

24. *Mahanaim.* This is an Israelite walled city in Transjordan.

25. *Ithra the Ishmaelite.* There are two different problems with the identification of Amasa's progenitors in the Masoretic Text. The Masoretic version has
"Israelite," but this national label (rather than identification by tribe) would be
strange here, and the same Ithra in 1 Chronicles 2:17 is said, more plausibly, to
be the son of an Ishmaelite. The fact that the father is a member of another
national-ethnic group accords with the report that he "had come to bed with

who had come to bed with Abigail daughter of Jesse, sister of Zeruiah,
26 Joab's mother. And Israel and Absalom camped in the land of Gilead.
27 And it happened when David came to Mahanaim that Shobi son of
Nahash from Rabbath-ammon and Machir son of Amiel from Lo-
28 debar and Barzillai the Gileadite from Rogelim brought couches and
basins and earthenware, and wheat and barley and flour and parched
29 grain and beans and lentils and honey and curds from the flock and
cheese from the herd. These they offered to David and the troops with
him to eat, for they thought, "The troops are hungry and exhausted and
thirsty in the wilderness."

Abigail," for that sexual term by no means necessarily implies marriage. The
Masoretic Text makes Nahash, an Ammonite, Abigail's father, but it looks as
though that name may have drifted into this verse in scribal transcription from
verse 27. 1 Chronicles 2 more plausibly reports that Jesse was Abigail's father.
She would then be the sister of David and of Zeruiah, Joab's mother; and so
Amasa and Joab, the two army commanders, are first cousins, and both of
them David's nephews.

28. *beans and lentils.* The received text adds "and parched grain" at the end of
the list, an apparent scribal duplication of the word that occurs just before
"beans and lentils." This detailed catalogue of vitally needed victuals, preceded by the utensils required to serve them and something like bedrolls, is a
vivid expression of loyalty to David's beleaguered forces on the part of the
Transjordanian Israelites and their Ammonite vassals. Barzillai's faithfulness
will be singled out when David returns.

29. *curds from the flock.* This reflects a very minor emendation of the
Masoretic Text, which says "curds and flock." In the next phrase, the Hebrew
word for "cheese" (*shefot*) has no precedent but is usually understood as
cheese because of the alimentary context and the likely root of the word.

CHAPTER 18

A nd David marshalled the troops that were with him and set over them commanders of thousands and commanders of hundreds. And David sent out the troops—a third under Joab and a third under Abishai son of Zeruiah, Joab's brother, and a third under Ittai the Gittite. And the king said to the troops, "I, too, will surely sally forth with you." And the troops said, "You shall not sally forth. For if we must flee, they will pay us no mind, and should half of us die, they will pay us no mind, for you are like ten thousand of us, and so it is better that you be a help for us from the town." And the king said to them, "Whatever is good in your eyes I shall do." And the king stood by the gate and all the troops sallied

---

2. *I, too, will surely sally forth with you.* The aging David, as we have had occasion to note (see comment on 11:1), has long been a sedentary monarch rather than a field commander. In the present crisis, he imagines he can rise again to his old role, but the troops, who diplomatically make no reference to age or infirmity, clearly recognize he is not up to it.

3. *should half of us die, they will pay us no mind.* Like Ahitophel, the troops assume that the real object of Absalom's attack is David. But they essentially propose an opposite scenario to Absalom's: David will remain safe inside the fortified town, well behind the lines, while the troops—not panicked, as Ahitophel would have had it, but strategically deployed—will do battle against Absalom's army.

for you are like ten thousand of us. This is the reading of numerous Hebrew manuscripts and the Septuagint and Vulgate. The Masoretic Text reads "for now we are like ten thousand."

4. *the king stood by the gate.* Fokkelman has noted a wry correspondence here with the beginning of Absalom's usurpation, when he took a stance by the gate of the city and accosted each man who came by in order to enlist him to his cause.

5 forth by their hundreds and their thousands. And the king charged
   Joab and Abishai and Ittai, saying, "Deal gently for me with the lad
   Absalom." And all the troops heard when the king charged the com-
6 manders concerning Absalom. And the troops sallied forth to the field
7 to meet Israel, and the battle took place in the forest of Ephraim. And
   the troops of Israel were routed there by David's servants, and great
8 was the slaughter there, twenty thousand. And the battle spread out
   over all the countryside, and the forest devoured more of the troops
9 than the sword devoured on that day. And Absalom chanced to be in
   front of David's servants, Absalom riding on his mule, and the mule
   came under the tangled branches of a great terebinth, and his head
   caught in the terebinth, and he dangled between heaven and earth,

---

5. *Deal gently.* This is the time-honored and eloquent rendering of the King
James Version. But some philologists derive the rare verb here from a root that
means "to cover" and hence construe it in context as "protect." This construction would make it a closer synonym of the verb used in the soldier's repetition
of David's injunction in verse 12, "watch over."

7. *the troops of Israel were routed there.* The elision of the precise details of the
battle is entirely consistent with the narrative treatment of battles elsewhere in
the Bible. One may assume that the three divisions of seasoned fighters, led by
their experienced commanders, attacked the Israelite army from three different sides, panicking it into disorderly flight—an outcome indicated in the
"devouring" forest, where presumably the fleeing soldiers lost their way, stum-
bled, became entangled in the undergrowth, perhaps even slashed at each
other in the dark of the wood. Throughout this episode, Absalom's forces are
"Israel" and David's are his "servants." The former are numerically superior, but
they behave like a poorly organized conscript army facing professional soldiers.

9. *his head caught in the terebinth, and he dangled between heaven and earth,
while the mule which was beneath him passed on.* This striking and bizarre
image of Absalom's penultimate moment provides a brilliant symbolic sum-
mation of his story. Most obviously, the head of hair that was his narcissistic
glory is now the instrument of his fatal entrapment, Absalom the commander
microcosmically enacting the fate of his army "devoured" by the forest. There
is nothing supernatural here—David's forces have shrewdly taken advantage
of the irregular terrain—yet there is a sense that nature is conspiring against
Absalom and his men. The mule is in this period the usual mount for princes
and kings (one should recall that all the king's sons ride away on their mules

while the mule which was beneath him passed on. And a certain man 10
saw and informed Joab and said, "Look, I saw Absalom dangling from
the terebinth." And Joab said to the man informing him, "And look, you 11
saw, and why did you not strike him to the ground there, and I would
have had to give you ten pieces of silver and a belt?" And the man said 12
to Joab, "Even were I to heft in my palms a thousand pieces of silver, I
would not reach out my hand against the king's son, for within our
hearing the king charged you and Abishai and Ittai, saying, 'Watch for

---

after Absalom has Amnon killed), so Absalom's losing his mule from under
him is an image of his losing his royal seat. Having climbed from exile and
rejection to the throne, he now dangles helplessly between sky and earth. The
mule's "passing on" (ʿavar), as Polzin notes, picks up the key verb ("cross over")
that has characterized David's flight from the royal city. Fokkelman brilliantly
shows that there is also a whole series of contrastive parallels between Absalom's fate and that of his counselor Ahitophel: "The counsellor rides calmly on
his ass to his home while the prince is abandoned by his mule, a fatal loss. He
is thrown into an unknown, nameless and ignominious grave while Ahitophel
is 'buried in his father's grave'. . . . With all these contrasts, they have one
detail in common: both finally hang."

he dangled. The Masoretic Text has "he was given," but ancient translations
into Aramaic, Syriac, Greek, and Latin, now confirmed by the Qumran Samuel
scroll, read "dangled," a difference of a single consonant in the Hebrew.

11. And look, you saw. The contemptuous Joab throws the soldier's own words
back into his face: if that's what you really saw, why didn't you have the brains
to finish him off on the spot and get the reward I would have given you? Joab,
in his unflinching resolution to kill Absalom in defiance of David's explicit
orders to the contrary, remains the consummately calculating political man—
something David once was but no longer is. When Joab thought it was politically prudent to reconcile David with Absalom, he took elaborate steps to
achieve that end. Now he realizes that an Absalom allowed to survive is likely
to be a source of future political dissension and that the only sure way to eliminate this threat is Absalom's death.

12. Were I to heft in my palms a thousand pieces of silver. The soldier responds to
Joab's contempt with righteous indignation, multiplying the hypothetical
reward a hundredfold and turning the general act of giving silver into a concrete
hefting of its weight in order to express how sacred he holds the king's injunction, which, we now see, has in fact been heard by "all the troops" (verse 5).

13 me over the lad Absalom.' Otherwise, I would have wrought falsely
with my own life, and nothing can be concealed from the king, while
14 you would have stood aloof." And Joab said, "Not so will I wait for you!"
And he took three sticks in his palm and he thrust them into Absalom's
15 heart, still alive in the heart of the terebinth. And ten lads, Joab's armor
bearers, pulled round and struck down Absalom and put him to death.
16 And Joab sounded the ram's horn, and the troops came back from pur-
17 suing Israel, for Joab held back the troops. And they took Absalom and
flung him into the big hollow in the forest, and they heaped up over it a
very big mound of stones. And all Israel had fled, each to his tent.

---

14. *he took three sticks in his palm.* Over against the soldier's palms hyperbolically hefting a thousand pieces of silver, Joab's palm grasps a blunt instrument
of violence. The Hebrew *shevatim* means "sticks," not "darts," as it is often
translated, and had they been darts, the blow would surely have been fatal.
On the contrary, it seems probable that Joab's intention is not to kill the
prince—after all, this military man is an experienced killer—but rather to
stun him and hurt him badly, and then to spread the responsibility for the
death by ordering the warriors to finish him off. Fokkelman proposes that the
three sticks jibe with the three divisions of the army, so that Joab performs a
deliberately symbolic act, "executing the rebellious prince on behalf of the
whole army."

   into Absalom's heart, still alive in the heart of the terebinth. The two hearts,
one a vulnerable human organ, the other the dense center of the tangle of
branches, produce an unsettling effect.

15. *lads.* The Hebrew *neʿarim,* "lads," in its sense of elite fighting men, rings
dissonantly against David's repeated paternal designation of Absalom as *naʿar,*
"lad."

16. *sounded.* The Hebrew reflects an untranslatable pun because the verb
taqʿa, "to make a piercing sound with a horn," also means to thrust or stab, and
is the word just used to report Joab's blow to the heart.

17. *the big hollow.* An alternative rendering is "pit," but "hollow" is used here to
preserve the verbal identity in the Hebrew between this moment and Hushai's
imaginary description in Chapter 17 of David's hiding in "one of the hollows."
To be flung into a hole in the field and covered with a heap of stones is a
shameful burial.

And Absalom had taken and heaped up a cairn for himself in his life- 18
time, which is in the Valley of the King, for he said, "I have no son to
make my name remembered." And he called the cairn after his name,
and it is called Absalom's Monument to this day.

And Ahimaaz son of Zadok had said, "Let me run, pray, and bear tid- 19
ings to the king that the LORD has done him justice against his
enemies." And Joab said to him, "You are no man of tidings this 20
day. You may bear tidings on another day, but this day you shall
bear no tidings, for the king's son is dead." And Joab said to the 21
Cushite, "Go, inform the king of what you have seen," and the
Cushite bowed down before Joab and ran off. And Ahimaaz son of 22
Zadok once again said to Joab, "Whatever may be, let me, too, pray,
run after the Cushite." And Joab said, "Why should you run, my son,

---

18. *Absalom had . . . heaped up a cairn.* This brief notice, in the pluperfect
tense, draws a pointed contrast with Absalom's ignominious grave. The same
verb, "to heap up," is used for both, and the cairn, or commemorative pile of
stones (*not* a "pillar") is the grandiose image that is transformed into the pile
of stones over Absalom's body.

I have no son to make my name remembered. Faulkner's *Absalom, Absalom!*, with reference to both its David figure and its Absalom figure, beautifully catches the pathos of these words. Those who have sought to
harmonize this verse with 14:27, where Absalom is said to have fathered
three sons, propose that the sons died, their early death explaining why they
are left unnamed.

21. *The Cushite.* This Nubian or Ethiopian is the third foreign messenger
introduced into the story (the other two are the Egyptian slave who informs
David of the whereabouts of the Amalekite raiding party and the Amalekite
who reports Saul's death to David). Joab appears to exhibit a certain paternal
concern for Ahimaaz, a priest and a faithful agent of David's during the insurrection—in the next verse he addresses him as "my son." Joab is keenly aware
that David has in the past shown himself capable of killing the bearer of ill tidings in a fit of rage, and so the commander prefers to let a foreigner take the
risk.

23 when yours are not welcome tidings?" "Whatever may be, I will run!"
And he said to him, "Run." And Ahimaaz ran by the way of the Plain,
and he overtook the Cushite.

24 And David was sitting between the gates, and the lookout went up on
the roof of the gate on the wall, and he raised his eyes and saw and,
25 look, a man was running alone. And the lookout called and told the
king, and the king said, "If he's alone, there are tidings in his mouth."

---

22. *yours are not welcome tidings.* The Hebrew—literally, "finding tidings"—is
anomalous, and has inspired both emendation and excessively ingenious
interpretation. The immediate context suggests "welcome" as the most plausible meaning, and this could easily be an idiom for which there are no other
occurrences in the biblical corpus, which, after all, provides only a small sam-
pling of ancient Hebrew usage. In fact, these two words, *besorah mots²eit,*
could well be an idiomatic ellipsis for *besorah mots²eit ḥen,* "tidings finding
favor (in his eyes)."

23. *by the way of the Plain.* The Plain in question is the Jordan Valley on the
east side of the river. Some have suggested that Ahimaaz overtakes the
Cushite not by speed but by running along a flatter, if less direct, route in the
Jordan Valley riverbed, but verses 25–27 indicate that Ahimaaz outruns the
Cushite.

24. *David was sitting between the gates.* Walled cities in ancient Israel and
environs often had double walls, with an inner and outer gate and a small
plaza between them. Moshe Garsiel neatly observes that David's ambivalence
about the armed struggle is spatially figured by his physical location: he
wanted to sally forth with the army; the troops wanted him within the city; he
stations himself in between. Before the battle he stood by the gate; now he is
seated by the gate, awaiting the news from the front—as Polzin notes, exactly
like Eli, who is told of the death of his two sons.
   the lookout went up on the roof of the gate . . . and he raised his eyes and saw.
This moment is quite exceptional, and striking, in representing the arrival of
the two messengers visually, from the perspective of the lookout on the wall
reporting to David down below in the gate plaza. David's troubles with all his
sons, it should be remembered, began when he himself looked down from a
roof and saw a woman bathing.

25. *If he's alone, there are tidings in his mouth.* A solitary runner is likely to be a
courier. Soldiers, whether in retreat or maneuvering, would travel in groups.

And he came on, drawing nearer. And the lookout saw another man 26
running, and the lookout called to the gatekeeper and said, "Look, a -
man is running alone." And the king said, "This one, too, bears tidings."
And the lookout said, "I see the running of the first one as the running 27
of Ahimaaz son of Zadok," and the king said, "He is a good man and
with good tidings he must come." And Ahimaaz called out and said to 28
the king, "All is well." And he bowed down to the king, his face to the
ground, and he said, "Blessed is the LORD your God Who has delivered
over the men who raised their hand against my lord the king." And the 29
king said, "Is it well with the lad Absalom?" And Ahimaaz said, "I saw a
great crowd to send the king's servant Joab, and your servant, and I
know not what . . ." And the king said, "Turn aside, stand by!" And he 30

---

27. *He is a good man, and with good tidings he must come.* This obvious non
sequitur suggests that the desperately anxious David is grasping at straws. In
fact, as revelatory dialogue, it shows us just how desperate he feels.

28. *All is well.* This is one word in the Hebrew, *shalom.* That word is the last
two syllables of Absalom's name in Hebrew, *'Avshalom,* a link David will reinforce when he nervously asks, "Is it well [*shalom*] with the lad Absalom
[*'Avshalom*]?"
    *Who has delivered over the men who raised their hands against my lord the
king.* Ahimaaz hastens to report, in terms that express both his Israelite piety
and his loyalty to the king, the general defeat of the usurper's army. He of
course says nothing of Absalom's fate.

29. *Is it well with the lad Absalom?* This seems to be David's overriding concern, not the military victory. Again and again, he insists on the term of affection, "lad," for the rebel son who would have killed him. The tension between
his political role, which, as Joab understood, requires Absalom's destruction,
and his paternal role, is painfully palpable. In this connection, it is noteworthy
that David, so much the emotionally vulnerable father here, is consistently
referred to as "the king," not as "David."
    I saw a great crowd to send the king's servant. This is nearly gibberish but not
because of any corruption of the text. Ahimaaz has been posed a question he
does not dare answer, and so he begins to talk nervously and incoherently
("and I know not what . . .").

30. *Turn aside, stand by!* David, realizing he is unlikely to extract anything from
the babbling Ahimaaz, decides to wait and interrogate the second messenger,
whose arrival is imminent.

31 turned aside and took his place. And, look, the Cushite had come and
the Cushite said, "Let my lord the king receive the tidings that the LORD
32 has done you justice against all who rose against you." And the king said
to the Cushite, "Is it well with the lad Absalom?" And the Cushite said,
"May the enemies of my lord the king be like the lad, and all who have
risen against you for evil!"

---

31. *Let my lord the king receive the tidings . . .* The Cushite is considerably
more brusque than his predecessor. He does not begin with a reassuring "All
is well." There is no indication of his bowing down before the king. He proceeds quickly to the report of the victory, and though the language of that
report approximately parallels Ahimaaz's language, it is briefer, and ends with
"against you" instead of the more deferential "against my lord the king."

32. *May the enemies of my lord the king be like the lad.* The Cushite promptly
and clearly responds by reporting Absalom's death, though even he has
enough sense to phrase it indirectly, neither mentioning Absalom by name nor
using the word "died." In referring to the usurper as "the lad," he is quoting
David, but without having picked up the crucial cue of David's paternal feelings reflected in the word. He blithely assumes that because Absalom was at
the head of "all who have risen against" the king, the news of his death will be
welcome. It strikes exactly the right note that the Cushite's very last word is
"evil" (or, "harm").

CHAPTER 19

And the king was shaken. And he went up to the upper room over ¹
the gate and he wept, and thus he said as he went, "My son,
Absalom! My son, my son, Absalom! Would that I had died in
your stead! Absalom, my son, my son!" And it was told to Joab, "Look, ²
the king is weeping and he is grieving over Absalom." And the victory ³
on that day turned into mourning for all the troops, for the troops
had heard on that day, saying, "The king is pained over his son."

---

1. *My son, my son, Absalom!* Much of the way experience transforms David
in the course of his story can be seen through his changing responses to the
deaths of those close to him. When Jonathan and Saul died, he intoned an
eloquent elegy. When Abner was murdered, he declaimed a much briefer
elegy, coupled with a speech dissociating himself from the killing. When
his infant son by Bathsheba died, he spoke somber words about his own
mortality and the irreversibility of death. Now, the eloquent David is
reduced to a sheer stammer of grief, repeating over and over the two
Hebrew words, *beni ʾAvshalom,* "my son, Absalom." Although the narrator
continues to refer to David only as "the king," in the shifting conflict
between his public and private roles the latter here takes over entirely:
Absalom is not the usurper who drove him from the throne but only "my
son," and David is the anguished father who would rather have died, that
his son might have lived.

3. *for the troops had heard on that day.* Before the battle they had all heard
David's admonition to his commanders to do no harm to Absalom. Now they
hear of his grief and are smitten with shame and apprehension—whether out
of empathy for their beloved leader, or guilt over the complicity some of their
number share in Absalom's death, or fear of potential violence between David
and Joab.

4 And the troops stole away on that day to come to the city as troops dis-
5 graced in their flight from the battle would steal away. And the king
covered his face, and the king cried out with a loud voice, "My son,
6 Absalom! Absalom, my son, my son!" And Joab came to the king within
the house and said, "You have today shamed all your servants who have
saved your life today and the lives of your sons and daughters and the
7 lives of your wives and the lives of your concubines, to love those who
hate you and to hate those who love you. For you have said today that
you have no commanders or servants. For I know today that were Absa-

---

4. *the troops stole away . . . as troops disgraced in their flight from battle.* This
striking image of victory transformed into the bitterness of defeat picks up
verbal threads, as Moshe Garsiel has perceptively noted, from the beginning
of Absalom's insurrection (Chapter 15). There, the usurper stood at the gate,
as David is here made to go out and sit in the gate. Absalom was said to "steal
the heart" of the men of Israel as here the men steal away, and in order to
recover dominion David is enjoined to speak to their heart (verse 8). The dis-
heartened slipping away of the troops suggests that Joab is addressing an
imminent danger of the disintegration of the army.

5. *the king covered his face.* The gesture makes perfect psychological sense,
while the verb used, *laʾat*, is the same one David chose when he said "Deal
gently [*leʾat*] with the lad Absalom."

6. *within the house.* The implication is that Joab speaks with David in private.
The thematic opposition to this term is "in the gate," where Joab will send David.
   You have today shamed all your servants who have saved your life today. Again
and again here Joab insists on the word "today." It is this very moment, he suggests, this crucial turning point, that you must seize in order to reestablish
your reign. You cannot allow yourself to think of the past, of your history as
Absalom's father: as king, you must confront *today*, with its challenge and its
political responsibilities.

7. *to love those who hate you and to hate those who love you.* Joab uses rhetorical
exaggeration in order to elevate David's paternal attachment to Absalom into a
generalized, perverse political principle: if you show such extravagant fondness for the usurper who sought your life, then you are behaving as though all
your enemies were your friends and your friends your enemies.
   For you have said today that you have no commanders and servants. That is,
by exhibiting such love for your archenemy, you are showing flagrant disregard
for the loyal officers and followers to whose devotion you owe your life.

lom alive and all of us today dead, then would it have been right in your
eyes! And now, rise, go out, and speak to the heart of your servants. For   8
by the LORD I have sworn, if you go not out, that not a man shall spend
the night with you, and this will be a greater evil for you than any evil
that has befallen you from your youth until now." And the king arose   9
and sat in the gate, and to all the troops they told, saying, "Look, the
king is sitting in the gate." And all the troops came before the king,
while Israel had fled each man to his tent.

And all the people were deliberating throughout the tribes of Israel,   10
saying, "The king rescued us from the clutches of our enemies and he

---

8. *speak to the heart of your servants.* This personal act of rallying the men is
deemed urgently necessary by Joab because the army has already begun to
disperse ("steal away").

    if you go not out . . . not a man will spend the night with you. These words
are a naked threat: if David does not follow Joab's order, the commander will
encourage the army to abandon the king, and he will be alone, without power
or troops, engulfed in "a greater evil" than any that has befallen him in his long
and arduous career. In all this, Joab's verbal assault on David, however motivated by pressing considerations of practical politics, is also a defense of his
own flouting of David's injunction to protect Absalom. David at this point
knows only the bare fact of his son's death, not who was responsible for it.
This is something that he will inevitably soon learn, and that bitter knowledge
is surely registered in his decision to replace Joab with Amasa (verse 14).

9. *the king arose and sat in the gate.* Fokkelman brilliantly observes the dispar-
ity between Joab's exhortation and the report of David's action. Joab had said,
"go out, and speak to the heart of your servants." Instead of these active gestures, we see David passively sitting in the gate while the troops come to him,
and we are given no reported speech for him. In Fokkelman's reading, this gap
between command and act "call[s] up the image of a man beaten to a pulp,
who can barely stand, and does only the minimum requested or expected of
him."

10. *deliberating.* The verb *nadon* in this verse is conventionally related to the
noun *madon,* "quarrel" or "contention." But in fact what the people say is not
contentious, and it is preferable to derive the passive (perhaps implicitly
reflexive) verbal form here from *dun,* to judge, consider, or deliberate.

11 saved us from the clutches of the Philistines, but now he has fled
the land before Absalom, and Absalom, whom we anointed over us,
has died in battle. And now why do you not speak up to bring back
12 the king?" And King David had sent to Zadok and to Abiathar the
priests, saying, "Speak to the elders of Judah, saying, 'Why should
you be the last to bring back the king to his house when the word of
13 all Israel has come to the king regarding his house? You are my brothers. You are my bone and my flesh, and why should you be the last to
14 bring back the king?' And to Amasa you shall say, 'Are you not my
bone and my flesh? So may the LORD do to me, and even more, if you
will not be commander of the army before me for all time instead of
15 Joab.' " And he inclined the heart of all the men of Judah as a single

---

12. *Why should you be the last to bring back the king?* Throughout this episode,
there is a central focus on who will be first and who will be last to show support
for the Davidic restoration. The northern tribes, Israel, have already evinced
support (verse 10), and David is concerned to enlist the backing of his own
tribe, Judah, which had largely swung to Absalom during the insurrection.

regarding his house. Or simply, "to his house." Many textual critics regard
this phrase as a mistaken scribal duplication of the same phrase earlier in this
verse.

13. *You are my bone and my flesh.* That is, you are Judahites, just as I am, and so
there is actual kinship between us.

14. *to Amasa . . . 'Are you not my bone and my flesh?'* Now the phrase is no
longer hyperbolic, for Amasa is David's nephew. The extraordinary offer of the
post of commander of the army to Absalom's general in the rebellion reflects
David's knack for combining personal and political motives. It is a slap in the
face to Joab, the killer of David's son, against whom David evidently does not
dare to take any more direct steps of vengeance. At the same time, the hesitation of the Judahites in rallying behind the restored king suggests that an act
such as the appointment of Amasa as commander may be required to enlist
their support. Joab, not surprisingly, will not quietly acquiesce in his abrupt
dismissal from the office he has held since the beginning of David's career.

15. *he inclined the heart.* It is not clear whether the Hebrew, characteristically
overgenerous in its use of pronouns, intends the "he" to refer to David or to
Amasa. In either case, David's overture succeeds in bringing the tribe of
Judah into his camp.

man, and they sent to the king: "Come back, you and all your servants."

And the king turned back, and he came to the Jordan, and Judah had   16
come to Gilgal to go to meet the king to bring the king across the Jordan. And Shimei son of Gera the Benjaminite from Bahurim hastened   17
and went down with the men of Judah to meet King David. And a   18
thousand men were with him from Benjamin, and Ziba, the lad of the
house of Saul and his fifteen sons and his twenty slaves with him, and
they rushed down to the Jordan before the king. And as the crossing   19
over was going on, to bring across the king's household and to do what
was good in his eyes, Shimei son of Gera flung himself before the king
as he was crossing the Jordan, And he said to the king, "Let not my lord   20
reckon it a crime, and do not remember the perverse thing your servant
did on the day my lord the king went out from Jerusalem, that the king
should pay it mind. For your servant knows that it was I who offended,   21
and, look, I have come today first of all the house of Joseph to go down
to meet my lord the king." And Abishai son of Zeruiah spoke out and   22

---

16. *to bring the king across the Jordan.* The verb *ʿavar*, "cross over," and its
causative form, *haʿavir*, "to bring across," which thematically defined David's
exodus from Jerusalem in Chapter 15, dominates this episode, too, as the
crossing over in flight to the east is reversed by the crossing over westward
back to Jerusalem.

17. *Shimei son of Gera.* There is an approximate symmetry between David's
encounters in his exodus from Jerusalem and those that now occur in his return.
Then he met a hostile Shimei, now he meets a contrite Shimei. Then he met
Ziba, who denounced his master Mephibosheth; now he meets Mephibosheth
himself, who defends his own loyalty. Then he spoke with Ittai, the loyalist who
insisted on accompanying him; now he speaks with Barzillai, the proven loyalist
who refuses to accompany him back to the capital. The encounter with Hushai,
who becomes David's secret agent, has no counterpart here.

21. *first of all the house of Joseph to go down to meet my lord the king.* Shimei,
who has rushed down to the Jordan in order to demonstrate his newfound loyalty to David, uses "the house of Joseph" loosely to refer to the northern tribes.
He is, of course, actually from the tribe of Benjamin. He "goes down" because
his hometown of Bahurim is in the high country near Jerusalem.

said, "For this should not Shimei be put to death? For he cursed the
23   LORD's anointed." And David said, "What do I have to do with you,
sons of Zeruiah, that you should become my adversary today? Should
today a man of Israel be put to death? For I surely know that today I am
24   king over Israel." And the king said to Shimei, "You shall not die." And
the king swore to him.

25   And Mephibosheth son of Saul had come down to meet the king, and
he had not dressed his feet or trimmed his moustache, and his garments he had not laundered from the day the king had gone until the
26   day he came back safe and sound. And it happened when he came
from Jerusalem to meet the king, that the king said to him, "Why did

---

22. *For this should not Shimei be put to death?* Abishai remains true to character, for the third time prepared to kill someone on the impulse of the moment.

23. *What do I have to do with you, sons of Zeruiah . . .* These words by now are a
kind of refrain, as David seeks to dissociate himself from the murderous sons
of Zeruiah. It is noteworthy that though Abishai alone has just spoken, David,
mindful of the killing of Absalom, includes Joab as well in his protest by using
the plural "sons of Zeruiah."
     Should today a man of Israel be put to death? David's "today" is an implicit
rejoinder to Joab's "today" in the confrontation over his mourning Absalom.
This day of victorious return is a moment for national reconciliation and
hence for a general amnesty for the Saulides and the supporters of Absalom.
In the course of time, it will appear that David in effect restricts his pledge
not to harm Shimei to an extended "today."

25. *he had not dressed his feet or trimmed his moustache, and his garments he had
not laundered.* These acts of mourning, reported to us by the authoritative narrator, are an indication that in fact Mephibosheth remained loyal to David
throughout the insurrection, and that Ziba's denunciation was a self-
interested calumny. (Some interpret "dressing"—literally "doing"—the feet as
cutting the toenails, though the parallel usage often cited from Deuteronomy
has "toenails," not "feet," as the object of the verb "to do.")

26. *when he came from Jerusalem.* The Masoretic Text simply says "Jerusalem"
but this encounter presumably takes place down by the Jordan. One version
of the Septuagint removes the word from this verse and places it at the end of
verse 25.

you not go with me, Mephibosheth?" And he said, "My lord the king!   27
My servant deceived me. For your servant thought, 'I'll saddle me the
donkey and ride on it and go with the king,' for your servant is lame.
And he slandered your servant to my lord the king, and my lord the   28
king is like a messenger of God, and do what is good in your eyes. For   29
all my father's house are but men marked for death to my lord the king,
yet you set your servant among those who eat at your table. And what
right still do I have to cry out still in appeal to the king?" And the king   30
said to him, "Why should you still speak your words? I say—you and
Ziba shall divide the field. And Mephibosheth said to the king, "Let   31
him even take all, seeing that my lord the king has come safe and
sound to his house."

---

27. *I'll saddle me the donkey . . . for your servant is lame.* The evident implication is that it would have taken the crippled Mephibosheth some time to get
ready to go after the fleeing king. Meanwhile, his servant headed out before
him in order to denounce him, perhaps actually leaving his master awaiting
his help to saddle the donkey.

29. *For all my father's house are but men marked for death to my lord the king.*
Mephibosheth's choice of words—the literal phrasing of the Hebrew is "men
of death"—is an oblique, perhaps inadvertent, concession that he shares what
must have been the general suspicion among the Saulides that David was
responsible for the chain of violent deaths in the house of Saul.

30. *Why should you still speak your words?* David cuts off Mephibosheth impa-
tiently, picking up the "still" that the anxious supplicant has just twice used.
    you and Ziba shall divide the field. This "Solomonic" judgment may actually
be another sign that David has lost his ruler's grip. For if Ziba has told the
truth about his master, Mephibosheth as a traitor would deserve nothing,
except perhaps capital punishment. And if Ziba was lying, then the servant
would deserve nothing except a harsh legal penalty for defamation. Perhaps
Mephibosheth is paying a price for having betrayed that he thought David was
responsible for the Saulide deaths: in this reading, David knows Mephibosheth is telling the truth, but he punishes him for assuming David was
involved in the killings by decreeing Mephibosheth will lose half his property.

31. *Let him even take all.* By this verbal gesture, Mephibosheth shows himself
loyal to David to the end, regardless of personal benefit. These words could
well be an implicit judgment on the unwisdom of David's decree.

32 And Barzillai the Gileadite had come down from Rogelim, and he crossed over the Jordan with the king to send him off from the Jordan.
33 And Barzillai was very aged, eighty years old, and he had provided for the king during his stay in Mahanaim, for he was a very wealthy man.
34 And the king said to Barzillai, "You, cross over with me, and I shall pro-
35 vide for you by me in Jerusalem." And Barzillai said to the king, "How many are the days of the years of my life that I should go up with the
36 king to Jerusalem? Eighty years old I am today. Do I know between good and evil? Does your servant taste what I eat and what I drink? Do I still hear the voice of men and women singing? And why should your
37 servant still be a burden on my lord the king? Your servant can barely cross over the Jordan, and why should the king give me this recom-
38 pense? Let your servant, pray, turn back, that I may die in my town by the tomb of my father and my mother, and, look, let your servant Chimham cross over with my lord the king, and do for him what is
39 good in your eyes." And the king said, "With me shall Chimham cross over, and I will do for him what is good in your eyes, and whatever you
40 choose for me, I will do for you." And all the troops crossed over the Jordan, and the king crossed over, and the king kissed Barzillai and

---

32. *Barzillai the Gileadite.* David's three encounters at the ford of the Jordan form a progressive series on the scale of loyalty: first Shimei, who has heaped insults on him and now pleads for forgiveness; then Mephibosheth, whose loyalty, though probably genuine, has been called into question by Ziba; and then the unswervingly devoted old man, Barzillai.

35. *How many are the days of the years of my life* . . . Though this rhetorical question literally echoes the question that Pharaoh asks the aged Jacob, the meaning is the opposite—not 'How long have I lived?' but 'How long could I possibly have left to live?'

38. *Your servant Chimham.* This is presumably Barzillai's son.

40. *the king kissed Barzillai.* This entire catastrophic sequence in the David story began with David's cold kiss to the son from whom he had been estranged, followed by Absalom's calculated kiss for every man he enlisted to his cause at the gate of the city. Now the king bestows a kiss of true affection upon the loyal old man who provided for him and his troops in their moment of need.

blessed him, and he went back to his place. And the king crossed over 41
to Gilgal, and Chimham crossed over with him, and all the people of
Judah, they brought the king across, and half of the people of Israel as
well. And, look, all the men of Israel were coming toward the king, and 42
they said to the king, "Why have our brothers, the men of Judah, stolen
you away, bringing the king across the Jordan with his household, and
all David's men with him?" And all the men of Judah answered the men 43
of Israel, "For the king is kin to us. And why should you be incensed
over this thing? Have we eaten anything of the king's? Have we been
given any gift?" And the men of Israel answered the men of Judah and 44
they said, "We have ten parts in the king, even in David, more than

---

41. *the king crossed over . . . and Chimham crossed over with him, and . . . they
brought the king across.* The crossing over eastward of the banished king, which
never should have occurred, is now decisively reversed, as David and all his
people come across the Jordan and head for Jerusalem. But, as the immediately following dialogue intimates, David's political troubles are far from over.

to Gilgal. This is the gathering place where Saul was consecrated as king
and later severed by Samuel from his role as God's anointed.

half of the people of Israel as well. In all likelihood, "half" is used loosely to
indicate simply that some members of the northern tribes took part in bringing David to Gilgal.

42. *and they said to the king.* Although their complaint is addressed to the king,
he never answers them. Instead, as Fokkelman notes, the scene breaks down
into a squabble between Israelite and Judahite. Once again, David appears to
be losing his regal grip.

43. *the king is kin to us.* That is, David is actually a member of the tribe of
Judah.

44. *We have ten parts in the king, even in David, more than you.* Though ten to
one might merely be idiomatic for great preponderance, it seems likely that
they allude to the fact that they are ten tribes to Judah's one—if David is king
of the entire nation, this gives them ten times the claim to the king that Judah
has. The phrase "even in David" (or, "also in David") is a little odd, and the
Septuagint reads instead, "also I am firstborn more than you." It should be
noted that all the pronouns in this dialogue in the Hebrew are cast in the first
person singular, referring to a singular, collective "man of Israel" and "man of
Judah," but that usage doesn't quite work in English.

you, and why have you treated us with contempt? Was not our word
first to bring back the king?" And the word of the men of Judah was
harsher than the word of the men of Israel.

---

the word of the men of Judah was harsher than the word of the men of Israel.
The episode concludes in a clash of words, to be followed by a clash of
swords. The implication of the greater "harshness" (or, "hardness") of the
Judahite words is aptly caught by the medieval Hebrew commentator David
Kimchi: "Their word was harsher and stronger than the word of the men of
Israel, and the men of Judah spoke harshly to the men of Israel, with the king
saying nothing to them. Therefore the men of Israel were incensed and they
followed after [the rebel] Sheba son of Bichri."

CHAPTER 20

And there chanced to be there a worthless fellow named Sheba son of 1
Bichri, a Benjaminite. And he blew the ram's horn and said,

> "We have no share in David,
> no portion have we in Jesse's son—
> every man to his tent, O Israel!"

And all the men of Israel turned away from David to follow Sheba son 2
of Bichri, but the men of Judah clung to their king from the Jordan to
Jerusalem.

---

1. *there chanced to be there*. The narrative is a direct continuation of the end of
the previous chapter, and so "there" is the national assembly grounds at Gilgal
where the northern tribes, Israel, and the tribe of Judah have just quarreled.
The northerners, resentful of the harshness of the Judahites' words, in which
the members of David's own tribe claimed a special proprietary relationship
with the king, are ripe for the appeal of a demagogue such as Sheba, who is at
once identified as "a worthless fellow."

We have no share in David. This is a defiant reversal of the claim just made
by the Israelites that they had "ten parts" in the king. Later, in 1 Kings, when
the monarchy actually splits in two, the same rallying cry will be used by the
secessionists.

2. *the men of Judah clung to their king*. David is, of course, "their" king because
he is from the tribe of Judah. The reach of the tribe stretches west to east,
from the Jordan to Jerusalem, and also to the south of Jerusalem, while the
rebel forces are to the north.

3 And David came to his house in Jerusalem, and the king took his ten concubine women whom he had left to watch over the house, and he placed them in a house under watch, but he did not come to bed with them, and they were shut up till their dying day in living widowhood.

4 And the king said to Amasa, "Muster me the men of Judah, in three
5 days, and you take your stand here." And Amasa went to muster Judah,
6 and he missed the appointed time that was set for him. And David said to Abishai, "Now Sheba son of Bichri will do us more harm than Absalom. You, take your master's servants and pursue him, lest he find him

---

3. *David came to his house in Jerusalem, and . . . took his ten concubine women.* The concubines have become taboo to David because they cohabited with Absalom his son. But this whole sad notice suggests that David now cannot fully "come back to his house." The women he left, perhaps foolishly and surely futilely, "to watch over the house" are now sequestered "in a house under watch." There is a wry echo in all this of that early moment of David's investment of Jerusalem when he was confronted by another wife he had left behind who had slept with another man—Michal. She had no child "till her dying day"—an image of interrupted conjugality that is multiplied tenfold here with the concubines.

4. *the king said to Amasa.* Amasa, Absalom's commander in the rebellion, has been designated by David to replace Joab. At the margins of the narrative report lurks the question, Where is Joab? The answer forthcoming will be savage.
    take your stand. That is, report to me.

6. *Now Sheba son of Bichri will do us more harm than Absalom.* Although it is not clear why Amasa is late for his appointed meeting with David (perhaps his appearance at Gibeon in verse 8 suggests that he decided, out of military considerations, to pursue Sheba at once without reporting back to the king), David's unjustified panic is another indication that he has lost his political composure. By sending out Abishai, Joab's brother, to give chase after Sheba, he sets up the circumstances for Joab's murder of Amasa and his subsequent return to power.
    You, take your master's servants. The obtrusively imperative "you" is very brusque, at the same time expressing David's intention to designate Abishai, and not his brother, to command the pursuit.

fortified towns, and elude our gaze." And Joab's men sallied forth after   7
him, and the Cherethites and the Pelethites and all the warriors. And
they sallied forth from Jerusalem to pursue Sheba son of Bichri. They   8
were just by the great stone which is in Gibeon when Amasa came before
them, and Joab was girt in his battle garb, and he had on a belt for a sword
strapped to his waist in its sheath, and as he came forward, it fell out.

---

and elude our gaze. The two Hebrew words here, *wehitsil ʿeynenu,* are problematic. They might mean: "and save [himself] [from] our eyes (the bracketed
words would be implied via ellipsis by the Hebrew); or, if the verb here is
vocalized differently, the words might mean "and cast a shadow over our eyes."
Needless to say, many emendations have been proposed. In any case, the idea
strongly suggested by the context is that Sheba would place himself beyond
the reach of pursuit by withdrawing into fortified towns. In the event, he is
trapped inside just such a town.

7. *Joab's men sallied forth.* J. P. Fokkelman must be credited with seeing what
an extraordinary designation this is. David has dismissed Joab. The elite warriors are in any case *David's* men (note how David has just referred to them in
addressing Abishai as "your master's servants"). The fact that they are here
called "Joab's men" suggests where the real power is, and where Joab's brother
Abishai assumes it must be. The clear implication is that the supposedly dismissed Joab is actually leading his men in the pursuit.

8. *They were just by the great stone which is in Gibeon.* Gibeon, it should be
recalled, is the very place where the civil war between the house of Saul
(Israel) and the house of David (Judah) began. That first battle (2 Samuel 2)
began with a choreographed duel between twelve champions from each side,
each warrior clasping the head of his adversary and stabbing him in the side.
Joab's posture in the killing of Amasa strikingly recalls those lethal gestures.
    *he had on a belt for a sword strapped to his waist, and as he came forward it fell
out.* The sword—often, as here, a weapon closer to a long dagger—was customarily strapped against the left thigh, for easy unsheathing across the lower belly
by a right-handed fighter. Joab may have deliberately fastened the sword to his
waist so that it would slip out of the scabbard as he leaned forward to embrace
Amasa. The last two verbs here are rather cryptic in the Hebrew: literally "he/it
went out and she/it fell." Since "sword" is feminine in Hebrew, that is the only
likely subject for "fell," and "he" (Joab) is the plausible masculine subject for
"went out" (or, "came forward"), though it could also be the scabbard. Josephus's
reading of this verse remains the most persuasive one: the wily Joab, deliberately allowing his dagger to slip to the ground as he bends forward, then
snatches it up with his left hand while his right hand grasps Amasa's beard.

9 And Joab said to Amasa, "Is it well with you, my brother?" And Joab's
10 right hand grasped Amasa's beard so as to kiss him. And Amasa did not
watch out for the sword which was in Joab's hand, and he struck him
with it in the belly and spilled his innards to the ground—no second
blow did he need—and he died. And Joab with Abishai his brother pur-
11 sued Sheba son of Bichri. And a man stood over him, one of Joab's lads,
and said, "Whoever favors Joab and whoever is for David—after Joab!"
12 And Amasa was wallowing in blood in the midst of the road, and the
man saw that all the troops had come to a halt, and he moved Amasa
aside from the road to the field and flung a cloak over him when he saw

---

9. *so as to kiss him.* We remember David's cool kiss to Absalom, then Absalom's
demagogic kiss, as we witness this kiss, which is a prelude to murder.

10. *Amasa did not watch out for the sword which was in Joab's hand.* His attention caught by Joab's gesture of affection, Amasa does not think to look at
Joab's left hand, which one would not normally expect to hold a weapon. (Has
Joab learned the lesson of Ehud, Judges 3, who takes the Moabite king Eglon
by surprise with a dagger thrust to the belly delivered by the left hand?) Joab's
manual proficiency as a killer reinforces the perception that he struck at Absalom in the heart with sticks, not "darts," in order to hurt him badly but deliberately not to finish him off. The phrase "did not watch out" rhymes ironically
with the plight of the ten concubines left to watch over the house and condemned to a house under watch.

he struck him with it in the belly and spilled his innards to the ground. It is by
a blow to the belly (*homesh*) that Abner's brother Asahel died at this same
place, Gibeon, and by a thrust to the belly that Joab killed Abner in revenge.
The spilling of the innards implies a horrendous welter of blood, and that
gruesome image of violent death will then pursue Joab through the story to his
own bloody end.

11. *Whoever favors Joab, and whoever is for David.* In dismissing Joab, David
had severed himself from his long-time commander. This henchman of Joab's
smoothly sutures the rift by bracketing Joab and David in these parallel
clauses, publicly assuming that Joab is once more David's commander.

12. *Amasa was wallowing in blood . . . and . . . all the troops came to a halt.* The
soldiers come to a halt because they are confounded by seeing their commander reduced to a bloody corpse, and they also recoil from the idea of treading
on the blood of the murdered man, who lies in the midst of the roadway.

that all who came upon him had come to a halt. When he had been 13
removed from the road, every man passed on after Joab to pursue
Sheba son of Bichri. And he passed through all the tribes of Israel to 14
Abel of Beth-maacah, and all the Bichrites assembled and they, too,
came in after him. And all the troops who were with Joab came and 15
beseiged him in Abel of Beth-maacah, and they heaped up a siege
mound against the town and it stood up against the rampart, and they
were savaging the wall to bring it down. And a wise woman called out 16
from the town,

"Listen, listen—speak, pray, to Joab,
Approach here, that I may speak to you."

---

14. *And he passed through.* The switch in scene is effected, in accordance with
an established technique of biblical narrative, by a repetition of the verb in a
slightly different meaning: the Judahite soldiers "pass on" beyond the corpse
at Gibeon; the object of their pursuit "passes through" the territories of the
northern tribes.

Abel of Beth-maacah. "Abel" means "brook." Thus "Beth-maacah" is
required in order to distinguish it from other place-names that have a brook
component. This fortified town is located near the northern border of ancient
Israel.

they, too, came in after him. That is, they withdraw with him into the shelter
of the fortified town.

15. *savaging the wall.* This is the first of several verbal clues intended to establish
a link between this episode involving a "wise woman" and the episode of the
wise woman of Tekoa that prepared the way for Absalom's return to Jerusalem,
which then eventuated in the rebellion. Both women seek to deflect an impulse
of vengeful violence. The Tekoite implores the king to take steps "that the blood
avenger not savage this much" (2 Samuel 14:11). She fears those bent on
"destroying me and my son together from God's heritage" (14:16), just as the
wise woman of Abel Beth-maacah asks Joab, "why should you engulf the LORD's
heritage?" He responds by saying "Far be it from me . . . that I should engulf and
that I should destroy [the same root as the verb rendered as "savage"].

16. *Listen, listen—speak, pray, to Joab.* As befits a professional wise woman in a
place evidently famous for its oracle (see verse 18), she speaks in poetry, in a
style that is elevated, ceremonially repetitive, hieratic, and at least a little
obscure.

17 And he approached her, and the woman said, "Are you Joab?" And he
said, "I am." And she said to him, "Listen to the words of your servant."
18 And he said, "I am listening," And she said, saying,

"Surely would they speak in days of old, saying:
'Surely will they ask counsel of Abel, and thus conclude.'
19 I am of the peaceable steadfast of Israel.
You seek to put to death a mother city in Israel.
Why should you engulf the LORD's heritage?"

---

18. *surely would they speak . . . surely will they ask counsel.* The Hebrew
expresses this emphasis by repeating the verbal root, first as infinitive, then in
conjugated form: *daber yedaberu, sha'ol yesha'alu.* Since the woman extravagantly uses this sort of initial reiteration three times in four clauses, the effect
is incantatory. The burden of what she says here is that Abel has long been a
revered city, so why would Joab think of destroying it?

and thus conclude. This might mean, come to a conclusion regarding the
question posed to the oracle at Abel, but the Hebrew is rather enigmatic, perhaps because the wise woman herself is quoting an ancient proverb, in
archaic language, about the city.

19. *I am of the peaceable steadfast of Israel.* She at once affirms her loyalty to the
national cause ("I am no rebel," she implies) and her commitment to peace
rather than violence. Some interpreters understand the first term of this con-
struct chain, *shelumey 'emuney yisra'el,* as "whole" (from *shalem*), but the context argues for a reference to peace.

to put to death a mother city in Israel. The literal Hebrew is "town and
mother," a hendyadis that clearly means something like "principal town." (The
phrase would remain idiomatic in later Hebrew.) Since in biblical Hebrew the
suburbs or outlying villages around a town are called "daughters," the logic of
the idiom is evident. It is, however, an idiom that appears only here in the
entire biblical corpus, and there is thematic point in its use. In this narrative
reflecting a male warrior culture and acts of terrible violence, from decapitation to evisceration, a series of female figures—Abigail, the Tekoite, the wise
woman of Abel—intervene to avert violence. The city itself is figured as a
mother; its destruction would be a kind of matricide, and the wise woman
speaks on behalf of the childbearers and nurturers of life in Israelite society to
turn aside Joab's terrible swift sword.

And Joab answered and said, "Far be it from me, far be it, that I should 20
engulf and that I should destroy. It isn't so. But a man from the high 21
country of Ephraim named Sheba son of Bichri has raised his hand
against the king, against David. Give over him alone, that I may turn
away from the town." And the woman said to Joab, "Look, his head is
about to be flung to you from the wall." And the woman came in her 22
wisdom to all the people, and they cut off the head of Sheba son of
Bichri and flung it to Joab. And he blew the ram's horn and they dispersed from the town, every man to his tent, but Joab came back to
Jerusalem.

---

20. *But a man from the high country of Ephraim.* This region is part of the territory of Benjamin, Saul's tribe. By providing this identification, Joab distinguishes the rebel who is the object of his pursuit from the non-Benjaminite
inhabitants of Abel Beth-maacah.

against the king, against David. By using this apposition (instead of the
usual "King David") Joab implicitly responds to some doubt as to whether in
fact it is David who is the king. Recent political events might well have trig-
gered general questioning about David's grip on the monarchy.

21. *Look, his head is about to be flung to you.* This decisive woman, instead of
using a simple future form, employs a participial form introduced by the presentative *hineh*, as if to say: it's already on the way to being done.

22. *in her wisdom.* The wisdom is her shrewdness in finding a way to avert a
general massacre (as the wise Abigail had done in mollifying David, bent on
vengeance) and perhaps also the aptness of rhetoric she no doubt employs to
persuade the people.

he blew the ram's horn, and they dispersed . . . every man to his tent. These
phrases echo the ones used in verse 1 to report the beginning of Sheba's
rebellion, and thus conclude the episode in a symmetric envelope structure.

but Joab came back to Jerusalem. He comes back to Jerusalem, not to his
house ("tent") in nearby Bethlehem. The implication, as Bar-Efrat notes, is
that he now resumes his post as David's commander. David evidently has little
say in the matter, being confronted with a *fait accompli* of military power. This
clause then provides a motivation for the introduction of the notice of David's
governing council in the next three verses.

23 And Joab was over all the army of Israel and Benaiah son of Johoiada
24 was over the Cherethites and the Pelethites. And Adoram was over the
25 corvée, and Jehoshaphat son of Ahilud was recorder. And Sheva was
26 scribe, and Zadok and Abiathar, priests. And Ira the Jairite was also a
priest to David.

---

23. *Joab was over all the army of Israel.* This list of David's royal bureaucracy
parallels the one in 8:16–18, with a couple of instructive differences. The two
serve as bookends to David's reign in Jerusalem. The first is introduced after
he has consolidated his miniempire, and this one after the suppression of two
successive rebellions and just before the account of David's last days in 1
Kings 1–2. (As we shall see, the remaining four chapters of 2 Samuel are actually a series of appendices to the story proper and not a direct continuation of
it.) In Chapter 8, Joab was simply "over the army." Here, after the defeat of the
secessionist northern tribes, he is said to be "over all the army of Israel." Adoram as supervisor of the corvée does not appear in the earlier list but is
inserted here to anticipate the role he will play in Solomon's grand building
projects, and he may in fact have been a much later appointment by David.
The name of the royal scribe, Sheva, is anomalous in the Hebrew, and may be
the same person identified in Chapter 8 as Seraiah.

25. *And Ira the Jairite was also a priest to David.* In addition to the hereditary
priests of the public cult just mentioned, David has a kind of special royal
chaplain. In Chapter 8, it is David's sons who are said to perform this service.
Either later editors were uneasy with this intimation of priestly dynasty in the
royal family, or David, after all the tribulations he has suffered because of two
of his sons, decided to designate someone else as his chaplain.

CHAPTER 21

nd there was a famine in the days of David three years, year after year. 1
And David sought out the presence of the LORD. And the LORD said,
"On account of Saul and on account of the house of blood guilt,

---

Chapters 21–24. These chapters appear to be a series of appendices to the David
story proper, manifestly written by different writers in styles that exhibit notable
differences from that of the main narrative, and also certain differences in ideological assumptions and even in what are presumed to be the narrative data of
David's history. It should, however, be kept in mind that creating a collage of disparate sources was an established literary technique used by the ancient
Hebrew editors and sometimes by the original writers themselves. Recent critics
have abundantly demonstrated the compositional coherence of Chapters 21–24
and have argued for some significant links with the preceding narrative. For that
reason, it may be preferable to think of this whole unit as a coda to the story
rather than as a series of appendices. The structure of the chapters is neatly chi-
astic, as follows: a story of a national calamity in which David intercedes; a list
(Chapter 21); a poem (Chapter 22); a poem; a list (Chapter 23), a story of a
national calamity in which David intercedes (Chapter 24). The temporal setting
of these materials is unclear but they seem to belong somewhere in the middle
of David's career, and do not follow from the late point in his reign reported in
the immediately preceding account of the rebellion of Sheba son of Bichri. The
editors placed these chapters here, rather than after David's death, and then set
the account of his last days which they interrupt at the beginning of 1 Kings in
order to underline the dynastic continuity between David's story and Solomon's,
which then immediately follows as the first large unit of the Book of Kings.

1. *David sought out the presence of the LORD.* The idiom means to seek an audience (with a ruler), though what is referred to in practical terms is inquiry of
an oracle. The rest of the verse gives God's response to the question put to the
oracle. At the very outset, a difference in idiom from the main narrative,
where people consistently "inquire of the LORD," is detectable. The idiom preferred by this new author emphasizes hierarchical relationship rather than the
practical business of putting a question to the oracle.

2 9

2 because he put the Gibeonites to death." And the king called to the
   Gibeonites and said to them—and the Gibeonites were not of Israelite
   stock but from the remnant of the Emorites, and the Israelites had
   vowed to them, but Saul sought to strike them down in his zeal for the
3 Israelites and for Judah. And David said to the Gibeonites, "What shall
   I do for you and how shall I atone, that you may bless the LORD's
4 heritage?" And the Gibeonites said to him, "We have no claim of silver
   and gold against Saul and his house, and we have no man in Israel
   to put to death." And he said, "Whatever you say, I shall do for you."

---

2. *and the Gibeonites were not of Israelite stock* . . . The syntactic looseness of
this long parenthetical sentence (compare the similar syntax in verse 5) is
uncharacteristic of the David story proper.

the Israelites had vowed to them. The story of the vow to do no harm to this
group of resident aliens is reported in Joshua 9:15.

but Saul sought to strike them down. There is no way of knowing whether this
massacre of Gibeonites by Saul reflects historical fact, but there is not the
slightest hint of it in the story of Saul recounted in 1 Samuel. As with the differences of style, one sees here the presence of a distinctly different literary source.

3. *What shall I do for you, and how shall I atone* . . . ? The speech and acts of
David in this story show nothing of the psychological complexity of the
experience-torn David whose story we have been following. He speaks in flat
terms, almost ritualistically, fulfilling his public and cultic functions as king.
And after this brief initial exchange with the Gibeonites, the writer entirely
abandons dialogue, which had been the chief instrument for expressing emotional nuance and complication of motive and theme in the David story.

4. *We have no claim of silver and gold* . . . *we have no man in Israel to put to
death.* The second clause is really an opening ploy in negotiation: they say they
have no claim to execute any Israelite ("claim" in the first clause is merely
implied by ellipsis in the Hebrew), suggesting that they are waiting for David
to agree to hand Israelites over to them in expiation of Saul's crime.

whatever you say, I shall do for you. David's submissiveness to the
Gibeonites reflects a notion of causation and the role of human action
scarcely evident in the main narrative. A famine grips the land because its former ruler violated a national vow. Collective disaster can be averted only by
the expiatory—indeed, sacrificial—offering of human lives. This archaic
world of divine retribution and ritual response is very far from the historical
realm of *Realpolitik* in which the story of David has been played out.

And they said to the king, "The man who massacred us and who   5
devastated us—we were destroyed from having a stand in all the
territory of Israel—let seven men of his sons be given to us, that we   6
may impale them before the LORD at Gibeah of Saul, the LORD's
chosen." And the king said, "I will give them." And the king spared   7
Mephibosheth son of Jonathan son of Saul because of the LORD's
vow that was between them, between David and Jonathan son of
Saul. And the king took the two sons of Rizpah daughter of Aiah,   8
whom she had born to Saul, Armoni and Mephibosheth, and the
five sons of Merab daughter of Saul, whom she had born to Adriel
son of Barzillai the Meholathite. And he gave them into the hands of   9
the Gibeonites, and they impaled them on the hill before the LORD,
and the seven of them fell together. And they were put to death in
the first days of the harvest, the beginning of the barley harvest.

---

6. *impale.* There is no scholarly consensus on the exact form of execution,
except that it obviously involves exhibiting the corpses. Some understand it as
a kind of crucifixion.

before the LORD *at Gibeah of Saul, the* LORD's *chosen.* "Before the LORD" is
an explicit indication of the sacrificial nature of the killings. Many scholars
have doubted that the Saulides would be executed in Saul's own town and
emend this to read "at Gibeon, on the mount of the LORD." If the phrase "the
LORD's chosen" is authentic, it would be spoken sarcastically by the
Gibeonites.

8. *Merab.* This is the reading of one version of the Septuagint and of many
Hebrew manuscripts. The Masoretic Text has "Michal," who had no chil-
dren and who, unlike her sister Merab, was not married to Adriel son of
Barzillai.

9. *the seven of them fell together.* Polzin neatly observes that this phrase precisely echoes "they fell together" of 2:16—the account of the beginning of the
civil war at this very same place, Gibeon. He also notes how this whole
episode is organized around recurring units of three and seven, the latter
number *shivʿah* punning on the reiterated *shevuʿah*, vow.

the beginning of the barley harvest. This would be in April. The bereaved
Rizpah then watches over the corpses throughout the hot months of the
summer, until the rains return—heralding the end of the long famine—in
the fall.

10　And Rizpah daughter of Aiah took sackcloth and stretched it out over herself on the rock from the beginning of the harvest till the waters poured down on them from the heavens, and she did not allow the birds of the heavens to settle on them by day nor the beasts of the field

11　by night. And David was told what Rizpah daughter of Aiah, Saul's con-

12　cubine, had done. And David went and took the bones of Saul and the bones of Jonathan his son from the notables of Jabesh-gilead who had stolen them from the square of Beth-shan, where the Philistines had

13　hung them on the day the Philistines struck down Saul at Gilboa. And he brought up from there the bones of Saul and the bones of Jonathan

14　his son, and they collected the bones of the impaled men. And they buried the bones of Saul and of Jonathan his son in the territory of

---

10. *Rizpah . . . took sackcloth and stretched it out over her.* The verb here is the one generally used for pitching tents, so the translations that have Rizpah spreading the cloth over the rock are misleading. What she does is to make a little lean-to with the sackcloth to shield herself from the summer sun.

　she did not allow the birds of the heaven to settle on them. The antecedent of "them" is of course the corpses. As in the ancient Greek world, leaving a corpse unburied is a primal sacrilege, a final desecration of the sacredness of the human person. Rizpah, watching over the unburied corpses, is a kind of Hebrew Antigone. David had delivered the seven descendants of Saul to the Gibeonites with the single-minded intention of expiating the crime that had caused the famine. Evidently, he gave no thought to the possibility that the Gibeonites would desecrate the bodies of the Saulides after killing them by denying them burial.

11. *And David was told what Rizpah . . . had done.* Rizpah's sustained act of maternal heroism finally achieves its end: the king is shaken out of his acquiescence in the Gibeonite inhumanity.

12. *David went and took the bones of Saul and the bones of Jonathan.* According to the account in 1 Samuel 31, they were cremated. Either this report reflects a conflicting tradition or "bones" here has to be understood as "ashes."

14. *he buried the bones of Saul and of Jonathan his son. . . . And God then granted the plea for the land.* It should be noted that the end of the famine does not come with the sacrificial killing of the seven Saulides but only after all of them, together with Saul himself and Jonathan, are given fitting burial in their own place (a biblical desideratum). In this strange story, David is seen handing over the surviving offspring of Saul to be killed, but only for the urgent good of the nation, after which he pays posthumous respect to the line

Benjamin in Zela, in the tomb of Kish his father, and they did all that
the king had charged. And God then granted the plea for the land.

And once again there was fighting between the Philistines and Israel,   15
and David went down, and his servants with him, and they did battle
with the Philistines, and David grew weary. And Ishbi-benob, who was   16
of the offspring of the titan, the weight of his weapon three hundred
weights of bronze, and he was girded with new gear—he meant to
strike down David. And Abishai son of Zeruiah came to his aid and   17
struck down the Philistine and put him to death. Then David's men

---

of Saul. It is conceivable that this story reflects an alternative narrative tradition to the more politically complex one of the David story proper through
which David is exonerated from what may well have been a widespread accusation that he deliberately liquidated all of Saul's heirs, with the exception of
Mephibosheth.

15. *David grew weary.* This phrase probably indicates an aging David, though
not yet the vulnerable sedentary monarch of the conflict with Absalom.

16. *Ishbi-benob.* This name looks as bizarre in the Hebrew as in transliteration
and probably betrays a corrupt text. (The textual obscurities that abound in
this section in all likelihood reflect the fact that this is an old literary document imperfectly transmitted.) There have been attempts to revocalize the
name as a verb, but those in turn necessitate extensive tinkering with other
parts of the verse.
   of the offspring of the titan. The Hebrew *rafah* (with a definite article here)
elsewhere means "giant." The ending is feminine and it is not clear whether
the reference is to a progenitrix or a progenitor.
   the weight of his weapon. The Hebrew for "weapon," *qayin,* appears only
here, and so the translation is merely inference from context. It might be
related to a word that means "metalsmith." The invocation of the titanic
weight of the weapon (spear?) is of course reminiscent of the earlier description of Goliath.
   girded with new gear. The Hebrew says simply "girded with new [feminine
ending]." Some assume the reference is to sword, which is feminine in
Hebrew.

swore to him, saying, "You shall not sally forth with us again to battle, lest you snuff out the lamp of Israel."

18 And it happened thereafter that once again there was fighting with the Philistines, at Gob. Then did Sibbecai the Hushathite strike down
19 Saph, who was of the offspring of the titan. And once again there was fighting with the Philistines at Nob, and Elhanan son of Jair the Beth-lehemite struck down Goliath the Gittite, and the shaft of his spear was like a weaver's beam.

20 And once again there was fighting, at Gath. And there was a man of huge measure, who had six fingers on each hand and six toes on each
21 foot, twenty-four in all, and he, too, was sprung from the titan. And he

---

17. *You shall not sally forth with us again.* This fragmentary episode is obviously remembered because it marks a turning point in David's career. It is at least consonant with the image of David at Mahanaim asked by his men to stay behind as they go out to the battlefield.

19. *Elhanan son of Jair.* So he is identified in the parallel report in Chronicles. The Masoretic Text here reads "Elhanan son of Jaᶜarey ᵓOrgim," but the last word, ᵓorgim, means "weavers," and seems clearly a scribal duplication of ᵓorgim at the very end of the verse.
    Elhanan . . . struck down Goliath the Gittite. This is one of the most famous contradictions in the Book of Samuel. Various attempts, both ancient and modern, have been made to harmonize the contradiction—such as the contention that "Goliath" is not a name but a Philistine title—but none of these efforts is convincing. Of the two reports, this one may well be the more plausible. In the literary shaping of the story of David, a triumph originally attributed, perhaps with good reason, to Elhanan was transferred to David and grafted onto the folk-tale pattern of the killing of a giant or ogre by a resourceful young man. The writer used this material, as we have seen, to shape a vivid and arresting portrait of David's debut.

insulted Israel, and Jonathan son of Shimei, David's brother, struck him down. These four were sprung from the titan, and they fell at the hand of David and at the hand of his servants.   22

---

22. *These four were sprung from the titan, and they fell at the hand of David* . . . Stylistically, the entire unit from verse 15 to the end of the chapter has the feel of a deliberately formulaic epic catalogue (rather than an actual epic narrative, which the earlier Goliath story in 1 Samuel 17 more closely approximates). Formally, the predominant number three of the famine story is succeeded by four here—just as in biblical poetic parallelism three is conventionally followed by four (e.g., Amos 1:3, "For three crimes of Damascus,/and for four, I will not revoke it.").

CHAPTER 22

Ａnd David spoke to the LORD the words of this song on the day the LORD rescued him from the clutches of his enemies and from the clutches of Saul, and he said:

---

1. *And David spoke to the* LORD *the words of this song.* It was a common literary practice in ancient Israel to place a long poem or "song" (*shirah*) at or near the end of a narrative book—compare Jacob's Testament, Genesis 49, and the Song of Moses, Deuteronomy 32. In the case of the Book of Samuel, David's victory psalm and Hannah's psalm, respectively a song of the male warrior's triumph and a song contextualized as an expression of maternal triumph, enclose the large narrative like bookends, and there is even some interechoing of language between the two poems. These long concluding poems were presumably selected by the editor or composer of the book from a variety of texts available in the literary tradition and then ascribed to a principal character of the story. There is, of course, a persistent biblical notion of David the poet as well as of David the warrior-king, and the idea that he actually composed this poem, though unlikely, cannot be categorically dismissed. In any case, most scholars (Albright, Cross and Friedman, Robertson) detect relatively archaic language in the poem and date it to the tenth century, David's time. The archaic character of the language makes the meaning of many terms conjectural. Even in the ancient period, some of the older locutions may already have been obscure to the scribes, who seem to have scrambled many phrases in transmission; but in contrast to the confident practice of many biblical scholars, caution in presuming to reconstruct the "primitive" text is prudent. It should be noted that this same poem occurs in the Book of Psalms as Psalm 18, with a good many minor textual variants. In several instances, the reading in Psalm 18 seems preferable, but here, too, methodological caution is necessary: Psalm 18 appears to be a secondary version of the poem, and its editor at least in some cases may have clarified obscurities through revision.

"The LORD is my crag and my fortress   2
   and my own deliverer.
God, my rock where I shelter,   3
   my shield and the horn that has saved me,
My bulwark and refuge,
   My savior Who saves me from havoc.
Praised! did I call the LORD,   4
   and from my enemies I was saved.
For the breakers of death beset me,   5
   the underworld's torrents dismayed me.
The snares of Sheol coiled round me,   6
   the traps of death sprang against me.
In my strait I called to the LORD,   7
   to my God I called,
And from His palace He heard my voice,
   my cry in His ears.
The earth heaved and quaked,   8
   the heavens' foundations shuddered,
      they heaved, for He was incensed.

---

2. *my crag and my fortress*. Albright notes that many of the Northwest Semitic gods were deified mountains. Thus the imagery of the god as a lofty rock or crag abounds in the poetic tradition upon which the biblical poet drew. It also makes particular sense for a poem of military triumph, since a warrior battling in the mountainous terrain of the land of Israel would keenly appreciate the image of protection of a towering cliff or a fortress situated on a height.

3. *horn*. The idiom is drawn from the goring horn of a charging ram or bull. In keeping with the precedent of the King James Version it is worth preserving in English in order to suggest the concreteness and the archaic coloration of the poem.

5. *for the breakers of death beset me*. The condition of being mortally threatened is regularly figured in the poetry of Psalms as a descent, or virtual descent, into the terrifying shadows of the underworld.

8. *The earth heaved and quaked*. God's descent from His celestial palace to do battle on behalf of his faithful servant is imagined as a seismic upheaval of the whole earth.

9   Smoke went up from His nostrils,
      consuming fire from His mouth,
        coals before Him blazed.

10   He bent the heavens, came down,
      dense mist beneath His feet.

11   He mounted a cherub and flew,
      He soared on the wings of the wind.

12   He set darkness pavilions around Him,
      a massing of waters, the clouds of the skies.

13   From the radiance before Him,
      fiery coals blazed.

14   The LORD from the heavens thundered,
      the Most High sent forth His voice.

15   He let loose arrows and routed them,
      lightning, and struck them with panic.

16   The channels of the sea were exposed,
      the world's foundations laid bare,
    by the LORD's roaring,
      the blast of His nostrils' breath.

---

9. *Smoke went up from his nostrils.* The poetic representation of God, drawing on premonotheistic literary traditions such as the Ugaritic Baal epic, is unabashedly anthropomorphic. One must be cautious, however, in drawing theological inferences from this fact. Modes of literary expression exert a powerful momentum beyond their original cultural contexts, as Milton's embrace of the apparatus of pagan epic in *Paradise Lost* vividly demonstrates. The LORD figures as a fierce warrior, like Baal, because that works evocatively as poetry. This God of earthquakes and battles breathes fire: in an intensifying narrative progression from one verset to the next and then from line to line, smoke comes out of His nostrils, His mouth spews fire, in His awesome incandescence coals ignite before Him, and then He begins his actual descent from on high.

11. *He mounted a cherub and flew.* The cherub is a fierce winged beast, the traditional mount of the deity.
    He soared on the wings of the wind. The translation reads with Psalm 18 *wayedaʾ* instead of the weaker *wayeraʾ*, "He was seen" (the Hebrew graphemes for *d* and *r* being very close).

He reached from on high and He took me,   17
  He drew me out of vast waters,
Rescued me from enemies fierce,   18
  from my foes who had overwhelmed me.
They sprang against me on my most dire day,   19
  but the LORD was a stay then for me.
He led me out to an open place.   20
  He freed me for He took up my cause.
The LORD dealt with me by my merit,   21
  by the cleanness of my hands, requited me.
For I kept the ways of the LORD,   22
  I did no evil before my God.
For all His statutes are before me,   23
  from His laws I have not swerved.
I have been blameless before Him,   24
  I kept myself from sin.
The LORD requited me by my merit,   25
  by the cleanness of my hands before His eyes.

---

19. *They sprang against me.* The verb here—its basic meaning is to meet or greet, sometimes before the person is ready—repeats "the traps of death sprang against me" in verse 6: first that act of being taken by surprise occurs metaphorically, and now again in the literal experience of the speaker on the battlefield.

21. *The LORD dealt with me by my merit.* It is often claimed that verses 21–25 are a Deuteronomistic interpolation in the poem—that is, seventh century or later. The evidence is not entirely persuasive because the theological notion of God's rewarding the innocence of the individual by rescuing him from grave danger is by no means a Deuteronomistic innovation, and adherence to "statutes" and "laws" (verse 23), though encouraged in the Deuteronomistic literary environment, is neither its unprecedented invention nor its unique linguistic marker.

25. *by the cleanness of my hands.* The Masoretic Text has merely "by my cleanness" *(kevori)* but the parallel version in Psalm 18 shows *kevor yadai* "by the cleanness of my hands," as do the Septuagint and other ancient translations of this line. The concrete juxtaposition of idioms anchored in body parts— "cleanness of hands" for "innocence" and "before Your eyes" for "in Your sight"—is characteristic of biblical usage.

26   With the loyal You act in loyalty,
           with the blameless warrior You are without blame.

27   With the pure You show Your pureness,
           with the perverse You twist and turn.

28   A lowly people You save,
           You cast Your eyes down on the haughty.

29   For You are my lamp, O LORD!
           The LORD has lit up my darkness.

30   For through You I rush a barrier,
           through my God I vault a wall.

31   The God Whose way is blameless,
           the LORD's speech is without taint,
               a shield He is to those who shelter in him.

---

26. *with the blameless warrior You are without blame.* Many textual critics consider "warrior" to be an interpolation and either delete it or substitute for *gibor,* "warrior," *gever,* "man." The parallelism of these four versets, in each of which God, in a verb, answers in kind to the adjectivally defined human agent, is better preserved without "warrior." The profession of blamelessness scarcely accords with David's behavior in the body of the story.

27. *twist and turn.* This English phrase represents a single reflexive verb in the Hebrew. It is the sole instance in this series of four versets in which the verb describing God's action has a root different from the adjective characterizing the kind of person to whom God responds, though there is still a manifest *semantic* connection between the two terms here, and this works quite nicely as a small variation on the pattern to conclude the series.

28. *A lowly people You save, / You cast Your eyes down on the haughty.* The opposition between low and high is conventional in the poetry of Psalms—it also figures in Hannah's Song—but is nonetheless effective. The speaker's people is "lowly" in the sense that it is miserable, afflicted, endangered by superior forces. God on high looks down on the lofty who seem to have the upper hand and, as the triumphant images from verse 39 onward make clear, brings them low.

30. *I rush a barrier . . . vault a wall.* The speaker who has just been seen among "a lowly people" and then vouchsafed a beam from God's lantern as he gropes in the dark now suddenly takes the offensive, charging the enemies' ramparts.

For who is god but the LORD,   32
    who is a rock but our God?
The God, my mighty stronghold,   33
    He has freed my way to be blameless,
Made my legs like a gazelle's,   34
    and on the heights He has stood me.
Taught my hands combat,   35
    made my arms bend a bow of bronze.

---

33. *The God, my mighty stronghold.* Although this phrase, *ma'uzi hayil,* is intelligible as it stands, the variant in Psalm 18, supported by the Qumran Samuel
scroll, is more fluent and sustains a parallelism of verbs between the two
halves of the line. That reading is *hame'azreni hayil,* "Who girds me with
might."
    He has freed my way to be blameless. The verb here, *wayater,* is problematic.
The most obvious construction would be as a term that generally means "to
loosen," though the syntactic link with "blameless" (there is no explicit "to be"
in the Hebrew) is obscure. The version in Psalm 18 substitutes *wayiten,* "He
made" (or "set") but the use of that all-purpose verb may simply reflect the
scribe's bafflement with the original verb.

34. *Made my legs like a gazelle's, / and on the heights He has stood me.* The
swiftness of the gazelle accords nicely with the image in verse 30 of the warrior sprinting in assault against the ramparts of the foe. Standing secure on the
heights, then, would mark the successful conclusion of his trajectory of
attack: the victorious warrior now stands on the walls, or within the conquered bastion, of the enemy. The *ai* suffix of *bamotai,* "heights," normally a
sign of the first-person possessive, is an archaic, or poetic, plural ending. The
sense proposed by some scholars of "my back [or, thighs?]" is very strained,
and destroys the narrative momentum between versets that is a hallmark of
biblical poetry.

35. *made my arms bend a bow of bronze.* The verb *nihat* has not been satisfacto-
rily explained, nor is its syntactic role in the clause clear. This translation, like
everyone else's, is no more than a guess, based on the possibility that the verb
reflects a root meaning "to come down," and so perhaps refers to the bending
down of a bow.

36   You gave me Your shield that saved,
        Your battle cry made me many.

37   You lengthened my stride beneath me,
        and my ankles did not trip.

38   I pursued my foes and destroyed them,
        never turned back till I cut them down.

39   I cut them down, smashed them, they did not rise,
        they fell beneath my feet.

40   You girt me with might for combat,
        those against me You brought down beneath me,

41   You showed me my enemies' nape,
        my foes, and I blotted them out.

---

36. *Your battle cry.* This noun, ʿanotkha, is still another crux. The least far-fetched derivation is from the verbal stem ʿ-n-h, which means either "to answer," thus yielding a sense here of "answering power," or "to call out," "speak up." Given the sequence of concrete warfare images in these lines, from bronze bow to saving shield, this translation proposes, conjecturally, "battle cry," with the established verbal noun ʿanot, "noise" or "calling out" in mind. Compare Exodus 32:18: "The sound of crying out of warrior's-might" (*qol ʿanot gevurah*). The battle cry would use God's name (perhaps something like "sword of the LORD and of David") with the idea that it had a potency that would infuse the warrior with strength and resolution and strike fear in the enemy. Thus the battle cry makes the solitary fighter, or the handful he leads, "many" against seemingly superior forces.

37. *You lengthened my stride beneath me, / and my ankles did not trip.* This focus on the long, firm stride jibes with the previous images of rapid running against the enemy and anticipates the evocation in the lines that follow of the victorious warrior's feet trampling the foe.

38. *Till I cut them down.* The English phrase, chosen to reflect the rhythmic compactness of the original, represents a Hebrew verb that means "to destroy them utterly," or, "to finish them off," but the former phrase is too much of a mouthful and the latter is the wrong level of diction. In any event, the narrative sequence of being provided with armor and weapons and charging against a fleeing enemy is now completed as the victor overtakes his adversaries and tramples them to death.

They looked round—there was none to save them,   42
   to the LORD, He answered them not.
I crushed them like dust of the earth,   43
   like street mud, I pounded them, stomped them.
You delivered me from the strife of peoples,   44
   kept me at the head of nations,
      a people I knew not did serve me.
Foreigners cowered before me,   45
   by what the ear heard they heeded me.
Foreigners withered away,   46
   crept trembling from their enclosures.

---

42. *there was none to save them, / to the* LORD, *He answered them not.* The frustration of the enemies' desperate prayers is meant to be a pointed contrast to the situation of the speaker of the poem, who calls out to the LORD and is saved (verse 4).

44. *the strife of peoples.* The translation follows the minor variation of the parallel reading in Psalm 18, *merivey ʿam,* literally, "the strife of people." The Masoretic Text here reads *merivey ʿami,* "the strife of my people," which may simply mean the battles in which my people is embroiled, but it also inadvertently suggests internal strife. Despite the presence of Saul in the poem's superscription, the immediately following lines here indicate external enemies.
   kept me at the head of nations. This phrase and the language of the next verset are perfectly consonant with David's creation of an imperial presence among the peoples of the Transjordan region.

45. *Foreigners cowered before me.* All that can be said in confidence about the Hebrew verb is that it indicates something negative. The common meaning of the root is "to deny" or "to lie." Perhaps that sense is linked in this instance with the foreigners' fawning on their conqueror.

46. *crept trembling from their enclosures.* The meanings of both the verb and the noun are in dispute. The verb *ḥagar* usually means "to gird," but the text in Psalm 18, more plausibly, inverts the second and third consonants, yielding *ḥarag,* which is generally taken to mean "emerge from," or "pop out from," a restrictive framework. The noun *misgerotam* is clearly derived from the root *s-g-r,* "to close," and "enclosure" seems fairly plausible. (The proposal of "collar" has little biblical warrant and makes rather bad sense in context.)

47 The LORD lives and blessed is my rock,
  exalted the God, rock who saved me!
48 The God who vouchsafes me vengeance
  and brings down peoples beneath me.
49 Releases me from my enemies,
  over those against me exalts me,
   from the wreaker of havoc You rescued.
50 Therefore do I praise You, LORD, among nations,
  and to Your name do I chant.
51 Saving tower to His king,
  standing steadfast by His anointed,
   by David and his seed, forever."

---

50. *Therefore do I praise You, LORD.* In keeping with a formal convention of the thanksgiving psalm, or *todah*, the poem concludes by explicitly stating that the speaker has praised or given thanks (the verb cognate with the noun *todah*) to God.

 and to your name do I chant. The pairing in poetic parallelism of the two verbs, *hodah*, "praise," and *zimer*, "chant," is common in the conclusion of thanksgiving psalms.

51. *Saving tower.* The variant reading in Psalm 18, supported by the consonantal text here but not by its Masoretic vocalization, is "He magnifies the saving [or victories]" of—(instead of the noun, *migdol*, "tower," the verb *magdil*, "to make big"). The one attraction of the Masoretic reading here of this word is that it closes the poem with an image that picks up the multiple metaphors of a lofty stronghold at the beginning.

 standing steadfast by His anointed, / by David and his seed, forever. Many critics have seen the entire concluding verse as an editorial addition, both because of the switch to a third-person reference to the king and because of the invocation of dynasty, beyond the temporal frame of the warrior-king's own victories. The inference, however, is not inevitable. Switches in grammatical person, even in a single clause, occur much more easily in biblical Hebrew than in modern Western languages, and if the triumphant speaker of the poem is actually David or in any event is imagined to be David, it is quite possible that he would conclude his account of attaining imperial greatness by a prayer that the dynasty he has founded will continue to enjoy God's steadfast support for all time.

CHAPTER 23

And these are the last words of David:

"Thus spoke David son of Jesse,
    thus spoke the man raised on high,
anointed of the God of Jacob,
    and sweet singer of Israel.

---

1. *these are the last words of David*. David's victory psalm in the preceding chapter is now followed by a second archaic poetic text, quite different in style, unrelated to the psalm tradition, and a good deal obscurer in many of its formulations. Although there is scholarly debate about the dating of this poem, the consensus puts it in or close to David's own time in the tenth century. The mystifying features of the language certainly suggest great antiquity, and it is just possible that the poet was really David. The exact application of "the last words of David" is unclear. In terms of the narrative, they are not literally his last words because he will convey a deathbed testament to Solomon (1 Kings 2). The phrase might be intended to designate the last pronouncement in poetry of David the royal poet.

Thus spoke David. This introductory formula is a mark of prophetic or oracular language—compare the beginning of Balaam's third oracle in Numbers 24:3.

raised on high. The two Hebrew words reflected in this translation, *huqam ʿal*, have a gorgeous strangeness as compacted idiom—so strange that both the Septuagint and the Qumran Samuel prefer a more common Hebrew locution, *heqim ʾel*, "God has raised up." In either case, the phrase refers to David's elevation to the throne.

sweet singer of Israel. The eloquent and famous wording of the King James Version seems worth retaining because the divergent proposals for understanding the phrase are scarcely more certain than that of the KJV. The literal meaning of *neʿim zemirot yisraʾel* is "sweet one [or, favorite] of the chants of Israel." The root *z-m-r* has a homonymous meaning—strength—which has encouraged some interpreters to construe this as "preferred of the Strong One

2   The LORD's spirit has spoken in me,
        his utterance on my tongue.
3   The God of Israel has said,
        to me the Rock of Israel has spoken:
     He who rules men, just,
        who rules in the fear of God.
4   Like morning's light when the sun comes up,
        morning without clouds,
            from radiance, from showers—grass from earth.

[or, Stronghold] of Israel" in parallel to "anointed of the God of Israel." It must be said, however, that there are no instances in which the root z-m-r in the sense of strength serves as an epithet for the deity.

2. *The LORD's spirit has spoken in me.* This does not mean, as some have understood, that David is claiming actual status as a prophet but rather that he is attesting to an access of oracular elevation as he proclaims his lofty (and enigmatic!) verse.

3. *He who rules men, just.* The translation reproduces the cryptic (elliptic?) syntax of the Hebrew, adding a clarifying comma (the Hebrew of course has no punctuation).
    who rules in the fear of God. The compacted syntax of the Hebrew has no "in," but most interpreters assume it is implied.

4. *from radiance, from showers—grass from earth.* The meaning of these images is much disputed, and some critics move "from radiance" altogether back to the preceding clause. The tentative reading presumed by the translation is as follows: The anointed king has been compared to the brilliant rising sun on a cloudless morning (solar imagery for kings being fairly common in ancient Near Eastern literature). The poet now adds that from the sun's radiance, coupled with rainfall, grass springs forth from the earth. Thus the rule of the just king is a source of blessed fruitfulness to his subjects.

For is not thus my house with God?   5
   An eternal covenant He gave me,
      drawn up in full and guaranteed.
   For all my triumph and all my desire
      will He not bring to bloom?
And the worthless man is like a thorn—   6
   uprooted every one,
      they cannot be picked up by hand.
Should a man touch them,   7
   he must get himself iron

---

5. *For is not thus my house with God?* The Hebrew grammar here is a little confusing. It is most plausible to construe both this clause and the one at the end of the verse not as negative statements but as affirmative questions. The image of bringing to bloom in the concluding clause suggests that David's dynasty in relation to God is to be imagined like the earth in relation to sun and showers and like the people in relation to the king: because of the everlasting covenant with David, God will make his house blossom.

6. *the worthless man is like a thorn— / uprooted every one.* The antithesis between flourishing soft grass and the prickly thorn torn from its roots is manifest (though it must be said that "uprooted" for the obscure *munad* is conjectural, if widely accepted).

7. *he must get himself iron.* The translation adopts the common proposal that the verb *yimalʾe* (literally, "he will fill") is an ellipsis for *yimalʾe yado,* "he will fill his hand, equip himself with"). Others emend it to read *ʾim lʾo,* "except [with]".

or the shaft of a spear.
And in fire they'll be utterly burned where they are."

8 These are the names of the warriors of David: Josheb-basshebeth,
a Tahchemonite, head of the Three—he is Adino the Eznite. He

---

or the shaft of a spear. The Hebrew is usually construed as "and the shaft,"
but the particle *waw* does occasionally have the force of "or," which is more
plausible here.

in fire they'll be utterly burned. The only suitable disposition of these nasty
thorns is to rake them up with iron tool or spear shaft and make a bonfire of
them, in order to get entirely rid of the threat they pose. The fact that *weapons*
are used for the raking suggests the political referent of the metaphor. Such
will be the fate of mischief makers ("the worthless")—evidently all who would
presume to oppose the legitimate monarchy.

where they are. This phrase reflects a single, highly dubious word in the
Masoretic Text, *bashavet.* That word may well be an inadvertent repetition by
a baffled scribe of the seventh Hebrew word in the following verse. That
whole phrase in which that term occurs is itself textually problematic.

8. *These are the names of the warriors of David.* This list of military heroes and
their exploits is perhaps the strongest candidate of any passage in the Book of
Samuel to be considered a text actually written in David's lifetime. The language is crabbed, and the very abundance of textual difficulties, uncharacteristic for prose, reflects the great antiquity of the list. These fragmentary
recollections of particular heroic exploits do not sound like the invention of
any later writer but, on the contrary, like memories of remarkable martial acts
familiar to the audience (e.g., "he . . . killed the lion in the pit on the day of the
snow") and requiring only the act of epic listing, not of narrative elaboration.
It should also be noted that the list invokes the early phase of David's career—
when the Philistines were the dominant military force in the land, when
David was at Adullam and in "the stronghold," and when Asahel, destined to
perish at the hands of Abner at the beginning of the civil war, was an active
member of David's corp of elite fighters.

Josheb-basshebeth a Tahchemonite. So reads the Masoretic Text. But this
looks quite dubious as a Hebrew name. One version of the Septuagint has
Ishbaal (alternately, Jeshbaal), which by scribal euphemism also appears as
Ish-bosheth and hence may have produced the confusion in the Masoretic
Text. Many authorities prefer as the gentilic "Hachmoni," in accordance with
the parallel verse in Chronicles.

the Three. Throughout the list, there are confusions between three, third,
and thirty. The received text at this point seems to read *shalishim,* "commanders of units of thirty" but "three" makes far better sense.

brandished his spear over eight hundred slain at a single time. And   9
after him Eleazar son of Dodo son of Ahohi, of the three warriors with
David when they insulted the Philistines gathered there for battle and
the Israelites decamped. He arose and struck down Philistines until   10
his hand tired and his hand stuck to the sword. And the LORD wrought
a great victory on that day, and the troops came back after him only to
strip the slain. And after him Shammah son of Agei the Ararite. And   11
the Philistines gathered at Lehi, and there was a plot of land there full
of lentils, and the troops had fled before the Philistines. And he took a   12
stand in the plot and saved it and struck down the Philistines. And the
LORD wrought a great victory. And three of the Thirty, at the head went   13
down in the harvest to David at the cave of Adullam, with the Philistine force camped in the Valley of Rephaim. And David was then in the   14
stronghold and the Philistine garrison then at Bethlehem. And David   15
had a craving and said, "Who will give me water to drink from the well

---

He brandished his spear. This whole phrase, which seems strictly necessary
to make the sentence intelligible, is lacking in the Masoretic Text but appears
in the parallel verse in Chronicles.

10. *to strip the slain.* No object of the verb "to strip" appears in the Hebrew, but
this may be a simple ellipses for a common military idiom rather than a scribal
omission.

11. *at Lehi.* The translation presupposes a minor emendation of the Masoretic
laḥayah (meaning obscure, though some understand it as "in a force") to *leḥi*,
a place-name, which the rest of the clause seems to require.
　　there was a plot of land there full of lentils. The homey specificity of the
detail is another manifestation of the feeling of remembered anecdote in this
catalogue of exploits.

13. *at the head.* The Hebrew says only "head," but the word seems to have an
adverbial function, and so "at the head" is not unlikely.

15. *who will give me water to drink from the well of Bethlehem . . . ?* Or, "Would
that I might drink water . . ." Bethlehem, of course, is David's hometown, at
this juncture a headquarters of the occupying Philistine forces. David
expresses a sudden yen to taste the sweet water he remembers from that well
by the gate of his native town, though he scarcely intends this as a serious
invitation to his men to undertake anything so foolhardy as to attempt breaking through the Philistine lines in order to get it. Presumably, the three war-

16 of Bethlehem which is by the gate?" And the three warriors broke
through the Philistine camp and drew water from the well of Bethlehem which is by the gate, and they bore it off and brought it to David.
But he would not drink it, and he poured it out in libation to the LORD.

17 And he said, "Far be it from me before the LORD that I should do such
a thing. Shall I drink the blood of men who have gone at the risk of
their lives?" And he would not drink it. These things did the three warriors do.

18 And Abishai brother of Joab son of Zeruiah—he was chief of the
Thirty. And he brandished his spear over three hundred slain, and he

19 had a name with the Three. Of the Thirty he was most honored and so

20 he became their captain, but he did not attain to the Three. And Benaiah son of Jehoida from Kabzeel, son of a valiant man, great in deeds—

---

riors—it is unclear as to whether they are identical with the Three just
named, for they are said to be part of the Thirty—do not misunderstand
David's intentions. Rather, as daring fighters, they decide to take him at his
word and risk their necks in raiding the Philistine garrison at Bethlehem in
order to prove they can execute a seemingly impossible mission. It is easy to
understand how such an exploit would be vividly recalled and registered in
the epic list.

17. *Shall I drink the blood of men* . . . The verb (one word in the Hebrew) "shall
I drink" is missing from the Masoretic Text, though present in both the parallel verse in Chronicles and in the Septuagint. It is possible that some ancient
scribe recoiled from an expression that had David drinking human blood,
even in a hyperbolic verbal gesture.

18. *he was chief of the Thirty.* The received text here and in v. 19 reads "Three," but
this makes no sense, as we are told that Abishai "did not attain to the Three."
  with the Three. Or, "in the three." Since Abishai is not a member of the
Three, this would have to mean that his prowess won him a reputation even
among the legendary Three. Another solution is to emend the initial *ba* ("in,"
"among") to *ka* ("like"), yielding "he had a name like the Three."

20. *son of a valiant man.* Many textual critics conclude that "son of" (*ben*) is an
erroneous scribal addition.

he struck down two sons of Ariel of Moab and he went down and
killed the lion in the pit on the day of the snow. And he struck down 21
an Egyptian man, a man of daunting appearance, a spear was in the
hand of the Egyptian. And he went down to him with a staff and stole
the spear from the hand of the Egyptian and he killed him with his
own spear. These things did Benaiah son of Jehoida do, and he had a 22
name with the Three Warriors. Of the Thirty he was honored but he 23
did not attain to the Three. And David put him over his royal guard.
Asahel brother of Joab was in the Thirty, and Elhanan son of Dodo of 24
Bethlehem. Shammah the Harodite, Elika the Harodite. Helez the 25, 26
Paltite, Ira son of Ikkesh the Tekoite. Abiezer the Anathothite, 27
Mebunnai the Hushathite. Zalmon the Ahohite, Maharai the 28
Netophathite. Heleb son of Baanah the Netophthite, Ittai son of 29
Ribai from Gibeah of the Benjaminites. Benaiah the Pirathonite, 30
Hiddai from Nahalei-gaash. Abi-albon the Anbathite, Azmaveth 31
the Barhumite. Eliahba the Shaalbonite, sons of Jashen Jonathan. 32

---

he struck down the two sons of Ariel of Moab. These words are among the
most enigmatic in the report of the exploits of David's heroes. The words "two
sons of" (*sheney beney*) are supplied from the Septuagint in an effort to make
this clause at least a little intelligible. "Ariel" is probably a cultic site or object
in Moab.

22. *he had a name with the Three Warriors.* See the comment on verse 18. The
same problem is reflected here.

25. *the Harodite.* All these identifying terms in the list designate the villages
from which the warriors come. A likely location of the biblical Harod would
be not far from Bethlehem. The earlier names in the list cluster geographically
in the territory of Judah, David's tribe. Some of the later names indicate
places in the territories of tribes to the north—perhaps reflecting new recruits
to the elite unit after the conclusion of the civil war. Toward the end of the list
there are also non-Israelites: these could have been mercenaries, or perhaps
rather naturalized subjects of the new monarchy.

32. *sons of Jashen Jonathan.* This identification definitely looks scrambled.
"Sons of" appears not to belong, and many textual critics omit it. "Jonathan" as
a second proper name immediately after "Jashen," is also problematic, and one
wonders whether Jashen (Hebrew *yashen* means "sleeping") was ever a name.

33, 34   Shammah the Hararite, Ahiam son of Sharar the Ararite. Eliphelet son
of Ahasbai son of the Maacathite, Eliam son of Ahitophel the Gilonite.
35, 36   Hezrai the Carmelite, Paarai the Arbite. Igal son of Nathan from
37   Zobah, Bani the Gadite. Zelek the Ammonite, Naharai the Beerothite,
38   armor bearer to Joab son of Zeruiah. Ira the Ithrite, Gareb the Ithrite.
39   Uriah the Hittite—thirty-seven in all.

---

34. *Eliam son of Ahitophel.* One notes that the son of the state counselor who
betrayed David for Absalom was a member of David's elite corps. He might
also be the same Eliam who is Bathsheba's father.

39. *Uriah the Hittite.* Is it an intended irony that the list of David's picked warriors concludes with the man he murdered? The irony may be an artifact of
the editor, if this list was composed after the events recorded in the
Bathsheba story.
    thirty-seven in all. As elsewhere in biblical tabulations, it is hard to make
this figure compute. One system of counting yields a total of thirty-six, and
the addition of Joab—rather surprisingly, omitted from the list—would produce thirty-seven.

CHAPTER 24

And once more the wrath of the LORD was kindled against Israel, and 1
He incited David against them, saying, "Go, count Israel and Judah."
And the king said to Joab, commander of the force that was with him, 2
"Go round, pray, among all the tribes of Israel, from Dan to Beersheba,
and take a census of the people, that I may know the number of the
people." And Joab said to the king, "May the LORD your God add to the 3
people a hundred times over with the eyes of my lord the king behold-

---

1. *And once more the wrath of the* LORD *was kindled against Israel.* The reason
for God's wrath is entirely unspecified, and attempts to link it to events in the
preceding narrative are quite unconvincing. In fact, this entire narrative unit
(which some scholars claim is itself composite) is strikingly different in theological assumptions, in its imagination of narrative situation and character,
and even in its style from the David story proper as well as from the tale of
David and the Gibeonites in Chapter 21 with which it is symmetrically paired.
Perhaps, indeed, there is no discernible reason for God's fury against Israel.
The God of this story has the look of acting arbitrarily, exacting terrible human
costs in order to be placated. Unlike the deity of 1 Samuel 1–2 Samuel 20, He
is decidedly an interventionist God, pulling the human actors by strings, and
He may well be a capricious God, here "inciting" David to carry out a census
that will only bring grief to the people.

2. *Joab, commander of the force.* A different vocabulary is another indication
that a different writer is at work here. Throughout the David narrative, Joab is
designated *sar hatsava* "commander of the army," but here the terminology
changes to the unusual *sar haḥayil*, "commander of the force." Similarly, the
verb for "go round," *sh-w-t*—it is attached to the Adversary in the frame story
of Job—is distinctive of this narrative.

4 ing. But why should my lord the king desire this thing?" And the king's
word prevailed over Joab and over the commanders of the force and
Joab, and the commanders of the force with him, went out from the
5 king's presence to take a census of the people, of Israel. And they
crossed the Jordan and camped in Aroer south of the town, which is in
6 the middle of the wadi of Gad and by Jazer. And they came to Gilead
and to the region of Tahtim-hodshi, and they came to Dan-jaan and
7 round toward Sidon. And they came to the fortress of Tyre and to all
the towns of the Hivite and the Canaanite, and they went out to the
8 Negeb of Judah, to Beersheba. And they went round through all the

---

3. *But why should my lord the king do this thing?* Underlying the story is both a
cultic and a superstitious fear of the census, reflected in Joab's objection to it.
Several commentators have noted that according to Exodus 30:12 every
Israelite counted in a census was required to pay a half shekel as "ransom"
(kofer) for his life. Since such payment could not be realistically expected in a
total census of the nation, masses of people would be put in a condition of
violation of ritual. But there is also a folkloric horror of being counted as a
condition of vulnerability to malignant forces. In Rashi's words: "For the evil
eye holds sway over counting." Beyond these considerations, Joab the commander may have a political concern in mind: the census served as the basis
for conscription (compare the notation in verse 9 of those counted as "sword-
wielding men"), and thus imposing the census might conceivably have pro-
voked opposition to the threatened conscription and to the king who was
behind it. It is noteworthy that the census is carried out by army officers.

5. *they crossed the Jordan and camped in Aroer.* Aroer is roughly fifteen miles
east of the Dead Sea. The trajectory of the census takers describes a large
ellipsis: first to the southeast from Jerusalem, then north through Transjordan
to Gilead and beyond, then west through the northernmost Israelite territory
to the sea, then all the way south to Beersheba, and back to Jerusalem. All
this, which will lead to wholesale death, is accomplished in nine months and
twenty days—the human gestation period.

6. *Tahtim-hodshi.* The name is suspect, but efforts to recover an original name
behind it remain uncertain.

7. *the fortress of Tyre.* Evidently a mainland outpost to the south of Tyre proper,
which was on an island.

land and returned at the end of nine months and twenty days to
Jerusalem. And Joab gave the number of the census of the people   9
to the king, and Israel made up eight hundred thousand sword-
wielding men, and Judah five hundred thousand men. And David   10
was smitten with remorse afterwards for having counted the people.
And David said to the LORD, "I have offended greatly in what I have
done. And now, LORD, remit the guilt of your servant, for I have been
very foolish." And David arose in the morning, and the word of   11
the LORD had come to Gad the prophet, David's seer, saying, "Go   12
and speak to David—'Thus says the LORD: Three things I have
taken against you. Choose you one of them, and I shall do it to you.
Seven years of famine in your land, or three months when you flee   13
before your foes as they pursue you, or let there be three days of
plague in your land.' Now, mark and see, what reply shall I bring back
to Him Who sent me?" And David said to Gad, "I am in great straits.   14
Let us, pray, fall into the LORD's hand, for great is His mercy, and into

---

9. *sword-wielding.* The Hebrew says literally "sword-drawing."

10. *I have offended greatly in what I have done.* In contrast to the cogent sense
of moral agency and moral responsibility in the David story proper, there is a
peculiar contradiction here: David confesses deep contrition, yet he has, after
all, been manipulated by God ("Incited") to do what he has done.

11. *Gad the prophet, David's seer.* Gad was mentioned earlier (1 Samuel 22:5).
His appearance here by no means warrants the claim of Kyle McCarter, Jr.
and others that this story is the work of a "prophetic" writer. Visionary intermediaries between king and God were a common assumption in the ancient
world. Gad is called "seer" (*hozeh*), not the way prophetic writers would ordinarily think of prophets (and also not the term used for Samuel in 1 Samuel 9).
Above all, the prophetic current in biblical literature does not presuppose
either this kind of arbitrarily punitive God nor the accompanying hocus pocus
with choices of punishment and divine messengers of destruction visible to
the human characters.

15   the hand of man let me not fall." And the LORD sent a plague against
Israel from morning until the fixed time, and from Dan to Beersheba
seventy-seven thousand men of the people died.

16   And the messenger reached out his hand against Jerusalem to destroy
it, and the LORD regretted the evil and said to the messenger who was

---

14. *Let us . . . fall in the* LORD's *hand . . . and into the hand of man let me not fall.*
There is a puzzle in David's choice because only one of the three punish-
ments—the flight from enemies—clearly involves human agency. Perhaps
David has in mind that an extended famine would lead to absolute dependence on those foreign nations unaffected by the famine, as in the story of
Joseph's brothers going down to Egypt. In all this, it should be noted that
David is scarcely the same character we have seen in the body of his story.
Instead of that figure of conflicting feelings and emotions so remarkable in
psychological depth, we have a flat character instigated to act by God, then
expressing remorse, then speaking in rather official tones in his role as political ruler and cultic chief responsible for all the people.

15. *the fixed time.* There is some question about what this refers to, though the
grounds for emending the text to solve the problem are shaky. The phrase
ought logically to refer to the end of the ordained three days of the plague. Yet
David's intercession to stop the plague short before it engulfs Jerusalem suggests that the plague does not go on for the full three days. The difficulty
might be resolved simply by assuming that the initial verb—"and the LORD
sent a plague against Israel"—refers to the initiating of the process according
to the promised time limitations: God sends a plague against Israel intended
to rage for the stipulated time of three days, but after it has devastated the
people on a terrible scale for a certain time (perhaps two days?), David, aghast
that these horrors should visit his own city as well, takes steps to induce God
to cut the plague short.

16. *And the messenger reached out his hand against Jerusalem to destroy it.* Once
again, the apparatus and the theology of this story reflect a different imaginative world from that of the main narrative about David, in which there are no
divine emissaries of destruction brandishing celestial swords. The text of the
Qumran Samuel scroll, paralled in 1 Chronicles 21, makes the mythological
character of this story even clearer: "and David raised his eyes and saw a messenger of the LORD standing between earth and heaven, his sword
unsheathed in his hand reaching out against Jerusalem, and David and the
elders fell on their faces, covered with sackcloth."

sowing destruction among the people, "Enough! Now stay your hand."
And the LORD's messenger was at the threshing floor of Araunah the
Jebusite. And David said to the LORD when he saw the messenger who   17
was striking down the people, thus he said, "It is I who offended, I who
did wrong. And these sheep, what have they done? Let your hand be
against me and my father's house." And Gad came to David on that day   18
and said to him, "Go up, raise to the LORD an altar on the threshing
floor of Araunah the Jebusite." And David went up according to the   19
word of Gad, as the LORD had charged. And Araunah looked out and   20
saw the king and his servants crossing over toward him, and Araunah
went out and bowed down to the king, his face to the ground. And   21
Araunah said, "Why has my lord the king come to his servant?" And

---

stay your hand. Literally, "let your hand go slack, unclench it."

the LORD's messenger was at the threshing floor of Araunah the Jebusite. In
this fashion, the last-minute averting of the destruction of Jerusalem is linked
with the etiological tale explaining how the site of the future temple was
acquired. (Although the temple is not explicitly mentioned, this acquisition of
an altar site in Jerusalem is clearly placed here to prepare the way for the story
of Solomon the temple builder that is to follow.) Thus, the first sacrifice
offered on this spot is associated with a legendary turning away of wrath from
Jerusalem—a token of the future function of the temple. The name Araunah
it is not Semitic and is generally thought to be Hittite or Hurrian. Some scholars claim it is a title, not a name. In any event, Araunah's presence indicates
that the conquered Jebusites were not massacred or entirely banished but
continued to live in Jerusalem under David as his subjects.

17. *It is I who offended.* The Qumran text reads here, "It is I, the shepherd, who
did evil." That, of course, neatly complements "these sheep" in the next
clause, but it is hard to know whether "shepherd" was original or added by a
later scribe to clarify the sheep metaphor.

21. *Why has my lord the king come to his servant?* Isaac Abravanel aptly notes
that it would not have been customary for the king to come to his subject:
"You should have sent for me, for the lesser man goes to the greater and the
greater does not go to the lesser." Abravanel, a councillor to Ferdinand and
Isabella who was in the end exiled by them, would have been keenly familiar
with such protocol.

22 David said, "To buy the threshing floor from you to build an altar to the LORD, that the scourge may be held back from the people. And Arau-nah said to David, "Let my lord the king take and offer up what is good in his eyes. See the oxen for the burnt offering and the threshing

23 boards and the oxen's gear for wood. All of it has Araunah, O king, given to the king." And Araunah said to the king, "May the LORD your

24 God show you favor." And the king said to Araunah, "Not so! I will surely buy it from you for a price, and I will not offer up burnt offerings to the LORD my God at no cost." And David bought the threshing floor

25 and the oxen for fifty shekels of silver. And David built there an altar to

---

to build an altar to the LORD, *that the scourge may be held back.* According to the ritualistic assumptions of this narrative, it requires not merely contrition but a special sacrifice to placate the deity. This leads one to suspect that the story, far from being prophetic literature, may have originated in some sort of priestly circle.

22. *Let my lord take . . . what is good in his eyes.* In this whole exchange, there is a distinct parallel to Abraham's bargaining with Ephron the Hittite for the pur-chase of a grave site at Hebron in Genesis 23. Ephron, too, first offers to make a gift to Abraham of what he requires, but the patriarch, like David here, insists on paying full price in order to have undisputed possession of the prop-erty.

the oxen for the burnt offering and the threshing board and the oxen's gear. What Araunah does not offer David is the land itself, which he clearly wants. Both the threshing board and the "gear" (presumably, the yoke) would have been wooden. Since the sacrifice needs to be performed at once in order to avert the plague, Araunah is quick to offer not only the sacrificial beasts but firewood on the spot.

23. *All of it has Araunah, O king, given to the king.* The Hebrew, with the repeated "king," looks peculiar, though it is intelligible if the first "king" is con-strued as a vocative. Some emend the verse to read "all of it has Araunah your servant given to my lord the king."

the LORD and offered up burnt offerings and communion sacrifices, and the LORD granted the plea for the land and the scourge was pulled back from Israel.

---

25. *the LORD granted the plea for the land.* This is, of course, a near-verbatim repetition of the words that conclude the story of David and the Gibeonites' execution of the descendants of Saul (21:14). The repetition may well be an editorial intervention intended to underscore the symmetry between the tale of a scourge averted by David's intercession at the beginning and at the end of this large composite coda to 1 and 2 Samuel. Although neither of these stories is especially continuous with the David story proper, both reflect a connection with it in the emphasis on guilt that the king incurs, which brings disaster on the nation and which requires expiation. But the writer of genius responsible for the larger David narrative imagines guilt in far more probing moral terms and does not assume that the consequences of moral offenses and grave political misjudgments can be reversed by some ritual act.

1 KINGS

CHAPTER 1

And King David had grown old, advanced in years, and they covered him   1
with bedclothes, but he was not warm. And his servants said to him,   2
Let them seek out for my lord the king a young virgin, that she may
wait upon the king and become his familiar, and lie in your lap, and my

---

1. *And King David had grown old.* Although an editor, several centuries after
the composition of the story, placed this episode and the next one at the
beginning of the Book of Kings, and after the coda of 2 Samuel 21–24, because
of the centrality in them of Solomon's succession, they are clearly the conclusion to the David story and bear all the hallmarks of its author's distinctive literary genius. There are strong stylistic links with the previous David narrative;
the artful deployment of dialogue and of spatial shifts is very similar; and
there are significant connections of phrasing, motif, and theme.

they covered him with bedclothes, but he was not warm. This extraordinary
portrait of a human life working itself out in the gradual passage of time,
which began with an agile, daring, and charismatic young David, now shows
him in the extreme infirmity of old age, shivering in bed beneath his covers.

2. *Let them seek out for my lord the king a young virgin.* The language used by
the courtiers recalls that of the mentally troubled Saul's courtiers, "Let them
seek out a man skilled in playing the lyre" (1 Samuel 16:16)—the very words
that were the prelude to the young David's entrance into the court.

became his familiar. The exact meaning of the Hebrew noun *sokhenet* is
uncertain. Some translate it as "attendant" on the basis of the context. The
verbal stem from which the word is derived generally has the meaning of "to
become accustomed," hence the choice here of "familiar"—of course, in the
social sense and not in the secondary sense linked with witchcraft. The only
other occurence of this term in the biblical corpus, Isaiah 22:15, seems to designate a (male) court official.

and lie in your lap. Nathan in his denunciatory parable addressed to David
represented the ewe, symbolic of Bathsheba, lying in the poor man's lap (2
Samuel 12:3).

3   lord the king will be warm." And they sought out a beautiful young
woman through all the territory of Israel, and they found Abishag the
4   Shunamite and brought her to the king. And the young woman was
very beautiful, and she became a familiar to the king and ministered to
him, but the king knew her not.

5   And Adonijah son of Haggith was giving himself airs, saying, "I shall be
king!" And he made himself a chariot and horsemen with fifty men run-
6   ning before him. And his father never caused him pain, saying, "Why
have you done thus?" And he, too, was very goodly of appearance, and
7   him she had born after Absalom. And he parlayed with Joab son of
Zeruiah and with Abiathar the priest, and they lent their support to

---

4. *the young woman was very beautiful . . . but the king knew her not.* David,
lying in bed with this desirable virgin, but now beyond any thought or capacity
of sexual consummation, is of course a sad image of infirm old age. At the
same time, this vignette of geriatric impotence is a pointed reversal of the
Bathsheba story that brought down God's curse on the house of David, trig-
gering all the subsequent troubles of dynastic succession. There, too, David
was lying in his bed or couch (*mishkav,* as in verse 47 here), and there, too, he
sent out emissaries to bring back a beautiful young woman to lie with him,
though to antithetical purposes.

5. *was giving himself airs.* The reflexive verb has a root that means to raise up
(hence the King James Version, "exalting himself"). Since a common noun
derived from that verb, *nasᵓi,* means "prince," the reflexive verb might even
have the sense of "acting the part of a prince."
   he made himself a chariot and horsemen with fifty men running before him.
These acts of regal presumption are the same ones carried out by the usurper
Absalom, Adonijah's older brother.

6. *his father never caused him pain.* The obvious sense of the verb in context is
"reprimand." The Septuagint reads "restrained him" (ᶜ*atsaro* instead of ᶜ*atsavo),*
either because the Greek translators had a better Hebrew version here or
were smoothing out the Hebrew.
   And he, too, was very goodly of appearance. As the second clause of this sentence makes clear, the "too" refers to Absalom, the son Haggith bore David
before Adonijah.

Adonijah. But Zadok the priest and Benaiah son of Jehoiada and 8
Nathan the prophet and Shimei and Rei and David's warriors were not
with Adonijah. And Adonijah made a sacrificial feast of sheep and oxen 9
and fatlings by the Zoheleth stone which is near En-rogel, and he
invited all his brothers, the king's sons, and all the men of Judah, the
king's servants. But Nathan the prophet and Benaiah and the warriors 10
and Solomon his brother he did not invite.

---

8. *Shimei and Rei.* The Septuagint reads "Shimei and his companions" (*re°aw*
instead of *re°i*).

9. *made a sacrificial feast.* The Hebrew verb z-b-ẖ refers both to the sacrifice of
the animals, the greater part of which was kept to be eaten, and to the feast.
This is clearly a ceremonial feast at which the monarchy is to be conferred on
Adonijah.

the Zoheleth stone which is near En-rogel. The spring (Hebrew °*ayin*) of
Rogel is within a couple of miles of Jerusalem. The spatial proximity becomes
important later in the story because Adonijah's supporters, after they finish
their feast, are able to hear the shouting from the city. Zoheleth means "creep-
ing thing," which has led some scholars to conjecture that this location was a
sacred site dedicated to the worship of a snake deity.

and all the men of Judah, the king's servants. Like his brother Absalom,
Adonijah draws on a base of support from his own tribe, Judah. In political
and royal contexts, the phrase "the king's servants" usually refers to courtiers,
members of the king's inner circle.

10. *But Nathan the prophet and Benaiah . . .* In keeping with the established
convention of biblical narrative, this list of the uninvited and the report of
Adonijah's self-coronation feast will be repeated more or less verbatim, with
subtle and significant changes reflecting who the speaker is.

and the warriors. One should remember that Joab, commander of the army,
was not listed in 2 Samuel 23 as a member of "the warriors," David's elite fighting corps. Though few in number, they would have been a formidable coun-
terforce in a struggle for the throne.

11 And Nathan said to Bathsheba, Solomon's mother, saying, "Have you
not heard that Adonijah son of Haggith has become king, and our lord
12 David knows it not? And now, come let me give you counsel that you
13 may save your own life and the life of your son Solomon. Go and get you
to King David and say to him, 'Has not my lord the king sworn to your
servant, saying: Solomon your son shall be king after me, and he shall
14 sit on my throne. And why has Adonijah become king?' Look, while you
are still speaking there, I shall come after you and fill in your words."

---

11. *Bathsheba, Solomon's mother.* After her fatal affair with David, she disappears from the narrative. Now, after some two decades of elapsed time, she
resurfaces. Whereas the beautiful young wife was accorded no dialogue
except for her report to David of her pregnancy, the mature Bathsheba will
show herself a mistress of language—shrewd, energetic, politically astute.

Adonijah . . . has become king and our lord David knows it not. Fokkelman
notes the play on words in the Hebrew between ²*Adoniyah* ("my lord is Yah")
and ²*adoneinu* ("our lord"). Playing also on the double sense of the Hebrew
verb "to know," the writer represents David in a state of both sexual and cogni-
tive impotence: he knows not Abishag and he knows not Adonijah's initiative
to assume the throne.

13. *Has not my lord the king sworn to your servant.* The script that Nathan dictates to Bathsheba invokes a central ambiguity which the writer surely intends
to exploit. Perhaps David actually made a private vow to Bathsheba promising
that Solomon would succeed him. There is, however, no mention of such a
vow anywhere in the preceding narrative, including the report of Solomon's
God-favored birth, where one might expect it. This opens up a large, though
by no means certain, possibility that Nathan the man of God has invented the
vow and enlists Bathsheba's help in persuading the doddering David that he
actually made this commitment.

Solomon your son shall be king after me, and he shall sit on my throne. The
verselike parallelism of David's purported vow has the effect of impressing it
on memory. It is repeated three times: here by Nathan, then by Bathsheba as
she carries out Nathan's orders, then by David, who will make one small but
crucial change in the wording of the formula.

14. *fill in your words.* Many translate the Hebrew verb that means "to fill" as
"confirm." But in fact what Nathan will do is to complement Bathsheba's
speech, adding certain elements and not repeating certain others.

And Bathsheba came to the king in the inner chamber, and the king 15
was very old, with Abishag the Shunamite ministering to the king. And 16
Bathsheba did obeisance and bowed down to the king, and the king
said, "What troubles you?" And she said to him, "My lord, you yourself 17
swore by the LORD your God to your servant, 'Solomon your son shall
be king after me, and he shall sit on my throne.' And now, look, Adoni- 18
jah has become king and my lord the king knows it not. And he has 19
made a sacrificial feast of oxen and fatlings and sheep in abundance
and has invited all the king's sons and Abiathar the priest and Joab
commander of the army, but Solomon your servant he did not invite.

---

15. *the inner chamber.* At an earlier moment, a figure from David's house,
Amnon, was seen lying ill (or pretending) while a beautiful woman came to
him in the inner chamber.

16. *Bathsheba did obeisance and bowed down to the king.* Whatever the actual
relationship between Bathsheba and David at this very late point in his life, it
seems reduced to a punctilious observance of palace protocol. In the background, silent, stands the beautiful young Abishag, now the king's bedmate
but not really his consort.

17. *My lord, you yourself swore by the LORD your God.* Bathsheba edits the
script Nathan has given her in two ways: the third-person address to the king
is switched to the second person, allowing her to introduce an emphatic, "you
yourself" (in the Hebrew the addition of the pronoun *'atah* before the conjugated verb); and the vow is said to have been made solemnly "by the LORD
your God." If in fact the vow is a fabrication, perhaps Nathan the prophet was
leery of invoking God's name in connection with it.

19. *oxen and fatlings and sheep in abundance.* The last term, "in abundance," is
added to the verbal chain from the narrator's initial report of the feast, a small
magnification of the scale of the event that Adonijah has staged.
  but Solomon your servant he did not invite. Nathan had not incorporated a
list of the excluded in his instructions to her. Bathsheba singles out only her
own son among the uninvited, but she is careful to identify him to David not
as "my son" but as "your servant," emphasizing Solomon's status as loyal subject.

20 And you, my lord the king, the eyes of all Israel are upon you to tell
21 them who will sit on the throne of my lord the king after him. And it
will come about when my lord the king lies with his fathers that I and
22 my son Solomon will be held offenders." And, look, she was still speak-
23 ing with the king when Nathan the prophet came in. And they told the
king, saying, "Here is Nathan the prophet." And he came before the
24 king and bowed to the king, his face to the ground. And Nathan said,
"My lord the king, have you yourself said, 'Adonijah shall be king after
25 me and he shall sit on my throne?' For he has gone down today and
made a sacrificial feast of oxen and fatlings and sheep in abundance,
and he has invited all the king's sons and the commanders of the army

---

20. *the eyes of all Israel are upon you to tell them who will sit on the throne.* Now
improvising, Bathsheba uses words that strongly evoke David's authority,
though in fact he has been out of the picture, failing and bedridden.

21. *when my lord the king lies with his fathers . . . I and my son Solomon will be
held offenders.* With admirable tact, she uses a decorous euphemism for dying,
and then expresses her perfectly plausible fear that as king, Adonijah would
take prompt steps to eliminate both her and Solomon. (Compare Nathan's
"save your own life and the life of your son.")

23. *Here is Nathan the prophet.* Nathan in his role as prophet is formally
announced to David by the courtiers. According to biblical convention, there
are no three-sided dialogues. Bathsheba presumably withdraws as soon as she
sees Nathan enter. In verse 28, after the conversation with Nathan, David has
to summon her back. All this takes place not in the throne room but in the
"inner chamber," where David lies in bed.

24. *have you yourself said, 'Adonijah will be king . . . ?'* Unlike Bathsheba,
Nathan makes no reference to a vow regarding Solomon, presumably because
it would have been a private vow to her. Instead, he refers to observable public
events: have you authorized the succession of Adonijah? He uses the identical
formula for succession that has already twice been attached to Solomon
("shall be king after me . . . shall sit on my throne").

25. *he has invited all the king's sons and the commanders of the army.* Nathan's
more political version of the unfolding usurpation adds to the list of Adonijah's
supporters the whole officer corps of the army, not just Joab.

and Abiathar the priest, and there they are eating and drinking before
him, and they have said, 'Long live King Adonijah!' But me—your ser-   26
vant—and Zadok the priest and Benaiah son of Jehoiada and Solomon
your servant he did not invite. Has this thing been done by my lord the   27
king without informing your servant who will sit on the throne of my
lord the king after him?" And King David answered and said, "Call me   28
Bathsheba." And she came before the king and stood before the king.
And the king swore and said, "As the LORD lives Who rescued me from   29
every strait, as I swore to you by the LORD God of Israel, saying,   30
'Solomon your son shall be king after me, and he shall sit on my throne
in my stead,' even so will I do this day." And Bathsheba did obeisance,   31

Long live King Adonijah. This vivid acclamation of Adonijah's kingship, not
reported by the narrator, is calculated to rouse David's ire. The evocation of
the coronation feast ("they are eating and drinking before him") is similarly
more vivid than Bathsheba's account.

26. *But me—me your servant.* Nathan takes pains, in righteous indignation as
prophet to the throne, to highlight his own exclusion, at the very beginning of
the list.

30. *just as I swore to you by the LORD God of Israel.* Whether or not David actually made this vow to Bathsheba, by now he is thoroughly persuaded that he
did. Note that he raises Bathsheba's language to still another level of politically efficacious resonance. Nathan had made no mention of God in invoking
the vow; Bathsheba had said "you . . . swore by the LORD your God"; David
now encompasses the whole national realm in declaring, "as I swore to you by
the LORD God of Isreal."

he shall sit on my throne in my stead. David introduces a crucial change into
the formula for the promise of succession, as Fokkelman shrewdly observes:
to the understandable "after me" of the first clause he adds "in my stead,"
implying not merely that Solomon will succeed him but that Solomon will
replace him on the throne while he is still alive. Accordingly, David then proceeds to give instructions for an immediate ceremony of anointment. In the
face of Adonijah's virtual coup d'état, David appears to realize that he is no
longer physically capable of acting as monarch and protecting himself against
usurpation, and that the wisest course is to put his chosen successor on the
throne without a moment's delay.

her face to the ground and bowed to the king and said, "May my lord
32 King David live forever." And David said, "Call to me Zadok the priest
and Nathan the prophet and Benaiah son of Jehoiada." And they came
33 before the king. And the king said to them, "Take with you your lord's
servants and mount Solomon my son on my special mule and bring
34 him down to Gihon. And Zadok the priest shall anoint him there, with
Nathan the prophet, as king over Israel, and sound the ram's horn and
35 say, 'Long live King Solomon.' And you shall come up after him, and he
shall come and sit on my throne, and he shall be king after me, him
36 have I charged to be prince over Israel and over Judah." And Benaiah
son of Jehoiada answered the king and said, "Amen! May thus, too, say
37 the LORD, my lord the king's God. As the LORD has been with my lord
the king, thus may He be with Solomon and make his throne even
greater than the throne of my lord King David."

38 And Zadok the priest, with Nathan the prophet and Benaiah son of
Jehoiada and the Cherethites and the Pelethites went down and

---

31. *May my lord King David live forever.* Bathsheba's tact remains flawless.
Now that she has extracted from David exactly the commitment she wanted,
she wishes him, hyperbolically, eternal life, even as he teeters on the edge of
the grave.

33. *your lord's servants.* That is, David's courtiers.
   my special mule. Literally, "the mule that is mine." Seating Solomon on the
royal mule is the first public expression of the conferral of the kingship on him.
   Gihon. This is a brook just outside the city walls. David enjoins his officials
to act rapidly in anointing Solomon while Adonijah's coronation feast is still
underway a couple of miles off.

35. *he shall come and sit on my throne.* This reiterated symbolic statement is
now literalized: after the anointment at the Gihon brook, Solomon is to be
brought to the palace and publicly seated on the throne.
   him have I charged to be prince. The term *nagid*, prince, previously attached
to Saul and now to David, appears for the last time to designate the monarch.
He is to be prince over Judah, where Adonijah has gathered support, as well as
over Israel.

38. *the Cherethites and the Pelethites.* These members of the palace guard of
Philistine origin provide a show of arms for the act of anointing Solomon.

mounted Solomon on King David's mule and led him to Gihon. And   39
Zadok the priest took the horn of oil from the Tent and anointed
Solomon, and they blew the ram's horn and all the people said, "Long
live King Solomon!" And all the people went up after him, and the peo-   40
ple were playing flutes and making such revelry that the very earth split
apart with their noise. And Adonijah heard, and all the invited guests   41
who were with him, and they had finished eating, and Joab heard the
sound of the ram's horn and said, "Why this sound of the city in an
uproar?" He was still speaking when, look, Jonathan son of Abiathar   42
the priest came. And Adonijah said, "Come! For you are a valiant fellow
and you must bear good tidings." And Jonathan answered and said   43
to Adonijah, "Alas, our lord King David has made Solomon king.

---

39. *took the horn of oil from the Tent.* The Tent in question is obviously the cultic site where the Ark of the Covenant is kept—the emphasis is that the oil of
anointment is sanctified oil.

40. *the people were playing flutes and making such revelry that the very earth
split apart with their noise.* This hyperbolic report of the public rejoicing over
Solomon's succession to the throne serves two purposes: the tremendous
clamor is so loud that the sound reaches Adonijah and his supporters at En-
rogel (verse 41), and it is a vocal demonstration that the choice of Solomon
immediately enjoys extravagant popular support. This latter consideration is
crucial for the politics of the story because it makes clear that Adonijah has no
hope of mustering opposition to Solomon.

41. *Adonijah heard, and all the invited guests . . . and Joab heard the sound of the
ram's horn.* As a couple of commentators have noted, Adonijah and his followers hear only the hubbub from the city, whereas Joab, the military man, picks
up the sound of the *shofar,* the ram's horn. This would be either a call to arms
or the proclamation of a king.

42. *For you are a valiant fellow and you must bear good tidings.* This obvious non
sequitur ominously echoes David's anxious words about Ahimaaz (2 Samuel
18), "he is a good man and with good tidings he must come." Jonathan's very
first word, "alas," shows how mistaken Adonijah is.

43. *our lord King David has made Solomon king.* Jonathan flatly begins with the
brunt of the bad news, then fleshes out the circumstances to make it all the
worse. He at once identifies David as "our lord," conceding that, after all,
David retains a monarch's authority to determine his successor.

44 And the king has sent with him Zadok the priest and Nathan the
prophet and Benaiah son of Jehoiada and the Cherethites and the
45 Pelethites, and they have mounted him on the king's mule. And Zadok
the priest and Nathan the prophet have anointed him king at Gihon,
and they have gone up from there reveling, and the city is in an uproar.
46 This is the sound you heard. And what's more, Solomon is seated on the
47 royal throne. And what's more, the king's servants have come to bless
our lord King David, saying, 'May your God make Solomon's name even
better than your name and make his throne even greater than your
48 throne.' And the king bowed down on his couch. And what's more, thus
has the king said, 'Blessed is the LORD God of Israel Who has granted
today someone sitting on my throne with my own eyes beholding
49 it.'" And all of Adonijah's invited guests trembled and rose up and
50 each man went on his way. And Adonijah was afraid of Solomon, and
he rose up and went off and caught hold of the horns of the altar.

46, 47, 48. *And what's more, Solomon is seated. . . . And what's more, the king's
servants have come. . . . And what's more, thus has the king said.* Jonathan's long,
breathless account of the installation of Solomon as king, with its reiterated
"what's more" *(wegam),* conveys an excited cumulative sense of the chain of
disasters that have destroyed all of Adonijah's hopes. He goes beyond what the
narrator has reported to depict Solomon actually seated on the throne, receiving his father's blessing.

48. *someone sitting on my throne.* Some textual critics propose instead of the
Masoretic reading "a son sitting on my throne."

49. *each man went on his way.* Terrified, the supporters of Adonijah's claim to
the throne disperse. This moment is reminiscent of the dispersal and flight of
"all the king's sons" from Amnon's feast after Absalom's men murder Amnon.

50. *caught hold of the horns of the altar.* The typical construction of ancient
Israelite altars, as archeology has confirmed, featured a curving protuberance
at each of the four corners, roughly like the curve of a ram's horn. The association of horn with strength may explain this design. Gripping the horns—
actually, probably one horn—of the altar was a plea for sanctuary: at least in
principle, though not always in practice, a person in this posture and in this
place should be held inviolable by his pursuers.

And it was told to Solomon, saying, "Look, Adonijah is afraid of King   51
Solomon and, look, he has caught hold of the horns of the altar, saying,
'Let King Solomon swear to me today that he will not put his servant to
death by the sword." And Solomon said, "If he prove a valiant fellow,   52
not a hair of his will fall to the ground, but if evil be found in him, he
shall die." And King Solomon sent, and they took him down from the   53
altar, and he came and bowed to King Solomon, and Solomon said to
him, "Go to your house."

---

51. *Let King Solomon swear . . . that he will not put his servant to death.* Adonijah, compelled by *force majeure,* fully acknowledges Solomon's kingship and
his own status as subject in his plea for mercy.

52. *And Solomon said.* Until this point, Solomon has been acted upon by others, and no dialogue has been assigned to him. Now that he is king, he speaks
with firm authority.
   if he prove a valiant fellow. In immediate context, the force of the idiom *ben
hayil* is obviously something like "a decent fellow." But its usual meaning is
worth preserving because it precisely echoes the term Adonijah addressed to
Jonathan (verse 42), and it also points up ironically that Adonijah now is trembling with fear.
   if evil be found in him, he shall die. The evil Solomon has in mind would be
further political machinations. He thus does not agree to swear uncondition-
ally, as Adonijah had pleaded, not to harm his half brother, and he will make
due use of the loophole he leaves himself.

53. *Go to your house.* This injunction concludes the episode on a note of ambiguity. Solomon is distancing Adonijah from the palace. He sends him to the
presumed safety of his own home, or is it to a condition of virtual house
arrest? In any case, Adonijah is surely meant to be kept under surveillance,
and Solomon has already put him on warning.

CHAPTER 2

Ａnd David's time to die grew near, and he charged Solomon his son, saying: "I am going on the way of all the earth. And you must be strong,
and be a man. And keep what the LORD your God enjoins, to walk in
His ways, to keep His statutes, His commandments, and His dictates
and His admonitions, as it is written in the Teaching of Moses, so that
you may prosper in everything you do and in everything to which you

---

3.–4. These two relatively long verses are an unusual instance of the intervention of a Deuteronomistic editor in the dialogue of the original David story
that was composed perhaps nearly four centuries before him. The language
here is an uninterrupted chain of verbal formulas distinctive of the Book of
Deuteronomy and its satellite literature: *keep what the* LORD *your God enjoins,
walk in His ways, keep His statutes, His commandments, and His dictates and
admonitions, so that you may prosper in everything you do and in everything to
which you turn, walk before Me in truth with their whole heart and with their
whole being.* The very mention of the Teaching [*torah*] of Moses is a hallmark
of the Deuteronomist, and as phrase and concept did not yet have currency in
the tenth century. The long sentences loaded with synonyms are also uncharacteristic of the author of the David story, and there is no one in that story—
least of all, David himself—who speaks in this high-minded, long-winded,
didactic vein. Why did the Deuteronomistic editor choose to intervene at this
penultimate point of the David story? It seems very likely that he was uneasy
with David's pronouncing to Solomon a last will and testament worthy of a
dying Mafia capo: be strong and be a man, and use your savvy to pay off all my
old scores with my enemies. In fact, David's deathbed implacability, which
the later editor tries to mitigate by first placing noble sentiments in his mouth,
is powerfully consistent with both the characterization and the imagination of
politics in the preceding narrative. The all too human David on the brink of
the grave is still smarting from the grief and humiliation that Joab's violent
acts caused him and from the public shame Shimei heaped on him, and he
wants Solomon to do what he himself was prevented from doing by fear in the

turn. So that the LORD may fulfill His word that He spoke unto me,   4
saying, 'If your sons keep their way to walk before Me in truth with
their whole heart and with their whole being, no man of yours will be
cut off from the throne of Israel. And, what's more, you yourself know   5
what Joab son of Zeruiah did to me, what he did to the two commanders of the armies of Israel, Abner son of Ner and Amasa son of
Jether—he killed them, and shed the blood of war in peace, and put
the blood of war on his belt that was round his waist and on his sandals

---

one case and by an inhibiting vow in the other. In practical political terms,
moreover, either Joab, just recently a supporter of the usurper Adonijah, or
Shimei, the disaffected Benjaminite, might threaten Solomon's hold on
power, and so should be eliminated.

5. *what he did to the two commanders of the armies of Israel.* David is silent
about the third murder perpetrated by Joab, and the one that caused him the
greatest grief—the killing of Absalom. Perhaps he does not mention it
because it was a murder, unlike the other two, that served a reason of state.
But it was surely the one act he could not forgive.
    *shed the blood of war in peace, and put the blood of war on his belt . . . and on
his sandals.* Both killings were done on the roadway, Joab approaching his victim with gestures of peace. In the case of Abner, his rival had come to make
peace with David, and the phrase "went in peace [*shalom*]" was attached to
Abner in a triple repetition (2 Samuel 3). In the case of Amasa, Joab's last
words to him before stabbing him in the belly were "Is it well [*shalom*] with
you, my brother?" (2 Samuel 20). The virtually visual emphasis of blood on
belt and sandals recalls in particular the murder of Amasa, who lay in the middle of the road wallowing in blood, while the mention of Joab's belt looks back
to his strategem of belting his sword to his waist so that it would fall out when
he bent over, to be picked up by his left hand. The reference to Joab's waist
and feet conveys an image of a man splashed all over with blood. Beyond this
integration of details from the preceding narrative in the words David
chooses, the concentration on blood reflects a general belief that blood shed
in murder lingers over not only the murderer but also over those associated
with the victim like a contaminating miasma until it is "redeemed" or "taken
away" by vengeance.

6 that were on his feet. And you must act in your wisdom, and do not let
7 his gray head go down in peace to Sheol. And with the sons of Barzillai
the Gileadite keep faith, and let them be among those who eat at your
table, for did they not draw near me when I fled from Absalom your
8 brother? And, look, with you is Shimei son of Gera the Benjaminite
from Bahurim, and he cursed me with a scathing curse on the day I
went to Mahanaim. And he came down to meet me at the Jordan, and
I swore to him by the LORD, saying, 'I will not put you to death by the
9 sword.' And now, do not hold him guiltless, for you are a wise man, and
you will know what you should do to him, and bring his gray head
10 down in blood to Sheol!" And David lay with his fathers and he was
11 buried in the city of David. And the time that David was king over

---

6. *you must act in your wisdom.* The wisdom of Solomon in the subsequent
narrative is proverbial, but what David already has in mind here is political
shrewdness: Joab is, after all, a formidable adversary, and Solomon will have
to choose the right time and place, when Joab is without allies or protection,
to dispatch him.

　　do not let his gray head go down in peace to Sheol. This proverbial phrase is
actualized here because we realize that Joab, after half a century as David's
commander—forty regnal years plus several years before that in David's
guerilla band—is now an old man. He who shed the blood of war in peace will
not be allowed to go down in peace to the underworld.

9. *for you are a wise man, and you will know what you should do to him.* In
regard to Shimei, the "wisdom" Solomon must exercise is to find some legal
loophole to obviate his father's vow not to harm the Benjaminite. In the event,
Solomon does this with considerable cleverness. David's vow to Shimei was
made at a moment when it seemed politically prudent to include the man who
had cursed him in what was probably a general amnesty after the supression
of the rebellion. It is understandable that later on David would regret this
binding act of forgiveness to a vile-spirited enemy.

　　bring his gray head down in blood to Sheol. Shimei had screamed at the
fleeing David, "man of blood." Now David enjoins Solomon to send him to
the netherworld in blood. In his long career, David has had noble moments
as well as affectingly human ones, but it is a remarkable token of the
writer's gritty realism about men in the vindictive currents of violent politics
that the very last words he assigns to David are *bedam She°ol,* "in blood to
Sheol."

Israel was forty years—in Hebron he was king seven years and in
Jerusalem he was king thirty-three years. And Solomon sat on the   12
throne of David like his father, and his kingdom was wholly unshaken.

And Adonijah son of Haggith came to Bathsheba, Solomon's mother,   13
and she said, "Do you come in peace?" And he said, "In peace." And he   14
said, "There is something I have to say to you." And she said, "Speak."
And he said, "You yourself know that mine was the kingship, and to me   15
did all Israel turn their faces to be king, yet the kingship was brought
round and became my brother's, for from the LORD was it his. And   16
now, there is one petition I ask of you, do not refuse me." And she said,
"Speak." And he said, "Pray, say to Solomon the king, for he would not   17

---

11. *forty years.* One may assume this is no more than an approximation of
David's regnal span since forty years, as the Book of Judges repeatedly shows,
is a formulaic number for a full reign.

13. *Adonijah son of Haggith.* The reappearance of Solomon's rival follows hard
upon the report that his kingdom was unshaken, introducing a potential dissonance. Adonijah was not included in David's list of enemies to be eliminated
because he is Solomon's problem, not David's.
   Do you come in peace? After Adonijah's attempt to seize the throne that was
then given to her son, Bathsheba is understandably uncertain about Adonijah's intentions in coming to see her.

15. *You yourself know that mine was the kingship . . . yet the kingship was
brought round and became my brother's, for from the LORD was it his.* Adonijah
tries to have it both ways in his overture to Bathsheba: on the one hand, the
kingship really was his, and he enjoyed popular support; on the other hand, he
is prepared to be reconciled with the idea that it was God's determination that
the crown should pass on from him to his brother. There may be a note of
petulance here: Adonijah speaks of his situation as though he deserved some
sort of consolation prize. It will prove a fatal imprudence that he should have
addressed this complaint to the mother of the man he sought to anticipate in
seizing the throne.

18 refuse you, that he give me Abishag the Shunamite as wife." And
19 Bathsheba said, "Good, I myself shall speak for you to the king." And
Bathsheba came to King Solomon to speak to him about Adonijah.
And the king arose to greet her and bowed to her and sat down on his
throne and set out a throne for the queen mother, and she sat down to

---

17. *that he give me Abishag the Shunamite as wife.* The promotion of fruitful
ambiguity through narrative reticence so characteristic of the author of the
David story is never more brilliantly deployed. What is Adonijah really up
to? He approaches Solomon's mother because he thinks she will have special influence over the king and because he is afraid to go to Solomon himself. Perhaps, Adonijah imagines, as a mother she will have pity for him and
do him this favor. But in taking this course, Adonijah betrays the most extraordinary political naiveté. Why does he want Abishag? The political motive
would be that by uniting with a woman who had shared the king's bed,
though merely as a bedwarmer, he was preparing the ground for a future
claim to the throne. (The act of his brother Absalom in cohabiting with
David's concubines stands in the background.) If this motive were transparent, as it turns out to be in Solomon's reading of the request, it would be idi-
otic for Adonijah to ask for Abishag. Perhaps he feels safe because Abishag
was not technically David's consort. Perhaps the political consideration is
only at the back of his mind, and he really is seeking consolation in the idea
of marrying a beautiful young woman who has, so to speak, a kind of association by contiguity with the throne. In any case, he will pay the ultimate
price for his miscalculation.

18. *I myself shall speak for you to the king.* As with Adonijah, there is no explanation of her motive. But given the shrewdness with which Bathsheba has
acted in the previous episode, it is entirely plausible that she immediately
agrees to do this favor for Adonijah because she quickly realizes what escapes
him—that it will prove to be his death sentence, and thus a threat to her son's
throne will be permanently eliminated.

19. *and bowed to her.* The Septuagint has "and kissed her" because of the
anomaly of a king's bowing to his subject.

his right. And she said, "There is one small petition that I ask of you, do 20
not refuse me." And the king said to her, "Ask, Mother, for I shall not
refuse you." And she said, "Let Abishag the Shunamite be given to 21
Adonijah your brother as wife." And King Solomon answered and said 22
to his mother, "And why do you ask Abishag the Shunamite for Adonijah? Ask the kingship for him, as he is my older brother, and Abiathar
the priest and Joab son of Zeruiah are for him." And King Solomon 23
swore by the LORD, saying, "Thus may God do to me and even more,
for at the cost of his life has Adonijah spoken this thing! And now, as 24
the LORD lives, Who seated me unshaken on the throne of David my
father, and Who made me a house just as He had spoken, today shall
Adonijah be put to death." And King Solomon sent by the hand of 25
Benaiah son of Jehoiada, and he stabbed him and he died. And to Abi- 26
athar the priest did the king say, "Go to Anathoth to your own fields, for

---

20. *There is one small petition that I ask of you* . . . In accordance with the
established convention of biblical narrative, she uses the very same words
Adonijah has spoken to her, adding only the adjective "small." This is just a
tiny request, she appears to say, full knowing that Solomon is likely to see it,
on the contrary, as a huge thing—a device that could be turned into a ladder
to the throne on which Solomon sits. One should note that this whole large
narrative begins when a woman who is to become a mother (Hannah) puts
forth a petition (*she'eilah,* the same word used here).

22. *as he is my older brother, and Abiathar and Joab are for him.* If he makes the
dead king's consort his wife, that, together with the fact that he is my elder
and has powerful supporters in the court, will give him a dangerously strong
claim to the throne. In the Hebrew, the second clause appears to say "and for
him and for Abiathar . . . and for Joab," which makes little sense, and so the
small emendation, deleting the second and third occurrence of "for" (a single-
letter prefix in the Hebrew), is presumed in the translation.

26. *to Abiathar the priest.* Throughout this episode centering on Adonijah,
Solomon shows himself to be decisive, emphatic, and ruthless—a worthy son
of his father. The moment he hears of Adonijah's pretentions to the late king's
nurse/bedmate, he orders him to be killed immediately. He then proceeds to
remove from office and banish the key priestly supporter of Adonijah, and he
will go on to deal with Joab as well.

you are a doomed man, but on this day I shall not put you to death, for
you bore the Ark of the LORD God before David my father and you suf-
27 fered through all that my father suffered." And Solomon banished Abiathar from being priest to the LORD, so as to fulfill the word of the
LORD that He spoke concerning the house of Eli at Shiloh.

28 And the news reached Joab, for Joab had sided with Adonijah, though
with Absalom he had not sided, and Joab fled to the Tent of the LORD,
29 and he grasped the horns of the altar. And it was told to the king that
Joab had fled to the Tent of the LORD, and there he was by the altar,
and Solomon sent Benaiah son of Johoiada, saying, "Go, stab him."
30 And Benaiah came to the Tent of the LORD and said to him, "Thus says
the king, 'Come out.'" And he said, "No, for here I shall die." And

---

on this day I shall not put you to death. There is a veiled threat in this formulation: right now I shall not kill you, and in any case you had better stay away
from Jerusalem on the farm at Anathoth.

*for you bore the Ark of the LORD . . . and you suffered through all that my
father suffered.* Solomon is circumspect in not ordering the execution of a
priest—in sharp contrast to Saul, who thought he might protect his kingship
from a perceived threat by massacring a whole town of priests who he imagined were allied with his rival. Solomon also honors the fact that Abiathar has
shared many years of danger and hardship with David, and during that time
never betrayed David, as Joab did.

27. *so as to fulfill the word of the LORD . . . concerning the house of Eli.* One sees
how this chapter concludes a grand narrative that begins in 1 Samuel 1, and is
not merely the end of a supposedly independent Succession Narrative.

28. *And the news reached Joab . . . and Joab fled to the Tent of the LORD.* With
Adonijah dead and Abiathar banished, Joab realizes that all who remain from
the recent anti-Solomon alliance have been isolated and cut off. This relentlessly political general recognizes that he has no power base left to protect
him against the resolute young king. He has only the desperate last remedy of
seeking sanctuary at the altar.

30. *Thus says the king, 'Come out.'* Solomon's blunt order was simply to stab
Joab, but Benaiah, steely executioner though he has shown himself, is loath to
kill a man clinging to the altar, and so he directs Joab to come down out of the
Tent of the LORD.

Benaiah brought back word to the king, saying, "Thus did Joab speak
and thus did he answer me." And the king said, "Do as he has spoken,   31
and stab him and bury him, and you shall take away the blood that Joab
shed for no cause, from me and from my father's house. And the LORD   32
will bring back his blood guilt on his own head, for he stabbed two men
more righteous and better than himself and he killed them by the
sword, unbeknownst to my father David—Abner son of Ner, commander of the army of Israel, and Amasa son of Jether, commander of the
army of Judah. And their blood will come back on the head of Joab and   33
on the head of his seed forever, but for David and his seed and
his house there will be peace evermore from the LORD." And Benaiah   34
son of Jehoiada went up and stabbed him and put him to death, and

---

31. *stab him and bury him.* Solomon's command is to take Joab's life in the very
place of sanctuary ("for here shall I die"), a decision that is in accordance with
biblical law: "When a man plots against his fellowman to kill him in cunning,
from My very altar shall you take him to die" (Exodus 21:14). But Solomon also
enjoins Benaiah to see to it that Joab, who was after all a stalwart soldier and
once David's boon companion, should have a proper burial and not be thrown
to the scavengers of sky and earth—the ultimate indignity in ancient Mediterranean cultures.

32. *for he stabbed two men more righteous and better than himself . . . unbeknownst to my father David.* Solomon in his "wisdom" has thus used the purported renewal of the Adonijah conspiracy to carry out the will of vengeance
his father conveyed to him, and for the precise reasons David stipulated.

33. *their blood will come back on the head of Joab and on the head of his son.* The
miasma of blood guilt settles on the house of Joab for all time: a curse on the
house of Joab was not part of David's injunction, but perhaps Solomon means
to ward off any prospect that resentful descendants of Joab will seek to mar-
shal forces against the Davidic line.

but for David and his seed and his house there will be peace evermore. There
is an emphatic contrast between permanent blessing on the line of David and
an everlasting curse on the line of Joab, with "peace" counterpointed to
"blood," as in verse 5.

35   he was buried at his home in the wilderness. And the king put Benaiah son of Jehoiada in his stead over the army, and Zadok the priest did the king put instead of Abiathar.

36   And the king sent and called to Shimei and said to him, "Build yourself a house in Jerusalem and dwell in it, and do not go out from there 37 hither and yon. For should you cross the Wadi Kidron, on the very day you go out, you must surely know that you are doomed to die, your 38 blood will be on your own head." And Shimei said, "The thing is good. Even as my lord the king has spoken, so will his servant do." And Shimei 39 dwelled in Jerusalem a long while. And it happened at the end of three years that two of Shimei's slaves ran away to Achish son of Maacah, king of Gath, and they told Shimei, saying, "Look, your slaves are in

---

34. *he was buried at his home in the wilderness.* This notation has puzzled commentators because one would assume that Joab's home (like David's original home) was in the town of Bethlehem. The Hebrew for "wilderness," *midbar,* has the basic meaning of pastureland, and it is not improbable that Joab would have had a kind of hacienda removed from the town. Nevertheless, the report of Joab's burial in the wilderness concludes his story on a haunting note. That resonance has been nicely caught by the medieval Hebrew commentator Gersonides: "he was buried in the wilderness, which was the home fitting for him, for it would not be meet for a man like him to be part of civil society [*lihyot medini*] because he had killed men by devious means and by deception."

37. *should you cross the Wadi Kidron.* This brook runs at the foot of Jerusalem to the east, and Shimei would have to cross it to go back to his native village of Bahurim.

    your blood will be on your own head. Again, behind these words lies the spectacle of Shimei reviling David with the epithet "man of blood" and asking that the blood of the house of Saul come down on his head.

38. *The thing is good.* Shimei has no alternative but to agree—better virtual confinement in the capital city than death.

Gath." And Shimei arose and saddled his donkey and went to Gath to   40
seek his slaves, and Shimei went and brought his slaves from Gath.
And it was told to Solomon that Shimei had gone from Jerusalem and   41
had come back. And the king sent and called Shimei and said to him,   42
"Did I not make you swear by the LORD and warn you, saying, 'The day
you go out and move about hither and yon, you must surely know that
you are doomed to die,' and you said to me, 'The thing is good. I do hear
it.' And why have you not kept the LORD's oath and the command with   43
which I charged you?" And the king said to Shimei, "You yourself know   44
all the evil, which your own heart knows, that you did to David my
father, and the LORD has brought back your evil on your own head.

---

40. *Shimei arose and saddled his donkey and went to Gath to seek his slaves.*
According to several ancient Near Eastern codes (though not Israelite law),
authorities were obliged to return a runaway slave. Evidently, by this point
peaceful relations obtained between Israel and the Philistine cities. Lulled
into a false sense of security by the passage of three years ("a long while"),
Shimei may be allowing his cupidity for recovering lost property to override
the concern he should have preserved about Solomon's injunction not to leave
Jerusalem. Or he may be a bad reader of Solomon's oral text, construing the
ban on crossing the Wadi Kidron as implicit permission to leave the city temporarily in the opposite direction, so long as he does not try to return to his
hometown.

42. *Did I not make you swear by the LORD . . . ?* In the actual report, only
Solomon swore (the Septuagint supplies an oath for Shimei), though perhaps
Shimei's taking a solemn oath is implied in verse 38.
   The thing is good. I do hear it. Solomon adds "I do hear it" (*shamaᶜti*) to the
actual report in verse 38 of Shimei's words, in order to emphasize that Shimei
gave full and knowing assent to Solomon's terms. Fokkelman notes that there
is a pun on Shimei's own name—*Shimᶜi/shamaᶜti.*

43. *And why have you not kept the LORD's oath . . . ?* Here, then, is Solomon's
wisdom in carrying out his father's will: he has set Shimei up, waiting
patiently until he violates the oath, which then frees Solomon of any obligation lingering from David's earlier oath to do no harm to Shimei.

45   But King Solomon shall be blessed and the throne of David shall be
46   unshaken before the LORD forevermore." And the king charged Benaiah son of Jeohaiada, and he went out and stabbed him, and he died.

And the kingdom was unshaken in Solomon's hand.

---

45. *But King Solomon shall be blessed* . . . As in the killing of Joab, the imprecation pronounced over the doomed man is balanced by the invocation of the
LORD's perpetual blessing on the house of David.

46. *And the kingdom was unshaken in Solomon's hand.* This seemingly formulaic notice at the very end of the story is a last touch of genius by that unblinking observer of the savage realm of politics who is the author of the David
story: Solomon's power is now firmly established, blessed by the God Who has
promised an everlasting covenant with David and his descendants; but the
immediately preceding actions undertaken so decisively and so shrewdly by
the young king involve the ruthless elimination of all potential enemies. The
solid foundations of the throne have been hewn by the sharp daggers of the
king's henchmen.

CAST OF CHARACTERS

Abiathar. Son of the priest of Nob, Ahimelech, who escapes to David in the wilderness after the slaughter at Nob; serves David as priest during his reign.

Abigail. Nabal's wife, who provisions David in the wilderness after her husband's refusal. After Nabal's death, David takes her as his third wife.

Abishag. The Shunammite woman recruited by David's courtiers to "warm" him in his old age. Adonijah asks help from Bathsheba to marry her after David's death.

Abishai. One of the three sons of David's sister Zeruiah and thus Joab's brother; one of David's notable warriors who saves him in battle from the Philistine Ishbi-benob and accompanies him on his secret raid of Saul's camp.

Abner. Son of Saul's uncle Ner; Saul's paternal cousin serves as his principal army commander, and also that of his son Ish-bosheth; in the civil war after Saul's death he kills Asahel, David's nephew.

Absalom. Renownedly handsome third son of David by princess Maacah of Geshur and brother to Tamar, plots for the throne and temporarily displaces his father as ruler in Jerusalem.

Achish. King of Gath, who provides sanctuary for David on two occasions when he is fleeing Saul; David plays the madman before him.

Adonijah. Handsome fourth son of David by Haggith; he attempts a coup in David's old age that precipitates Solomon's ascension to the throne.

Agag. King of Amalek, whom Saul fails to kill and whom Samuel ultimately executes.

Ahimaaz. Son of Zadok the priest and renowned for his running.

Ahimelech. Son of Ahitub and so Zadok's brother; a priest of the Nob sanctuary who assists David in his flight from Saul.

Ahinoam, daughter of Ahimaaz. Saul's wife; to be distinguished from Ahinoam of Jezreel, David's first wife and mother of Amnon.

Ahitophel. Most clever co-conspirator in Absalom's cabal.

Amasa. Son of Ithra and Abigal (Zeruiah's sister), maternal cousin to Joab, and nephew of David; appointed army commander in place of Joab by Absalom, and reappointed so by David.

Amnon. Firstborn son of David by Ahinoam of Jezreel; rapes his half-sister Tamar and subsequently pays with his life.

Araunah. The Jebusite owner of a threshing floor purchased by David. At this site David sacrifices to stop the plague precipitated by his census.

Asahel. One of the three sons of David's sister Zeruiah and thus Joab's brother; killed by Saul's army commander Abner during the battle at Gibeon.

Barzillai. The Gileadite octogenarian and friend of David who provisions him after Absalom's coup d'état.

Bathsheba. Daughter of Eliam and wife of Uriah the Hittite who becomes David's eighth named wife; mother of the heir to the throne, Solomon.

Benaiah. Son of Jehoiada from Kabzeel, commander of David's bodyguard, the Cherethites and Pelethites, and highly regarded among David's warriors; he remains loyal during Adonijah's coup attempt and is subsequently appointed army commander by Solomon.

Chimham. Servant or perhaps son of Barzillai, David's ally during Absalom's coup; sent to serve David as Barzillai's proxy.

David. Son of Jesse, a Bethlehemite; hero of the Philistine war who becomes King Saul's son-in-law; through many twists and turns he finds his way to the throne for which Samuel anoints him; rules first from Hebron, and then from Jerusalem.

Doeg. The Edomite, Saul's chief herdsman, who observes David's encounter with the priest, Ahimelech, at the Nob sanctuary.

Eli. Priest in the regional sanctuary at Shiloh and father of the impious Hophni and Phinehas; he accepts Samuel, dedicated by his mother Hannah, as a temple servant.

Eliab. Firstborn son of Jesse and eldest brother of David; he follows Saul to war.

Elkanah. Son of Jeroham, an Ephraimite from the hills, and husband of Hannah and Peninnah; he sires Samuel.

Goliath of Gath. A champion of the Philistines whom, in one tradition, David fells, and in another, Elhanan, son of Dodo the Bethlehemite, defeats.

Hannah. The childless but favorite wife of Elkanah ultimately bears Samuel and dedicates him to the sanctuary at Shiloh.

Hophni. Eli's son and scoundrel priest at Shiloh; together with his brother Phineas, has charge of the Ark of God.

Hushai the Archite. Friend of David who, under pretense of fealty to Absalom, attempts to undermine the revolt by thwarting clever Ahitophel's counsel.

Ichabod. Son of Phinehas, son of Eli; named "Inglorious" after the death of both his father and grandfather and the capture of the Ark of God by the Philistines.

Jesse. An Ephrathite of Bethlehem in Judah and father of eight sons, the youngest of whom is David.

Joab. One of the three sons of David's sister Zeruiah; his comrade-in-arms during David's period as guerilla chieftain and subsequently his field commander.

Jonadab. Son of Shimah and clever nephew of David; helps plan Amnon's plot to "seduce" Tamar.

Jonathan. The most important of the six named sons of Saul, brother in law to and comrade-in-arms with David; he dies with his father and two brothers at the battle of Mount Gilboa.

Mephibosheth. Crippled son of Jonathan, whom David politically rehabilitates and brings to his court.

Michal. Younger daughter of Saul given to David as wife; although she assists David in an escape from her father, she later exhibits her contempt for him when he brings the Ark of God to Jerusalem.

Nabal. The Calebite husband of Abigail, who refuses David aid in the wilderness.

Nahash. Ammonite King, who besieges Jabesh-gilead, providing the occasion for newly "elected" King Saul to demonstrate his military prowess.

Nathan. David's court prophet noted for his prophecy about building the Temple and the dynastic rule of David's heirs, and for his rebuke to David over the incident with Bathsheba.

Obed-edom the Gittite. He houses the Ark of God for three months after the incident with Uzzah.

Palti(el), son of Laish. Saul gives him Michal, David's wife, after David flees into the wilderness.

Peninnah. Co-wife with Hannah of Elkanah; she taunts her rival about her childlessness.

Phineas. Son of Eli and father of Ichabod; along with his brother Hophni, an impious priest in the sanctuary at Shiloh responsible for the Ark of God.

Rechab and Baanah. Sons of Rimmon the Beerothite and assassins of Ish-bosheth, who briefly succeeds to Saul's throne.

Rizpah. Daughter of Aiah and Saul's concubine; Abner, over Ish-bosheth's objections, takes her as his concubine too; David impales her two sons.

Samuel. Son of Elkanah and Hannah; an Ephraimite dedicated by his mother to the sanctuary at Shiloh; becomes seer and priest, anointing both Saul and David as kings-designate.

Saul. Son of Kish and nephew of Ner, a handsome Benjamite member of a wealthy family who stands a head taller than everyone else; becomes an ecstatic "prophet" after his anointing as king by Samuel; his kingship is confirmed by lot and is inaugurated after he relieves the Ammonite siege of Jabesh-gilead; he rules from Gibeah.

Sheba, son of Bichri. A Benjamite and leader of the Israelite rebellion against David after the defeat of Absalom.

Shimei, son of Gera. A member of Saul's tribe who encounters David retreating from Jerusalem after Absalom's revolt.

Solomon. David's eighth son (and third child born in Jerusalem), by Bathsheba; eventual heir to David's throne; rules from Jerusalem.

Tamar. Daughter of David by his fourth wife Maacah and a sister to Absalom; her half-brother Amnon rapes her, precipitating a cycle of revenge in David's family.

Uriah the Hittite. One of David's renowned warriors and husband of Bathsheba; David arranges his death in battle to cover up the adultery with his wife.

Uzzah. Member of the parade escorting the Ark of God to Jerusalem, who makes the mistake of touching the Ark as it falls.

Zadok. Son of Ahitub and brother to Ahimelech, the priest of Nob, uncle to Abiathar and father to Ahimaaz; serves as a priest for David along with Abiathar and David's sons; part of the pro-David faction during Absalom's revolt.

Ziba. Saul's steward who reveals Mephibosheth's whereabouts.

REFERENCES

The following list is limited to modern authors referred to in the commentary. Comments cited from exegetes of Late Antiquity, the Middle Ages, and the Renaissance can be located at the relevant verse and chapter of their commentaries, most of which are available only in Hebrew. Page references to the modern texts seemed superfluous because most are commentaries, where, again, turning to the verse and chapter at issue is all that is needed.

Avramsky, Shmuel. In *The World of the Bible: 2 Samuel* (in Hebrew). Tel Aviv: Revivim, 1989.

Bar-Efrat, Shimon. *1 and 2 Samuel: With Introduction and Commentary* (in Hebrew). Tel Aviv: Am Oved, 1996.

Faulkner, William. *Absalom, Absalom!* New York: Vintage Books, 1990.

Fokkelman, J. P. *Narrative Art and Poetry in the Books of Samuel.* 4 vols. Assen: Van Gorcum, 1981–1993.

Garsiel, Moshe. In *The World of the Bible: 1 and 2 Samuel.* 2 vols. (in Hebrew). Tel Aviv: Revivim, 1984, 1989.

Gevaryahu, Haim. In *The World of the Bible: 1 Samuel* (in Hebrew). Tel Aviv: Revivim, 1984.

McCarter, P. Kyle, Jr. *The Anchor Bible: 1 and 2 Samuel.* 2 vols. New York: Doubleday, 1980, 1984.

Perry, Menahem, and Meir Sternberg. "The King through Ironic Eyes" (in Hebrew). *Hasifrut* 1(1968):263–292.

Polzin, Robert. *David and the Deuteronomist.* Bloomington: Indiana University Press, 1993.

———*Samuel and the Deuteronomist.* Bloomington: Indiana University Press, 1989.

von Rad, Gerhard. "The Beginnings of History Writing in Ancient Israel." In *The Problem of the Hexateuch and Other Essays,* trans. E. W. Trueman Dicken. New York: McGraw-Hill, 1955.

Rost, Leonhard. *Die Ueberlieferung von der Thronnachfolge Davids.* Stuttgart: W. Kohlhammer, 1926.

Shalev, Meir. *The Bible Now* (in Hebrew). Jerusalem: Schocken, 1985.

Shklovsky, Viktor. "Art as Technique." In *Russian Formalist Criticism*, ed. L. T. Lemon and M. J. Reis. Lincoln: University of Nebraska Press, 1965.

Speiser, E. A. *The Anchor Bible: Genesis*. Garden City, N.Y.: Doubleday, 1964.

Sternberg, Meir. *The Poetics of Biblical Narrative*. Bloomington: Indiana University Press, 1985.

Yadin, Yigal. *The Art of Warfare in Biblical Lands*. 2 vols. New York: McGraw-Hill, 1963.

INDEX